HUMAN INTERACTION
WITH COMPUTERS

HUMAN INTERACTION WITH COMPUTERS

Edited by

H.T. SMITH

Department of Psychology
University of Nottingham
Nottingham, England

T.R.G. GREEN

MRC Unit of Social and Applied Psychology
The University
Sheffield, England

1980

A Subsidiary of Harcourt Brace Jovanovich, Publishers
London   New York   Toronto   Sydney   San Francisco

ACADEMIC PRESS INC. (LONDON) LTD.
24/28 Oval Road,
London NW1

United States Edition published by
ACADEMIC PRESS INC.
111 Fifth Avenue
New York, New York 10003

British Library Cataloguing in Publication Data
Human interaction with computers.
    1. Data processing   2. Man-machine systems
    I. Smith, Hugh T.   II. Green, T. R. G.
    001.6'4   QA76   79-42930
    ISBN 0-12-652850-0
    ISBN 0-12-652852-7 Pbk.

Printed in Great Britain by
Whitstable Litho Ltd., Whitstable, Kent

CONTRIBUTORS

Arblaster, A., Logica Ltd., 64 Newman St., London W1A 4SE., England.

Bjørn-Andersen, N., and Bloch Rasmussen, L., The Copenhagen School of Economics and Business Administration, Jul. Thomsens Plads 10, DK-1925 Kobenhavn V, Denmark.

Fitter, M. J., and Sime, M. E., MRC Social and Applied Psychology Unit, University of Sheffield, Sheffield, S10 2TN, Yorkshire, England.

Green, T.R.G., MRC Social and Applied Psychology Unit, University of Sheffield, Sheffield, S10 2TN, Yorkshire, England.

Hartley, J. R., Computer Based Learning Project, University of Leeds, Leeds 2, England.

Jackson, M. A., Michael Jackson Systems Ltd., 101 Hamilton Terrace, London NW8 9QX, England.

Martin, T., Annenberg School of Communication, University of Southern California, University Park, Los Angeles, California 90007, U.S.A.

Maver, T., Abacus, University of Strathclyde, Department of Architecture, 131 Rottenrow, Glasgow, G4 0NG, Scotland.

Rasmussen, J., Riso National Laboratory, Post Box 49, DK-4000, Roskilde, Denmark.

Scott Morton, M. S., and Huff, S., Alfred P. Sloan School of Management, Massachusetts Institute of Technology, 50 Memorial Drive, Cambridge, Massachusetts 02139, U.S.A.

Smith, H. T., Department of Psychology, University of Nottingham, University Park, Nottingham NG7 2RD, England.

Taylor, T., Department of Family Medicine, School of Medicine, University of Washington, Seattle, Washington 98195, U.S.A.

PREFACE

Computers have a potential flexibility that makes them seem infinitely adaptable to different tasks. And yet often this adaptability is more project- ed than real. Getting a computer to do what you want is exceedingly difficult; the computer is rigid and unyielding, unable to cope with excep- tions, and demanding of its users. Too often the computer system is like a superb road that lies at the end of a pitted cart-track; to reach the road you first have to experience the cart-track. In order to use computers effectively, people have had to make quite considerable changes in their habits and values. Why this is the case and what, if anything, is being done about it is the subject of this book. The intent has been to focus on the general characteristics and requirements of people-oriented computer systems from the differing perspectives provided by different tasks and their associated disciplines.

Many people from many disciplines are struggling to narrow the gap between the computer and the user, to produce packages that do what the user wants in ways that the user can grasp. Unfortunately, communication between one discipline and another is, as ever, rather poor, so that what goes on in one area misses the insights and experience gained in another. Our intention in this book was to provide a focus for this unconnected body of people, to show how researchers in the different disciplines approached problems of the impact of computer systems on human behaviour. We were sure that a number of problems would turn out to be common to several research areas, notably the problems of communication, of the interface between the computer and its users.

The contents of this book have confirmed our belief. For example, Taylor examines the state of semi-automated patient history taking systems and finds that one problem is their clinical effectiveness and another problem is whether clinicians will accept them. Rasmussen, looking at decision sys- tems for process control, also finds that both their performance and their acceptability are important factors. Fitter and Sime examine the issues of responsibility and accountability, using examples drawn from similar areas.

Despite the common problems, there is no substantial agreement about solutions, only about the appropriate criteria to apply. Frequently the problems are many-faceted, problems of sociology as well as of technology. What conclusion can possibly be drawn about computer-aided instruction without explicitly considering the status and role of teachers in education? This is the dilemma in compiling a book of this nature. It was not intended to be comprehensive and it has certainly not turned out to be. Current research on sociological implications of computer systems alone would fill a book twice this size, not merely one chapter. The aim has been instead to give the reader a general feeling for the different research approaches. Again the research chosen is representative rather than complete—for example, Maver's chapter on computer-aided design concentrates on architectural design but encompasses methods used in other design fields, such as engineering and circuit design.

The book is split for convenience into three sections which inevitably overlap to some degree. The first section looks at general approaches to the study of people-oriented computer systems. The second is concerned more specifically with the techniques that have been adopted in a number of application areas. Finally, in the third section we turn to the nuts and bolts of computing, the programming languages, to consider how their design and use could be improved. Each section is previewed more fully in its introduction.

To get the most out of the last section, the reader will need to have some modest experience of writing programs and of coping with the attendant problems; the first two sections make no such demands. Anyone who has praised or excoriated, designed, dreamed of, or vetoed an attempt to make computers useful to non-specialist people will find the first sections comprehensible and, we hope, rewarding. And if there is one message that we hope comes through loud and clear, it is this: It's not enough just to establish what computer systems can and cannot do; we need to spend just as much effort establishing what people can *and want to* do.

Both editors would like to thank the following people. Agnes Uy for retyping the manuscript and coping with the vagaries of the computer system, Cheri Dubey and Isabel Rivero for the graphics and the paste-up, Janet DeLand for overviewing the computer typesetting process. Finally, Judy Sibley for help and extreme fortitude. In addition, the first editor would like to acknowledge the contribution of the Annenberg School of Communication, University of Southern California, who provided facilities to complete the book during a visiting appointment.

Hugh Smith
Thomas Green
March 1980

CONTENTS

PART 1

PEOPLE IN COMPUTER SYSTEMS

INTRODUCTION

The chapters in part one are devoted to an examination of the general issues surrounding human interaction with computers. The first chapter is intended to provide an introduction to many of the subjects that are discussed in detail elsewhere in the book. It opens with a review of the more important social and technical factors underlying the evolution of computer systems. The discussion of technical factors highlights how the process of instructing computers to perform specific functions is still relatively primitive. Social factors considered include the place of technology in society, the fascination that computers hold for the individual, and the emotional attitudes that people exhibit towards computer systems. This is followed by a description of the types of users and task characteristics that are encountered in computer systems. The next section deals with the nature of the processes involved in human-computer communication and the requirements it engenders. The chapter concludes with a discussion of the difficulties that beset attempts to use natural language for human-computer communication.

In the second chapter, Mike Fitter and Max Sime discuss the problems of creating people-responsive computers. They develop some of the questions raised in the previous chapter concerning the actual limits of human-computer co-operation. The chapter is concerned with the changing role and responsibilities of the decision-maker in computer systems. One of the key problems is accountability, i.e., if something goes wrong with a semi-automatic (or automatic) system, who is liable? The question is examined from a moral and a legal viewpoint. The authors then outline characteristics of the decision process that should be taken into account when introducing computer systems. One of their themes is that people need to be able to comprehend the rationale and workings of computer-based decision systems if they are to place reliance in them. In the more complex applications, this means that the computer system should be able to explain its behaviour to the user, possibly by adopting strategies which are natural to the user. Approaches to the implementation of such control structures are investigated with examples drawn from the fields of medicine, process control and planning.

Jens Rasmussen similarly considers the nature of human response in a control system environment; however, he is primarily concerned with the detailed description of operator behaviour. Although the examples and discussion largely concentrate on process control, the chapter is included in the first part of the book because it attempts to develop a systematic view of human actions in a technical system. The theme is whether it is possible to describe human performance in terms of the type of functional specifications that could be utilised by an industrial system designer. A model of the basic human information processor is presented which differentiates between conscious and sub-conscious mental functions. This is followed by an analysis of the strategies which control operators use. Rasmussen describes the inter-relationship between data originating from the control system and the mental models constructed by these operators. The implications of this analysis for the design of human-oriented computer systems are then discussed. Finally, the topic of human error analysis is outlined. The question of whether it is possible to predict errors and take steps to make their consequences less serious is investigated.

The fourth chapter turns to the somewhat wider subject of the sociological implications of computer systems. Recent years have seen a great deal of interest in this area; however, much of what has been written has been based on conjecture rather than fact. Niels Bjørn Andersen and Lief Bloch Rasmussen review the available empirical evidence in an attempt to confirm or refute some of the more established suppositions. Much of their data comes from the field of organisational studies. They divide their treatment of the subject between two main themes, direct and indirect effects of computer systems. Direct effects include such topics as employment, work role and power. In each of these a distinction is made between effects on managerial employees and effects on non-managerial employees. The discussion of power deals with the issues of centralisation, discretion and influence. The indirect effects cover job satisfaction, alienation and privacy. The first two of these are constructs, i.e., there is still much debate about their definition and effects; privacy is a rather more concrete issue. The authors discuss both the reasons why privacy has become such an important topic in computer system design and the safeguards that are necessary.

Chapter 1

HUMAN-COMPUTER COMMUNICATION

Hugh Smith

Contents

1.0 Introduction

The growth of computer systems has been truly remarkable. Estimates suggest that in the USA alone there will be around 700,000 computers in 1980 and that by 1985 the figure will have increased to some 1,100,000 (Dolotta et al., 1976). This contrasts markedly with a figure of 5,500 in the mid-1960's. In fact, the projected figure is probably conservative, given the rise of the microprocessor system and its rapid diffusion into the small business and home computer market. However, the number of computers alone does not reveal the full extent of their impact. The industrial and commercial effort involved in designing, supporting and utilising such systems is very large; the previous study estimates that by 1980 the total USA data processing industry expenditure will be around 82 billion dollars, or some 5.2% of the Gross National Product. Similar growth patterns are observable in the rest of the western world. These figures serve to underline the increasing orientation of western society to information and information processing activities. Indeed, they appear to reflect an active trend towards the much heralded post-industrial society—a society in which the socio-economic system is tailored towards services rather than manufacturing systems.

The utilisation of computers is not of course limited to business; increasingly, they are finding their way into education, health and other public services and utilities. So much so that it is becoming difficult to find instances where their use does not impinge, directly or indirectly, on some aspect of individual lifestyle—whether it be banking, travel reservations or telecommunications. Such a widespread adoption underlines how dependent we have become on computers and their associated systems. Some people would say that this dependence has been bought at a high price, a change in basic work practices and social habits. Whether this is true or not, it is clear that as well as benefits, there have also been problems associated with the utilisation of computers. Even when heavily utilised they have not necessarily always been accepted. This chapter is concerned with the exploration of one facet of acceptance—human-computer communication. In discussing this topic we shall examine some of the general questions that have arisen in the development of computer systems. This will involve reflecting a little on the nature of computers, the needs they fulfill, the side-effects they produce and the psychology of human nature. One disclaimer should be made: sometimes we will refer to the 'computer' performing some action, but this does not imply purposiveness of the machine; rather it is shorthand for saying 'the computer has been programmed to perform x'.

It has frequently been observed that computers are a tool, in many ways similar to previous although less complicated tools such as the engine, the telephone or the radio. Each of these devices was developed to satisfy a demand; the engine to supply a form of continuous energy, the telephone for interpersonal communication and the radio to reach mass audiences. The history and development of each may be regarded from a technological *or* a sociological standpoint. In a technological description the emphasis would rest on the physical characteristics and capabilities of a device, including its efficiency in meeting design requirements, its immediate ancestors and descendants. A sociological description might discuss the utilisation of such devices for social purposes, their reinforcement of the political establishment, and their commercial exploitation. Both views are important —tools have attributes which shape and are shaped by the total environment.[1] However, it is the case that technological goals are more easily set

---

[1] There is a story, perhaps apochryphal, that reflects on the general issue of the value of technological artifacts. George Bernard Shaw, on hearing that a gentleman by the name of Alexander Graham Bell had invented a device that allowed him to communicate over a wire with an assistant, was asked "Didn't he think this was a marvellous invention?". "Well", he replied "it all depends upon what was said."

and carried through than social ones. Consequently social studies of the effects of technology tend to resemble a post mortem, i.e., a search for cause and effects which can seldom be used to benefit the patient. Computers, through their nature and use, tend to generate larger social effects than any pre-existing tools. This derives from the way in which they can be utilised to construct large and complex systems. One of their basic properties is that they are more analagous to 'building blocks' than tools—they serve to tie together systems consisting of many components, systems which could not exist were computers to be removed. Weizenbaum (1976) points out the result, a commitment to computers verging on the irreversible that has made it impossible for modern society to function without them. Another outcome of this integrative role in constructing large systems is that frequently there are large indirect side-effects. For example computer-based public record data bases facilitate efficient management of government resources; however, they also provide the potential means to more closely monitor individuals. Although serious abuses are probably rare, there are many ways that small incursions in the individual's right to privacy can occur with such systems. One area of difficulty is that there is no widespread agreement as to what privacy rights individuals have. In some states in the USA public information is sold to commercial establishments that specialize in mail listings, a practice that many in Europe would regard as dubious. More serious implications of the scale of proposed federal data banks in terms of control, accountability and cost are examined by Loudon (1979). Bjørn Anderson & Bloch Rasmussen (Chapter 4) also discuss many of the direct and indirect sociological effects of computer systems, including centralisation of power, employment effects and privacy.

There is another characteristic that distinguishes computers from traditional tools—flexibility. The computer is an apparently amorphous object that may be tailored to fit any particular application. However, this tailoring is not accomplished easily; complex systems utilising computers tend to be constructed in such a way that graceful incremental change is difficult. Frequently life histories of such systems show sharp discontinuities as new technology, new software and new people are introduced. Until recently the importance of the control and management of this life-cycle process has been underemphasised.

We will now turn to a description of the development of computers and computer systems in which the more important technical and social factors pertinent to human-computer communication will be outlined. The topics covered below are only representative of some of the general issues that computer systems present. For example, Gotlieb & Borodin (1973), in discussing the questions raised by computer systems, identify nine overlapping problem areas: managerial, economic, legal, political, ethical, social, philosophical, technical, and pedagogical. Most computer applications will generate concerns in several of these areas, the relative importance of each varying with the application. Many (but not all) of these topics are covered in other parts of this book. This chapter provides a brief sightseeing tour; the other chapters must be read to fill in the gaps.

2.0 The Evolution of Computer Systems

2.1 Technical Factors

In the history of their development, the exponential growth of computer systems has almost always been underestimated, even by the developers. Arblaster (Chapter 12) points out that even IBM at one time considered that ten machines would be able to satisfy the United States' demands. Nor was this atypical; similar size estimates were made by European manufacturers for their own markets. The primary error was an inadequate realisation of the potential applications for this new tool; the original estimates were correct in that they focussed on the requirements of government and military for scientific calculation. The realisation that these devices could also be used by organisations for management accounting, control and record keeping opened up the market enormously.[2] This trend of increasing applicability has continued with entry into the word processing market and, more recently, the emergence of electronic data transfer networks. As these networks extend into the home and small business the growth will continue in its upward spiral.

Not only did the early predictions about the scope of computer applications prove to be inadequate, the degree and ease of progress within the areas which were an early concern was overestimated. The potential for (what was then thought to be) almost unlimited computational power was seen to be the significant factor in promoting new discoveries. For example, one of the early predictions was that language translation of books would be readily achievable through the use of computer systems, as would speech recognition. Indeed, not only popularist science writers but people inside the emerging discipline also underestimated some of the difficulties and the direction computing would take. The Association for Computing Machinery (the pre-eminent USA professional computer society) included in their original 1947 definition of objectives the following paragraph

"The purpose of this organization would be to advance the science, development, construction, and application of the new machinery for computing, reasoning, and other handling of information."

In 1972 the phrasing was

[2] It is interesting to note a parallel with a firm who invented a device for copying engineering drawings. Projections of possible sales were low enough to suggest it was not worth marketing —the firm was Xerox.

"... to advance the sciences and arts of information processing ... the study, design, development, construction, and application of modern machinery, computing techniques and appropriate languages for general information processing, for scientific computation of all kinds, and for the automatic control and simulation of processes."

The striking substitution is that information processing has now become a goal and occupies the first, rather than the last, position in an expanded list of goals. Where information handling was once seen as the means to an end, it has become the end. Notice also that not only is information handling apparently now considered an 'art' as well as a 'science, the specific phrase 'reasoning' has been omitted. One could conclude that, in part, this omission reflects the shift in emphasis as the Society moved from being primarily an interest group to a professional institution concerned with the *process* of information handling, and that science per se has been de-emphasised. However, this would not be totally accurate; another cause for omitting reasoning might be that no one is really sure what defines it any more (although everyone is pretty sure it's hard). What tends to cloud the issue is that once acceptable synonyms for reasoning, such as 'knowledge' or 'intelligence', no longer prove to be adequate. For example, there have been demonstrations of experimental computer programs making limited inferences about objects in tightly defined environments. Few people would agree that this is an exhibition of reasoning that parallels human intellect. We shall discuss later what the limitations of these programs are.

The power of computers has been so emphasised that many people find it hard to understand how it is that computers can perform well in situations such as chess, yet are not currently involved in governmental policy decision making. In part this arises from a misunderstanding of both the nature of decisions and of intelligent behaviour. For example, intelligence is frequently defined casually in terms of what most people find it hard to do (we almost always assume chess players are very intelligent). However, attempts to make computers mimic people's abilities in a variety of 'everyday' tasks such as sensory motor activities (walking, catching, lifting etc.) or recognition (faces, places, and races) reveal real sources of difficulty initially unsuspected. Simon (1979) puts this rather nicely:

"The area in which the human being retains his largest competitive advantage, I believe, is in the coordination of a pair of eyes, a mind, and a set of hands in dealing with an external environment (for example, writing a computer program to simulate a college professor is a lot easier than writing programs to simulate a bulldozer driver)."[3]

Except in the most specific and limited of situations, computers have not

---

[3] However, perhaps this is to overly emphasise the intellect. Simon also points out that for most of the population the most creative use of their facilities is that of driving to work rather than the object of work itself.

been programmed to display "intelligent" behaviour. The problem has been that we don't understand what must be done to make computers display such behaviour. In other words, *how* to go about instructing the computer. Feigenbaum (1974) has summarised the problem in terms of the *What-to-How* spectrum:

"The potential uses of computers by people to accomplish tasks can be 'one-dimensionalized' into a spectrum representing the nature of instruction that must be given to the computer to do its job. Call it the *What-to-How* spectrum. At one extreme of the spectrum, the user supplies his intelligence to instruct the machine with precision exactly *How* to do his job, step-by-step. Progress in Computer Science can be seen as steps away from the extreme *How* point on the spectrum: the familiar panoply of assembly languages, subroutine libraries, compilers, extensible languages, etc.. At the other extreme of the spectrum is the user with his real problem (*What* he wishes the computer, as his instrument, to do for him). He aspires to communicate *What* he wants done in a language that is comfortable to him (perhaps English); via communication modes that are convenient for him (including, perhaps, speech or pictures); with some generality, some vagueness, imprecision, even error; without having to lay out in detail all necessary sub-goals for adequate performance—with reasonable assurance that he is addressing an intelligent agent that is using knowledge of his world to understand his intent, to fill in his vagueness, to make specific his abstractions, to correct his errors, to discover appropriate sub-goals, and ultimately to translate *What* he really wants done into processing steps that define *How* it shall be done by a real computer."

Although Feigenbaum was talking about the goals of artificial intelligence research, these views seem to represent what many believe communication with a computer should aspire to. Such phrases as 'symbiosis' have been bandied about as the goal of this communication. However, it is worth remembering that we still do not know much about the *How* of some of the more 'natural' basic human skills mentioned above. A review of progress in computer science in the last twenty or so years would reveal few steps away from the basic tools that provide the *How* instructions. There are bigger, faster, cheaper machines; better programming languages, better packages and system utilities. Yet the basic process of instructing the machine has changed little. (Part 3 of this book discusses issues in programming research.)

The reasons for this state of affairs are primarily technical. However, there are other non-technical factors that are important in evaluating the goals of computer science. Many of these concern social processes and the role of computers in society, and it is to these that we now turn.

2.2 Social Factors

It is not possible to discuss the evolution of computer systems without reference to their social symbolism and political significance. As instruments of technology computers may be viewed against the backdrop of many generations of other forms of technological development. The changes in society that have occurred during this time have been the concern of many social commentators and philosophers—Mumford, Ellul, Marcuse, Arendt and others. Most of the writings that have emerged from this group have stressed the negative consequences that have attended the adoption of technology and have fueled the flames of the 'Antitechnology' movement. Particular themes have been that technology is an uncontrollable force; the progenitor of unrewarding work; producer of unwanted and undesirable material goods; and a political instrument for repression. A survey of many of the approaches to the question of the value of technology to society is given by Langdon Winner in his book, *Autonomous Technology* (Winner, 1978). There have been fewer voices raised against the antitechnologists, among them Persig (1975) and Florman (1976), who support the notion of technology as a potential force for existential experience by the individual. The most well known treatment of the particular effects of computers is provided by Weizenbaum (Weizenbaum, 1976), who reflects the opinions of the former group in detailing some of the unintended consequences of computer use. It is not possible to represent even partially all these views here; the following discussion focusses on those attitudinal factors which particularly impinge upon human-computer communication.

The act of interacting with a computer holds a good deal of fascination for many people; this is evidenced by the growth in sales of home computers. People frequently have very ill-defined goals when purchasing these machines, although manufacturers usually stress the positive educational implications for children. In fact, the quality of educational software usually available with such systems is very poor. A typical pattern of activity of buyers is to spend a lot of time redesigning the software for their own use. This situation closely parallels what has been happening in more professional circles ever since computing devices gained popular currency. Software is often deficient, but equally often the motive for redesign is less than clearly stated; the fact that the individual gains considerable gratification from the intellectual process of wrestling with the machine is of great relevance. There is some quality to the interaction that produces positive reinforcement in a manner analagous to that used for animal behaviour shaping in a psychology laboratory. Ironically the difference is that here the computer is shaping the user's behaviour rather than vice versa. The root of this fascination may lie in a number of areas, both in what computers *do* and *how people think of them*. (Turkel (1979) provides an analysis of how and why people project their emotions and fantasies onto computers.) Certainly one of the explanations of such fascination is the deeply rooted desire of mankind to create autonomous artifacts that incorporate aspects of their creators. Such desire is not only evidenced by the fictional concerns of

Frankenstein but by a long history of attempts to create machines to play chess, to play musical instruments and to play games.[4]

Whatever the deep-seated roots of this fascination, it is a fact that one of the sources of the computer's attraction as an automaton is the infinite variety of possible outputs that can be exhibited. The very malleability of the environment is a source of attention. The instant power to change some facet of the system's response produces almost a commitment to that change. It is as though a student learning to play the piano found that the chromatic scale of the instrument could be adjusted and constantly engaged in a process of trying to modify it in the hope that it would dispense with the necessity to practice chords. Insight may be enhanced perhaps, but not performance. However this malleability is tempered by the 'resistance' that the system exhibits to change—error messages, unpredicted behaviour, etc.. The feeling that one is almost there, 'but'. Many programmers have been seduced by this effect into a condition (*hacking*) that in its worst form resembles a psychosis. Weizenbaum summarises the compunction that is experienced by these individuals:

"Unlike the professional, the compulsive programmer cannot attend to other tasks, not even to tasks closely related to his program, during periods when he is not actually operating the computer. He can barely tolerate being away from the machine. But when he is nevertheless forced by circumstances to be separated from it, at least he has his computer printouts with him. He studies them, he talks about them to anyone who will listen—though of course, no one else can understand them. Indeed while in the grip of his compulsion, he can talk of nothing but his program. But the only time he is, so to say, happy is when he is at the computer console." (Weizenbaum, 1976).

It is the very tightness of the person-computer feedback loop that sucks in the user; one small change may generate unpredicted effects that may take many hours to resolve. Without careful forethought and resolve, users can find themselves continuously battling to stay afloat. The more profligate the energy put in, the more dissipated.

A measure of this fascination is now being seen in the introduction of computation into the educational process. Computer programming courses have begun to find their way into junior schools. Classroom practice in the logical procedure of formalising and developing an algorithm is accorded roughly the same status that geometrical theorem proving or trigonometry used to have a few years ago. Proponents of such instruction argue that the computational metaphor is an important aid to understanding the modern world. Several people (e.g., Boden, 1978) have also argued that there is justification for this process in that it may prevent the emergence of a

[4] Lighthill (1973), in a review of the state of AI research in Great Britain, chided researchers' interest in Robotics as reflecting an urge to have mechanical children. The comment was much resented.

computer elite. Seemingly, without subjecting these tenets to any form of scrutiny, the usefulness of computer programming instruction seems to have been accepted. However, as we shall discuss, there are many more aspects to computers than the coding of algorithms. Certainly more consideration of the application limitations and social deployment of computers seems indicated.

While the programmer may find fascination, the person just introduced to a computer for the first time may exhibit a markedly different set of emotions based on fear, awe and general uncertainty. Sometimes the emotions involved may be more positive; they are in any event seldom neutral. Taylor (Chapter 9) reports studies that found that medical out-patients subjected to automated history taking via a computer terminal were highly positive towards the process, despite the question subject matter being highly personal. (This may have been novelty; it could equally well be a comment about the satisfactoriness of the patient-doctor contact.) One of the reasons that people form strong preconceptions about computers is that their workings are invisible. Without much evidence they may be quite prepared to defer to, or put trust in, the computer, believing it has superior intelligence. Weizenbaum (1976) discusses his experiences with a group of individuals who interacted with a primitive program (ELIZA) that simulated the sorts of non-directive response that a psychotherapist might make. He observed that people were only too ready to attribute human qualities to the program, to anthropomorphise it. They wished to confide in it and be alone with it and generally empathised with it. This tendency is frequently observed with other sorts of mechanical objects, from cars to airplanes. However, the effect seems particularly strong with computers. Turkel (1979) points out one explanation related to the epistemological irreducibility of computation: "The computable, the 'essential' computer has no antecedents, presents no easy analogies with other objects in the world (as the airplane does to birds) except ... for its analogies with people". That is, shorn of physical referents, people have to resort to attributing purposiveness and other human attributes to the computer.

One final issue that will be mentioned is the amount of responsibility that the user places on the computer system and vice versa. Computers are often used as scapegoats for essentially human failings—"the computer's broken down" constitutes an impenetrable barrier to further awkward questions. The computer can also be used as a means of individuals avoiding their obligations to think—"but the computer said so". However, this may also result from the human being placed in an untenable position when monitoring a system whose working he or she barely understands. Fitter & Sime (Chapter 2) and Rasmussen (Chapter 3) examine this problem from a number of viewpoints.

3.0 Communicating with Computers

Communicating with a computer is typically a very unsatisfying experience. Most of the communication is constrained to rather clumsy devices like alphanumeric or graphic display terminals and usually consists of exchanges involving short, serially ordered strings of commands or messages. The onus is on the users to check that their input and the responses of the computer are meaningful and, in terms of the actions desired, correct. The contrast with the humanoid robot characters that appeared in such films as "Star Wars" and "2001" is painfully obvious. In these fictional incidents not only do the robots understand and converse in English, they are capable of undertaking complex series of tasks in response to simple requests. (Their creators underline their humanness by giving by giving them an acceptable tinge of idiosyncracy, humour or insanity.) Such thinking mechanical artifacts are far beyond anything that can currently be produced. At the moment, real life attempts to produce speech recognising machines that have even a fraction of this sort of understanding are very limited, as we shall discuss later. For the time being, we shall turn to wider considerations of what is involved in the human-computer communication process.

Why do people (need to) communicate with computers? Principally to perform some pre-planned function or set of actions. Computers are supposed to offer ways of performing these functions that are more convenient (e.g., faster, less error prone) than would be the case if they were not available. In order to examine this assumption we have to look at what is typically involved in the act of communicating with computers. This involves a consideration of the sorts of activities which are undertaken with computers and who undertakes them. In fact it is useful to distinguish three components:

- Tasks
- Users
- Communication Interfaces

We will examine these in some detail. These components are not independent; they exist within a common environment and each influences the other and thereby itself. In the following discussion relatively little will be said about other interacting forces within this environment, particularly the social culture which the environment produces and reflects. Computers do not exist in a vacuum; there is always some sort of administrative and support structure. This is not just confined to large data processing centres, it exists even with minicomputers, though it is usually less formal and less visible. Consequently the act of communicating with a computer system draws on a whole set of underlying factors. Much of the research work in this area has focussed on the social processes attendant on introducing computers into organisations. Such factors as the centralisation of power, impact on jobs, and attitudes to automation have been investigated. Bjørn Andersen and Bloch Rasmussen (Chapter 4) discuss many of these studies. Kling (1978b) examines a set of public policy strategies for insuring the social accountability of computer systems. The study of sociological effects of computer systems constitutes a growing and important body of knowledge; however, there still exists much uncertainty in the literature about common definitions of terms, constructs and methods of investigation.

One further observation bears making at this point. Any discussion of human-computer communication highlights two quite distinct types of activity: programming, i.e., providing a very specific definition of a task and user interaction in a computer language, and the act of interacting with an executing program. The analogy can be made with the activities of designing and building a car and the very separate activity of driving it.

3.1 Tasks

It would be rather difficult to detail a list of all the application areas in which computers are used. Within this book examples cover such topics as process control, medical decision-making, information retrieval, planning, computer-aided design and several others. Although diverse, many of these applications can be described in terms of a similar task structure. On the one hand we have tasks which are tightly defined and can be thought of as being 'closed' as opposed to 'open-ended'. A closed task could most easily be typified as one which admits of precise description in terms of its goals and behaviour under different input and output conditions. The program held in an elevator controller to determine which floors are given priority would be such a task. Another, more complicated example would be the automatic control of industrial processes. Such tasks often do not require human intervention, except in the case of malfunction.[5] On the other hand, we have simple action tasks whose goal structure is quite clearly defined but specific instances of the task differ slightly. In this case we utilise computers as straightforward tools as we would use screwdrivers or typewriters. Thus, calculation, editing, and word processing are all tasks that can be more conveniently performed using computers. There are some tasks which have elements of both these two types but differ because of the amount of knowledge required. Thus segments of a car assembly plant might be technically straightforward to automate if the assembly operations were constrained to precisely fix the locations of tools and materials in space and recognition of defective performance did not have to proceed with the same flexibility

[5] Humans are often used to monitor and back up such automatic processes, a job which is very difficult to perform well when the opportunities for practice are confined to infrequent moments when things go wrong.

as a human could provide. Similarly, it would be possible to replace a filing clerk with a computer system *if* the job consisted only of retrieving documents and not answering questions about them from inexperienced users. When we want to attempt these more difficult options the going becomes very tough indeed.

There are factors present in each of these tasks which determine their ease or difficulty—the degree of complexity, the amount of determinism, the nature of the operating constraints and the types of evaluation criteria. By *complexity* we imply the number of states (number of events or ways of arranging them) in a particular application; and by *determinism*, the extent to which the occurrence of events or their sequence can be predicted in advance. Generally speaking, task difficulty can be defined as the product of these two factors. Thus when a task has few states and is completely predictable it is relatively straightforward. Simple numerical calculation would be an example of one such task. Conversely when something is very complex and subject to random or unforeseen circumstances it is very difficult to encompass. An example here would be economic forecasting. Computer systems are very successful when applied to the first of these examples and can (though not as easily as is sometimes claimed) help in exploring the possible outcomes of systems governed by chance events. Computers are most useful when task complexity is high and the situation is 'almost' deterministic—the case for most industrial and commercial systems. For example, airline reservation systems could not possibly exist in their present form without computer support.

However, airline systems have one sort of complexity, huge numbers of planes, passengers and requirements; but another aspect which makes them conceptually simple is the nature of their *operational constraints.* There are a small number of actions which can take place only at prescribed times, e.g., booking, cancelling, confirming and a host of other constraints that effectively limit the potentially enormous number of system states. What characterises these and other similar systems, then, is controllability or manageability—even though they are large aggregated systems composed of many components. (This is *not* to say that computer-based real time reservation systems are simple; on the contrary, they are equivalent to a tour de force in the computing world—for the reason of operational reliability, if for no other.) There are other resource management tasks which do not allow such a degree of control; production scheduling is a good example of a task where it is almost never possible to work out the optimal solution to a particular problem fast enough to apply it because of the complexity of the environment. Approximation techniques based on 'heuristic' rules are frequently employed in these situations.

An example of the importance of *evaluation* procedures is given in Chapter 8. Maver discusses the use of simulation programs to investigate differing solutions to the building design process. Here the task is deterministic but very complex. Computers are useful because very small changes to an element of a proposed design can have an enormous effect on the total structure and therefore its performance on the evaluation criteria (e.g., cost). Typically there are large numbers of changes that can be made to these elements, e.g., site, room sizes, materials, etc., and therefore the set of possible actions is large enough to be considered, for all practical purposes, infinite. In this instance the computer can be used as a vehicle for assessing the outcome of changes in a tightly coupled system that would normally either be very laborious or beyond the information processing capacity of a human to predict. Sometimes the amount of information produced by computer-aided systems in these situations can also exceed the handling capacity of the user. Whether or not this happens will depend upon how difficult it is to evaluate success (or failure), i.e., whether one discards unessential information. Sometimes it is not possible to decide *when* we have a satisfactory answer to a problem, or even when we have the best answer. In real life, notions of what is 'good' are frequently gleaned from relative comparisons—"This year's performance is better than last year's, but can we do better?". Unless there is a very adequate model or understanding of the cause-effect relationships in a task *and* a defined set of evaluation criteria, there is a good chance that a computer system will not improve performance.

Each of the examples given above differs in terms of its functional requirements. At the moment it is still relatively easy to partition task functions into those which can be almost completely automated and those which require human participation, whether it be for reasons of intellect, manipulative skill or simply backup. However, even in the latter tasks, we are witnessing a drift away from direct human involvement towards a 'computer-mediated' supervisory role. Whereas contact with the task environment used to be through direct sensory experience, the computer now acts as an intervening screen. This has implications not only for task performance but also for all the users that come into contact with the system. It is to the description of these users that we now turn.

3.2 Users

The majority of public utilities and commercial institutions process information using computers. Practically any individual in society can be classed as a user, even though his/her experience of 'contact' may have been only the dubious priviledge of returning an incorrect transaction and receiving the explanation that "the computer made a mistake". At the other extreme are the rapidly growing ranks of the professional programmer or systems analyst who provides services for a whole spectrum of users. This range encompasses a tremendously different variety of experience and expectancies regarding the use of computers. The issue of designing computer systems for specific groups within the user community is complicated by the inherent adaptability of the human; today's tyro is tomorrow's informed user, or even expert. This transiency accounts for much of the difficulty of focussing on a particular category of user—they won't stay in their category long without changing their requirements. Nevertheless, in talking about users in computer systems it is useful to focus on three basic groups provided by Dolotta et al. (1976): the end-user, mid-user and system support-user. The end-user may be defined as the consumer of computer services provided by the other two groups. The mid-user corresponds roughly to what could be described as the programmer/analyst whose job is to develop application packages for the end-users. The mid-user relies on the system support-user to provide and maintain the computer system facility on which the end-user's application package can be constructed. These three groups have been mentioned in order of decreasing size (and, if we were to believe that computer systems are demand driven, importance). This chapter is principally concerned with the first two groups, although the influence of the third group is frequently paramount, for this group has the power to constrain the other two.

System Support-Users.   System support-users (to use a somewhat anachronistic analogy) are the high priests of computer systems. They tend the operational requirements of the computer, administer resources amongst the user community and, when necessary, ritually exorcise bugs and glitches from the operating system. A more precise statement of their goals would include such phrases as maintaining the integrity of the system, safeguarding privacy and preventing illegal modification. In most computing situations they perform both an administrative and an operational function. This involves the art of balancing between the position of a user service agency and an autocratic supplier of those services. Unlike many administrative groups, they understand the technology they provide at a level far beyond the other two groups. This may give them the ultimate fiat ("it's not technically possible") on both their overlords and their users.

Nor is their position without problems. Resources have to be spread over the user requirements as efficiently as possible. Sometimes this necessitates shaping user behaviour: variable shift charges, connection rates, introducing and supporting only particular kinds of packages. Their role includes the difficult matter of making decisions about new technology; deciding when speed and potential flexibility are worth the cost, period of uncertainty and inconvenience that follows a decision to 'upgrade'.

One psychological phenomenon which this user has to recognise and deal with is that of software 'invisibility'. The components from which computers are made (the hardware) are now cheap. The writing of programs (the software), maintenance, and documentation continually increase in cost. Most organizations have few problems with the purchase of hardware because it can be seen, heard and touched. Software by its very nature is more difficult to experience. People who have no hesitation in sanctioning the purchase of hardware tend to become uneasy at a similar commitment to software. Furthermore, the concept that software ages and becomes more difficult (and costly) to change and maintain—just like hardware—is somehow difficult to accept. (What happens is that a piece of software tends to closely embody the facilities available at the time of its implementation; since these change relatively frequently with new machines or operating systems, etc., the software can be seen to be 'aging'.) The consequences of this state of affairs can be observed in most computer installations, particularly academic institutions, as decisions to re-write existing packages from scratch rather than adapting them to meet new circumstances.

Most of the research on system support-users has concentrated on power aspects and the move towards centralisation of function. Some of this material is discussed in Chapter 4.

Mid-Users. For most practical purposes this group of users can be considered to have the determining influence on whether a particular computer application is successful or not. The mid-user corresponds to the person who has had some limited experience with the vagaries of computer systems and understands what it is relatively easy, and not easy, to do. For example, the mid-user will typically know something about interacting with an operating system and editing files and will perhaps be familiar with one or two languages (such as PASCAL or FORTRAN) or know about data base design and the operation of statistical and other packages. Dolotta et al. (1976) list five main task areas to which this group devotes time: understanding end-user requirements, system design, implementation, testing, and maintenance.

Apart from the smallest ventures, these activities are usually performed by several individuals, sometimes structured into groups under project leaders. A term which has become synonymous with the management of this set of activities is "software engineering". Much of the literature in this area concerns the structuring of groups and individual work tasks to achieve *efficiency*. Efficiency is usually measured as the number of errors generated prior to and during installation tests or the time to complete the project. The pursuit of efficiency has concentrated on three areas: splitting the programming process into structured components, examining programming languages for their contribution to programming difficulty, and evaluating programmers and their training. By far the largest amount of computing literature is devoted to the first of these components. In this area a variety of techniques have been proposed, the basic aim usually being to decompose the task into independent sub-tasks (or modules) that are more 'intellectually manageable' by one person (or a small group of programmers). The philosophy's success depends upon constraining the decomposition process so that the modules share a common, highly specified control and communication structure. The term which has become generic for this process is Dijkstra's 'structured programming' concept (Dijkstra, 1972). (Jackson discusses some of this material in Chapter 11.)

The tools which are used to build these modules comprise the basic set of programming languages. Several of the features provided in these different languages have been the subject of empirical investigation. The intention has usually been to determine which set of features make it easy or difficult to program, and to further discover whether some are more suited to the novice than the expert. For example, investigations have centred on whether language syntax obscures the control structure of a program, thereby making it difficult to comprehend, how much semantic help the language terms provide to the programmer or whether there are too few or too many features in a language. Green (Chapter 10) provides a thorough analysis of the insights that can be offered by the tools of applied psychology. The third component, programmer selection and training, has received the least general attention. Some discussion of the issues is given by Weinberg (1971). The general attitude in computer science seems to be that programming should, if anything, make fewer demands on the individual than at present.

So far what has been discussed focusses almost exclusively on the traditional viewpoint of programming: the process of designing an algorithm to perform a task and then specifying it in terms of programming language instructions. As was indicated in the second section, the basic process has not changed in thirty years; the only difference has been the trend to 'higher level' languages which are more convenient than assemblers and other primitive facilities. There is increasing dissatisfaction with this process. Winograd (1979) points out that the nature and requirements of programming have changed as computers have become incorporated into complex systems—that solving well-structured mathematical problems is less important than utilising packages or sub-systems in the integration and modification of existing programs. Traditional programming languages do not lend themselves well to the support of such activities. There has been a good deal of conviction that programming should become more of a *description* of computational processes and objects than the creation of series of detailed instructions. As Arblaster (Chapter 12) says, "... that programming may be done by functional specification rather than the manipulation of machine words, even when, as in present programming languages, these are disguised as 'variables'.". What this functional specification should look like is unclear. Winograd (1979) points out that one can talk about formal program specification (as now, the process details), result specification (inputs and outputs) and behaviour specification (the temporal activity of a program on a machine). Thus programming by 'description' might be more analagous to detailing the behavioural specification than the program specification.

One of Winograd's distinctions that is particularly germane to the subject of human-computer communication is the notion of description domains. Using the construction of a university classroom assignment system as an example, he defines the *subject, interaction* and *implementation* domains. The subject domain represents knowledge about the task world and a description of the properties of objects in this world (buildings, classrooms, etc.). The interaction domain represents the viewpoint of the user in that it defines the communication aspects (questions, answers, statistical techniques, etc.) that will be used. (It also covers inter-communication between different parts of the system.) The implementation domain incorporates things that range from parts of the hardware, the operating system, to the exact form of data structures. This approach is an interesting one in that it brings more clearly into focus the importance of the (end-) user's specification of the form of the communication as something rather more than an afterthought tacked onto the basic control structure. However, there are substantial areas of difficulty yet to be resolved before such schemes can be thought of as practical. At the very least, some or all of this world knowledge has to be provided for, or assimilated by, machines.

A major point has been passed over in reviewing this material, i.e., how much attention is paid to the process of eliciting the end-user's requirements in constructing systems. Since this user does not usually know what he or she wants in other than very general terms, and the process of obtaining the information is typically at best described as ad hoc, very often the system reflects the mid-user's idea of the end-user's requirements rather more than the end-user's. Very little research has been devoted to how well systems meet *end-user* expectations. There is considerable need for research into improved methods in this area. Such research would probably have to be based on techniques of formative evaluation by external groups.

Another aspect of the mid-user's task relates to testing and maintenance. Incidents which occur from both simple and complex errors in computer systems are not uncommon. Not surprisingly, errors in complex systems tend to be more catastrophic when they occur but are usually very difficult to discover in advance.[6] It may be that errors are the inevitable conse-

---

[6] This is typified by the discovery in 1979 of a design flaw that caused the shutdown of five nuclear power stations in the USA. The flaw was caused by an error in a sub-routine that was part of a modelling program used in the initial design process. The error resulted in core pipes not being made thick enough to withstand potential earthquake forces. The interesting point is that the error was not discovered until the stations had been in operation several years and long after the original design program had been discarded in favour of a newer program. (ACM, 1979).

quences of building complex systems. Whether or not this is the case is a matter of debate. However, the amount of effort devoted to the process of error *correction* has been a cause of concern. The operation and maintenance of computer systems and packages usually receives far less attention than the process of their design. The consequence is that errors persist throughout the lifetime of some systems. This seldom troubles the mid-user directly because he or she either knows enough to get around the system or is not affected by the error. However the end-user often has a much more difficult time trying to get errors corrected.

When systems develop errors which cause injuries or material loss the question of accountability comes up. Who should be blamed in such a situation, the computer, the operators of the computer system or the designers of the package? Or is no single one of these accountable? In most countries strict legal liability has not yet been fully established for computer controlled systems. Moral (as opposed to legal) liability is perhaps a more difficult concept yet. Fitter and Sime explore both problems in Chapter 2.

End-Users. There are two basic categories of end-user, *indirect* and *direct.*[7] The indirect user is the customer of the computer service providers, the person who writes a cheque, uses a credit card or receives a gas bill. Although this group are customers of such services they have almost no direct power to influence them. For example, the end-user often has a difficult time trying to get errors corrected, particularly when they are in favour of the system. Sterling (1979) reports that approximately 40% of the respondents to a British Columbia survey reported computer errors (mostly in billings). Not only was it difficult to get the organisations responsible to fully correct these errors, it was sometimes impossible. Frequently such faults are attributed to the nature of the computer system making correction difficult. Although similar errors have been reported in other types of system, they seem to be more prevalent and resistant with computers. Often this reflects a disinclination on the part of the organisation running the system to take up user complaints. The causes are various. Sometimes the real problem is one of technical expertise; the people who designed and built the particular system have left, and literally nobody knows, or remembers, how to modify it. Sometimes the problem comes down to finance; the operational budget does not cover corrections and adjustments. Sometimes it is both of these reasons and the fact that an external complainant does not have the power to influence the organisation. Seemingly the only sure means to achieve change is through regulatory control. Some of the social issues mentioned in first section (e.g., privacy, right to inspect personal data records, right to

---

[7] Dolotta et al. (1976) identify a third category, those people who specify the requirements of a computer system to the mid-users. In practice this group can usually be considered as belonging to one of the other two.

demand changes) are slowly being tackled by such means. New issues continually arise, a recent example being the status of traditional customer practices in electronic funds transfer—the potential disappearance of the 'float' caused by the delay in processing cheques as instant debits and credits become common (for wider considerations of this topic see Kling, 1978a). General sources of social issues are Mumford & Sackman (1975) and Gotlieb & Borodin (1973).

The second category are those people who directly interact with a computer system. The *direct* user tends to fall into one of two types, depending upon job role and/or knowledge of the system. The first type are those people who operate a terminal as part of their job, e.g., clerks in banking and reservation systems. These are the people who the mid-users typically would like to automate out of the system. Although there are gloomy prognostications about future unemployment in this group, many of the jobs have an interpersonal component (e.g., interacting with a client) which is likely to preserve them (that is, perhaps as long as the economic price for choosing to have someone else type into a machine remains invisible). Certainly the jobs without this interpersonal component, e.g., data entry, are in a more precarious position.

The other type of direct users are those people who interact with a computer system in a less constrained way and understand how to use particular software packages. They may be managers, accountants, doctors, librarians and other professional groups. Because these users are not computer experts (in the mid-user sense), they depend upon mid-user products being intelligible and easy to operate. Furthermore, they require consistent communication interfaces, good documentation and access to advisors. This group of users are those who are the subject of the application research in the second part of this book. Many of their requirements are discussed in the next section.

3.3 Communication Interfaces

Each of the users mentioned in the previous section needs very different types of interaction dialogue, documentation, and other aids in cases of difficulty. However, it also has to be borne in mind that users *within* each of these categories also need different kinds of communication; for example, systems which give detailed prompts appear to be very helpful to the inexperienced user, but quite soon that same user will find the dialogue irritatingly verbose as he or she becomes more practiced. We will use the term 'communication interface' to describe all the communication processes that go on concerning user interaction with a computer. What constitutes good communication interface design? Sometimes the principles have been stated succinctly as providing 'natural' communication facilities for the user. What this means in practice is seldom clear. Although there are some general guidelines arising from the human factors literature for the design of hardware displays and input devices (e.g., Martin, 1973), it is difficult to make prescriptive comments about the detailed design of the communication interface on a general basis as much depends upon the particular situation.

Earlier in this chapter we quoted Feigenbaum (1974) describing what a computer should be able to do. He noted that the user would like the computer to have a number of characteristics: a discourse language which is comfortable *for the user*, appropriate communication modalities, and computer responsiveness to user vagueness, imprecision and error. All of these characteristics should ideally be encapsulated (implicitly or explicitly) in the communication interface for any type of task. Although intuitively reasonable, defining what each of these means for particular users and tasks is not easy. Seemingly the yardstick for the design of the communication interface ought to be that of human communication, i.e., of a discourse between two people. However, one of the properties of good human communication is that it represents a transactional process in which the speaker and listener alternate roles, spend a good deal of their time anticipating what the other will say, or noting any reaction to what is being said. The basic act of communication also embodies a social transaction component, even in cases where 'factual' information is being imparted. The two participants could be said to share the following attributes:

- Representation—similar modalities, language capability and underlying thought mechanisms.
- Knowledge—about each other's background, about the subject of the communication, about correct social norms of behaviour (e.g., honesty and reliability).
- Adaptability—modifying the discourse to take account of what has happened in the present and previous communications.

Such an array of qualities constitutes a formidable challenge to any notion of making the computer responsive to the same degree as a human. In fact some of these attributes would be impossible to assimilate into the computer, since they are physical and not just cognitive properties. For example, body language conveys a great deal of information about the progress of a communication—impatience, frustration, boredom, etc.. Even if it were possible for a machine to recognise such attitudinal states, it would not be possible for it to signal their recognition back to a human. This basic unresponsiveness to the user's 'state of mind' cannot be overcome. Furthermore, there are other social considerations in the exchange such as authority, role status and responsibility, which are also very difficult to encompass. Clearly, all that is part of human communication cannot be reproduced in the communication interface. The most reasonable expectation would seem to be to make it as responsive to as many of the above factors as possible *and* delineate carefully what can and cannot be done. Some of these unattainable components are very important and should be defined as part of the external environment (e.g., accountability).

In discussing the issue of representation we must separate out the underlying subject of a discourse and the language tokens that are exchanged as part of the communication process. Languages differ as tasks differ; as Green (Chapter 10) points out, algebraic notation evolved because it was laborious to use ordinary written language for mathematical manipulation. Similarly, inadequacies in artistic representations of physical objects prompted designers to evolve languages for representing three-dimensional forms on a two-dimensional surface—paper. There are also a number of special-purpose languages available for differing kinds of computer tasks such as manipulating record structures or text strings. Each has a set of properties that tend to make it uniquely suitable for specific applications. Although there have been many attempts to design completely general purpose computer languages (the DOD language ADA being a recent example), not many people would argue that it is worthwhile or even desirable.

The difficulty of adequately talking about representation comes in the distinction between the overt process of communication and the underlying processes of meaning or intent. For example, communication dialogues are usually intended to convey information, perhaps clarify meaning and/or evoke actions from the participants. However, the *type* of representation tends to be determined by the task and the *level* of representation by the amount of knowledge the participants share. If a teacher is explaining something to a student, what is said and how it is said will naturally differ from what happens when the teacher is talking to a colleague. People are particularly adept at making transitions between these levels of shared understanding, based upon their prediction of what is being, or will be, comprehended by the other party. The process of communication ultimately cannot occur unless there is this comprehension. In human-computer communication the representation is similarly crucial, but the dissimilarities of the components form an obstacle. When interacting with a computer, the human has a model of the task environment, a set of goals and (typically) a diffuse model or image of how the computer represents the task. For its part, the computer is usually provided only with a formal model of the task process and a control structure that is operated on by the communication interface. It does not have a model of the users, their expectancies and preferred ways of reaching their goals, nor can it adapt to them. Such accommodation as there is normally has to be built into the system at the time of its inception.[8] Since the communication is therefore primarily one-sided, it becomes very important for the user to have an adequate understanding of the range of behaviours of the computer.

This behaviour can be represented at a number of levels. Situations in which the user gives *simple commands* and the computer responds with *unique actions* facilitate the user's classification and control of the machine's behaviour. The more immediate and direct the relationship between the command and action, the easier it will be for the user to comprehend. How the underlying process in the machine maps the command into the action need not necessarily be the user's concern; indeed it may often be beyond his capability to comprehend. As long as there is a unique and observable response of the system to each user input, this will not necessarily matter. This is a description which fits much computer use at present because of the low level and *imperative* style of most interactive computer languages and packages. For example, any use of computer driven graphic displays in design activities involves the positioning of objects on a display screen. The user can indicate the intended placement by utilising a light pen, mouse, tabiet or similar device and can observe the outcome on the display. Foley (1978) and Foley & Wallace (1974) describe many of the desirable characteristics of such action/outcome languages for graphic display. In this type of situation it is often possible to conduct experiments to decide what is the most suitable format and modality for the communication.

One distinction that occurs in these and more complicated interactive dialogues is that of 'state' information versus 'control' information—that is, separating the communication of the control instructions and responses from their effect on the machine's task model. This applies whether the situation is querying a database, editing text or running a simulation program. The distinction applies to higher levels of representation also. In particular, state information is necessary to tell the users where they are, have been, and are going. In many interface activities it is easy for the computer to keep a record of this information, but not so easy for the human to keep track of it. Indeed, it is possible to get lost in exploring systems which can take on many states. (This is surely going to happen with teletext information systems in the home—e.g., Prestel—where information in vast data bases is accessed one page at a time and the user crawls through the system page by page.) Various suggestions have been made for helping the user that employ novel representations for state location and evaluation (e.g., Rasmussen 1976; Smith, 1976; Bolt, 1978).

So far we have been talking about situations which have the character-

---

[8] Recent computer aided learning programs have in fact attempted to include a simple model of the user's strategies so that the program can deduce why particular sorts of errors are being made. See Hartley (Chapter 5).

istics of a generalised finite state automaton—that is, each state transition has associated with it a condition and response. Fitter (1979) and Cheriton(1976) discuss how such systems should be controlled. For more complicated degrees of communication involving some degree of adaptability on the part of the participants, the idea of being confined to a dialogue consisting entirely of simple commands is less than attractive. This is not because such commands are unable to express quite complex ideas or actions; they can. However, as far as the user is concerned, the efficiency of such a process is low. The analogy is to completing a jigsaw without looking at the picture on the box; there are lots of pieces, they have to be put together in the right sequence, and an incorrect sub-assembly means the picture cannot be completed. In other words, this is both a time-consuming and highly specialised task requiring extensive practice. The designers of data base query languages have grappled with this problem for some time. A review of data base research is given in Mohan (1978), and human factors aspects are considered by Martin (Chapter 6) and also Shneiderman(1978). Data base query languages have varied from procedure-type formalisms, through template selections, to subsets of natural language. No totally satisfactory solution to the problem has been found. One of the chief difficulties is that users have to limit their queries to forms that are valid for the data model used (i.e., a query may be 'correct' yet not meaningful because it uses terms that have not been defined for the data model). Therefore, in the absence of a discourse facility, the user has to spend some time planning how to break a particular question down into carefully phrased query statements.

An illustration of the importance of discourse in this type of task specification is given by Mann (1975). He provides an extract of a hypothetical conversation between two people concerning the design of an office index system that one individual wants the other to implement:

Goals and Purposes

"I want to be able to find things I have already read, and maintain a list of stuff I haven't read yet by topic, so that I can easily pick things to read."

Examples

"So you would index Speech Acts under Searle, and Ordinary-language Philosophy and Illocution."

Description

"The index should include several entry regions, by author and title and so forth, and a region of citations."

Clarifications

"I want all papers indexed."

"Do you mean the papers in the journals too?"

"No."

Hypothetical Conditions

> "Suppose I find two different papers with the same title and author."

Functional Descriptions

> "The location code tells where the item is physically, within a couple of feet of shelf."

Analogies and Comparisons

> "The authors section is like the white pages, and the subject section is like the yellow pages."

Similarities and Differences

> "It's like a library card catalog, except that we're not using code numbering or cards."

Refused Commands

> "I can't index the papers this week."

Mann's hypothetical example illustrates the importance of both participants having a common body of knowledge to identify the exact requirements of the task. Most of the above comments would be difficult to translate into command form irrespective of the type of representation. This underlines comments made earlier—that to have a truly co-operative system there must exist some sort of model of the intended subject shared by all components in the system. This model must, as in the example above, be capable of being extended or made more specific to the task at hand through the process of communication. This does not mean that the only acceptable form of communication between people and computers is natural language. The argument has been that to mimic the flexibility of humans, the computer component has to be an active rather than a passive member of the dialogue. However, the optimistic belief in the 'natural language' solution to the communication interface problem is very appealing at first sight. Since second sight is a prerequisite for computer system design, we will examine the promise of such solutions in more detail.

4.0 (Un)Natural Language Communication

The need for natural language 'understanding' systems has been argued by many authors in the field of computer science over the years. The main justification cited is that natural language capability is of fundamental importance if computers are to be fully utilised by end-users (i.e., those who do not have the time, capability or inclination to learn and use formal computer languages). Furthermore, it is suggested that natural language is the ideal communication medium for many applications. In fact, the application area which has attracted the most theoretical interest has been that of information retrieval, primarily because it is possible to closely define the scope of the language system in terms of the underlying data base. Complicated systems involving discourse and problem solving have proceeded at a much slower pace than at first anticipated. Systems which also attempt to incorporate general speech recognition, as opposed to textual input, have been the most difficult of all to build.

The fundamental problem has been generalising successful experimental projects involving very limited domains to more realistic situations. As we shall see, it has turned out that the solution to even very specific natural language problems involves a great deal of general comprehension or understanding about the world. A distinction should be made here between research attempts to make use of Natural Language for *writing* programs in the conventional sense (i.e., to implement algorithms and/or sets of actions) and its use to explain or qualify the subject matter of a discourse (sometimes somewhat misleadingly referred to as question-answering). Although one can conceive of situations in which these activities amount to the same thing, the distinction reflects different strands of work in the research literature. Thus several attempts have been made to design computer programming languages which look like English—COBOL being an early example. By and large, the consensus seems to be that this is not possible without imposing undue constraints on language terms that have to reflect underlying control structures. One result is that although procedures couched in such languages often read acceptably, the act of writing procedures is far from the straightforward employment of natural forms of English. Halpern (1966) rather succinctly summed up this approach; "Combining the wordiness and noisiness of a natural language with the rigidity and arbitrariness typical of programming languages ... exhibits the worst features of both and the virtues of neither". Green (Chapter 10) discusses in detail these and other considerations in the design of programming languages.

In what follows we will primarily consider interactive discourse language systems. However, in some of these the distinction between question-answering and programming is rather obscure since the systems are extensible, e.g, terms and special cases can be added. Attempts to employ natural language have encountered a number of difficulties. Petrick (1976), in reviewing features of several natural-language-based systems, summarises the more important objections to the natural language movement:

- The most difficult aspects of a problem are formulating it precisely, analyzing it, and planning the method of solution in detail. Actual code production is relatively straightforward and easy.
- Natural language is inherently too loose, vague, and ambiguous to serve as a computer language. For this reason its use would lead to processing inefficiency and possible error due to misunderstanding of intended meaning.

- Allowing the use of unrestricted natural language is technically infeasible and likely to remain so in the foreseeable future. Consequently, subsets of natural languages must be used for communicating with computers. These subsets would be harder to learn and use than traditional formal computer languages because of interference with natural language usage habits.
- Providing a large enough subset of a natural language to be useful is an exceedingly difficult intellectual activity, requiring not only a far greater command of linguistics than is likely to be available for many years, but also requiring capabilities for representing an enormous quantity of information about the world and for efficiently drawing deductive and inductive conclusions from that information.

It is worthwhile to examine these objections in a little more detail. The first of these is relatively clear. Most problems can be specified to a point where the translation to any form of programming language is simple. Thus, for example, if one could anticipate all the questions that users of a particular database would ask, the questions and forms of suitable responses could be 'built-in' to the system. Particular questions could then be invoked by selection of items from a pre-stored menu. In this instance the full power of a natural language processor becomes unnecessary, since the potential variety of terms that it offers is not required. Although sometimes reasonable, there are many situations in which it would be hard, tedious, or even impossible to pre-specify the dialogue. There are also cases, for example in computer aided learning, where it is very desirable to have a discourse capability to allow clarifying questions to be phrased or to enable extensions to the facilities to be easily defined. The second objection is that natural language is inherently not a suitable vehicle for communication due to its ambiguousness and imprecision. This is obviously true for many purposes. In cases where rules or instructions have to be couched in English, difficulties often arise in trying to make them unambiguous. When achieved, it is usually at the expense of clarity and parsimony. (Because of this problem, attempts have been made to substitute artificial languages or representational structures for the involved convolutions that typify legal documents, e.g., Stamper, 1976). Hill (1973) presents a number of amusing illustrations of the ambiguities of English:

"You would scarcely recognise little Johnny now. He has grown another foot."

or the office notice

"During the present fuel shortage please take advantage of your secretary between the hours of 12 and 2."

Hill also points out several other forms of difficulty in natural language—

idiomatic expressions which may be used to imply the reverse of what they say, words with multiple meanings, and problems of scope. The latter present a particular problem — in computer languages the boundaries of clauses are usually well marked by delimiters (such as *begin* and *end*). Furthermore, which external terms can and cannot affect the expressions within the delimiters is well defined. In natural languages no such explicit markers exist (or are regularly used) and correct interpretation depends on the recipient of a communication having a body of shared knowledge with the sender that includes likely patterns of actions and values. This problem is particularly pertinent to the third of Petrick's objections. The third objection is concerned with the consequences of the fact that it is technically infeasible at present to use other than a subset of natural language for communication (i.e., unnatural languages). So far we have not described the technical difficulties in constructing natural language processors, and these will now be briefly outlined. Martin (1978) succinctly summarises these difficulties and we will present some of his examples. There at least four components that typically appear in descriptions of the problems of natural language processing:

- Syntax
- World knowledge
- Discourse context
- Problem solving

Syntactic rules that identify correct or incorrect grammatical constructions are well known. The phrase

"I reached for it"

is clearly acceptable, whereas

"I reached it for"

is not. However, the phrase "I reached it for the first time" is acceptable. The number of permissible syntactic rules constructions that would be needed to define most constructions in a language would be very large. Although it would be conceivably possible to incorporate many of them in a computer data base as an aid to decoding utterances, it is doubtful whether the effort would be worthwhile since, through semantic cues, world knowledge often appears to allow people to understand sentences which are syntactically incorrect. However, most natural language programs utilise syntactic knowledge in one form or another. World knowledge is clearly useful in divorcing intended meaning from a whole host of other possibilities. Thus, in reading

"I rode down the street in the car"

one does not consider the possibility of the street being in the car, even though this is syntactically correct. Despite the fact that most natural language systems deliberately have a very limited domain, world knowledge is still a problem. This is because there are no formal rules for generating likely relevant knowledge about a subject at a given level of specificity. Therefore provision has to be made for more complete knowledge to be added. Martin (1978) specifies a hypothetical dialogue between a user and a question-answering system (QAS) that exemplifies the problem quite well.

> *(User) What was the most profitable plant in 1977?*

(QAS) I'm afraid I don't know the word "profitable". Is it a noun, verb, or adjective or adverb?

> *Adjective*

Does "profitable" come from adding "able" to "profit"?

> *Yes*

Is "profit" a noun, verb, adjective or adverb?

> *Noun*

Can you state a condition involving "profit" and "plant" that tells when a plant is profitable.

> *Profit of plant greater than 0*

I see that profit is a numerical quantity. What are the units of measure?

> *Dollars*

Is a plant more profitable when the profit of the plant is greater?

> *Yes*

Can you define the profit of a plant in terms of quantities I am familiar with?

> *The profit of a plant equals the revenue minus the expenses*

I'm afraid I don't know the word "revenue". Is it a noun, verb, adjective, or adverb?

As Martin says, this would be fairly tedious. However, systems which are short of world knowledge have a lot of catching up to do. Therefore some convenient means of specifying such knowledge must be found.

Discourse knowledge is also required so that the present (and past) context of the communication can be used to guide interpretations. At the simplest level this might be used to determine pronoun referents. With question/answer systems contextual information will be used to guide the answer. Kaplan (1978), in discussing natural language systems, identifies a number of relevant contextual features that they must have if they are to be co-operative. For example:

Q: Which departments that sell scissors also sell blade sharpeners?

R1:   No departments sell scissors.

R2:   None.

R1 can be described as being more co-operative than R2. As was mentioned earlier, in human communication the respondent is co-operative in usually providing information that is *not* requested by the question. Siklossy (1978) discusses the need for such facilities in computer systems, entitling them 'impertinent' question-answer systems. He identifies an important failing in present QAS systems—that they frequently only return answers to literal contents of the question, not the focus of the subject. The following details another hypothetical result of a system lacking impertinence.

> (User) *I want to make a trip from Chicago to London by air, then return to Chicago.*

(QAS) When do you wish to leave?

> *June 1.*

Will you fly first class?

> *No, economy.*

I can book you on TWA flight 746, leaving 9:30 p.m. on June 1, and returning TWA 753, leaving London Heathrow on June 14 at 10 a.m.

> *Fine. Thank you. Bye.*

The continuation of our scenario shows that User was "had!" On the plane on June 1, User's neighbor also flies to London, but returns 1 day later, on June 15. Her ticket cost $250.00 less than User's. While in London, User meets a fellow Chicagoan who left 1 day earlier, on May 31, and returns also a day earlier, on June 13. Her ticket cost $175.00 less than User's. On the return flight, on June 14, User's neighbor mentions that she left Chicago 1 day before User, on May 31. Her ticket cost $375.00 less than User's. In Chicago, User calls up his trusty QAS:

> *Why didn't you tell me that if I returned 1 day later I would save $250.00?*

Let me check. You are *so* right. But, you know, you didn't ask!

> *Why didn't you tell me that if I moved my entire trip back by 1 single, lousy day, I could save $175.00?*

Let me check. You are *so* right. But, you know, you didn't ask!

> *Why didn't you tell me that if I left 1 day earlier, returning on the same day as I did, I would have saved $375.00?*

Siklossy proposes that an impertinent QAS can be constructed by building a system that notices when a small change in the wording of a question will produce a large change in the 'answer space' that is favourable to the user. However, the technical difficulties here are immense. Such a mechanism must not only know what constitutes a sensible change to the question but must also have a problem solving capability tied to a representation of the user's goals and values. We are back in the realm of deducing meaning from information that is not present in the communication dialogue, i.e., having an 'appropriate' model of the user.

Before concluding this section, we should mention the computer processing of spoken, as opposed to textual, input. If text processing is difficult, the spoken form is much harder. Text is already segmented into words; speech has to be similarly broken down before it can be understood. However, research has shown that it cannot be easily broken down until it has been understood! The goals of a five-year ARPA research project that started in 1971 were 90% accuracy in recognition of a 1000-word vocabulary with several speakers. (Klatt (1977) reviews this project.) Only one system succeeded in meeting the principal performance specifications, even though there were considerable syntactic and semantic constraints. In the intervening period no dramatic breakthroughs have been reported. Nevertheless, although true speech recognition has so far been unattainable, a number of so-called speech recognition devices are on the market. These recognise short utterances (e.g., numbers or one word commands) drawn from a small vocabulary. Such systems require the user to 'tune' the system by enunciating the complete vocabulary. Apart from demonstrations, the potential use of these devices seems limited.

Speech synthesis has been less of a problem; it is possible to have a 'canned' set of words or phrases delivered in a style only slightly reminiscent of a cybernaut. Spontaneous generation of speech in real time with natural inflection has so far been elusive. There are applications in which sound output is useful, for example, repeating back commands that have been punched or typed in. However, apart from its use in the performance of straightforward routine tasks, it is not yet clear how often this is a truly decisive advantage.

In summary, what has been emphasised in this section is the difficulty of proposing completely (or even partially) *general* purpose natural language systems. There have been several successful data base systems which employ limited subsets of natural language. The important point being made here is that these are most beneficial when the user sticks to a fairly small range of questions *or* understands the underlying data structure to the point that any ambiguities in the language translation process can be resolved. This does bring one back towards wondering whether, under these restrictions, a natural language capability is required. Undoubtedly a natural language system seems attractive for many applications. However, there is a dearth of evidence to say that in real, as opposed to the sort of limited domains that exist in experimental, situations end-users need such capability. Perhaps they would indeed be better off employing a human intermediary who understood the system's restrictions and who did not require anything as broad as natural language capability.

5.0 Conclusion

This chapter has attempted to review briefly many of the factors that influence human-computer communication and set the scene for the other contributions in this book. It has ranged across both technical and social characteristics, from computer capabilities to human preferences. The need for better understanding and integration of the requirements of tasks, users and communication procedures has been presented. Underscoring the urgency of this need is the steady advance of computer systems into every aspect of life. Soon the home computer terminal will take its place alongside the stereo as another indispensable component of modern living. A large number of technical and pedagogical problems will need to be solved if these devices are to be used by other than that subset of the population that speaks 'computerese'.

Equally important, or perhaps more so, is the question of what role we wish computer systems to play in our society. There is a need to take careful stock of what sorts of values we wish to preserve, to carefully balance technical prowess with human interests. Sometimes conflicts arise which make this balance difficult. For example, Taylor (Chapter 9) discusses the positive effects of computer diagnostic systems in clinical medicine. He also points out that there are many influences at work in computer adoption, e.g., physicians being more responsive to computer systems than to trained paramedics capable of doing the same job—the latter threaten professional status. There are other areas where similar political factors enter into decisions. There will always be such factors; the only satisfactory solution is to make sure that they are made explicit in any decision process regarding computer adoption.

Another area of concern is the conflict between technical fascination and pragmatism. An example here is the continued commercial interest in speech synthesizers and speech recognition equipment. Except in certain situations (e.g., for those people who are handicapped) there is little efficiency to be gained from using speech input and output unless it is combined with formidable problem solving power. No one (I hope) would dream of using a speech recognition system to drive a car—what if you coughed at a vital moment! If it ever becomes possible to say "drive me to San Francisco" and then sit back, that will be another matter, but not before.

In the meantime it might be worthwhile to spend more time thinking how we might build humans *into* systems rather than designing them out in the pursuit of technical advances. The human still has no rival for explanation; most people who have learned anything about computer systems would confess to having greatly benefitted from access to expert advisors. It might continue to be a better technical and social strategy to train someone to understand the system *and* the user requests, so that person can act as the user's agent, rather than pursuing the goal of training the system to understand the user. The rise of the information broker (see Chapter 6) is perhaps a harbinger of such a trend. The problems are still formidable, but so are the consequences of not doing anything.

References

ACM. (1979). An editorial on software correctness and the social process. *ACM SIGSOFT (Software engineering notes)*, **4**, 2.

Boden, M.A. (1978). Social Implications of Intelligent Machines. *Proceedings ACM Annual Conference*, ACM, New York.

Bolt, R.A. (1978). Spatial Data Management-Interim Report. Architecture Machine Group, MIT. (DARPA MDA903-77-c-0037).

Cheriton, D.R. (1976). Man-machine interface design for time-sharing systems. *Proceedings ACM Annual Conference*, ACM, New York.

De Millo, R.A., Lipton, R.J., & Perlis, A.J. (1979). Social processes and proofs of Theorems and Programs. *Communications ACM*, **22**, 5, 271-280.

Dijkstra, E.W. (1972). Notes on structured programming. In *Structured Programming* (eds.) Dahl, O.J., Dijkstra, E.W. & Hoare, C.A.R. Academic Press, New York.

Dolotta, T.A. et al. (1976). *Data Processing in 1980-1985.* John Wiley, New York.

Feigenbaum, E.A. (1974). 'Artificial Intelligence Research: What is it? What has it achieved? Where is it going? *Symposium on Artificial Intelligence*, Canberra, Australia.

Fitter, M. (1979). Towards more "natural" interactive systems. *International Journal Man-Machine Studies*, **11**, 339-350.

Florman, S.C. (1976). *The Existential Pleasures of Engineering.* St. Martin's Press, New York.

Foley, J.D. & Wallace, V.L. (1974). The art of natural graphic man-machine Conversation. *IEEE Proceedings 62*, 4, 462-470.

Foley, J.D. (1978). The human factors-computer graphics interface. Paper presented at Annual ACM Conference, Washington, DC.

Gotlieb, K.C. & Borodin, A. (1973). *Social Issues in Computing*. Academic Press, New York.

Halpern, M. (1966). Foundations of the case for Natural Language Programming. *AFIPS Fall Joint Computer Conference Proceedings 29*, 639-649.

Heidorn, G.E. (1976). Automatic programming through natural language dialogue: a survey. *IBM Journal of Research and Development*, 20, 302-313.

Hill, I.D. (1972). Wouldn't it be nice if we could write computer programs in ordinary English or would it? *Computer Bulletin*, 16, 306-312.

Jackson, M.A. (1975). *Principles of Program Design*. Academic Press, London.

Kaplan, S.J. (1978). On the differences between Natural Language and High Level Query Languages. *Proceedings ACM Annual Conference*, ACM, New York.

Klatt, D.H. (1977). Review of the ARPA Speech Understanding Project. *Journal Acoustic Society of America*, 62, 6, 1345-1366.

Kling, R. (1978a). Value Conflicts and Social choice in Electronic funds Transfer System Developments. *Communications ACM*, 21, 8.

Kling, R. (1978b). Six Models for the social accountability of Computing. ACM Computers and Society, 9, 2.

Lighthill, J. (1973). *Artificial intelligence:a paper symposium*. Science Research Council, London.

Loudon, K.C. (1979) Complexity in large federal Data Banks: The FBI and IRS Systems. Paper presented at *UC Irvine Conference on Social Issues and Impacts of Computing*, Lake Arrowhead, California. August.

Mann, W.C. (1975). *Why things are so bad for the computer-naive user*. ISI Institute, 4676 Admiralty Way, Marina Del Rey, California.

Martin, J. (1973). *Design of Man-Computer Dialogues*. Prentice-Hall, New Jersey.

Martin, W.A. (1978). Some comments on EQS, A Near Term Natural Language Data Base Query System. *Proceedings Annual ACM Conference*, ACM, New York.

Mohan, C. (1978). An Overview of Recent Data Base Research. *ACM SIGBDP*, 10, 2.

Mumford, E. & Sackman, H. (1975). *Human Choice and Computers*. North-Holland Publishing Co., Amsterdam.

Persig, R.M. (1974). *Zen and the Art of Motorcycle Maintenance*. Bantam Books, New York.

Petrick, S.R. (1976). On Natural Language Based Computer Systems. *IBM Journal Research & Development*, 20, 314-325.

Rasmussen, J. (1976). *The Human data processor as a System Component: bits and pieces of a model*. Riso-M-1722

Shneiderman, B. (1978). Improving the human factors aspect of database Interactions. *ACM Transactions on Database Systems*, 3, 4.

Siklossy, L. (1978). Impertinent Question-Answering Systems: justification and theory. *Procdings Annual ACM Conference*, ACM, New York.

Simon, H. (1979). Decision Making is a Satisficing Experience (Interview). *Management Review*, 68, 1.

Smith, H.T. (1976). Perceptual Organization and the design of the man-computer interface in process control. In *Monitoring Behaviour and Supervisory Control* (eds.) Sheridan, T.B. & Johannsen, G. Plenum press, New York.

Stamper, R.K. (1976). *The Legol project: a survey*. IBM UKSC Report 0081. Peterlee, County Durham, England.

Sterling, T.D. (1979). Consumer difficulties with computerized transactions: An empirical investigation. *Communications ACM*, 22, 5, 283-289.

Turkel, S. (1979). Computers as Rorschach: Subjectivity and Social responsibility. Paper presented at *UC Irvine Conference on Social Issues and Impacts of Computing*, Lake Arrowhead, California. August.

Weinberg, G. (1971). *The Psychology of computer programming*. Van Nostrand Reinhold, New York.

Weizenbaum, J. (1976). *Computer Power and Human Reason*. W.H. Freeman, San Francisco.

Winner, L. (1977). *Autonomous Technology*. MIT Press, Cambridge, Mass.

Winograd, T. (1979). Beyond Programming Languages. *Communications ACM*, **22**, 7, 391-401.

Chapter 2

CREATING RESPONSIVE COMPUTERS: RESPONSIBILITY
AND SHARED DECISION-MAKING

Mike Fitter & Max Sime

Contents

1.0 Introduction

One of the major considerations when developing computer software has
been to produce a responsive system. In the past emphasis has tended to
be on the speed of response, and a considerable amount of human factors
research has concerned what would be an *acceptable* response time to the
user in a variety of contexts (Miller, 1968). With the development of the
field of 'Software Engineering' over the last ten years, the *quality* of the
response has become a matter of concern. Herb Grosch (1978) has characterized the field as "the technology of making very complex computer
programs responsive to user needs, free of errors, and economical". This
has, in part, followed from developments in interactive software due to
improved graphics and manual input facilities which have permitted the
user to be (and feel) in control of the system in a manner analogous to a
driver being in control of his car. As Brooks (1977) has stressed, "Moving
images on a screen have great power to inform; images that move *in response* to one's manipulation seem to be perceived more as real things and

studied more intently. Such systems achieve a high degree of transparency." (p. 629). When these systems have been developed for the purposes of decision making (often at the level of corporate or project planning) they have been referred to as Decision Support Systems (Scott Morton and Huff, Chapter 7), and as their very name suggests, they offer an aid to the decision-maker to enable him to devise higher quality solutions to what are often only partially formulated problems.

This chapter is concerned with the changing role and responsibilities of the decision-maker (be it an individual or a collective decision) when *automated decision aids are introduced*. If the decision-maker is not to be placed in a stressful, or even impossible position, some of the following factors need to be taken into account when designing such systems:

- The status of the user:—Does the user have the authority to override the automated decision on some or all issues? Do the persons to whom he is accountable for his decisions have an adequate understanding of the automated system? Is the decision-maker being placed in a position where the only sensible strategy is to 'opt-out' rather than risk overriding the automation?

- The seriousness of the consequences of a decision:—If the consequences of a wrong decision are potentially very great (as in medical diagnosis or Air Traffic Control) the decision-maker is likely to look for cautious (and probably inefficient) strategies, especially if he/she does not fully comprehend the automated decision process. The decision-maker is likely to be placed in a very stressful situation if not also of high status (unless he/she opts out).

- The complexity of the information required to make a decision:—In complex problem domains, decision aids are likely to be essential for effective decision-making. In such a situation the decision-maker can only reasonably be regarded as accountable for decisions if he/she is capable of understanding the functional properties of the model specified in the decision aiding program.

- The speed at which decisions must be made:—Again it may be essential to use a decision aid if the decision-maker cannot make sufficiently rapid decisions unaided. Clearly there is a trade off between decision speed and decision complexity. There are two aspects of decision speed: (a) the distance of the planning horizon which can, for example, be a few seconds for some decisions in process control, a few minutes in Air Traffic Control, or a few months in production planning; (b) the permissible response time to make a modification when things don't go according to plan, which can be a second or two in process control, a few seconds in Air Traffic Control, or a few minutes in production control.

- The specificity of stated objectives and the structure of the problem domain:—This chapter looks in some depth at the types of decision model which can be incorporated into a computer program, depending on how well the problem domain is understood. Even when the domain is well understood, if the decision objectives are not clearly defined it will not be possible to make effective automated decisions. In these circumstances the user will be required, as best he/she can, to interpret the decision objectives and instruct the system accordingly.

- The quality of the interaction:—Most of the above factors combine so that when 'each is at its most demanding' the user, if he/she is to remain sane and stay in the job, will need a high quality interaction with the automated decision processes. There must in some sense be a genuine *dialogue* between the user and the computer.

Even with sophisticated systems that control complex processes the assumption is that somewhere there is someone who is responsible for the system. This person, it is also assumed, will spot system malfunctions, or decide when the automated system can no longer cope, and will then take over manual control, perhaps by 'closing down the system'. We will examine the first assumption in the legal context and the second in the context of what can reasonably be expected of a person from our knowledge of human information processing.

The existence of well established fears of computers has been illustrated both in science fiction and in the more academic literature (for example Martin, 1976, Chapter 25—Resistance to Rational Systems; or Marcuse's *One Dimensional Man*, 1964 in which he argues that the sweeping rationality of technology which propels efficiency and growth is itself irrational.) Although some fears may be exaggerated we believe that the feeling that automated systems can and will get out of control is indeed valid. This is *not* because the computer may develop a will of its own and attempt to satisfy its own purposes in some monstrous manner, but because the people responsible for its use may not be in a position to comprehend the workings of the system. In other words the 'cognitive coupling' between the user and the computer is too impoverished. For example, to what extent can the user query the computer's reasoning or proposed solution? And what mechanisms are available to either override the computer or intervene in the decision process?

There has been considerable anticipation of better communication between human and machine (as indicated by phrases such as man-machine symbiosis, and man-machine synergism), and several authors have talked of sharing responsibility for decisions between human and computer. However, an assumption which underlies the arguments of this chapter is that a computer is not, and should not, be capable of interacting with its user on an equal footing. The computer is a conceptual tool and the user should always be its master. (The authors apologize to any reader offended by any anthropomorphic implications in the master/servant relationship—we hope we are not misled by it.) Thus responsibility for the behaviour and use of a computer system must always rest entirely with people if responsible decisions are to be made; but a critical question is to what extent a user might be expected to override a computer recommendation or decision if there is reason to believe it may be in error.

2.0 Responsibility for Decisions

What do we mean when we talk of allocating responsibility? Our dictionary defines 'responsible' as "liable to be called to account or render satisfaction: capable of discharging duty: able to pay: respectable looking". From this definition it is difficult to imagine how a computer could be given responsibility although it has been stated in scientific papers that "Alternative levels of interaction between man and computer and the allocation of responsibility to each can also be evaluated", and that, ". . . .if human and computer are both allocated responsibility for all tasks. . . .". Clearly these authors are not using responsibility in the usual and correct sense (perhaps *this* is a disturbing consequence of anthropomorphization) but the question of who can reasonably be expected to accept responsibility for the decisions resulting from use of a computerized decision system remains. The alternatives that immediately spring to mind are the users of the system or the people who developed the system (software and hardware). Normally allocation of responsibility will only become an issue when something has gone wrong and some injury (either to persons or property) has occurred. Then, there may indeed be recriminations as the courts attempt to place liability somewhere. For example, following a UK motorway pile-up in December 1976 in which several people were killed, the jury decided that the computer controlling the motorway fog signals might have contributed to the accident. The Department of Transport considered the computer system "not to have failed", while the jury was told that a correctly entered instruction to the system had been rejected by the computer "for no apparent reason". There was no evidence available as to why the computer rejected the command correctly entered by the police (Voysey, 1977).

Immense difficulties surround the problem of establishing whether software describing a complex process is faulty or not. Large programs have invariably been produced by a team of specialists, no one of whom is likely to comprehend precisely what the program will do in a representative set of circumstances. Norbert Wiener perceptively foresaw the problem,

"It may well be that in principle we cannot make any machine the elements of whose behaviour we cannot comprehend sooner or later. This does not mean in any way that we shall be able to comprehend these elements in substantially less time that the time required for operation of the machine, or even within any given number of years or generations.

An intelligent understanding of (a machine's) mode of performance may be delayed until long after the task which (it) has been set has been completed. . .This means that, although machines are theoretically subject to human criticism, such criticism may be ineffective until long after it is relevant." (Quoted in Weizenbaum, 1976, p. 232).

A more recent assessment of the same problem has been made by Minsky,

"When a program grows in power by an evolution of partially understood patches and fixes, the programmer begins to lose track of internal details, loses his ability to predict what will happen, begins to hope instead of know, and watches the results as though the program were an individual whose range of behaviour is uncertain. This is already true in some big programs. . . it will soon be much more acute. . . large heuristic programs will be developed and modified by several programmers, each testing them on different examples from different (remotely located computer) consoles and inserting advice independently. The program will grow in effectiveness, but no one of the programmers will understand it all. (Of course, this won't always be successful—the interactions might make it get worse, and no one might be able to fix it again!). Now we see the real trouble with statements like 'it only does what its programmer told it to do'. There isn't any one programmer." (Quoted in Weizenbaum, 1976, p. 235).

The point is illustrated by the findings resulting from a human factors evaluation of the Hoogovens hot steel rolling mill sponsored by the European Coal and Steel Community (we shall draw upon the findings of this evaluation several times in this chapter and shall refer to it as the Hoogovens Report, 1976). Large parts of the steel milling process were fully automated and as well as describing the resulting benefits the report highlights several problems. One such problem resulted from breakdowns,

"Diagnosing the cause of a breakdown is very difficult in an installation of this complexity, but is extremely important to reduce the chance of subsequent breakdowns with the same cause.
There were notable differences between the operators in their descriptions of the functioning of certain parts of the automation. . . This reflects a poor formal understanding of the automation, though not necessarily a poor operating practice. However it is reasonable to assume that lack of understanding will inhibit the best use of the facilities available in the automation. . . .
The position was made more difficult because of the poor documentation of parts of the automation; in certain cases automation engineers had to 'experiment' with the systems in order to find out how they worked. In addition, because responsibility for maintenance and development of automation was divided among a number of departments no one group had a full overview of the functions of all the systems."

As a result of these shortcomings and the lack of overview of the system (hardware and software), the burden of responsibility for its satisfactory operation inevitably fell on the user as the report comments,

"Paradoxically, only the operator was in a position, because of his responsibilities, to gain an understanding of the control systems as a whole, but the information required was not available to him, nor was he equipped with the necessary educational background and training required to fully analyze the systems."

It seems likely that an appreciation of such difficulties has contributed to the development of 'structured programming' techniques (Dijkstra, 1972; Sime, Arblaster & Green, 1977) whose explicit intent is to produce well-structured programs which will be easier to comprehend, less likely to contain errors, and render errors that they do contain easier to find. Just how susceptible a computer system can be to even the smallest of programmer errors has been illustrated by Hoare (1973), who reports that the first American space probe to Venus is said to have failed because a comma was left out of a Fortran program. Should the programmer be responsible for the failure? Or should the designers of the Fortran compiler be held responsible for designing such an unforgiving language? Furthermore, because very often a program will be used in ways not explicitly foreseen by its creators, we need to know, "when. . . . programs are operating outside an acceptable range of behaviour or when, for any reason, they no longer deserve our trust" (Weizenbaum, 1976, p. 236). And the question remains as to who will be responsible for decisions in such circumstances.

2.1 Legal Liability

Thus far we have really been discussing the allocation of 'moral' responsibility for the outcomes of specific decisions. It has been implicitly assumed that it would be unreasonable to decide someone was responsible for an act over which they had no influence. Yet this may not coincide with the allocation of 'formal' responsibility and legal liability for an act. There is, as yet, very little case law on liability for injury attributed to defects in computer software or brought about by the use of a computer (that which there is, is mainly from the U.S.A.). Nevertheless, such cases are likely to become much more common in the law courts in the future, and the indications are that the issues will be certainly complex and in some cases disturbing. One might even speculate whether at some time an Act might be passed which could make a computer liable for its own decisions! Perhaps this is not entirely fanciful because, following the Companies Act of 1856, a company in the UK is a distinct legal entity, or 'personality' as it is called in English law (Barratt Brown, 1978). The purpose of the Act is to make a company liable for any debts or damage it might create. For these the company is responsible, not the individuals who own the company (although managers now have certain responsibilities under the Health and Safety Act). Could the circumstances ever arise when a computer system was made a distinct legal entity?

At the moment issues of computer liability are quite unclear. Enborg & Treadway (1975) distinguish a number of grounds for liability of the software supplied to the user. In the absence of any specific contracts, warranties or claims made about the system, it is likely that an injured user could sue either for negligence or for strict liability. In a case of negligence the user may have the burden of showing exactly what event caused the injury, even though the software might be extremely complex, and nobody could understand its behaviour. A court might however decide to favour the consumer and accept evidence of inference that defective software must have led to the injury. In a claim for strict liability it may not be necessary to show negligence if the software is regarded as a product on the market containing a defect which causes injury. However, the "software supplier will attempt to show that he is providing a service involving a degree of expertise, calling for professional judgement and that he should not be held to be the insurer of his judgement." (Enborg & Treadway, 1975, p. 289).

Petras & Scarpelli (1975) raise some important questions about the rapidly changing situation of medical practitioners in the United States and the extent to which they might be compelled to use computers for diagnosis in the future. Traditionally if a physician followed the standard practice of other doctors in the locality he could not be found negligent, nor his hospital found liable. However recently what is known as the 'rationale of the T.J. Hooper' [1] has been applied to medical cases. This enables a court to rule that if a new measure or device exists, the use of which could have avoided the injury, then a doctor can be negligent for not using it, *even* if it is not the normal accepted practice to do so. Thus the possibility exists that failure to use a computer might be judged negligent if, for example, a physician neglected to ask a question, the answer to which was crucial to a correct diagnosis, *and* a computer system would have asked the question. Petras and Scarpelli go on to say, "Where computer performance of diagnosis related tasks is superior to that of a doctor, a finding of negligence for non-use may be justified" (p. 42). There seems to be cause of concern here bearing in mind, for example, the claim of De Dombal (1975) that a computer aid to differential clinical diagnosis of acute abdominal pain, on average, produces more accurate diagnoses than does a doctor alone.

Such arguments could lead the physician into a most unenviable position. He may become obliged to at least consider a computer's advice; but what if he considers the computer is wrong? Can he interrogate the system or understand how and why it produces its proposals? If not, and difference

---

[1] In the case of the T.J. Hooper, the owner of two tugs was found negligent for failure to equip them with radio receiving sets. Had the tugs been equipped, the court reasoned, the skipper would have heard disturbing weather reports which would have persuaded a reasonably prudent master to put into port, thus averting the loss of barges which the tugs had in tow. The events surrounding the case took place in 1928 at a time when only one tugboat company provided radios to its tugs. The court concluded that even if the custom was not to provide radios this would not relieve the tugboat owner of liability since whole callings may unduly lag in adopting new and available safety devices (Petras & Scarpelli, 1975, p. 22).

of opinion cannot be resolved, should he follow his own judgement or the computer's advice? It seems likely at the moment that a physician would follow his own judgement and would be unlikely to be found culpable for doing so, but will this situation always be true? And what if he follows the computer's advice and the decision is the wrong one? Who is responsible then?

The position of a decision-maker obliged to use a computer, unsure of the basis for its advice, unable to find out, and yet responsible for the decisions, is not a reassuring one. The situation is exacerbated by legal arguments which may protect the software producers. It has been argued (Freed, 1977) that software programs are not 'products' but are 'processes', and are analogous to industrial processes generally. The distinction is important because by classifying them as processes it becomes more difficult to establish the burden of liability on the supplier. Similarly, the actual output from a computer (data values, advice, etc.) might be considered as a 'product' or as 'information'. Freed argues that the output is most appropriately considered to be analogous to the output from *human* information processing, using a quaint line of reasoning reminiscent of some early discussions on the subject of machine intelligence. As a consequence of such a classification, legal liability would parallel the professional liability of the appropriate professional activity, e.g., medicine, engineering, law, accounting, secretarial work, or be dealt with under the rules of ordinary negligence. Again the result is that the supplier would be less likely to be legally liable for faults in his software. Freed somewhat disturbingly concludes by recommending that,

"Until greater perfection can be achieved in software program design, if it ever can, there might be good reason to avoid saddling that new industry with intolerable liability responsibilities. Since computer output vulnerabilities stem in large part from software program deficiencies, it might be appropriate to spare the data processing industry from the broad exposure as well. Both industries, still infants, are extremely important to contemporary society and should not be stunted by such burdens " (p. 478).

Many people may find it difficult to take such a charitable view, especially a doctor obliged to use a computer system he cannot trust, or a patient who may be the end recipient of advice resulting from a program bug! Perhaps the apparent reasonableness of Freed's position will be severely tested when it comes into conflict with the emotions of both judges and jury.

3.0 Automating the Decision Process

Important and complex decisions take time and usually involve a considerable amount of information processing. Making a decision is a process of reducing uncertainty about which state of affairs exists, which state of affairs is in fact preferred, what courses of action are possible, and about the actual consequences of any course of action. In practice, reducing uncertainty can involve a great deal of work: a search for information, inventing possible courses of action, and exploring the properties of the environment to deduce its likely response. (See Sime & Fitter, 1978a, for a more detailed analysis of the decision process.)

All decisions involve *prediction* of the likely consequences of actions. To make a prediction the decision-maker must have a *model* of the environment which is being influenced. (In most cases this model will be implicit and not sufficiently complete to make predictions with any degree of certainty.) In a discussion paper (Sime & Fitter, 1978b) we have developed a conceptual framework to describe the essential properties of the decision process: A diagram of the decision process based on this analysis is shown in Figure 1, which we shall use to consider the automation of components of the decision process.

There are many reasons why we may wish to automate parts of the decision process. By 'automate' we mean prescribe and implement a procedure which will give a functionally satisfactory emulation of a process normally performed by a human decision-maker. To do this does not necessarily mean that we understand the process by which the human reaches a decision (although it would clearly help) but that we can specify *some* procedure which can be shown (either logically or empirically) to produce satisfactory results.

Sometimes we will wish to automate a process because the environment in which the decision-maker must work is unsuitable for a human being. For example, it may be too small, too hot, or too dangerous. Alternatively, the task may be so complex or the decision needed so rapidly that some sort of decision aiding is essential. The computer can be seen as a conceptual tool which is used to offload some of the more routine aspects of decision making. Viewed in this way a pocket calculator would offer a low degree of automation, enabling decisions to be made that would not otherwise be possible in the time available. Towards the other end of the spectrum would be the automated selection of a treatment for a range of potential illnesses. Clearly if a person is to take responsibility for decisions, he/she needs to either have total faith in the system implemented by the designers or have sufficient access to the programmed decision process as it unfolds to evaluate its decisions. We believe that in any but the most simple and routine decision systems the latter strategy is necessary.

Each of the interacting sub-processes in Figure 1 is a candidate for partial or total automation, although some will be more readily automated than others. For example, the inputs marked by broad arrows are potentially highly creative, likely to be difficult to define and will depend on 'human values and judgements'.

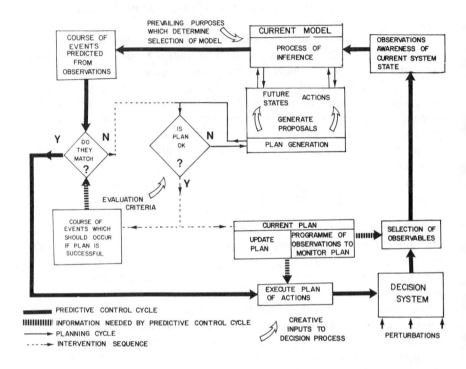

Fig 1. The Decision Process. The decision process models, analyses and controls the decision system. The broad continuous lines show the predictive control cycle which incorporates a monitoring function, an evaluation procedure and an executive procedure to exercise control on the decision system itself. The thin dotted lines indicate the intervention sequence which initiates the planning cycle, and comes into use when things seem to be going wrong, as indicated by a mismatch between the planned course of events (aspiration) and those predicted from the current state (expectation). The planning cycle, indicated by a thin continuous line, is heavily dependent upon a model of the decision system. It takes proposed actions or desired states and iterates until the resultant plan is acceptable, or until some stopping rule terminates the process and leads to a modification of the criteria for success. The wide arrows indicate 'creative inputs' from outside of the decision process which are, in general, difficult to define and will depend on 'human values and judgement'.

In the rest of this chapter we are concerned, not with whether automation is desirable but, given that it has been decided that it is desirable, with the ways in which the decision process can benefit from automation and yet retain the means of permitting responsible decision making.

For any process, the alternatives available to the systems designer are that it could be performed:

- Manually—i.e., by a human operator.
- Automatically—i.e., by a prescribed procedure.
- Automatically with switching to manual—i.e., the operator can monitor and if necessary switch off the automated process taking total control himself.
- Automatically with supervisory control—i.e., the human operator can monitor the automated decision process and augment or overrule it when he considers it necessary. In this manner he is exercising supervisory control 'on top of' the automated process rather than switching it out. However, for supervisory control to be effective the operator must be able to understand the mechanisms of the automated process and thus a high degree of 'communication' between the automated system and the operator will be essential.

It should be clear to the reader by now that we are arguing that in many situations this fourth alternative is necessary for responsible decision making. The Hoogovens Report observes, for example, that when automation is introduced into a plant, "The need for the operator to intervene directly in the process is much reduced, but the requirements to evaluate information and supervise complex systems is higher." (p. 14). It is further argued that in many respects the automated system fails to permit adequate supervisory control. For example, sometimes the operator has to wait while the computer makes its own choice or abrogates control to the operator, thus making the operator subservient to the computer. At times when control is passed to the operator he is unable to modify the computer settings (supervisory control) but has to use manual operation. In fact, "there were very few opportunities for the operators to interact with the automatic systems in order to improve their performance." (p. 21).

The extent of user control in automation can be illustrated by considering a somewhat hypothetical dimension of 'degree of user control' and examining how effective control of the decision system is likely to be affected by the level of automation for various types of system. At one end of the dimension the system is controlled completely manually, and at the other the system is fully automated. The first stage of automation is the use of tools such as stop watches, calculators and temperature gauges to provide information for the human decision-maker. The use of a tool of this sort is liable to restrict the decision-maker to some extent (and thus decrease his control over the problem domain) because it may, for example, require that an observation is made, or a calculation performed, in a particular manner. As these tools become more sophisticated the system approaches total automation where the operator will have no effective control other than starting or stopping the process, but this state can be 'held back' by providing facilities which permit supervisory control and allow the less well-defined or unexpected aspects of decision making to be performed by the user. Supervisory control may entail the user monitoring all activities and intervening when he considers it to be desirable, or the automation may itself have inbuilt criteria for deciding when to alert the user to the possible need for an intervention. Nevertheless, an automated system which only allows the user to supply information or control actions when requested to do so (as described in the Hoogovens Report) is, in effect, at the same position on the degree of control dimension as a fully automated system.

Somewhere toward the centre of the dimension one might expect to find the relationship of 'equal partners' in the decision making. The realization of such systems has been the aspiration of human factors researchers for a considerable time. However, equal partnership between man and computer may be mythical because, for a truly co-operative relationship, both participants must share a common conceptual model of the problem domain and jointly accept responsibility for outcomes. It seems doubtful whether such systems are in practice feasible, bearing in mind how little is currently understood of human problem solving skills.

In a complex problem domain a human decision-maker is unlikely to comprehend all of the consequences of a decision unaided. Hence, although he/she may be able to make decisions without restriction, the decisions are unlikely to be completely effective. A tool which restricts the range of possibilities available to the decision-maker, but also gives more information about the probable consequence of decisions will lead to a more effectively controlled decision system. For a decision system of any given complexity it seems likely that there is an optimal level of automation which will produce the most effective decisions. In the same way that the desirable level of automation increases with the complexity of the decision system, it will also increase with the speed with which a decision needs to be made. In many situations the human decision-maker cannot reach an effective decision unaided in the time available.

We may decide to automate just part of the decision process illustrated in Figure 1, in which case it will be necessary for information to cross the boundary between the manual and automatic processes. The sub-processes most likely to be automated are the ones in direct contact with the decision system e.g., temperature gauges for smelting furnace controllers or secondary radar for air traffic controllers; and the use of automatic effectors for controlling the system e.g., speed governors on engines or the complex transducers needed to enable pilots to control modern fighter planes.

When we decide to automate a component of the decision process we must recognize that the human decision-maker may quite possibly be performing a sub-process in parallel to the automated function. For example, although sensory transducers may be used to observe the current state of the decision system, the operator himself may be making judgments based on his own direct observations. The Hoogovens Report comments that, "The operators felt that the information they received from the process (both visual and auditory) was of paramount importance, and they placed more trust in this direct sensory information than the pulpit displays." (p. 24). In fact, the operators seemed to take pride in using 'informal' sources of information, which it would almost certainly be impossible to automate.

It is clear that automation has a constraining effect on the decision process. In the case of observation, if the operator is accustomed to using sensory data for which the techniques of automation are not available then, to achieve automation, alternative observations must be used. For example, an operator who makes judgements based on the colour or smell of a process may have considerable difficulty adapting to measures of temperature or acid content etc.. Although it may be possible to use also the more 'informal' observations, unless the system has been designed to integrate them in a way that enables the operator to interact with and override the formal system (i.e., in a supervisory manner, perhaps by changing the value of an observation), the choice will be between manual and automatic observations.

Furthermore, automation will not only constrain the sub-process in question but it is also likely to constrain sub-processes with which it interacts. For example, only states of the decision system for which observations are available can be used as evidence in the prediction of future states. This may well limit feasible solution strategies. Similarly there is little point in making a decision to change the state of the system if the necessary control actions are unavailable because control has been restricted by automation.

3.1 Automated Plans and Predictions

A crucial step in the decision process is the prediction of the effects of a proposed course of action. If it is possible to produce a computer model which simulates the causal structure of a system it becomes possible to evaluate proposed actions or changes by observing their effects on the model itself. Experimentation on the real system is often not practical and a simulation can have many advantages in cost, time and safety. However, the development of a successful simulation in some respects appears paradoxical. One builds a simulation to help understand a system, yet to build the simulation one must first understand the system. The paradox vanishes when it is recognized that one can understand the rules which govern a system without understanding the implications of the rules or how they will combine to determine the system's behaviour. Here a working model can be a great aid to understanding, and the ability to make trial actions and explore their effects should lead to improved problem-solving.

In Figure 1 the predicted future states are generated by the process boxes labelled *Current Model* and *Plan Generation*. The model must contain information on the *constraints* of the problem domain. For example in the simulation of an industrial workshop they might include the routes which products must follow, or in Air Traffic Control the legally required separations between planes. In addition, to generate plans, *rules of change* (or heuristics) are needed to derive the possible future states. For example, these might be the priorities for particular jobs in the industrial workshop or, in the traffic control, the preferred trajectories on which a plane should travel and the rules by which potential conflicts are resolved. A plan can be produced by applying the *rules of change* iteratively within the *constraints* of the problem domain.

For a variety of tasks it has proved possible to automate the generation of plans (although they may be called control actions or diagnoses in some problem domains), and some specific applications are discussed below. The issue of particular concern in this chapter is whether the user of the automated system can understand the rationale behind the mechanisms which generated the plan and the specific circumstances which led to a specific plan. To do this the user must comprehend the rules and constraints embodied in the computer program which models the problem domain. Thus we believe *the critical issue is one of program comprehension,* and there are two distinct approaches to making a process comprehensible. Firstly, the program may be written in such a way that its structure is readily perceived and is 'natural' to the user, and secondly, various aids may be provided so that the user can either directly observe the behaviour of the program or be given information on how and why various actions are taking place.

The difficulty with the development of well-structured programs is that they require a fundamental understanding of the problem domain, whereas unstructured programs can be written in a piecemeal fashion and do not necessarily require an overview of the problem domain so long as adequate facilities can be provided to explain the program's behaviour. The structured procedural approach will often try to create a single structure which, as far as possible, combines both the user's and program's model of the problem domain. Unfortunately in many applications, especially those characterized as requiring human insight and judgement, there is an insufficient understanding of the user model to create a program structure for generating plans. This does not mean that automated plans cannot be produced, there are many examples to the contrary, but it may be necessary to resort to other techniques to provide a formal model of the decision process.

3.2 Behavior, Explanations and Introspection

One approach, characteristic of the operations researcher, is to provide a formal (and often in some sense optimal) solution based on statistical theory. It is not the intent to model closely the techniques that may be employed by people, and so a user may well not be familiar with the methods employed by the program. Thus he would probably have difficulty understanding explanations of the program's behaviour even were they to be provided.

1. *If* there is wine on the table *then* have a drink.
2. *If* there is food on the table *then* eat some.
3. *If* tired *then* go to bed.

Fig. 2. Some simple rules of a *production system*. If the predicate of a rule is true it will fire and its action will be obeyed. Rules will continue firing until no predicates are true. Normally the programmer has to decide on how a conflict will be resolved if more than one predicate is true at a time. If, for example, the rules are ranked for priority (1,2,3 above) and there is both food and wine, rule 1 will continue to fire until all the wine is gone, then rule 2 will fire until all the food is gone, and then rule 3 will fire.

Another approach to modelling the decision process is to build up a set of rules by a trial and error procedure until they produce a satisfactory output. Here there are two distinct criteria as to what constitutes a satisfactory output. Psychologists have attempted to develop sets of rules and control mechanisms known as *production systems* (Newell & Simon, 1972) which are refined until they capture the *behaviour* of a human decision-maker. (See Figure 2 for an example of a basic production system.) Whether or not the program maps directly onto a decision-maker's own model of the problem domain, or is comprehensible to him, seems to be relatively unimportant. The objective is to simulate the behaviour and infer the mechanisms that might have produced it in terms of the psychologists own model of the decision process. However another criterion, used when creating and refining *production systems*, is that they should produce a satisfactory *performance*. That is, the prediction or advice output from the program should be judged useful and satisfactory by the decision-maker, and be proved correct as events unravel on a sufficiently frequent number of occasions. Note that the aim is for a satisfactory rather than an optimal performance. (Simon, 1969, has referred to this distinction as between satisficing and optimizing). As a consequence of this criterion, even if the model embodied in the program is not comprehensible to the user, its behaviour must be explainable to him via an interactive dialogue. Such rule-based consultation systems, have been written as *production systems* for a number of problem domains. (Davis, Buchanan & Shortliffe, 1977; Aikens, 1977; Davis & Buchanan, 1977).

Each rule in a *production-system* is completely modular and independent of all other rules. Rules are not usually permitted to refer to other rules. Such modularity permits a relatively uncomplicated control structure, and makes the addition of new rules easy since no other rule need be changed. (In a highly structured procedural language a lot of restructuring may be required when adding a new piece of code if the program is to remain well-structured; see Fitter & Green, 1979). To ensure that the modification has the *desired* effect may be rather more difficult. The program's behaviour will be hard to infer by simply reading a print-out of the rules due to the control structure. Moran (1973), for example, has said that a programmer cannot predict a *production system's* behaviour as well as with a structured language, because whereas a structured programming language expresses the relations between its primitive actions formally (via the syntax of the language) a production system expresses them functionally (via the conditions for the actions). Furthermore, Davis (1976) observes that even experts acquainted with the program tend to think of a sequence of operations in procedural terms and find the conversion to a set of rules difficult.

However, notwithstanding the disadvantages, the fact that a *production system* structures information as a collection of rules allows the system to generate explanations of its actions fairly easily. (Some examples are given in the next section). The techniques in general involve rather literal explanations of what the program is doing or has done; for example, which rule is being invoked and the events which occurred to satisfy the preconditions which led to it being invoked. The explanations are literal in the sense that an action is explained in terms of a set of values of program variables (possibly expressed in natural language) rather than any intentions or purposes that may be imputed to explain why the program is producing a particular piece of behaviour. Although this approach may not give an entirely satisfactory explanation, because it will not be at the same conceptual level as would occur in a conversation between two people, at least the user can be sure he is being informed about the program's *behaviour*.

Goldstein & Grimson (1977) have suggested that 'second order knowledge' in the form of annotations should be added explicitly to production rules. These annotations include caveats, rationales, plans and control information. Goldstein and Grimson argue that rationales in particular would provide the underlying justification for why a rule is being invoked and thus provide a higher level of explanation. Higher level explanations involve *inference* which may be supplied directly by the programmer when the software is written, or by inference rules built into the program and invoked at run-time. Clearly it would be essential that the rationale was in fact correct otherwise the explanation could be misleading. The possibility seems to exist whereby the explanation could, in principle, become divorced from the behaviour of the program if, for example, an error occurred when relating the rationale to the rule. Thus although the program might be performing correctly it might be misleading the user as to its reasoning. This would not be possible with the simpler, literal explanations. One is reminded of the dissatisfaction with psychological interpretations of behaviour at the beginning of this century which led (with such a vengance) to a spell of hard line behaviourism. The feeling was that introspection had become too divorced from behaviour; one hopes that the same could not happen to programs capable of introspecting at a higher level than simple explanations of action.

These alternative approaches to the design of a decision aid are shown in Figure 3.

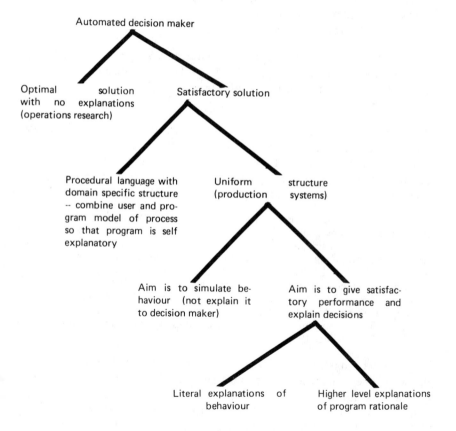

Fig. 3. Various objectives for automated decision-makers and their ability to give explanations.

3.3 Medical Advisors

There are many types of aid to medical decision making available. The earliest ones used actuarial data and produced recommendations derived from statistical decision theory. These would, in the main, fall into the optimal solution category of Figure 3 and will not be discussed in this chapter. (See Chapter 9).

The MYCIN consultation system (Shortliffe, 1976) is designed to prescribe antibiotic drugs for patients with infectious diseases. Explanation facilities are an important part of MYCIN because of the issue of responsibility discussed earlier and because rational antimicrobial therapy decisions rely upon the accurate identification of the micro-organisms causing the infection, and studies have shown that physicians will often reach therapeutic decisions which differ significantly from those that would have been suggested by fellow infectious disease experts.

A MYCIN consultation has four stages:

• Decide which organisms, if any, are causing significant disease.
• Determine the likely identity of the significant organisms.
• Decide which drugs are potentially useful.
• Select the best drug or drugs.

The system has a 'goal rule' to ensure the above stages are carried out, and when the goal rule has been applied the consultation is over. MYCIN first tries to evaluate the PREMISE of the goal rule and the first condition requires that it knows whether there is an organism that requires therapy. MYCIN reasons backwards in a manner informally paraphrased as:

"How do I decide whether there is an organism requiring therapy? Will RULE 090 tell me that organisms associated with significant disease require therapy. But I don't even have any organisms in the context tree yet, so I'd better ask first if there are any organisms and if there are I'll try to apply RULE 090 to each of them. However, the PREMISE of RULE 090 requires that I know whether the organism is significant. I have a bunch of rules for making this decision (RULE 038, RULE 042, etc.). For example RULE 038 tells me that if the organism came from a sterile site it is probably significant. Unfortunately, I don't have any rules for inferring the site of a culture, however, so I guess I'll have to ask the user for this information when I need it. . . ." (Shortliffe, 1976)

The consultation is controlled by the program in that MYCIN only asks the physician questions when there is a reason to do so. The goal-orientated approach is automated via two interrelated procedures, a MONITOR which analyses rules and a FINDOUT that searches for data needed by MONITOR. When FINDOUT returns a value to MONITOR it marks the clinical parameter as having been traced, and the MONITOR also adds the conclusion of the rules (whose premises are true) to the ongoing record of

** HOW DID YOU DECIDE THAT ORGANISM-1 MIGHT BE
E. COLI?

I USED RULE 021 TO CONCLUDE THAT THE IDENTITY OF
ORGANISM-1 IS E.COLI.
THIS GAVE A CUMULATIVE CF OF 0.47.
THEN I USED RULE 084 TO CONCLUDE THAT THE IDENTITY
OF ORGANISM-1 IS E.COLI.
THIS GAVE A CUMULATIVE CF OF 0.55.
FINALLY I USED RULE 003 TO CONCLUDE THAT THE
IDENTITY OF ORGANISM-1 IS E.COLI.
THIS GAVE A CUMULATIVE CF OF 0.74.

** WHY DIDN'T YOU CONSIDER STREPTOCOCCUS AS A
POSSIBLE FOR ORGANISM-1?

THE FOLLOWING RULE COULD HAVE BEEN USED TO DETERMINE
THAT THE IDENTITY OF ORGANISM-1 WAS STREPTOCOCCUS:
RULE 033. BUT CLAUSE 2 ("THE MORÉHOLOGY OF THE
ORGANISM IS COCCUS") WAS ALREADY KNOWN TO BE
FALSE FOR ORGANISM-1, SO THE RULE WAS NEVER TRIED.

Fig. 4. Some sample questions that the user can ask the MYCIN system. (From Davis, Buchanan & Shortliffe, 1977). A CF is a measure of the confidence of the conclusion being valid.

the current consultation. Thus the rules allow a reasoning chain to grow dynamically on the basis of the user's answers to questions. This chain can then be used to explain the program's behaviour in chunk sizes determined by the user. In this way MYCIN can explain both why things happened and also why a particular action failed to take place. (See Figure 4.)

Another consultation system which has similarities to MYCIN but is designed as a procedural system using hierarchical structures, is known as the OWL Digitalis Therapy Advisor (Swartout, 1977). Digitalis is prescribed mainly to patients who show signs of congestive heart failure or conduction disturbances of the heart. The therapeutic effect of digitalis is achieved by maintaining a level in the patient's body within certain bounds which are patient-specific. Thus prescriptions need to be adjusted based on feedback from previous ones and the program constructs a patient-specific model. Explanations of the program's advice are based on the code of the program and a trace of its execution. Swartout argues, "The chief advantage of this approach is its simplicity. If a program can be written in a sufficiently structured, close-to-English style, very little additional work need to be done to produce explanations of the code. Additionally, if the program is modified, the changes are immediately reflected in the explanations. Because of this simplicity, this approach is most applicable to those programs which closely model methods employed by humans." (p. 824). Thus the aim is for programs to be self-documenting. But the rub is—*can* the program be written in such a way, or indeed is the problem domain sufficiently well understood to pre-define a program in any form.

The structure of the program is intended to reflect the structure of methods used by doctors in prescribing digitalis, although when explaining the program to the user, it is necessary to take into account the possibility that the user's model of the problem is very different from the program's. The program is structured hierarchically, the higher level procedures expressing more general goals and actions, and the lower levels more specific procedures. When an explanation is given of the higher level procedure, the lower levels are summarised, although the user can ask for details of the lower levels to any depth.

One of the explanation routines, DESCRIBE-METHOD, takes a procedure and translates it into an English-like language whilst preserving the sequential and nested structure by using subsection numbering and line indenting. Calls to other procedures are named but not expanded. (It is not stated in Swartout's account how repetition, the other basic building block of well-structured programs, is expressed). Another explanation routine, DESCRIBE-EVENT, gives explanations of what is happening in a consultation with a particular patient. The principle difference between explaining events and explaining methods is that when methods are explained, all possible paths through the method are outlined, but when events are explained, only the specific path taken during the event is displayed. Thus predicate values of conditional statements must be checked and if the predicate succeeds, it is given as the reason for the action taken. An example of an explanation of an event is given in Figure 5.

At the moment, *medical* advisor programs are the most advanced in terms of explanation facilities. This is perhaps not surprising bearing in mind the responsibility that rests on a physician. Although we know of no advisor program in general use as yet, the provision of satisfactory explanations seems to be a prerequisite condition. It is perhaps too soon to know whether the rule-based or procedural programs will on balance be preferable; as with most issues it will probably depend on the specific application area. It seems likely that rule-based systems will be easier to write and modify (at least clerically if not conceptually) but that procedural systems will be easier to comprehend provided the problem domain and decision process do not defy description. These differences between these two procedural and rule-based models are outlined in Figure 6.

(DESCRIBE [(CHECK (SENSITIVITY (DUE (TO THYROID = $\geqq$ FUNCTION)))))])

DO YOU ONLY WANT TO SEE EVENTS FROM THE CURRENT SESSION? (YES OR NO) **no**

DURING THE SESSION ON 9/2/76 AT 11.10, I CHECKED SENSITIVITY DUE TO THYROID-FUNCTION BY EXECUTING THE FOLLOWING STEPS:

1. I ASKED THE USER THE STATUS OF MYXEDEMA. THE USER RESPONDED THAT THE STATUS OF MYXEDEMA WAS PRESENT.

2. SINCE THE STATUS OF MYXEDEMA WAS PRESENT IT DID THE FOLLOWING:

2.1 I ADDED MYXEDEMA TO THE PRESENT AND CORRECTABLE CONDITIONS. THE PRESENT AND CORRECTABLE CONDITIONS THEN BECAME MYXEDEMA.

2.2 I REMOVED MYXEDEMA FROM DEGRADABLE CONDITIONS. THE DEGRADABLE CONDITIONS THEN BECAME HYPOKALEMIA, HYPOXEMIA, CARDIOMYOPATHIES-MI, AND POTENTILA POTASSIUM LOSS DUE TO DIURETICS.

2.3 I SET THE FACTOR OF REDUCTION DUE TO MYXEDEMA TO 0.67. THE FACTOR OF REDUCTION DUE TO MYXEDEMA WAS PREVIOUSLY UNDETERMINED.

2.4 I ADDED MYXEDEMA TO THE REASONS OF REDUCTION. THE REASONS OF REDUCTION BECAME MYXEDEMA.

Fig. 5. An explanation of the event of checking for sensitivity due to myxedema in the Digitalis Therapy Advisor. (From Swartout,1977).

It is yet to be seen whether Aikens' (1977) proposal of a rule-based consultant based on a model of the decision process expressed in a frame-like structure (Minsky, 1975) will provide a half-way house which combines the advantages of both approaches.

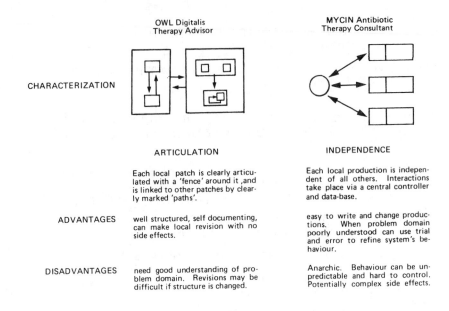

Fig. 6. The differences between procedural and rule-based models.

3.4 Process Controllers

In process control (or regulatory control, as it is sometimes called) the planning component of the decision process tends to be quite straightforward; usually to maintain the process variable within a given tolerance. However, the control necessary to remain within the required tolerance can be rather complex and any formal model which predicts the effects of a control action on the system is likely to be incomplete and inadequate. Although it is fairly common to automate process control systems, the more complex ones need a human operator supervising the process to achieve safe and efficient control. Often the system is modelled in such a way that its supervisor has difficulty in comprehending the program and following its behaviour. For example, of the automation controlling the hot strip mill processes, the Hoogovens Report observes,

"The philosophy of the present systems is based on the computer surveying certain data (temperatures, desired gauges, etc.) and producing recommended set-ups on the basis of various calculations. The operator has the job of accepting or rejecting this advice, on the basis of a rather different set of data, and his own skill. Because the operator does not have access to the computer's sources of information he occasionally cannot understand what the computer is recommending. He can choose between accepting the computer's set-up and hoping for the best, or intervening to modify the set-up. In future designs more consideration should be given to providing information to help the operator understand the decisions being taken by the automation. This is in contrast to the present use of information to advise operators of process states." (p. 40).

It is just this type of difficulty that led Macvicar-Whelan (1976) to urge that, "one ought to observe the actions taken by the human operator and only then make serious efforts to model the process." (p. 692). Although Mamdani and Assilian (1975) believe such an approach is possible they also believe it is not generally being aimed for. They argue that,

"Most control engineers would accept intuitively that the mathematical computations they perform in translating their concept of a control strategy into an automatic controller are far removed from their own approach to the manual performance of the same task, and that there seems to be a fairly direct relationship between the loose linguistic expression of control strategy and its manual implementation." (p. 2).

Rule based production systems have recently been developed to control industrial processes (Mamdani and Assilian, 1975; Kickert and Van Nauta Lemke, 1976). Interestingly, because of the "loose linguistic expression" used by many controllers these rules have been expressed in fuzzy logic (Zadeh, 1973). The fuzzy logic allows both the predicates and the control actions in the rules to be expressed as 'fuzzy variables'. That is, a temperature can be referred to as 'fairly hot' or a control action as 'very small'. These 'fuzzy values' must of course, be converted to a numeric form at some stage, but this can be done 'behind the scenes' and by defining a membership function which maps a 'fuzzy value' onto a set of dial or control values. Examples of such rules are:

1. *If* time is small *and* deviation is negative big *then* desired change is big.
2. *If* time is big *and* deviation is positive zero *then* desired change is zero.

Fuzzy rule systems have been shown to be satisfactory process controllers (but so far only for fairly simple machines) and the rules can be modified by the operator with little difficulty to give improved performance. (Mamdani, 1976). A reason why rule-systems are well suited to process control may be that the control actions require little sequential information but have many complex contingencies which determine their application. The rule-systems used in process control bear a close resemblance to decision tables, which, it has been claimed (Montalbano, 1974), provide a good representation for problems involving a high ratio of conditions to actions. For the purposes of process control it looks as if fuzzy logic may provide a unique marriage between a 'natural' representation of control rules, readily comprehensible to the operator, and a powerful underlying formalism capable of giving effective control. Whether fuzzy rule-systems could offer such a combination to other problem domains, that have a larger planning component, is rather doubtful.

'Well-structured' control programs based on operator models do not seem to have been developed for process control purposes as yet. This may be due to the fact that regulation requires a closed test-act-retest loop rather than long sequences of operations or hierarchical structuring. However, the development of high level languages especially designed for specific application areas (such as the COMPASS, a real-time software system currently being developed by the UK Central Electricity Generating Board) may encourage the production of well-structured programs, suitable for sequential control problems and capable of being modified on-line by their operators.

3.5 *Planning Aids and Progressive Automation*

To create a plan, decisions must usually be made between competing possible actions. If an automated decision aid is required rules must be stated which will lead to the desired decision and produce a satisfactory plan. If the problem domain is analyzed and understood it may be possible to define a well-structured process which captures the essentials of the decision-maker's own model and is comprehensible to him/her. More commonly, only heuristics (or rules of thumb) are available which the decision-maker can use to select actions and create a possible plan. For the task of planning a sequence of jobs through an industrial workshop (e.g., a job shop) scheduling heuristics have been used (Gere, 1966), some of which are relatively simple (e.g., when jobs are queueing select the one most urgently required), and others much more sophisticated (e.g., Holloway & Nelson, 1973). A similar task for which highly sophisticated man-computer decision systems have been developed is the production of school timetables (e.g., Platts, 1974). Here the planning component is the only relevant part of the decision process because the timetabler's job is complete before the execution of the plan commences. In most planning tasks however, a major complication stems from discrepancies between a planned course of events and the *actual* course of events. This leads to a continual need to review and revise the plan in the light of events as they unfold.

We have carried out some laboratory research on interactive job-shop scheduling aids (Fitter, 1976a; 1976b). In this area the formal techniques of operations research do not usually provide adequate solutions which can replace a human scheduler, and the decision process of a scheduler is insufficiently understood to produce a well-structured procedural model. We decided therefore, to use a rule-based *production-system* which would help the user produce a plan to schedule products through a simulated job-shop. In an attempt to avoid the problem of the user not understanding how plans were being produced by the rules, we allowed the user to devise his own rules and insert them into the system. Initially the system had just one rule (first-come-first-served) but as the user learned more about the problem domain (by using the simulation to make exploratory actions) rules could be devised and inserted. In addition the simulation could be interrogated to evaluate the success of, and if necessary modify, the rules in use. If the user wished, the rule system could be overriden by making a *manual move*. That is, at any point in the simulation the user could directly change the job-shop (e.g., load or unload a product onto/from a machine) thereby making a 'one-off' decision to create a future state different from the one that would have occurred from the rule system alone. In addition, a *slowmotion* facility was provided which allowed the user to run the simulation and observe a display of the job-shop changing one discrete event at a time. The user could thus see which rule was responsible for each event in the job-shop. This was useful when trying to trace the behaviour of the program to understand why a particular event had occurred. This explanation facility proved particularly helpful and allowed the user to debug the rule-system. Similar visual traces of program states have been used to aid understanding of program behaviour in LOGO (Papert, 1971) and for LISP animation (Dionne & Mackworth, 1978). If they are to prove useful to program comprehension the visual trace must be capable of reflecting all program constructs in a visual analogue. There is plenty of scope for ingenuity in developing visual representations capable of explaining a program's purposes or rationale as well as its dynamic behaviour.

Our subjects had several problems in getting their rules to produce the behaviour they had in mind; in particular they sometimes had difficulty coping with a rule that would fire several times in succession without allowing another rule to be tried. The problem was to identify a condition which would cease to apply when the rule had fired. Problems also arose from the difficulty of devising rules which would prevent an action occuring. Subjects wanted to give instructions which would prohibit a particular action being performed, although they were uncertain as to which positive action should take place, e.g., they knew that a particular product should *not* be loaded onto a machine in the current circumstances. A simple solution would have been to extend the production system to allow 'demons' which would prohibit actions. A somewhat similar facility exists in MYCIN which checks the drugs appropriate to the identified disease, to see if any are likely to have undesirable side effects on the particular patient under consideration (Shortliffe, 1976).

Production systems have the disadvantage of being difficult to control, but perhaps have the compensating advantage because of their simple control structure, of allowing simple explanations of their behaviour. Furthermore, when the problem domain is poorly understood, it is relatively easy to program by trial and error—modifying the program's behaviour until it seems to be acceptable. However this may produce dangerous side-effects if not performed rigorously.

4.0 Conclusions

In this chapter we have examined the role of decision-makers and their responsibilities and possible liabilities when using automated decision aids. These aids are becoming increasingly necessary for the understanding and control of complex systems. Thus, man's increasing dependence upon them. A need exists for improved 'cognitive coupling', based (in some sense) on a genuine dialogue between the decision-maker and decision aid. It is necessary for complex automata to be able to explain their own behaviour in terms readily understandable to the decision-maker. This is best achieved by attempting to incorporate the user's model of the decision process into the program model. Where this is not possible, because the decision process or the problem domain is insufficiently understood, the explanations need to be simple reports based on a trace of the program's behaviour.

As systems undoubtedly become more complicated, more sophisticated mechanisms will be needed by which the behaviour of an automated process can be explained. In the systems of the future it will also be more tempting to delegate responsibility to the computer. However, future designers would be wise to bear in mind the belief of an eminent software engineer that,

"...the man is always the master, and bears total responsibility; the computer is only a machine, and must never deviate from absolute subservience. Such a one-sided communication should probably not be called a dialogue; in which you expect a human partner to give essentially uncontrolled and even unpredicted responses— and take responsibility for them." (Hoare, personal communication.)

References

Aikens, J. (1977). The Use of Models in a Rule-Based Consultation System, *Proceeding of the 5th International Joint Conference on Artificial Intelligence.* Cambridge, Massachusetts.
Barratt Brown, M. (1978). *Information at Work.* Arrow Books, London.
Brooks, F.P. (1977). The Computer 'Scientist' as Toolsmith: Studies in Interactive Computer Graphics. In *Information Processing '77* (Ed.) Gilchrist. IFIP, North Holland Publishing Company
Davis, R. (1976). *Applications of Meta-Level Knowledge to the Construction, Maintenance, and use of Large Knowledge Bases.* Stanford HPP Memo, 76-7.

Davis, R. & Buchanan, B.G. (1977). Meta-Level Knowledge: Overview and Applications. *Proceedings of the 5th International Joint Conference on Artificial Intelligence*. Cambridge, Massachusetts.
Davis, R., Buchanan, B. & Shortliffe, E. (1977). Production Rules as a Representation for a Knowledge-Based Consultation Program. *Artificial Intelligence*, **8**, 15-45.
De Dombal, F.T. (1975). Computer-Assisted Diagnosis of Abdominal Pain. In *Advances in Medical Computing* (Eds.) J. Rose & J.H.Mitchell. Churchill Livingstone, London.
Dijkstra, E.W. (1972). Notes on Structured Programming. In *Structured Programming* (Eds.) O.J. Dahl, E.W. Dijkstra & C.A.R. Hoare. Academic Press, New York.
Dionne, M.S. & Mackworth, A.K. (1978). Antics: A System for Animating LISP Programs. *Computer Graphics and Image Processing*, **7**, 105-119.
Enborg, K.D. & Treadway, A.E. (1975). Liability for Defects in Computer Software. *Journal of Urban Law*, **53**, 279-303.
Fitter, M.J. (1976a). *Computers as aids to forecasting and control*. M.R.C. Social and Applied Psychology Unit, Memo 117, University of Sheffield.
Fitter, M.J. (1976b). Towards a Design for an Online Scheduling Aid. To apppear in *Proceedings of NATO ASI on Man-Computer Interaction* (Ed.) B. Shackel. Noordhoff International Publishing, Leiden (NATO Series E: Applied Sciences).
Fitter, M.J. & Green, T.R.G. (1979). When do Diagrams make Good Computer Languages?. *International Journal of Man-Machine Studies*. (In Press).
Freed, R.N. (1977). Products Liability in the Computer Age. *The Forum*, **12**, 461-478.
Gere, W.S. (1966). Heuristics in job-shop scheduling. *Management Science*, **13**, 167-190.
Goldstein, I.P. & Grimson, E. (1977). Annotated production Systems: A Model for Skill Acquisition. *Proceedings of the 5th International Joint Conference on Artificial Intelligence*. Cambridge, Massachusetts.
Grosch, H. (1978). Article in *Computing Europe*, **6**, 30, Haymarket Publishing Ltd., London.
Hoare, C.A.R. (1973). *Hints on Programming Language Design*. Stanford Artificial Intelligence Laboratory, Memo AIM-224.
Holloway, C.A. & Nelson, R.T. (1973). Alternative Formulation of the Job Shop Problem with Due Dates. *Management Science*, **20**, 65-75.
Hoogovens Report (1976). *Human Factors Evaluation, Hoogovens No. 2 Hot Strip Mill*, British Steel Corporation, B.S.C./HOOGOVENS, London. FR251.
Kickert, W.J.M. & Van Nauta Lemke, H.R. (1976). Application of a Fuzzy Controller in a Warm Water Plant. *Automatica*, **12**, 301-308.
Macvicar-Whelan, P.J. (1976). Fuzzy Sets for Man-Machine Interaction. *International Journal of Man-Machine Studies*, **8**, 687-697.
Mamdani, E.H. (1976). *Application of Fuzzy Logic to Approximate Reasoning using Linguistic Synthesis*. Fuzzy Logic Working Group, Research Report 3. Queen Mary College, London.
Mamdani, E.H. & Assilian, S. (1975). An Experiment in Linguistic Synthesis with a Fuzzy Logic Controller. *International Journal of Man-Machine Studies*, **7**, 1-13.
Marcuse, H. (1964). *One Dimensional Man—Studies in the Ideology of Advanced Industrial Society*. Routledge and Keegan Paul, London.
Martin, J. (1976). *Principles of Database Management*. Prentice-Hall, New Jersey.

66   M.J. Fitter and M.E. Sime

Miller, R.B. (1968). Response times in computer conversational transactions. *Proceedings of AFIPS Fall Joint Computer Conference*, 33, 267-277.
Minsky, M. (1975). A framework for Representing Knowledge. In *The Psychology of Computer Vision*. (Ed.) P. Winston. McGraw-Hill, New York.
Montalbano, (1974). *Decision Tables*. Science Research Associates, Chicago.
Moran, T.P. (1973). The Symbolic Nature of Visual Imagery. *Proceedings of the 3rd International Joint Conference on Artificial Intelligence*. Stanford Research Institute Publication Department.
Newell, A. & Simon, H.A. (1972). *Human Problem Solving*. Prentice-Hall, New Jersey.
Papert, S. (1971). *A Computer Laboratory for Elementary Schools*. Massachussetts Institute of Technology A.I. Lab. Logo Memo 1.
Petras, D.D. & Scarpelli, S. (1975). Computers, Medical Malpractice, and the Ghost of the T.J. Hooper. *Journal of Computers and Law*, 5, 15-49.
Platts, R.W. (1974). An Interactive Approach to School Timetabling. *Man-Machine Studies Progress Report* UC-DSE/4, 24, 14-75. Department of Electrical Engineering, University of Canterbury, Christchurch, New Zealand.
Shortliffe, E.H. (1976). *Computer Based Medical Consultations: MYCIN*. American Elsevier, New York.
Sime, M.E., Arblaster, A.T. & Green, T.R.G. (1977). Structuring the Programmer's Task. *Journal of Occupational Psychology*, 50, 205-216.
Sime, M.E. & Fitter, M.J. (1978a). Computer Models and Decision Making, In *Psychology at Work* (Ed.) P.B. Warr. Penguin (2nd edition), Harmondsworth, London.
Sime, M.E. & Fitter, M.J. (1978b). Automating the Decision Process—a conceptual framework. M.R.C. Social and Applied Psychology Unit, Memo no. 213, University of Sheffield.
Simon, H.A. (1969). *The Sciences of the Artificial*. MIT Press, Cambridge, Massachusetts.
Swartout, W.R. (1977). A Digitalis Therapy Advisor with Explanations. *Proceedings of the 5th International Joint Conference on Artificial Intelligence*. Cambridge, Massachusetts.
Voysey, H. (1977). Problems of mingling men and machines. *New Scientist*, 18th August, IPC, London.
Weizenbaum, J. (1976), *Computer Power and Human Reason*. W.H. Freeman & Company, San Francisco.
Zadeh, L.A. (1973). Outline of a New Approach to the Analysis of a Complex System and Decision Process. *IEEE Transactions on Systems, Man and Cybernetics SMC-3*, 28-44.

Chapter 3

THE HUMAN AS A SYSTEMS COMPONENT

Jens Rasmussen

Contents

1.0 Introduction

During recent decades there has been an increasing interest in the study of human operators in complex industrial systems. Within aviation and vehicle control in general, there is a tradition of modelling the human as a component in continuous control loops. In industrial systems, however, continuous control has long been performed by automatic controllers, and instrumentation systems have typically consisted of arrays of measuring channels displaying individual variable states. In this situation, studies of human operators have focussed quite naturally on "knob-and-dial" ergonomics and on the selection and training of operators. Only a limited effort has been made to analyse the mental information processing performed by the operators. However, for several reasons, this situation is now rapidly changing. The introduction of the digital computer into process control systems has supplied the system designer with an extremely flexible component for the design of the human-machine interface. To be effective, however, the design must be based on compatible models of human information processes as well as the functions of the control system. Furthermore, as the unit size of technological systems has increased, so has the potential for drastic consequences of malfunctions. Hence the designer must consider not only the typical performance in planned functions—for which the design can be validated empirically—but also the response of the system, *including the human operators*, to specific rare conditions and events.

In the following discussion the term "operator" is used in its general meaning of a human interacting with a physical system. Generally speaking, even in an automated system, operators have two kinds of role: On the one hand, they are movable, multipurpose manipulators taking care of a variety of preplanned control actions, adjustments, tests and maintenance tasks. On the other, they are adaptive, learning data processors able to cope with ill-defined and unforeseen situations; they have both a monitoring and supervisory task. There are of course individual characteristics to consider, for example, depending upon the task and operating conditions, the operators will have different professional backgrounds. In some industrial systems the range spans from unskilled workers to university-trained engineers. The human operator is therefore a very complex and varied system component, and any attempt to develop a model of the human operator to serve as a guide for systems design must include knowledge from several scientific fields. Given this diversity it is difficult at present to identify useful research results and establish how they may be combined to form a model. The aim of the present chapter is to discuss a general frame of reference in this situation, to outline a map of the woods rather than to describe the individual trees.

2.0 A Model of the Human Data Processor

The system we consider is shown in Figure 1. A system performing some kind of physical process is controlled by an information-processing system that includes an automatic control system and a human operator. The human operator receives information on the operational state of the system; transforms it and as a result performs some physical actions upon the system. An operator is basically an extremely adaptive data processor. When he/she responds to a familiar environment in a well adapted mode, the behaviour largely reflects properties of the environment in the light of current goals (Simon, 1969). Only when the limiting properties are exceeded, will inner mechanisms become more evident. The basic aim in modelling human data processes will be to identify those internal mechanisms which are activated in different task environments and to determine their limiting properties.

When human performance in a uniform and well defined task condition is modelled, for example manual control, the limiting properties of his/her inner mechanisms can be properly identified and described in terms referring to external task concepts. If however, the model is to be useful for work

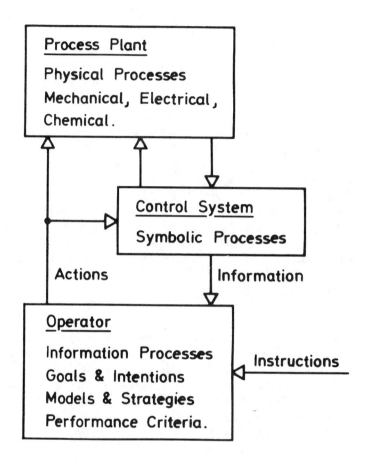

Fig. 1. A model of the human operator in a control system. The task is to transform information obtained from the display system into manual actions upon the system.

situations such as those found in process plant environments, where tasks vary widely and where different types of task may interfere and compete for the operator's resources, the limiting properties of operators must be identified and described in terms referring to internal human functions or mechanisms at a level which is reasonably task independent. Even though such models may be rather qualitative and ambiguous, they can serve as efficient guides to the design of work situations in which the operator can adapt efficiently, and the adaptability of the operator will often serve to compensate for inaccuracies of the model. Attempts to outline a model of a human operator have been discussed elsewhere (Rasmussen 1974, 1976).

In the present context some features of the human data processor which we have found important from analysis of the behavior of control room operators will be mentioned (see Figure 2).

First of all, since manual actions are almost always the output of human data processing, bodily skills are important elements of the human function. To be useful in the present context, a model of the human data processor must represent sensorimotor functions as well as higher level cognitive processes. Secondly, a model must consider the observations stressed in Miller's (1956) classic paper, where he points out that the individual's data processing capacity in certain situations is very low, even though one is able to recognize faces immediately and to drive a car in crowded traffic. Such behavior can be accounted for by considering human data processing as a co-operation between a high-capacity, parallel processing system, which functions subconsciously, and a sequential conscious processor of limited capacity. The subconscious processor takes care of routine tasks, and only in unfamiliar environments and tasks is there need for higher level control of the processing by the versatile, but slow sequential processor.

2.1 The Subconscious Processor

The subconscious processing system comprises several functions that are important in the present context. For example, the possession of an efficient internal dynamic world model must be assumed if we are to account for several features of human behavior: In familiar situations, complex and precise sequences of actions can be released by simple cues and performed at a pace too fast for simple sensory feed-back control. Furthermore, human attention is very selective. The operator is not continuously scanning the environment in order to obtain information; generally he/she predicts very well when and where in the environment changes may make observations necessary, i.e., operators have "process-feel" (Bainbridge, 1974b). The existence of an internal world model has important implications. An operator cannot be considered merely as a data channel transforming input information into actions. Instead, in a specific situation, the input information synchronizes the internal model, and complex responses may be generated from primitive inputs. In highly trained situations it can be extremely difficult to predict the information which is used to synchronize the internal model. Often it can be secondary sources, utilizing such auditory information as relay clicks and motor noises.

What are the elements of the internal, dynamic world model? The model is apparently formed by extracting and storing dynamic patterns from the input information, and therefore in some sense it stores a time-space representation of the behavior of the environment. The precision of fast movements and the efficient transfer between similar environments almost sug-

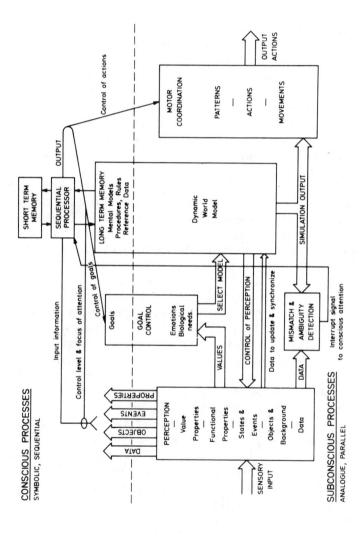

Fig. 2. Schematic map of the human data processing functions which illustrates the important role of the subconscious dynamic world model as part of a complex loop of interactions in conjunction with the perception and goal systems. The world model also forms the basis for a high-capacity efficient feed-forward control of physical actions and serves as a reference for the mismatch detector which activates the conscious processor.

gests an internal world structure similar to an analogue model with generic types of objects and object behavior. Here "objects" refer to time-space data patterns representing physical objects, as well as artifacts such as signs and symbols on paper and displays.

Closely connected to the internal world model is a mis-match detection system which alerts conscious attention and control if the input information deviates from the predictions of the internal model. This occurs if/when the internal model loses synchronization or is not properly updated due to unfamiliar or unexpected behavior of the environment. The efficiency of this mis-match detection is demonstrated clearly by the "Bowery El" phenomenon mentioned by Pribram (1969): When the noisy train was torn down, people awakened periodically at the times the train had formerly rumbled past to call the police about some strange occurrence they could not properly define. "The strange occurrences were of course the deafening silence that had replaced the expected noise . . .".

The information input to the human data processes is structured by the perceptive system which extracts relevant higher level features from the information received from the environment. In fact, the environment is a continuum of information sources. To cope with this great variety, the human data processor must structure the environment into manageable higher level elements. Thus, the perceptive system aggregates data sources into familiar objects separated from the background and assigns to these objects functional and value properties relevant to the particular situation. The correct level of activation of objects and properties depends upon the context of the situation and the immediate goal. Therefore observed selectivity must be based on an internal model, otherwise one would need to be perpetually scanning and sorting information from the environment. In our context, this leads to the important conclusion that the human is not an unbiased, neutral observer. Instead, information selection proceeds by asking those questions of the environment which are needed to update the internal model and verify its predictions. The necessary feature extraction in the perceptive system appears to rely upon parallel processing in a preconditioned high capacity network, and its efficiency depends upon simultaneous presence of items of information which are correlated with, and can be structured in terms of, familiar time-space patterns. Overload of the input system is not directly related to the amount of information; but rather to masking effects from irrelevant information.

In a given task environment proper initiation and activation of the relevant dynamic world model depends upon the immediate goal and intention. In real-life work situations, a large degree of freedom is left to the human even though the overall goal is stated unambiguously. This means that subjective performance criteria and emotional preferences are important factors which, depending upon value properties assigned to the situation, will control initiation and activation of the internal world model.

2.2 The Conscious Processor

The high capacity of the subconscious sensorimotor functions protects the low capacity of the higher level conscious cognitive functions from overload in familiar routine tasks. Conscious attention may be considered as a single channel function which has to be switched between different items, objects, or tasks. Therefore the conscious data processor may be thought of as a sequential processor which normally runs different tasks on a time-sharing basis. The limiting properties of the conscious data processor are related to the capacity of its short term buffer memory which is generally taken, as a rule of thumb, to be between 2 and 7 items of information (Miller, 1956, Simon, 1969). The effectiveness of the conscious processor, in spite of these limitations, is due to both its ability to operate on efficient information codes at high levels of abstraction and to its large repertoire of different data processing models and strategies. (These are discussed in the following sections). The role of the conscious processor in overall performance varies widely. It can be used for passive monitoring of the performance of the subconscious processor in routine tasks. When initiated by "interrupts" caused by less familiar situations, it can be used to bridge mismatches of the subconscious processor by categorizing the input set and adding verbal labels to situations; thereby switching "states" of the subconscious processor. It can also perform problem solving in unique situations by evaluating alternatives and by making decisions and plans based on predictions, etc.. During problem solving the conscious data processor is capable of operating in several basically different modes, which behavior implies co-operation with the subconscious processor at different levels. For example, it can simulate the external world in the domain of the sensed information—e.g. make "visual experiments" in which a visual imagination of a process is used to "foresee" the response of the environment to planned manipulations. Or it can process symbolic data by following a prescribed plan, a sequential procedure—e.g. to make numerical calculations and abstract logical reasoning.

There is an important difference between the internal models or representations of the environment which are used by subconscious sensorimotor responses and those of the higher level cognitive processes; a difference which has a fundamental influence upon the kind of description which can be used to model operator behavior. Subconscious, sensorimotor responses appear to depend upon an active, dynamic model which simulates the behavior of the environment. This means that the data processes are determined by the structure and elements of the models, conceptually in the same way as the processes of an analogue computer are determined when it is initialized and activated. Accordingly, when modelling this kind of data process it may perhaps best be simulated or represented by a mathematical set of time functions. Several such mathematical models of trained operators in specific situations have been developed: Young (1969) describes manual control of vehicles, Curry (1976) and Sheridan (1976) model attention in a monitoring task using optimal Kalman filters to represent the internal world model, Senders & Posner (1976) model the control of information selection by means of sampling and queueing theory.

Typically, the sequential, conscious data processes are based on stationary (static) models or representations of the functional properties of the system to be controlled, in the form of cognitive, functional maps. Process rules or strategies are therefore necessary to activate and control the steps in a sequential data process and descriptions of these in terms of flow diagrams provide feasible analysis tools (Bainbridge, 1974a, Newell & Simon, 1972). However a major problem in the study of behavior in human-machine systems is that the higher level cognitive processes called upon in infrequent unique situations cannot be considered independently from the sensorimotor skills developed to respond to routine situations, and yet the models developed so far are difficult to interrelate.

3.0 Structure Of Task Sequences

In order to study mental models and strategies, we have to refer to a specific task and environment. In our context, however, the problem is to derive guidelines for the design of human-machine interfaces suitable for a large repertoire of tasks related to a specific system. Therefore reference can only be made to a generalized description of typical task sequences. This description must be based on analyses of the performance of skilled operators in their normal work situation, and frequently an effective way to distinguish their internal processes in this situation is to obtain and analyse verbal protocols supported by observations, interviews, etc.. As has been mentioned the efficiency of skilled performance results from the ability to compose the process needed for a specific task as a sequence of familiar sub-routines that are useful in different contexts. This implies the existence of links in the sequence at standard key points, or "states of knowledge", which are characteristic of the specific skill. The data process stops at such links, the mode of processing and frequently the level of abstraction changes, and to study and identify the processes, the activity must be structured according to such key points. In familiar situations, the sub-routines depend upon subconscious or non-verbal processes, and verbal protocols from such situations typically express a sequence of such states of knowledge without any indication of the connecting data processes. However, the structure of the sequence of verbal statements gives important

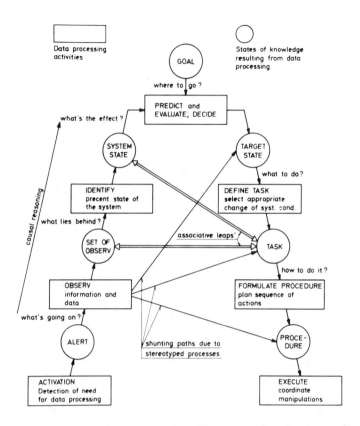

Fig. 3. Schematic map of the sequence of mental activities used between initiation of response and the manual action. Rational, causal reasoning connects the "states of knowledge" in the basic sequence. Stereotyped mental processes can bypass intermediate states. Associative leaps can connect any states of knowledge.

information on the strategies used for control of mental processes. Only in unfamiliar task situations when operators have to improvise and generate new subroutines will verbal protocols reflect data processes at a more detailed level. The verbal statements of the task sequence reflect "states of knowledge" in different categories representing plain observations, properties of the environment, goal, plans, etc.; i.e., knowledge at different levels of abstraction and associated with different roles in task strategies. It follows that the type of data process needed to derive one state of knowledge from the preceding one depends upon the categories of these states.

In a situation where the operator uses rational data processes based on knowledge of the causal structure of the system being controlled, the different states of knowledge follow each other in an apparently logical order, which has been represented in Figure 3. In this figure, the steps of the basic sequence form in a way a "ladder of abstraction."

To be able to predict the behavior of a system and its response to operator actions, its internal state must be known to the operator. The process necessary to derive this knowledge from the observations is basically one of abstraction, of induction. In practice this process can be a complex set of elementary processes including search, hypothesis generation and test, model transformation, performance evaluation, etc.. The top of the ladder dealing with the determination of the target state of the system from the present state and of the overall operational goal implies a prediction of system behavior, performance evaluation and value judgements. In general, the operator will not climb to this level of abstraction. The goal will be implicitly defined by the situation; the internal model will be controlled by the subconscious value/goal system and a specific system state will immediately associate to a target state or a task. When a target regarding the system state is chosen, the operator must determine the task, i.e., the proper control actions to perform, by a process of deduction. The operator now moves down from the higher levels of abstraction to more specific technical details; identifying the possible changes of the plant, such as switching, valve manipulation, or adjustments which will lead to the desired plant state.

In the basic sequence of mental processes based on knowledge of the causal structure of the system, the different states of knowledge may be expected to follow each other in a logical sequence. This is not necessarily the case if the data processes are stereotyped or proceduralized—if they follow "cook book" prescriptions, which may be the case in familiar or preplanned activities. Then, there may be no logical connection between subsequent states of knowledge, and some of the higher level processes of the basic sequence can be bypassed as shown in Figure 3. Regardless of which of these two cases apply, the operator must follow a sequential, conscious data process when a problem is recognized, i.e. an uncertainty needs to be resolved. This applies only if an immediate association does not lead from one state of knowledge to the next. Such direct association between states of knowledge is the typical process in familiar situations and leads to very efficient bypassing of low-capacity, higher-level processes. Such direct association does not follow logical rules; it is based on prior experience and can connect all categories of "states of knowledge." Some typical examples of the associations found in verbal reports from skilled operations are given in Figure 4.

In everyday tasks, evolution has fitted the human for an efficient interaction with a time-space environment where high-capacity parallel processes take care of the lower functions of the ladder of abstraction. An abundance of redundant information supports feature extraction and the formation and synchronization of the internal world model. In process control, however, an operator controls a physical process from which only preselected infor-

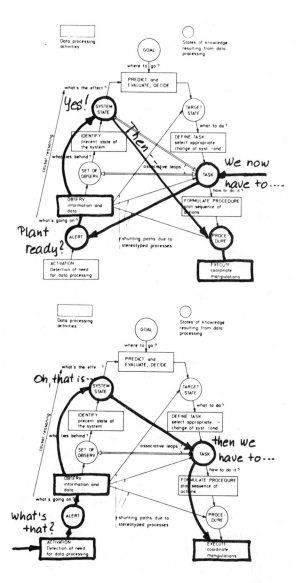

Fig. 4. Sample of typical routine sequences from skilled operator performance.

mation is presented and typically as symbolic representations of individual variables. Often designers suppose that the operator uses rational, conscious processes—even in lower level tasks—which would lead to complex time-sharing between tasks at different process levels. An important task when

studying process-operator performance is to identify the repertoire of in-
genious tricks developed by operators to avoid this situation. Thus, for
example, the operator adopts focussing strategies (Bruner et al., 1956) based
upon a model of normal state and leading to separate judgements based on
individual observations. He/she relies on these intuitive judgements which,
due to the nature of the subconscious world model, may be based on
representativeness rather than on a rational foundation (Tversky & Kahneman, 1974) etc..

4.0 Analysis of Real-Life Strategies

Human data processes in real-life tasks are extremely situation and person dependent and a detailed process description is difficult to obtain. This
is even the case when an unfamiliar situation forces the operator into a
process of detailed functional reasoning from which a good verbal protocol
can be obtained. In most tasks, several different strategies are available by
which the operator may solve the problem. These strategies may all be
rational, but differ according to different performance criteria. However, in
actual work situations, these different strategies are typically not followed
systematically. The mental processes seem to follow the law of least resistance, and a shift between strategies will take place whenever a momentary
difficulty is encountered in the current strategy, or special information is
recognized that makes another strategy look more promising (Rasmussen
& Jensen, 1974). See Figure 5. Even when it is possible to obtain detailed
verbal protocols from a single task sequence, it is very difficult to identify
general features of the data processes due to frequent spontaneous shifts
between different basic process strategies, shifts which are initiated by
minute details in the situation. One cannot see the wood for the trees.

A simultaneous analysis of several process descriptions (e.g., from verbal
protocols) at the level of types of data, models and procedural rules supports
a more efficient identification of consistent strategies. This leads to a description in terms of information transformations between different categories of "states of knowledge", in the form of an information flow map rather
than a sequence description. When this analysis has led to the fundamental
structure of different strategies used in a mental sub-task, it may be possible
logically and rationally to complete the description of a strategy and to
generate a full set of possible strategies. In this way a description of what
the operator *can do* is obtained. This information enables the formulation
of precise questions to be used for an analysis of the sequence in a specific
protocol in terms of the information coding, the type of models, and operations used. Furthermore, a detailed analysis can lead to identification of the
leaps between formal strategies.

A description of what the operator *will do* in a specific situation can then

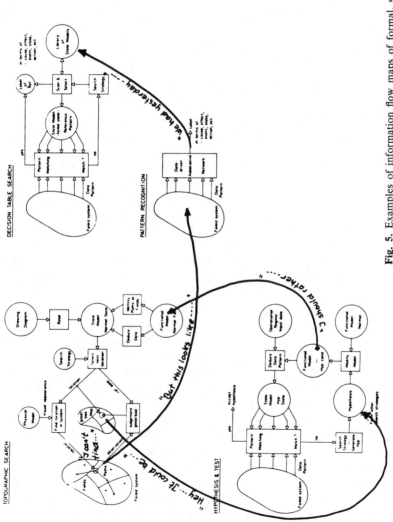

Fig. 5. Examples of information flow maps of formal, systematic strategies found in a diagnostic task. The actual sequence consists of pieces of such strategies because of the frequent "jumps" in between them.

only be obtained in terms of a set of typical, systematic strategies and the heuristic rules controlling the transitions between these strategies.

4.1 Data, Models and Strategies

In considering the human data processor as a system component, it is necessary to describe mental processes in a frame of reference compatible with the decisions to be made by the interface designer. In this respect a description related to the properties of the data processes as discussed above is advantageous. Identification of the data, i.e. the representation of the variables describing the actual state of the system, used in the mental processes should indicate the appropriate preconditioning of the system variables to be presented. The mental model, representing the interrelationship between variables resulting from the internal causal structure of the system, specifies the appropriate structure and format of the data displays. Finally, the strategies preferred by the operator must be encapsulated in some way in the automatic system so that it will be readily accepted as a proper support. The following discussion aims at a tentative morphology of models and related types of data and strategies. A system operator meets a wide spectrum of tasks in dealing with a system subject to changing operating conditions and internal faults. An important aspect of the sets of models, data and strategies used is the ease with which they can be updated to take into account changes in the task environment.

Every observation yields information identifying the information source and information representing the actual state of this source. The environment is, of course, a continuum of information sources, but it is normally aggregated in frequently appearing sets or "objects" at a level convenient in the specific situation. The most primitive and ever necessary model of the environment is a map representing the physical information sources and their location, *a physical model*. For direct encounters with the physical environment, such models are typically iconic: pictorial representations, "scale models", topographic maps. For technical process systems controlled from a control console, this physical model can refer to the display surface as well as to the physical system behind this surface. The physical model only supplies information on "where is what".

In order to support mental data processes, information on functional system properties must also be available. Functional system properties can be represented in a data domain as state models; in the domain of structures and relations as a functional model; or in the process domain as an algorithmic model. The *algorithmic model* represents system properties implicitly by a sequence of specific observations and actions leading the system to the desired end-state; as, for instance, a cook-book recipe or work instruction peculiar to a specific system and task. *State models* represent functional properties of the system by coherent sets of states of system variables labelled in terms of system states—"operation normal"—or related actions —"boiler now ready for start". Such models are related to specific systems but are useful in different task contexts—to monitor or recognize system states, to verify the result of actions, or as a reference during a search to locate changes in the system. The usefulness of algorithmic and state models is limited. They are based on stored results from previous operations and do not contain the information needed when new situations call for improvisations and problem solving. Such cases demand more general and explicit representation of the constraints imposed upon system variables by the anatomy and the physical process of the system. Such *functional models* must describe system properties in terms of a map identifying the data sources and their structural relationships together with rules representing the relation between the magnitudes of the variables. A functional model can be monolithic, i.e., it can represent the information sources and specify the relation between them at the surface of the system. Generally, however, a functional model explicitly reflects the internal structure of the system. The model is then a structured set of frequently used items; i.e., frequently encountered sets of data sources labelled as physical objects or components; or frequently used sets of relations—labelled as functions, e.g., feed-back loops, heat balances.

This distinction between a functional model representing the environment by a set of interacting objects or components and a model representing it by a set of variables connected by a network of relations or rules is similar to Russell's (1913) distinction between causal, commonsense reasoning and deterministic, scientific reasoning. The distinction is important since the system designer can use the latter, while, according to our studies, a skilled operator will prefer the former type of model. In the causal, commonsense model the objects are ascribed functional properties relating to what they can do or what can be done to them. The physical variables of the system are represented collectively in sets labelled as states of objects. Causal reasoning then is an associative chaining of events through the system from the initiating event to its ultimate effect. Events are *changes* in object states influencing the states of other objects. Initiating events can be human actions or spontaneous changes in object states (faults). This kind of functional model has been studied by computer linguists in an attempt to find language-independent representations of the semantic content of verbal messages (Rieger, 1976; Scragg, 1976). In the deterministic, more formal type of model, the state of the system is represented by the magnitude of measurable or observable variables, and the functional properties of the system are represented by a set of rules or relations describing the interrelationships among the variables. These rules can have the form of basic physical laws, technical component specifications, or symbolic conventions, depending upon the actual system and task condition.

In philosophical discussions the causal model based on objects and events is generally characterized as an ambiguous and fuzzy representation of realities in comparison to the more formal model. This is not quite fair. As the basis for communication and actions in a specific system context where skill has evolved—i.e. the internal world model is well developed, verbal statements have a very precise meaning. This is clearly demonstrated by recordings of conversations between operators, which frequently show the very precise effect of rather rudimentary verbal messages. The quantitative accuracy that can be obtained by more formal models is not required, because actions on a system are considered relatively with reference to the actual state or normal state, etc.. The lack of quantitative accuracy is normally compensated through feed-back effects during the ultimate action.

However, the distinction between object/property-based and variable/relation-based models is not quite as clear as it may seem. Typically, frequently used sets of relations and the corresponding variables are often represented collectively as functions that are ascribed properties and potential for actions. They then become pseudo-objects and are treated as such in verbal reasoning. This way of "chunking" several variables into higher level abstractions as states is an efficient way to counteract the low capacity of conscious reasoning.

The functional model can represent the properties of a system at different levels of abstraction leading to advantages in different task conditions. It can refer to the basic physical properties of the system, dealing with the physical properties of the components (transistors can saturate, capacitors discharge, multivibrators fire, etc.) or expressing relations in basic physical laws (Ohm's and Kirchof's laws, etc.) or their graphic representations (transistor characteristics, transfer function plots, etc.). This level of modelling is necessary when dealing with the effects of physical changes (faults) in the system, and if the physical process itself is the ultimate purpose (industrial process plants). In a large class of systems, especially computers and other electronic systems, the physical process is only of interest as a carrier of information. A description at the level of physical functioning of this kind of system is too detailed for most purposes, and the significance of the physical function cannot be derived from basic physical laws. In this case a model representing system variables and properties by information content and processes is necessary. An example of this is logic diagrams of electronic circuits together with coding and process conventions. At the symbolic functional level, information systems, such as electronic control systems and computers, do not behave according to general physical laws. Instead they execute stored human decisions, which makes it difficult to "understand" their properties and to deduce their behavior under infrequently encountered circumstances. In process control, this causes difficulties for the operators when rarely seen, abnormal plant states initiate more subtle automatic actions or protective interlock conditions. Case stories of such situations sometimes resemble records of a struggle between control system and operator to gain control of the system. This difficulty diminishes if the function is not modelled in concepts and terms referring to the physical internal functioning of the information system, or in general, formal information concepts, but in concepts referring directly to the external effects on the environment. In the case of a control system, this could relate to the operations it performs upon the process. This type of model is similar in structure and content to flow diagrams of the function of a computer program. Such models support the prediction of the response of the system to changes in its environment, but they cannot be used to judge the effect of changes within the system itself, because there is no longer any explicit relation between physical parts of the system and the content of the model.

In the case of systems with an autonomous internal organization originating from adaptive or learning capabilities, a mental model cannot be based on information on the internal anatomy and function, nor on a deterministic sequence of operations. In this case it is generally necessary to use "intentional models." That is, from knowledge of the input information and the actual intention of the system (designer), the response of the system can be predicted because it can be assumed to act rationally as long as the actual task does not surpass the capability limits of the system. The term *intentional model* is more precise in our context than teleological or purposive models and is taken from a discussion by Dennett (1971). This kind of model is not only used when dealing with complex, adaptive and goal-oriented systems, but can also be used effectively to recollect degenerated functional models of less complicated systems. These are then obtained by a "redesign" of the system based on assumptions of the design intentions combined with general professional technical knowledge. The types of model discussed so far are stationary models used for sequential conscious processes. The subconscious *dynamic world model* has been characterised in previous sections as an active, dynamic analogue model capable of simulating the time-space behaviour of items perceived in the environment.

The need for a set of rules or procedures to control the cognitive data processes varies widely depending upon the processes in question. Processes in the data domain performed by active, parallel processing models (such as subconscious simulation of world behavior, recognition and perception) are completely specified by the dynamic model and no procedural rules are necessary to control the process. The process is determined when the proper model is initiated and activated. The mental processes in the functional domain depend upon process rules or strategies for proper sequencing of the conscious sub-routines. Whereas associations can directly connect any two states of knowledge in the ladder of abstraction, regardless of their logical connection, different processes must be used to relate states of different kinds of knowledge if they are to be based on logical reasoning. Typical sub-processes are those of deduction and induction as well as performance evaluation and value judgements; processes that all depend on different types of strategies. The strategies can only be discussed with reference to a specific task and system; the point here is that the strategy can be of a very general nature if the functional model represents the properties of the system closely and specifically. The more rudimentary the model, the more specific must be the procedural rules. The different categories of data process that are available to an operator involve very different requirements of mental effort, time, type and amount of input information, and knowledge of system properties. Accordingly, the operator will be able to meet the different constraints in a specific task by a proper selection of the mental process. It also follows that a description of human behavior in real-life work situations must be based on explicit formulation of either process models or process rules or both, depending upon the situation. A strong emphasis upon the process rules which are effective in the analysis of symbolic problem solving (Newell & Simon, 1972) is not feasible in the present context. (See chapter 2 for a discussion of this approach).

5.0 Data Processes and Human-computer Co-operation

When a computer and a computer-controlled interface are placed between a human and the system, human and computer share a data-processing task and must necessarily co-operate. To make the data processes performed by both partners compatible, some of the requirements that can be derived from the preceding discussion should be considered. Expectations and intuitions are important factors even in rational thinking, and it is therefore important to supply the operator with the means to properly update and synchronize his/her dynamic world model and not only to display information in response to conscious requests. It is well known that skilled operators monitor a system continuously and subconsciously by means of characteristic, often secondary information, such as noise from relays, recorders, and teleprinters. Computer operators sometimes listen to the actual CPU operations from loudspeakers. Curiously enough, the possibility of a qualitative topographic display from well planned stereophonic auditive systems to indicate the operating state of different functions and parts of a system does not seem to have received serious attention for this purpose.

The human and computer will only be able to share the data-processing task in co-operation if they are using compatible processes and strategies for solving a task. The operators should understand and accept the strategy of the computer, and not be allocated a part of the task that exceeds the limiting properties of their data-processing mechanisms. This is generally expressed as a demand to keep the mental load sufficiently low. However, as also discussed by Bainbridge (1974a), the concept of load and stress is useful in physical systems, but for information systems it is misleading. The problem is more complex. The data processes that can be used for a task are subject to constraints determined by process mechanisms (e.g., short-term memory capacity, time for retrieval, characteristics of the available mental model, etc.), and by the task environment (time requirements, information supplied, quality of references, etc.). The characteristics of different strategies related to the constraints vary widely, and a strategy must be chosen from a trade-off between the different limiting properties and task demands. This means that the operator should be free to chose the proper strategy without losing support from the computer. Furthermore, the codes used for human-machine communication must be compatible with the mental processes of an operator. Criteria for interface design sometimes refer to interface transparency, i.e., the operator should be able to see the physical process through the data processing and display system. However, as we have seen, the operator will only occasionally operate at the level of the physical process itself. The human has different data processes related to different functional levels in the system. Instead, the guiding principle should be that no mental task should be forced into a level of consciousness higher than the task in itself justifies, (due to some inappropriate coding of information or choice of strategy in the computer). If this principle is not followed, the operator may have to time-share the main task with the extra, irrelevant task of data recoding. This is perhaps one of the great problems in conventional systems where the magnitudes of process variables—selected not only in accordance with their importance to the operator's tasks, but largely according to the availability of reliable measuring probes—are displayed individually by meters or indicators. When the system state, therefore, cannot be identified by direct perception but by the cognitive process of diagnosis, skilled operators will typically replace functional reasoning by the use of single cues as signs for system states. This is a very efficient solution during a normal work situation, but becomes somewhat of a trap in not-seen-before situations. This situation can be drastically changed by computers—but unfortunately not only for the better.

The problem then is to match the code used in the information display to the mode of human data processing preferred in the specific task. It is *not*, as frequently stated, to reduce the amount of information displayed. As Newman (1966) concluded:

"(It was) found that properly formatted displays allowed people to tolerate and absorb much more information than would normally be expected. There seems to be an important principle operating here, one of considerable generality: People don't mind dealing with complexity if they have some way of controlling or handling it. .... (If) a person is allowed to structure a complex situation according to his perceptual and conceptual needs, sheer complexity is no bar to effective performance." (p. 14)

This is another way of saying that inappropriate coding of information should not force a task from the level of high-capacity perceptive functions to the level of low-capacity cognitive functions.

In a discussion of human data processes we can distinguish between operations in the data domain, in the different functional domains, and in the physical domain, according to the different types of mental models used. Operations in the *data domain* are typically based on processes such as association, recognition, matching of sets of observations to stored state models, etc.. Such data processes depend on stored data sets, state models, used as reference sets and labelled according to their operational significance as system states, properties, tasks, etc.. The operations in the data domain can be performed by the high-capacity subconscious functions if all information is available in parallel and the operations can be performed directly on the presented symbols constituting a time-space configuration rather than on their functional meaning. The subconscious processes operate by the "expression on the face of the system"—which does not necessarily have any logical connection to the internal processes. This feature was used literally by Chernoff (1971), who applied computer-generated human faces to the control of mineral sample classification. Smith (1976) uses manipulation of boxes (rectangles) to solve scheduling problems. Direct perception of system states can be facilitated if patterns of data are presented in formats where normal, expected or specified states form regular figures from which deviations are easily perceived, such as straight lines, symmetrical patterns (Coekin, 1969; Affinito & Wohl, 1966). Effective support can be given by computerized collection, storage and presentation of reference data sets classified and labelled according to system state, operating regime or related task.

Operations in the *functional domain* are related to the internal causal processes of the system, and data presentation should be related to the structure of mental models of the functional category. Typical processes implied in operations at the functional level are those of abduction, deduction and induction (Fogel, 1961). Abduction and deduction are respectively the processes of backward and forward cause-and-effect tracing through a system having known internal properties and structure. Such processes are used to generate non-observable data; to predict the response to intended actions upon the system; to predict the course of events in a system subject to known disturbances; and to select the proper means of action to reach a specific system state. Such operations can be supported by computer-generated maps of the causal pathways of the system, i.e., the flow paths of matter, energy or information through the system. The data measured in the system should not be presented directly, but converted and displayed according to their significance to the state of the flow system, such as information on flow and level magnitudes. The level variables of energy or mass balance systems (such as temperature and pressure) are typical, critical variables subject to specified limitations and should be identified in the display, as should also potential means for manual action in the different causal paths. The data conditioning needed for this kind of display implies computerized deductions for information recoding. Complete computerization of deductive processes is readily feasible by automatic cause-effect tracking programs and predictive displays (Taylor & Hollo, 1977), as long as the functional model behind the processes is known, which is the case for deductions related to normal states of the system or models modified by a reliable diagnosis. Nevertheless, even when completely computerized deductions are used, a display should indicate causal flow level to allow operators to follow the processes.

The process of induction is involved in the task of identifying the structure and properties behind an observed system response. This is a difficult task with creative overtones, and it is one that leads to trouble in practice (Rasmussen, 1969). In the human-machine context, the inductive task can be solved in the data domain by recognition of previously experienced system states. In the functional domain, it takes the form of a search to locate a change in system conditions or structure. In order not to force the identification of the system state onto the conscious level, unless the situation presents a genuine diagnostic problem, the computer must either present information that leads to identification by direct perception, as discussed above, or it must do the identification automatically by search through a library of data patterns labelled in terms of system states. In the case of infrequent, unfamiliar system conditions, operation by association at the level of the familiar system-state/task level is not sufficient. Perceptive identification becomes unreliable and must be replaced by more conscious diagnostic procedures. This diagnostic task is a search to locate changes of system conditions with reference to a state of normal operation. This search can take place in different domains depending upon the circumstances. Critical plant situations are typically related to disturbed mass or energy balance functions, resulting in "pile up", i.e., abnormal level magnitudes endangering system integrity. Search in the data domain will lead to identification of endangered critical level variables and directly to appropriate actions if safety procedures are preplanned. Search to locate the change in the functional domain will be used for a more detailed judgement about the functional effects of the change and to plan compensatory actions. Direct search by good/bad mapping of the system can readily be supported by computer-generated maps in the proper domain as discussed above, especially if data are presented as deviations from the normal state. The reference values—being "normal" values—can be predetermined or generated by automatic data collection in the relevant regimes of operation. This direct visual search may be even more effective if computers are used to store and replay the spread of changes through the system following the initial change or fault.

During search by hypothesis and test, the computer can be used to *generate* hypotheses by automatic diagnostic procedures. This, however, should be done with great care. Automatic diagnosis of infrequent situations must also consider events and combinations of events with drastic consequences and therefore—in well designed systems—of very low probability. If hypothesis generation starts at the most probable end of the spectrum of possible system states, it can cost the operator valuable time on trivialities. On the other hand, if it starts from the possible, but low probability, risky end of the event spectrum it will generally be too conservative. In both cases, acceptance of the hypothesis by the operators will be endangered. Typically, computer-generated hypotheses must be based on a repertoire of stored functional or state models related to a large number of abnormal system states and will only take into account causes that have been conceived by the designer. On the other hand, the computer has a great capacity for complex causal deductions, for collecting, storing and searching through data patterns and for testing of relations such as energy and mass balances by quantitative calculation. The fact that such tests can be based on functional and state models related to known, or normal system states, makes it possible to give the operator reliable, trustworthy support in rapid, complex test operations. Leaving the task of identifying the state of the system, which is a rather unpredictable and badly structured task, to an operator supported by effective information displays, and using the computer to test the operator's hypotheses brings into use the special advantages of co-operative partnership. Importantly, it also leaves the operator in control of the situation. Thus the operator should be able to follow his/her natural tendency to first test the most probable hypothesis—without necessarily getting lost in preconceived ideas resulting from ineffective tests.

Finally, a few words on operations in the physical domain, which is typically related to the question of "where is what" in terms of physical parts and components, sources of information, and means for action. The results of mental operations in the functional domain can be directly related to the physical domain, if the functional map is structured in physical components and variables refer to the physical state of components. This is not necessarily the case, as the concepts of the functional domain may have no reference to the physical domain. Mental models related to the physical domain are therefore in general necessary in order to transfer the results of functional reasoning to actions upon the physical system. Operations directly in the physical domain are typically tied to the execution of preplanned procedures, cook-book recipes for operations on the physical system, adjustments, assembly tasks, etc.. As a result of the constructive nature of human long-term memory, preplanned procedures and work instructions are often stored by an intentional model and tend to degenerate in that they become *operationally* optimized, e.g., they may leave out the more subtle safety considerations. Furthermore, analysis of accidents (e.g., Bartlett, 1943) indicates a break-down of proper sequencing prior to any deterioration in the execution of the skilled sub-routines in the case of stress and fatigue. Accordingly, support of operators by computer presentation of special, preplanned and critical work procedures should be considered.

6.0 Human Error Analysis and Prediction

Case stories describing human errors are important sources of information on human data processes and their limitations. The external behaviour of a human operator, or of any other adaptive system, does not reflect the inner organization as long as the task requirements are within the functional limitations. When limitations are exceeded, rationality of behaviour breaks down, and the way in which this happens gives important information on the inner organization. The term "human error," however, is very ambiguous. Basically, a human error is committed if the effect of human behaviour exceeds a limit of acceptability. Of course, the classification of a specific behavior as an error depends as much upon the limits of acceptability as it depends upon the behaviour itself. In practice, the limits are often defined after the fact by someone who can base their judgements on a careful consideration of the functional properties, while the specific behavior was possibly a rapid response to a stressed, dynamic situation. Therefore, as argued by Swain (1969), it is necessary to distinguish clearly between errors induced by inappropriate limits of acceptability, i.e. by the design of the work situation, and errors caused by inappropriate human behavior. Furthermore, as discussed by Rigby (1969), errors can be classified as *random errors*, due to random variability of human performance, *systematic errors*, which are causally connected to the situation and which can be caused by personal abnormalities or inappropriate system design, and, finally, *sporadic errors*, occasional "blunders" that are infrequent and often inexplicable erroneous actions, i.e., they are not likely to recur even if the same situation is repeated.

Random errors can be eliminated only to the extent to which the limits of acceptability can be arranged to span the range of natural variability of performance of the people selected for the task. Systematic errors can be related deterministically to specific properties of the work situation and can be eliminated if the causal relations can be identified and changed. This is a very important category of errors within the context of monitoring and supervisory tasks in automated systems. Typically, the operators have to respond to changes in system operation by corrective actions, and in a properly designed system there should be an inverse relationship between the probability of the occurrence of a change and its potential effect in terms of loss and damage. In modern, large centralized systems, the consequences of faults can be extremely serious and therefore the effect of human errors in situations of extremely low probability must be considered. In such cases, the potential for systematic errors cannot be identified from experience, but only by a systematic functional analysis of the process plant and of the operator's actions.

In the present general discussion, two types of systematic error are important and must be considered. First, human responses to changes in a system will be systematically wrong if task demands exceed the limits of capability. Demands and capability may conflict in several aspects of a task such as time required, availability of state information, background information on system functioning, complexity of data processes, etc.. The operator must be able to trade-off demands and limitations by choice of a proper strategy. Secondly, systematic human errors may be caused by a kind of procedural trap. During normal work conditions, human operators are extremely efficient due to their very effective adaptation to convenient, representative signs and signals; on the other hand these signs very probably lead them into difficulties when the behavior of the system changes. An operator will only make conscious observations if his/her attention is alerted by an interrupt from the subconscious processes. Consequently a change will only be detected in the environment if the convenient, representative information modelled by the dynamic world model also includes the defining attributes of the actual state of the environment. Likewise, someone cannot be expected to cope correctly with a unique event in the system if their attention is alerted by information that immediately associates to a familiar task or action. It is very likely that familiar associations based on representative, but insufficient information will prevent the operator from realizing the need to analyze the situation. An operator may more readily accept the improbable coincidence of several familiar faults in the system rather than realize the need to investigate a new and complex fault of low probability. Thus although the efficiency of the internal world model allows one to be selective, and therefore cope effectively with complex systems in familiar situations, it at the same time leads into traps that are easily seen after the fact. Davis (1958) concludes from an analysis of traffic accidents:

"It is usual for a person to have expectations, or to hold to what may be called an hypothesis about every situation he meets, even when information is notably incomplete. This hypothesis, which is in some degree the product of his previous experience of similar situations, governs the way in which he perceives the situation and the way in which he organizes the perceptual material available to him. As he receives further information, his hypothesis tends to be modified or amended or abandoned and replaced. Sometimes, however, a hypothesis and the expectations which go with it, appear to be unduly resistant to change."

The failure of human operators to identify abnormal states of a plant or system plays an important role in accidents and incidents in complex systems (Cornell, 1968; Rasmussen, 1969). However, even if the state of the system is correctly identified, the operator may still be caught in a procedural trap. A familiar, stereotyped sequence of actions may be initiated from a single conscious decision or association from the system state. If the corresponding procedure takes some time—e.g., it is necessary to move to another location to perform it—the mind may return to other matters, and the subconscious actions will become vulnerable to interference, particularly if part of the sequence is identical to steps in other stereotyped sequences. Systematic human errors in unfamiliar tasks are typically caused by interference from other, more stereotyped, situations and therefore the potential for systematic errors depends very much upon the level of the operator's skill. The fact that operators can control a system successfully during a commissioning and test period is no proof that they will continue to do so during the lifetime of the plant.

There is a trend towards the situation where a major industrial concept will only be acceptable if it can be demonstrated by a systematic analysis that the safety and reliability requirements will be met by the operating staff. The unit size of modern systems implies high risk potential, and the rapid development of new processes and equipment makes it increasingly difficult to ensure the fulfillment of stringent safety requirements by means of specific technical norms and standards. To be susceptible to systematic analysis, a system concept is subject to several constraints related to the limitations and assumptions of the accepted methods of analysis. Guidelines for system design can therefore be derived by an analysis of the assumptions and limitations underlying the methods for reliability and safety analysis. Currently the systematic methods for such analysis of technical systems are quite well developed. The basic method is a break-down of the system into parts or components to a level at which component properties are recognized from widespread use; empirical fault data can then be collected. At this level probabilistic models of system function can be formed and the resulting reliability and safety figures for the total system can be computed.

In a discussion of the problems related to the quantification of human errors, a distinction must be made between reliability analysis and safety analysis. The definition of the reliability of a system or system component is generally stated in terms of the probability of specified function versus time, such as: "Reliability is defined as that characteristic of an item expressed by the probability that it will perform its required function in the desired manner under all relevant conditions and on the occasion or during the time intervals when it is required so to perform" (Green & Bourne, 1972). Reliability analysis therefore is related to the effects caused by the absence of a specified function. In the case of a process plant, reliability figures are used to judge the expected average loss of production; in the case of a safety system, to judge the expected average loss of protection.

However, human elements cause problems when considering the basic aspects of reliability analysis. The human is an adaptive and learning system element and will very probably respecify a function or task related to certain observations. Consider, for example, a monitoring task at a power plant. The specified task is: "If the frequency meter indicates a frequency below 58 C/S, disconnect load to save the generator.". If an operator has only seen readings below 58 C/S that result from poor meter performance, he may well respecify his task: "If . . . ., then calibrate meter"—and lose a generator (as happened in the US power black out in 1965). Unless such respecifications are known, reliability prediction will be systematically wrong. Furthermore, a human operator is a multi-purpose element. He/she may be occupied by another task, and the omission of a specified function may be due to other events in the system rather than human failure mechanisms.

In the methods of human reliability prediction in practical use (Meister, 1971; Swain, 1976), the method of technical reliability, in which a system is broken down into components to a level where functions are invariate with application, has been transferred to the analysis of human performance. The complex and often very system-specific human functions are broken down into typical elements for which reliability data can be collected. Such elementary functions are in practice only distinguishable by their external effects, and are therefore generally characterized as "sub-tasks." This technique must be used, however, with extreme caution. The operator is in many respects a holistic data processor responding to total situations rather than to individual events or system states. Complex functions may be performed by skilled operators as one integrated and automated response. In this case, fault data can only be obtained by a realistic simulation of the total function (Regulinski 1973). Break-down of complex functions is only acceptable if the performance is paced by the system, i.e., cues from the system serve to initiate elementary, skilled sub-routines individually and to control their sequence. This is the case in many manual tasks, e.g., mechanical assembly, but can probably also be arranged in more complex mental tasks by properly designed interface systems.

Another basic difficulty arises when human error data are collected and categorized according to the external effects of human functions, i.e., tasks. As discussed in the previous sections, the internal function used to perform a specific external task depends strongly upon training and skill, prior experiences of system behavior, subjective performance criteria, etc..

Therefore, failure mechanisms and the probability of error related to the performance of a sub-task may change drastically when the work condition changes. In particular, it will be difficult to justify a prediction of the reliability of a sub-task in a rare work condition from failure data collected from the performance of the task in more normal situations. Finally, the failure properties of a specific internal function also depend upon the operating conditions, and for technical components weighting functions are generally used to modify fault data according to load and environmental effects. The great variability of human performance makes a similar weighting of fault data by "performance-shaping factors" mandatory (Swain, 1973), but the application is difficult because "operating conditions", such as motivation, stress, fatigue, etc., are badly defined and difficult to quantify; "expert judgements" are generally the only method available.

At the present state of the art, therefore, human reliability prediction is only feasible if the "specified function" of human operators is synonymous with a familiar task performed with a skill maintained through frequent use or exercise. In complex task sequences, the elements must be individually cued by the system. The reliability of tasks requiring more complex mental operations, improvisations, etc., can only be quantified if the result of the task is verified by test or inspection based on predictable human performance. Prediction of test and inspection reliability will give the lower limit to the reliability of the total task.

Whereas reliability figures are related to the probability of specified operation, safety considerations are related to the effects of the terminal state into which the system is brought by a fault. System safety is a measure of the risk—the expected average loss—related to the direct effects of the transitions from specified function into a state of accidental maloperation, in terms of human injuries or damage to equipment or environment. System safety has to be judged from an extensive accident analysis. To identify the course of events following the initiating fault, and to determine the ultimate effect and its probability, it is necessary to use a detailed functional description of the system including functional properties both within and outside the normal operating regimes of the plant. In the analysis of accidents, the human element is the imp in the system. Human inventiveness makes it impossible to predict actions after errors, and it is impossible to predict reactions in a sequence of accidental events, as an unfamiliar situation will very probably be misinterpreted. Some illustrative case stories are found in Rasmussen & Taylor (1976).

In practice, human variability makes a quantitative safety analysis unrealistic, unless the system design satisfies a number of conditions. If a potential for an unacceptable consequence of faults in a system has been identified, and the probability of the different chains of events leading to such a consequence is unacceptably high, or cannot be determined, e.g., due to the possibility of human interference, the design must be changed. This can be done either by inserting barriers or interlocks blocking the course of events, or by detecting the advent of risky courses of events at an early phase and initiating countermeasures. In a way, such monitoring and safety functions solve the variability problem by introducing feed-back paths in the course of events. If this can be realized and the protective function does not in itself introduce potential risks, an upper limit to the probability for a large set of chains of events leading to the monitored effect can be derived from a reliability analysis of the barrier or the protective function, which can be automatic or based on human actions. The general rule then is: If the reliability of a complex human task or the probability of unacceptable human actions must be predicted, it is necessary to apply a feed-back design concept. The effect of the human actions must be monitored or inspected and errors must be observable and reversible. The lower limit of the reliability of the total task or the upper limit of the frequency of unacceptable actions can then be determined from the frequency of error opportunities together with the reliability of the monitoring function. This function can be performed automatically or by humans.

Automation and a policy of thorough inspection and monitoring do not remove humans from the system—or turn them into trained apes. Instead they lead to a philosophy of shared responsibility. The designer takes the responsibility for system safety during acute, abnormal situations, while the operators have the responsibility for optimizing operation within the limits of automatic protection and for testing, calibrating and maintaining the system in an optimal state. Unexpected tasks during stressed situations will be replaced by tasks that can be planned and performed under more optimal conditions. This approach will not necessarily degrade the responsibility and opportunity for qualified decision-making of the operator. It opens the possibility for a strict formalization of some critical tasks, such as testing, inspection and verification, while other types of task are left unconstrained and can draw upon all the mental resources and imagination of the operator.

7.0 Conclusion

The preceding discussion has mainly considered the functional aspect of human data processing, such as mental models, codes and strategies. It has been pointed out that the human operator must be considered an intentional data processor, and that within process limitations he performs rationally— seen in the light of the subjective goal and performance criteria. The importance of a positive attitude towards computer assistance in complex systems has only been touched upon in passing. Although a prerequisite for appropriate goals and positive attitudes is a fit between the codes and strategies of the operator and a computer, this is only part of the problem, and a careful consideration of the emotional and social aspects of the work conditions of human operators in complex automated systems is necessary but this is outside the scope of the present paper. To recapitulate, the human is only considered as a system component in the present discussion; nevertheless it is equally important to consider the system as the working environment of the human. The qualities of the system in functional terms and in terms of working life quality are intimately connected.

References

Affinito, F.J. & Wohl, J.G. (1966). *Data Conditioning and Display for Apollo Prelaunch Checkout.* Dunlap and Associates, Inc. Report 675-TM-7; SSD-66-353.
Bainbridge, L. (1974a). The Representation of Working Storage, and Its Use in the Organization of Behavior. In *Measurement of Human Resources* (Eds.) W.T. Singleton, R.G. Taylor, & P. Spurgeon. Taylor and Francis,London.
Bainbridge, L. (1974b). Problems in the Assessment of Mental Load, *Le Travail Humain*, **37**, 2, 279-302.
Bartlett, F.C. (1943). Fatigue Following Highly Skilled Work. *Proc. Royal Society B.*, **131**, 247-257.
Bruner, J., Goodnow, J.J., & Austin, G.A. (1956). *A Study of Thinking.* Wiley, New York.
Chernoff, H. (1971). *The Use of Faces to Represent Points in n-Dimensional Space Graphically.* AD-738-473.
Coekin, J.A. (1969). A Versatile Presentation of Parameters for Rapid Recognition of Total State. In *International Symposium on Man-Machine Systems.* Cambridge, 8-12 September 1969. IEEE Conference Record 69 (58-MMS 4).
Cornell, C.E. (1968). Minimizing Human Errors. *Space Aeronautics*, **49**, March, 72-81.
Curry, R.E. & Ephrath, A.R. (1976). Monitoring and Control of Unreliable Systems. In Sheridan and Johannsen, 1976.
Davis, D. & Russel (1958). Human Errors and Transport Accidents. *Ergonomics*, **2**, 24-33.
Dennett, D.C. (1971). Intentional Systems. *Journal of Philosophy*, **LXVIII**, 4, Feb. 25.
Fogel, L.J. (1961). Levels of Intelligence in Decision Making. *Annals of the New York Academy of Sciences*, **89**, 5, 732-751.
Green, A.E. & Bourne, A.J. (1972). *Reliability Technology.* Wiley—Interscience, New York.
Meister, D. (1971). *Comparative Analysis of Human Reliability Models.* Human Factor Dept., Bunker Ramo Corp., Westlake Village, California, AD-734-432.
Miller, G.A. (1956). The Magical Number Seven Plus or Minus Two. *Psychology Review*, **63**, 81-97.
Newell, A. & Simon, H.A. (1972). *Human Problem Solving.* Prentice Hall, New Jersey.
Newman, R.J. (1966). *Extension of Human Capability Through Information Processing and Display Systems.* AD-645-435.
Pribram, K.H. (1969). The Neurophysiology of Remembering. *Scientific American*, **220**, 1, 73-82.

Rasmussen, J. (1969). Man-Machine Communication in the Light of Accident Records. *Int. Symp. on M-M Systems, Cambridge.* IEEE Conference Records 69 (58-MMS. 3).

Rasmussen, J. (1974). *The Human Data Processor as a System Component: Bits and Pieces of a Model.* Ris0-M-1722.

Rasmussen, J. & Jensen, A. (1974). Mental Procedures in Real Life Tasks A Case Study of Electronic Trouble Shooting. *Ergonomics,* **17,** 3, 293-307.

Rasmussen, J. & Taylor, J.R. (1976). *Notes on Human Factors Problems in Process Plant Reliability and Safety Prediction.* Ris0-M-1894

Rasmussen, J. (1976). Outlines of a Hybrid Model of the Process Operator. In Sheridan and Johannsen, 1976.

Regulinski, T.L. (1973). Human Performance Reliability Modelling in Time Continuous Domain. NATO—Conference, Liverpool 1973. In *Generic Techniques in System Reliability Assessment* (Eds.) Henley & Lynn. (1976). Nordhoff,Holland.

Rieger, C. (1976). An Organization of Knowledge for Problem Solving and Language Comprehension. *Artificial Intelligence,* **7,** 89-127.

Rigby, L.V. (1969). *The Nature of Human Error.* Sandia Laboratories, SC-DC-69-2062, Oct.

Russell, B. (1913). On the Notion of Cause, *Proc. Aristotelian Soc.,* **13,** 1-25.

Scragg, G. (1976). Semantic Nets as Memory Models. In *Computational Semantics* (Eds.) E.Charniak & Y. Wilks. North Holland Publishing Company.

Senders, J.W. & Posner, M.J.M. (1976). A Queuing Model of Monitoring and Supervisory Behavior. In Sheridan and Johannsen, 1976.

Sheridan, T.B. (1976). Toward a General Model of Supervisory Control. In Sheridan and Johannsen, 1976.

Sheridan, T.B. & Johannsen, G. (Eds.) (1976). *Monitoring Behavior and Supervisory Control.* Plenum Press, New York.

Simon, H.A. (1969). *The Sciences of the Artificial.* M.I.T. Press, Cambridge, Mass.

Smith, H.T. (1976). Perceptual Organization and the Design of the Man-Computer Interface in Process Control. In Sheridan and Johannsen, 1976.

Swain, A.D. (1969). *Human Reliability Assessment in Nuclear Reactor Plants.* Sandia Laboratories, SC-R-69-1236.

Swain, A.D. (1973). *Improving Human Performance in Production.* Industrial and Commercial Techniques Ltd., 30-32 Fleet St. London EC4.

Swain, A.D. (1976). *Sandia Human Factors Program for Weapon Development.* Sandia Laboratories SAND 76-0327, June.

Taylor, J.R. & Hollo, E. (1977). Experience with Algorithms for Automatic Failure Analysis. *International Conference on Nuclear Systems Reliability Engineering and Risk Assessment.* Gatlinburg, Tennessee, June 1977.

Tversky, A. & Kahneman, D. (1974). Judgement under Uncertainty: Heuristics and Biases. *Science,* **185,** 1124-1131.

Young, L.R. (1969). On Adaptive Manual Control. *Ergonomics,* **12,** 4, 635-675.

Chapter 4

SOCIOLOGICAL IMPLICATIONS OF COMPUTER SYSTEMS

Niels Bjørn-Andersen & Leif Bloch Rasmussen

Contents

1.0 Introduction

The past fifteen to twenty years has witnessed an enormous growth in the use of computer systems for administrative and management purposes. This development has primarily been driven by the old dream of technology as a means to free humanity from toil, strongly embedded in a desire to reap economic benefits. Accordingly, we have come to see the use of computer systems primarily as a technical and economic matter. The real benefits of striving for the ideals are yet to be seen, and in the meantime a growing awareness of possible unexpected negative consequences is posing serious questions about our technological optimism. Some of these questions are sociological and it is the main aim of this chapter to present and investigate current knowledge about sociological effects of computer systems. In doing so we also hope to be able to show that computer technology does not always cause inevitable changes in the social environment.

The following discussion will be based on an analysis of empirical studies. The reason for this is twofold. Firstly, the present level of knowledge about the sociological aspects of computerization prevents us from giving detailed prescriptions about their design apart from the general one, to take social aspects into account. (For a review of current prescriptions, however, see

Bjørn-Andersen & Hedberg, 1977). Secondly, in spite of a large number of empirical studies of the sociological effects of computer systems which we try to present in a systematic fashion, a large group of researchers and practitioners hold that flaws in existing systems are to be attributed to technical/economic omissions or poor implementation strategies, not to the computer technology itself. We are therefore not trying to make any specific statements about computer technology being either good or bad. What we do suggest, however, is that computer technology offers society a number of choices, quite a few of which employees, managers or politicians are not prepared to make. Unless these choices are made the salesmen of the computer industry will, by default, be the sole decision-makers for organizations and society as a whole.

The chapter will be divided between two main themes, the direct and indirect sociological effects of computer systems. By direct effects we mean the ways in which computer systems change the role of man in relation to organizations, i.e. the "objective" behavioural characteristics of his situation. By indirect sociological effects we denote the ways in which computer systems change man's relation to others and himself, e.g. the attitudes, feelings, and emotions encountered as a result of the introduction of the computer system. The direct effects will be grouped into those concerning employment, those concerning the formal relationships between man and the organization, and those concerning power relationships. Furthermore, when necessary, we subdivide organizational man into two main groups: non-managerial employees (i.e. workers, clerks) and managers (i.e. decision-makers, supervisors, etc.). The indirect effects include three issues which have turned out to be very important in the contemporary scene; job satisfaction, alienation, and privacy. These particular issues are chosen in an effort to make an overwhelming but fragmented amount of empirical data fit into a coherent picture.

Our frame of reference is illustrated in the model shown in Figure 1. This model depicts the variables most often investigated in empirical studies of the sociological implications of computer systems and the main interrelationships between these variables. In an area like this, one of the main problems is methodological; it is virtually impossible to distinguish the effects of technology from other changes in society. Political changes, changes in economic climate, changing norms and values, and governmental policies are interwoven into a complex web where one set of changes will have direct or indirect effects on every other. It might also be worth noting that there is an almost total lack of consensus about definitions of concepts, operationalization of concepts, interpretations of empirical data, etc. It should therefore be emphasized that the above model and the following discussions are our way of making a path through the jungle. A path which is not authorized by any of the authors referred to. And even worse,

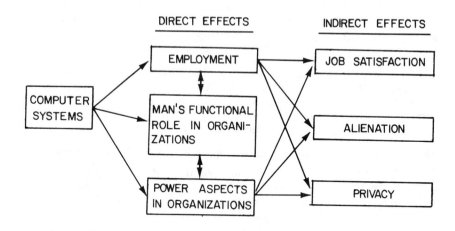

DIRECT EFFECTS   INDIRECT EFFECTS

Fig. 1. Classification of Effects of Computer Systems.

the jungle has not been authorized either.

2.0 Direct Effects Of Computer Systems

In making our path through this part of the jungle of direct effects of computer systems we are using a modified version of the conceptual scheme developed by the Aston Group (see Pugh et al., 1963). The Aston Group has made a classification of variables in the organizational structure: functional and role specialization, standardization, formalization, centralization, configuration, and flexibility (traditionalism). We are drawing on these variables (in the spirit of the aforementioned lack of agreement in the literature about concepts) to represent aspects of organizational structure perhaps not inherent in the original use. Through this free interpretation of their terms we get a more comprehensive frame of reference for our special analysis. Accordingly we take the concept "employment" to be part of role specialization and configuration. The concept "functional role" is taken to be a wider term for the three structural dimensions: functional specialization, standardization, and formalization. Furthermore, we take the concept "centralization" to be part of the power aspects in organizations. Finally, power aspects are further subdivided into discretion and influence. The detailed definitions of these terms will be given in the following sections.

2.1 Employment Level

The relationship between technology and employment is a very complex one. The increases in productivity experienced in this century are almost entirely due to the mechanization and automation of physical and mental work. Mowshowitz (1976, p. 98) observes,

".... the question of whether or not technological change results in unemployment is misleading. Work can be redistributed in many ways. Productivity increases can be absorbed by decreasing the number of hours people work. The critical observation is that new machines and methods are introduced for the purpose of increasing worker productivity and reducing labor requirements."

The validity of this statement is illustrated in the service industries where the replacement of labour has been dramatic. For example Danish banks estimate that in the seventies the introduction of advanced computer systems enabled the banks to keep staff level constant in spite of a 15% annual increase in transactions. If computers had not been used, an increase in the labour force of approximately 40% would have been necessary. Similarly Whisler (1970) found that in life insurance companies, were computers to disappear, the estimated average magnitude of additional clerical personnel needs was 65%.

In an early and much cited article by Leavitt & Whisler (1958) it was predicted that the middle managers would disappear and that the number of top-managers and staff personnel would increase through the coming use of computer systems. But later investigations have shown that the substitution of managerial labour is far less profound than for the workers/clerks. In the study by Whisler (1970) the estimated magnitude of additional personnel needs, were computers to disappear, is only 9% in supervisory personnel and 2% in managerial personnel. In a large study by Stewart (1971) only very few examples were discovered where managerial tasks have been taken over by the computer. The only type of tasks taken over were simple control and other routine activities.

The following reasons might account for this relatively minor impact on managerial employment level:

- Firstly, we are only seeing the beginning of the development of computer systems in the managerial area. The glorious prediction of what MIS (Management Information Systems), DSS (Decision Support Systems) etc., might accomplish in helping, and for some in substituting managers, are only now slowly coming into effect.
- Secondly, we might probably find some kind of cuckoo effect meaning that managers will be able to stay in their jobs for simple power reasons. The reduction in overall staff will therefore come first with the subordinates.

- Thirdly, it ought to be noted that computer systems are normally introduced to increase the level of control in the organization in order to
monitor the utilization of resources better, and often new managerial
tasks are associated with this development.

However one illustration of the possibility of the Leavitt & Whisler's prediction coming true was found in a study by Bjørn-Andersen & Pedersen
(1977) of an advanced materials handling system in an electronic equipment company in Denmark. Close to two-thirds of the production planners
and one factory manager were made redundant as a direct consequence of
the introduction of the computer system into the organization.

What does seem certain is that the nature of many managerial tasks will
change as a consequence of computer technology and that many managers
will not be able to adjust rapidly enough. Considerable unemployment will
therefore occur for this group. As Gotlieb & Borodin (1973, p. 188) remark:
"Just as a low unemployment rate does not preclude displacement because
of technology, the constancy of average skill levels does not preclude people
becoming obsolete." This view is supported by the currently available data
and raises serious doubts about the validity of the prediction by Jaffe &
Froomkin (1968, p. 69)

" . . . it is only possible to generalize that the impact of technological changes on
unemployment is temporary and generally self-corrective."

Their conclusion seems fairly plausible in a historical context; for example
the early cotton-weavers prevented the introduction of machinery for several decades until other employment was generated. This type of self-
corrective action based on mere resistance to change was possible in the
past when the rate of technological development was so slow that changes
might remain unnoticed in a person's lifetime. However, the speed of advancement of computer systems seems to destroy the notion that a gradual
transfer of the labour force is possible from the production industries into
service industries (or from actually carrying out the jobs to being in super-
vision of some production process).

Several very careful analyses have been carried out by governmental
commissions suggesting the notion of some technological unemployment.
Naturally, one has to consider the primary effects (reductions in present
staff) as well as possible new jobs. In the main these will come in the data
processing industry and in data processing departments. But also the competitive advantage one company might get because of an effective use of
technology could generate new jobs in that particular company if more
goods and services can be sold.In a British report (cited in SOU, 1974) from
the Department of Employment it is estimated that by 1969 158,000 jobs
had been saved, and approximately 100,000 new positions have been estab-

lished. The forecast made by the Swedish government commission is a net technological unemployment of 78,000–114,000 by 1979 (SOU, 1974).

In our opinion it is not unlikely that we shall soon reach the point of no return where Norbert Wiener's (1950) prediction will come true, that we shall see an end to full employment and the obsolescence of all but small fractions of the work force caused by computers. Certainly the employees in the printing industry and in the general workers unions as a whole are experiencing these tendencies. However, optimistically this may not necessarily be a bad development. Having a job eight hours a day has for a long time been considered a prerequisite of a good life. But if man could be relieved of the boring and strenuous work and at the same time given a possibility of carrying out jobs better fitted to his needs and possibilities, then eight-hours-a-day-jobs may not be a goal in itself but a challenge to more qualified interests. In our opinion this possibility is to be seen in relation to a shift in attitudes especially in the younger generation against consumerism and materialism; if not for any other reason than our growing awareness of the limits to natural resources and energy. Demand may of course still increase in directions like better health, better education, recreational services, etc. which might necessitate substantial labour elements without substantial use of natural resources and energy. But such preaching and optimism needs to be checked by reflection on the built-in need for major changes in the political and economic systems in the Western world. Given the available evidence, it is not difficult to believe that the speed at which computer systems are introduced—for the benefit of the individual organization—is so high that western society will not be able to adjust its political and economic structure fast enough. Inevitably mass unemployment is going to be the result, at least for some transitional period.

2.2 Functional Role

One of the important foci of attention of research has been the extent to which computer systems have changed the job itself, often labelled job content, work content, role task, etc.. In order not to get into lengthy theoretical discussions about the different terms we shall use the concept "functional role" to represent this area of research. This concept includes the way and the degree to which work is divided within the organization (specialization); the way and the degree to which work is carried out according to prescribed rules, regulations, procedures etc. (standardization); and the extent to which these prescriptions are formalized, i.e. documented one way or another (formalization).

The diversity of studies is substantial. It ranges from single case studies of changes experienced by one group of employees to large-scale survey type studies. The depth to which the jobs have been changed ranges from looking at one dimension (e.g. whether the job is more or less repetitive) to investigations of up to fifty dimensions. We will attempt to identify any general trends in the effect of computer systems on these dimensions, but at the same time we shall try to demonstrate the diversity of impacts of computer systems and scrutinize the underlying arguments. As this variable involves job content and as job content is different for different kinds of employees we shall distinguish between implications for non-managers and managers.

Non-Managerial Employees. Most studies concentrate on clerical functions and the white-collar workers, but blue-collar workers also experience completely new working procedures as numerically controlled machines and production scheduling systems are becoming more widely used. Early studies by Hoos (1960) and Mann & Williams (1962) suggest that the introduction of computers tends to make general clerical and office work become more organized, more like factory floor procedures. These conclusions are reinforced by more recent work. For example, Whisler (1970) investigated the effects of computer systems on employees in insurance companies by using interviews and questionnaires with top-management. He does not directly report on major changes in the functional role of non-managerial employees, but he confirms the findings in the above-mentioned studies by stating that strong influences on the functional role dimensions are caused by the fact that "...it is critical in computerised systems that employees perform precisely as the system demands, greater reliability in performance is required". He also observed that the introduction of computer systems caused a decrease in the communication between employees and furthermore that interpersonnel communication was dominated by giving and receiving impersonal information to and from the computer system.

Mumford & Banks (1967) made detailed studies in one bank and one production firm in England and they report on a parallel study in an American firm. On the standardization and formalization dimensions their studies show that the introduction of computer systems in the bank raised the demand for precision and planning of work. In the production firm the effect was more demand for planning of work and in the American firm more demand for precision. The results obtained in an international comparative study "Systems Change in Organizations" (Bjørn-Andersen et al., 1980) point in the same direction. This study is based on interviews with employees in eight banks in four European countries. The study investigates 38 different job variables and the extent to which changes are seen on these as a result of the introduction of computer systems on different levels of technological complexity. One of the main findings is a unanimous trend in the direction of a reduction in the employee's possibility of choosing work methods and sequence of work operations themselves in all banks. A clear step in the direction of the jobs becoming more structured and preplanned. Furthermore both of these studies found that the introduction of computer systems caused a higher degree of division of work (functional specialization). The effects of the computer system were markedly different for the so-called direct and indirect users of the computer systems; the former being the cashiers and others primarily responsible for data entry using terminals, and the latter being those primarily concerned with using output. The introduction of the computer system caused an increase in the routinization and repetitiveness of the jobs especially of the direct users, the jobs of the indirect users were left approximately unchanged. Most important, however, this tendency appears to be more pronounced the more advanced the computer technology is, i.e. with the real-time systems. This is particularly regrettable in view of the fact that most systems seem to be moving in this direction.

There is no universal pattern delineating which work groups get the worst deal. Jaffe & Froomkin (1968) report that they have evidence suggesting that banking and insurance companies which have experienced high increases in worker productivity show a corresponding growth of skilled positions. The contrary holds true for organizations which have not undergone high increases in worker productivity as a result of automation. Mowshowitz (1976) explains this tendency by stating: "This difference may be attributed to the degree of 'technological saturation' characteristic of an industry. The absence of large productivity gains indicates a relatively stable situation in which automation is not likely to have a pronounced effect on jobs.".

Another way this tendency may be seen is reported by Crossman & Laner whose main results are presented in Gotlieb and Borodin (1973). They show that skill requirements immediately essential to job performance tend to increase, while skill requirements in maintenance and support functions tend to decrease. Again this may be related to different effects in different industries. Mowshowitz observes (1976) ". . . in banking and insurance, computer systems eliminate many jobs connected with support functions, while introducing new operating jobs with higher skill requirements. In some areas of manufacturing, on the other hand, automated methods shift the balance in favour of maintenance type jobs.". It might be added that Whisler's study shows the same controversy without a clear tendency in one or the other direction.

The conclusion to be drawn from these differing results seems to be rather optimistic as it seemingly leaves room for choice. It might only be a matter of consciously working on the possibilities of making jobs less routinized and repetitive when introducing computer systems. On the other hand, the options for using scientific management techniques for creating specialized and very routinized and repetitive jobs are there too. The general trend is that the effects on the functional role of non-managerial employees have the following characteristics:

- *Increased standardization* with 1) more demand for accuracy in carrying out jobs according to standards (often set by the computer), with 2) less opportunity for the employees to choose their own work-methods and sequence of work-operation for themselves.
- *Increased formalization* with 1) an increased proportion of the communication being impersonal and 2) with more planning in advance.
- *Increased specialization* as repetitive and routinized tasks are eliminated and the remaining manual tasks are grouped together (e.g. all tasks performed at a particular terminal are grouped into one job).

Managers. The managerial group is even more heterogeneous than the workers/clerks group. The traditional distinction has been between the layers in the hierarchy singling out top-managers, middle managers, and first-line supervisors. Other researchers have chosen to distinguish the specialists (normally staff personnel) from more traditional line-managers, this distinction being close to differences between the supervisory and decision-making role of managers. The latter distinction has perhaps been the most decisive as the majority of researchers have either taken a supervisory point of view (Bjørn-Andersen & Pedersen, 1977; Eason et. al., 1974; Jangård, 1974; Mumford & Banks, 1967; Stewart, 1971; Stymne, 1966) or a decision theory point of view (Hedberg, 1970; Morton, 1971; Simon, 1965). We shall discuss the findings in these two lines of research and try to integrate them in order to arrive at possible common results.

As mentioned earlier a prerequisite of any computer assisted data processing is a formalization and a standardization of whatever data there is to be processed. This cannot be avoided when data are to be fed in and stored away from where they originated and are to be used. Output might be individualized, but only very rarely have managers been successful in getting personalized output designed for their personal style of inquiry. This in spite of the fact that different cognitive/personality styles do have different demands on the information system (e.g. see Mason & Mitroff, 1973). Jangård (1974) confirms the tendency to standardize part of the communication of the role of first-line supervisors in her analysis of the introduction of a production control system in a small company within the iron and steel industry. Bjørn-Andersen & Pedersen (1977) found concurrently that procedures and reporting had to be standardized between three assembly plants and two manufacturing plants to a far greater extent than in the manual system. Also Stewart (1971) found in her study of the effects of administrative and production planning systems that a "... higher degree of accuracy (exactness) was demanded of the managers in order to work with a computerized system.".

As regards formalization Mumford & Banks (1967) as well as Jangård (1974) point towards a higher degree of structuring and planning of the role of supervisors when the decision-making was moved to the headquarters and higher levels in the management hierarchy. This coincides with the findings of Stymne (1966) from an insurance company where "extensive changes were directed towards the creation of a more rational structure where insurance-professional orientation was replaced by conscious planning and control of production.".

One of the main results given by Whisler (1970) concerning managers at the supervisory level is that ". . . the number and variety of responsibilities were increased for most supervisors", considerably increasing the demand for training and experience of the supervisor. These tendencies seem even more pronounced in Jangård's study (1974). (She does point out, however, that parallel with the introduction of the computer system, other changes in the organization took place from an overlapping group system to a traditional line organization). The changes connected with the introduction of the computer system had a pronounced effect on the role of the foremen. They had in their role ". . . fewer tasks demanding a personal evaluation and real decisions.". This did reduce their role conflict, but the ever increasing number of work instructions (ever increasing standardization and formalization) will also reduce the supervisor's personal freedom and hamper their possibilities of shaping their own job situation.

We therefore see that the general impact of computer systems on the supervisor's role is mixed, just as we found with workers/clerks. Two tendencies emerge:

- Automation of certain lower level managerial jobs takes place, potentially clearing the way for a job enlargement as it is mostly the routine tasks that vanish.
- The higher degree of standardization and formalization of the role of the supervisors means a reduction in the supervisor's possibility of shaping their own jobs.

The actual effect of these mixed tendencies will be determined by the area of application, the more or less explicitly expressed philosophy of control and the way in which the computer systems are implemented.

The effect of computer systems on the higher managerial level has mostly been discussed in the literature either in relation to the decision-making process or to the authorization of the decisions (the last-mentioned often discussed under the label centralization/decentralization). The former we will briefly discuss here as *functional specialization*. (See chapter 7 for a detailed discussion of management decision-making). Hedberg (1970) discovered in a laboratory situation that managers increased their activities for seeking information when an advanced information system with visual display terminals was put at their disposal. This is in accordance with Morton (1971) who designed a MDS (Management Decision System) for a large manufacturing company. MDS was a combination of interactive visual display terminals, computers, and models for operational analysis and it was used in short and medium term planning decisions within marketing as well as production. Morton discovered that the managers preferred to work with the new system and used it as a tool for budgeting and planning. As a result the general definition and solution of problems improved and communication between different decision makers was facilitated.

He concludes that previously the decision-making process "was constrained by the manager's ability to manipulate data. Therefore, it was a serial process with few feedback loops ... The structure resulting after the MDS is one that matches management's notion of natural problem solving —it was flexible enough to match what the managers wanted to do.".

An extensive study of 254 users of 26 computer systems was carried out in England (Eason et al., 1974). The so-called "task fit" (the congruence between the task of the manager and the service of the computer system) varied between 82% to 37% for the computer systems examined. The systems at the lower end suffer from a number of weaknesses. The authors indicate that this is especially the case when the form of interaction was inflexible and predefined, e.g. where the user received his output in the form of standardized print-outs at fixed intervals. Furthermore, they found the following changes in the work role as a consequence of the computer system (the percentage of the managers choosing the alternative is quoted in brackets):

- Possibility of developing new skills, ideas, methods (72%)
- Task has been made more routine (17%)/less routine (21%)
- The scope of the job has been increased (96%)/decreased (4%)
- The work load has been increased (74%)/reduced (26%)
- Communication with others has increased (56%)/decreased (44%)

Eason et al. (1974) conclude "the overwhelming finding ... is that the computer system had very little effect upon the general character of management. In most cases the computer system remained a peripheral part of the manager's work, taking only little of his time and attention. If there is to be a revolutionary change in methods of management and organizational structure as a result of the use of computer system, it is not apparent in these results.".

The final study to be mentioned here was carried out by Stewart (1971). In ten case studies she investigated how administrative systems, production planning systems and investment models influenced the role of the individual manager and the management structure.

Despite quite large variation from company to company she was able to draw several general conclusions: that effects were minor except for some junior level managers, that operations research models seem to have a long term effect in promoting an analytic approach to management decision, and that in several cases the most important effect was that managers were encouraged to reflect on their policies or activities.

Our conclusion on the effects on the degree of functional specialization on higher level managers cannot be a clear and unequivocal one. On one hand we have a representative for a type of research whose main concern is the construction of a MIS (Morton) pointing at the revolutionary effect that computer systems may lead to. On the other hand we have examples of sociologists (e.g. Stewart and Eason et al.) whose conclusions indicate that up to now such effects have been rather sporadic. We shall thus suggest firstly, that the potential of computer systems might be very significant but there is a lack of knowledge preventing us from realizing this potential. Secondly, that there will be a significant variation in the impact of the systems depending on the application, philosophy of design, type of company, capabilities of the designers to realize the needs of the users, etc. Thirdly, that the impact of a system is not pre-determined but depends on the use managers make of the system and their willingness to be encouraged to revise their policies and methods. Fourthly, that the systems so far have had a small impact on the role of top management and fifthly, that to the extent that there has been an effect, this has mainly been of a positive nature and in general the new system has been preferred to the old one.

2.3 Power

The question of power has been given more and more attention in relation to computer systems. Our discussion of power will be divided into structural aspects and behavioural aspects. The former being termed centralization which is especially related to organizational structure, i.e. the organizational hierarchy and the level at which decisions are taken, and the way and degree to which control is exercised. The behavioural aspects of power are much more concerned with the individual and his possibilities for shaping his own work environment. In order to encompass the most important aspects we shall, when necessary, subdivide the behavioural aspects of power into discretion (the power to decide on one's own role, the absence of power from everybody else on one's role) and influence (the power to change the behaviour of somebody else).

Effects on Centralization. The consequences of introducing computer based information and operational systems at an organizational level have often been discussed as a question of centralization/decentralization. This is the case in Whisler's (1970) study in insurance companies where he discovered that "with a small number of exceptions, companies reported that the effect of using computers is to push decisions (choice-making) to a higher level in the organization.". Schultz & Whisler (1960) and Hoos (1960) studies also report similar findings. Stymne (1966) reports from a study of a life insurance company that the most significant organizational changes were:

- A certain amount of centralization of functions in the computer department. Although this originally was planned as a service function, work flow, education, long-term organizational planning, etc. were soon assigned to it.
- The data processing was also centralized and "there are certain indications in this study that some decision-making sources were also centralized. E.g. the computer department was made responsible for the judgement of certain types of financial problems.".
- The control system and the criteria of success were changed. Previously the quality of an insurance broker was estimated according to his professional knowledge but with the new system success was measured by the number of task units produced.
- Options of directing and controlling employees on lower levels of the hierarchy were increased and
- At the same time the number of control impulses received from other departments was increased.

Finally, Stewart (1971) concludes that,

- The case studies "provide no evidence on whether computerization will, as Leavitt and Whisler suggested, make for greater centralization" because of the ability to establish greater control of the employees. (Only in a single case did Stewart find such a centralization and she ascribes it to a new management policy. On the other hand we would add that she did not find any examples of less control being exercised).
- "The level at which specific decisions are taken may be changed. Some may become more structured and consequently be taken by a lower level of management. Fuller information can reveal the complexity of particular decisions and some may result in their being taken at a higher level in the hierarchy than before.".
- The time-span before decisions are reviewed is not changed. Only in one case did she find a reduced time-span of discretion. Better and faster information can enable the manager to check up sooner on the performance of his subordinates. This, it can be argued, makes for more centralization as it reduces their discretion. Whether it does so will depend on who is given the information.

Our conclusion on these and other findings is that although we agree that computer systems potentially can be used to further a decentralization as well as a centralization the vast majority of the existing research indicates that any change that occurs will be towards centralization.

Discretion and Influence of Non-Managerial Employees. When the majority of computer systems were administrative systems primarily automating large volume repetitive tasks, the influence and discretion of employees was not changed significantly. When computer systems are introduced gradually into the communication and decision-making processes of an organization, the behavioural aspects of power become extremely important. It has often been said that information is power, and the introduction of a computer based information system is an occasion where power may be shifted around. A new information system is a way of rocking the boat, and weak groups might very easily lose power.

Changes in discretion and influence accompanying the introduction of batch computer systems of the more administrative type were investigated by Hoos (1960) and Mann & Williams (1962). They found that these systems introduced an increased control of the performance of the individual employee. This was partly because these earlier systems introduced repetitive and fairly standardized tasks as earlier mentioned (e.g. punching operations) which could easily be measured. Later studies do not confirm these changes. Mumford & Banks (1967) did find some reduction in the control of own workpace in banks, but in more recent studies, e.g. Bjørn-Andersen and Borum (1979) there is no unanimous trend in the direction of higher degrees of controls of the individual employee; at least not as perceived by the employees.

One has to realize, however, that the most advanced real-time terminal systems rapidly being placed at an increasing number of work places provide previously unknown opportunities for controlling the individual operating the terminal. This is even emphasized by the manufacturers of computers/terminals when they state that their terminals "give far better opportunities for controlling the production factors". In plain words the new cashier terminals, e.g. in supermarkets, give possibilities of comparing the different cashiers (who is fastest, who is the most reliable, who are taking breaks, when and for how long, etc.) in a far more detailed way than ever experienced before. Even though some might argue that an employer may have the right to obtain this kind of information, there is a serious risk that decisions might be taken on behalf of the "objective " information picked up by the terminal, forgetting aspects like helping the old lady, giving a smile, some customers being attracted to certain cashiers etc. This raises numerous validity problems. But goal displacement with the cashiers could be even more serious. When told how they are evaluated—if told at all—

they they will most likely try to perform well on these dimensions and forget the rest of the job dimensions, with the employees adjusting their activities even closer to the given minimum norms, or worse, using their creativity and initiative to beat the system instead of carrying out their task.

Another example of the use of computer systems for control is given by a French insurance company which, for security and control reasons, introduced a personal identity card instead of keys. These cards were to be used to open all doors in the organization, and the old-fashioned door handles were removed. Even the doors to the toilets could only be opened by entering the card into a small terminal. Obviously this control of the individual—whether it is used regularly, on an ad hoc basis or held in reserve—provides the owner of the system (manager, department or whoever) with a possibility of controlling the individual which goes far beyond what is now normally considered acceptable. It brings us dangerously close to the descriptions in Orwell's "1984". In this particular case the trade union called out a strike against the system and management cancelled the entire project.

As might be seen from these examples there is a great danger that employees may lose power when computerized information systems are introduced because they are (potentially) more controlled. As a consequence trade unions have begun to play an increasingly dominant role in this area as they have started to become concerned about these problems. In the Scandinavian countries they have started research projects themselves, e.g. Nygård & Bergo (1973) in order to negotiate better work role conditions in computerised environments. German trade unions have embarked on a different set of activities and have started to develop Workers Information Systems (Hedberg, 1977).

A couple of serious problems might arise for trade unions in relation to computer technology. First the issue raised by Gotlieb & Borodin (1973). "Are automation and concurrent shifts in labour force from blue-collar to white-collar endangering the strength and bargaining power of unions?" The underlying hypothesis being that white-collar workers are traditionally more often against unionization than blue-collar workers. And—if this tendency is correct—this leaves the non-managerial employees individually, and as a group, with less power than before. No clear-cut answer is in sight, but the level of white-collar unionization is rising rapidly (at least in the Scandinavian countries) and spokesmen of these unions today demand influence on systems design in several countries. Secondly, trade unions have been concerned about whether automation will eliminate possibilities for strikes and thereby again leave workers and clerks with less power. Gotlieb & Borodin (1973) on this question conclude that automation may weaken the effectiveness of strikes but that it is certainly premature to sense an end to them. On the other hand it must be emphasized that it cannot be taken for granted that personnel employed for operating, planning, and developing computer systems will not strike. The concentration of data-processing activities on fewer and fewer machines and computer operators will most certainly lead to organizations and societies getting more and more vulnerable to industrial action, just as the large computer installations are getting more vulnerable to terrorism.

Discretion and Influence of Managers. Given that non-managerial employees have lost power and apparently are going to lose more in the future (unless we are going to witness unions making a forceful attempt at influencing system developments), it could be asked where does this power go to? Despite the fact that we do not assume a zero-sum of power (if one person gains power someone else will have to lose it) it might be expected that at least some power will shift to various groups of managers.

To verify this hypothesis, let us first look at the discretion issues. Bjørn-Andersen & Pedersen (1977) point to a loss of discretion for all groups of managers as a consequence of the introduction of a production and scheduling system in an electronics company. The organizational hierarchy in each of the three assembly plants studied consisted in principle of a plant manager and under him a line hierarchy (work managers, foremen) and three parallel staff functions (production planning, production technique and production control), each of these headed by a section manager. The system primarily changed the job content of the production planners by taking over a large part of the planning task. One consequence of the introduction of this system was that all groups of managers involved with the system had lost discretion as they were now receiving more "goals, policies, and plans" and worked with more "rules, procedures, and preplanned methods". Furthermore, they were more "dependent on the work of others" than before, and they felt more "controlled in their tasks".

Similar changes were found by Jangård (1974) in a small production company. After the new system had been introduced there were fewer tasks in the role of the foreman which "will necessitate a personal evaluation and real decisions". She goes on to state that "in general it could be concluded that more and more specified prescriptions were introduced in such a way that the personal freedom of the foreman to shape his own role was reduced". Further support for this finding appears in the study by Eason et al. (1974). 32% of the respondents claimed that the computer now determined the work procedures to a large extent while 42% claimed that their computer system determined work procedures to a small extent in their company. The unanimous trend in these studies was a loss of discretion caused by the fact that the computer systems were introduced to obtain more effective utilization of capital, humans and natural resources. This was done through the standardization and formalization of all work roles including those in charge of the system. Nobody gained more freedom in his organizational role.

As regards the influence aspects of power quite a few studies are concerned with the question of whether the introduction of computerized information systems gives the computer specialists more influence. This hypothesis is supported in the study by Stymne (1966) where the computer department acquired control of a number of different company functions. However, very often the winners in the struggle for influence are not the computer specialists but the staff departments for whose benefit the system was designed. This effect was found in the study by Bjørn-Andersen and Pedersen (1977) where the production planners in charge of the system were, in everybody's opinion, considered to have become more influential. At the same time works managers, foremen (and to a smaller extent the factory manager and other staff functions) appeared to lose influence. That information is power and the control of the computer systems resource is by no means unimportant is also emphasized by Gotlieb & Borodin (1973): "It makes a difference *where* the computer is. The processing and planning capabilities of the computer impart authority to the division in charge of it, and this is particularly true, if, as so often happens, the arrival of the computer is accompanied by a functional reorganization."

We have tried to show how information systems may be used by smaller groups in the organization to change influence structure. In relation to systems development, the power to influence other groups is often available for the asking. However, the general trend, that most computer systems seem to further bureaucratization and specialization, will almost inevitably lead to loss of discretion in the work role for the benefit of higher productivity.

In order to explore the extent to which the changes reported so far could be said to have a mostly positive or negative value, let us turn our attention to the indirect sociological effects of computer systems, in part mediated through the direct effects.

3.0 Indirect Sociological Effects Of Computer Systems

By indirect effects of computer systems we understand the concepts job satisfaction, alienation, and privacy. These are all of major importance in contemporary society. But when one moves "further away" from the computer system, the possibilities of isolating the effects caused by computer systems become problematic. Furthermore, it becomes difficult to investigate empirically the links between direct effects and indirect effects. In the following discussion we will try to draw attention to the role of computer systems in society and organizations over and above the changes in direct effects. These indirect effects of computer technology we feel are the most important. Unfortunately, there is a shortage of empirical evidence.

3.1 Impact on Job Satisfaction

The potential dangers posed by computer systems have fortunately not always materialized. The most negative reports about job satisfaction deteriorating as a consequence of computer systems stem from the introduction of the early batch systems. But job satisfaction is a thorny concept; it is normally defined as the relationship between the expectations of the holder of the job and what he gets from the organization in which he works (e.g. Mumford, 1972). This means of course that if only the expectations of a person are low enough, any job will do. For example shift work is generally accepted even though it has been proved that it causes sleeplessness, sexual problems, higher consumption of medicine, etc.

There are few examples of computer systems causing physical hazards to employees. One exception is the current concern about radiation emission from visual display units. Most physical problems which do arise are of an ergonomic nature in that they relate to work place layout (for example eye fatigue caused by visual displays, back and neck pains resulting from working with poorly laid out equipment, etc.). Substantial efforts by (the better) computer manufacturers have provided solutions to many of these problems, but unfortunately there are still terminals and other computer hardware which by ergonomic measures are substandard. Unfortunately, this is impossible to avoid when the only regulating mechanism is the "free market competition".

Psychological and sociological problems are more difficult to handle. Most of these originate from the direct effects of computer systems as previously discussed. A person may accept a very monotonous, repetitive job because it is easy to perform and it does not demand any particular skills. Then after five years the job is changed because the computer system is changed. The job may now be quite different. Would we expect this person to accept and fulfill the new job, will he be able to cope with the change and even understand it? Or is it more plausible that the development will go along the lines suggested by a manager when asked why he had made no attempts to strive for participative system design ". . . the present employees do not know much about the present system as such, and when we get the new system, it will work as some kind of selection mechanism. Those who cannot cope with the new system will be substituted, those who can cope with the new system may keep their jobs." (Pedersen, 1977).

Of course man is a very adaptable creature. If absolutely necessary he can adapt to any job and even be satisfied. Perhaps then it is not surprising that many researchers have found that, on the average, people are very well satisfied with their new jobs in computerized environments and that computer systems have not had any substantial effects on job satisfaction. This may be the case despite marked negative changes e.g. a tightening of the organizational structure and a shifting of power from man to computer or from middle managers to the top-echelons in the organization.

Most empirical studies of the impact of computer systems have one or more measures of job satisfaction. In a small study of job satisfaction among 18 clerks working with an on-line customer service system in a Danish insurance company Kjaer (1977) found that job satisfaction in the computerized environment had increased. All the clerks interviewed found that the system was better for the organization than the old one. A large majority felt that it was just as good or better for the employees. Similar results were obtained in an international study of the introduction of computer systems in banks in Denmark, England, France, and Sweden (Bjørn-Andersen et al., 1980). In spite of the fact that the computer applications were fairly different and the banks used very different types of computer technology, the clerks were almost unanimous in favour of the new system. From 59% to 100% of the clerks in each of the five banks found the system better for the bank. In fact in three banks the majority of the clerks found that work was now more interesting, while the clerks in the remaining two banks reported no change in level of work interest.

In order to look for possible reasons for the apparent conflict or paradox between the often negative impact on organizational structure and power on the one hand and the positive change in job satisfaction on the other, we have to go to the broader and more elusive concept of alienation.

3.2 Impact on Alienation

Within the context of the work role Blauner (1964) defines alienation in the following way: "Alienation exists when workers are unable to control their immediate work processes, to develop a sense of purpose and function which connects their job to the overall organization of production, to belong to integrated industrial communities, and when they fail to become involved in the activity of work as a mode of personal self-expression. In modern industrial employment, control, purpose, social integration, and self-involvement are all problematic."

Blauner does try to limit alienation to people and their work environment, and even in this rather restricted sense he sees the work environment of today as leading to some kind of alienation in general. Powerlessness, meaninglessness, and self-estrangement are the terms most often used to describe the situation. The empirical findings reported above do indicate that many employees run the risk of becoming alienated in their work, in spite of the fact that they respond positively on job satisfaction scales.

But work is not the total life. One might ask whether it is possible to be alienated in one's work and at the same time not be alienated towards society as a whole? Can one say that computer systems do play a role in what might be called work alienation but not in alienation in general? And in the same sense can computer technology be separated from technology in general? One can hope that computer technology will mark a shift in relation to our historic experience with technology by turning out to be humanistic; but the opposite keeps calling upon our attention. What then are the human consequences of technology? Erich Fromm (1955) gives a terrifying answer, "Alienation as we find it in modern society is almost total; it pervades the relationship of man at his work, to the things he consumes, to the state, to his fellow man, and to himself. Man has created a world of man-made things as it never existed before. He has constructed a complicated social machine to administer the technical machine he built. Yet the whole creation of his stands over and above him. He does not feel himself as creator and centre but as the servant of a Golem, which his hands have built." Many other creators have more or less pointed to the same effects of technology; Norbert Wiener warned against the dangers of computers (e.g. 1960, 1964).

A similar line of argument is pursued by another computer scientist/philosopher—Weizenbaum (1976) in his attempt to explain the most likely relationship between man and computer. Based on his experiences of people's reactions to a crude simulation of a psychiatrist (Eliza) he tries to answer these fundamental questions related to his understanding of computers and alienation,

- "What is it about computers that has brought the view of man as a machine to a new level of plausibility?"
- "Is the fact that individuals link themselves with strong emotional ties to machines to be taken as surprising?"
- "It is perhaps paradoxical that just when in the deepest sense man has ceased to believe in—let alone to trust—his own autonomy, he has begun to rely on autonomous machines, that is, on machines that operate for long periods of time entirely on the basis of their own initial realities."

The central part of his argument—and the new warning—is that although man can be viewed as another information processing machine, just like a computer, it is dangerous to view man as being nothing but a machine. Furthermore, as man is able to adapt himself to almost everything, he can internalize aspects of the technology he uses in the form of kinesthetic and perceptual habits and at the same time "... accept as authentically natural (that is, as given by nature) such technological bases for his identity."

Weizenbaum points out the difficulties for man to build a free conception of the internal realities of computers except through the single analogy readily available: his model of his own capacity to think. This view might lead one to believe that computers possess much better thinking capabilities than man. In the end we might be running the risk of making the perfect self-controlling machine as the limit of human capabilities.

The counter argument of course must be that technology itself, and computer technology especially, is neutral, and only bad use of the neutral technology is the cause of alienation. This issue has a long history of debate, and agreement is as little in sight today as it has ever been. However, one tendency seems clear. We are witnessing a shift from general belief in technology as neutral to at least a growing awareness of what the technology is used for and by whom. Therefore it is imperative that all technological choices are brought out in the open and that the general level of consciousness on these matters is raised. But in the words of Samuel Butler it may already be too late (Mowshowitz, 1976, p. 102): "The servant glides by imperceptible approaches into the master; and we have come to such a pass that, even now, man must suffer terribly on ceasing to benefit the machines."

3.3 Impact on Privacy

The concept of privacy has accounted for most of the public debate on computer impact. Right or wrong as this predominance may be, it is a concept which we shall no doubt be confronted with more and more often with the growing use of computers in private and public organizations. Our hypothesis is that this confrontation is mediated by the changes in bureaucratization and power as a result of computer systems. The hypothesis is based on the following observations about possibilities in the use of computer systems:

- Large amounts of personal data can be collected (and are collected) in machine readable form.
- Previously scattered data can be brought together.
- Data may be accumulated in a cheap, easy accessible form.
- Faster integration (e.g. sorting, comparing, selecting) of data on request.
- More secure, permanent records.
- Mistakes are greatly reduced by error checking, but when they do occur they are no longer local and are propagated through-out the system.

It may readily be seen that these possibilities allow decisions to be taken on (more) complete pictures of the individual, instead of very fragmented and nearly always less valid pictures. But do we want that? Are all "relevant" data accepted as legitimate in each decision situation? For example, an applicant for a position in the public sector will accept that his previous experience is taken into account, but what about when his military records, his financial records or even worse his medical records are available to the hiring officer. This example illustrates the fact that there might be a fundamental conflict between the hiring officer trying to find the best person for the job and the applicant trying to create the most positive image of himself. (To some extent they have similar interests in finding a good match, but we leave that discussion for elsewhere). In the wider social context there is a basic conflict between the individual's need for privacy and society's need for information. We have to admit that the complexity of our modern society is such that an extensive exchange of information is necessary. In saying that, the definition of privacy and the actual amount of privacy left to individuals cannot be separated from its socio-cultural context.

Westin (1967) identifies four main reasons for a high level of privacy in a western democratic society:

- The need for personal autonomy.
- To allow emotional relaxation by shedding one's various masks.
- The need for, and right to, self-evaluation.
- Limited and protected communications about oneself.

We might add an extension to the last aspect as this in effect implies the possibility of not suppressing the past from interfering with the individual's present and future.

All these aspects of privacy may be attacked by computer systems which involve the handling of personal information. To what extent this happens or is going to happen, is hard to say for a lack of empirical data. On the other hand judging from the level of public debate, and the fact that legislation in many countries has been passed to prevent the dangers, there seems to be adequate evidence to indicate that the fear is perceived to be real. These legislative efforts can give a picture of the relationship between computer systems and privacy; the main content of such laws in western democracies can be summarized as follows:

- There must be no personal data record-keeping systems whose existence is secret. There must be a way for each individual to find out what information is stored and used about him or her.
- There must be a way for each individual to prevent information gathered for one purpose being used for another.
- There must be a way for each individual to correct or amend information about him or her.
- There must be a way of ensuring that any organization creating, maintaining, or accessing personal data takes sufficient precaution to prevent its abuse.

The last rule usually has to be enforced by a public institution of some sort which has the right (and duty) to investigate personal records and in some cases question their existence.

In his 1967 book Westin expressed great concern about the possible dangers of privacy being eroded and subsequently he conducted one of the first empirical studies into these matters in the USA for the US National

Academy of Science (Westin & Baker, 1972). Westin and his associates visited fifty five organizations, government agencies, private enterprises, and non-profit organizations. Furthermore, they surveyed many other organizations and individuals. Their conclusion was that at that time the dangers many were foreseeing as a consequence of computer data banks had not come into existence. This was primarily due to the small number of data banks then established and also due to previous enthusiasm about data banks as a means of better control. At about the same time one other major survey was conducted by the American Federation of Information Processing Societies (AFIPS) and TIME Magazine in 1971. This survey represented cross sections of the US population (1001 individuals). Almost half of the respondents said that they had some contact with computers in their work. The interviews were related to questions concerning computer problems observed by the respondents, computers and consumers, computer use in business, computer use in government, etc. The survey revealed the following characteristics related to privacy according to Gilchrist & Schiller (1971):

- 38% of those surveyed believed computers represented a real threat to people's privacy versus 54% who disagreed.
- 62% were concerned that some large organizations keep information about millions of people.
- 53% believed computerized information files might be used to destroy individual freedom.
- 58% felt computers will be used in the future to keep people under surveillance.
- 42% believed there was no way to find out if information stored in a computer about one was accurate.

As can be seen from this data more than half of the respondents disagree with computers posing a real threat to privacy. On the other hand the responses to the rest of the questions suggest the opposite. This inconsistency, however, may perhaps be explained by the fact that people perceive threats towards themselves differently than threats towards others (or more abstractly—society as a whole). In any event, the main impression is that roughly half of the respondents perceive the threats described in Orwell's "1984" as real.

However, as mentioned above we cannot discuss privacy without basing it on a model of society and on our cultural background. The information collected and communicated about a person can never be the total picture, it will always be fragmentary. But we must realize that our fear of computer systems as intruders may be wrongly founded—perhaps we should accept more freedom in the dissemination of personal data in order to be more fully human. One might argue that a higher information level is a necessary prerequisite for accepting our fellow human beings for what they really are, instead of the artifact we see. After all, most of our facade is created in order to protect ourselves from a society which expects us to be a little better than we are. And while everybody pretends, society will not change in the direction of being more tolerant of deviances.

4.0 Conclusion

We have tried to summarize current knowledge about the sociological effects of computer systems. In so doing we have tried to identify primarily empirical data concerning the effects on organizational structure and the power aspects in organizations, and more speculative discussions as related to effects on job satisfaction, alienation, and privacy. In sum we have noted the following:

- At least temporary unemployment.
- A bureaucratization of organizational structure.
- A shift in power to those in control of computer resources.
- Whether they be workers, clerks or managers, people are not particularly more dissatisfied with their jobs following the introduction of computer systems than previously.

It seems to us that there is some kind of paradox in these findings. Of course, the more bureaucratic structure might be appreciated especially if one is seeking security. Similarly, giving up control to someone else or to the impersonal technology may have some attraction, at least in the short run. But as current speculations on alienation and privacy may suggest, job satisfaction can be seen as the surface of a much deeper problem. As Mowshowitz (1976) warns, "The particular effects of automation on job content, skill levels, education requirements, and other aspects of work may be less important than the general changes effected by technology itself in the organization of work. It is our love affair with technology itself that makes the issue so problematic. We are inclined to accept technological change in spite of our fears and misgivings."

What is called for is a far broader perspective on the system design process. We have to stop thinking of systems design in terms of just writing programmes, establishing databases and designing output. Computer systems design must be seen on the organizational level as one way of accomplishing organizational change. And on the social level it must be seen in relation to the issues of alienation and privacy. Space does not permit a lengthy discussion about normative suggestions for improving on systems design from a sociological point of view. We shall just point to three areas where improvements are needed, and refer the reader to other publications (Bjørn-Andersen & Hedberg, 1977; Bjørn-Andersen & Borum, 1979) for a more detailed discussion.

Firstly, it seems necessary to improve on the structure within which systems design is carried out. Many countries have introduced data laws, but for all practical purposes these are only concerned with privacy issues. More important are the laws/agreements securing employees the right to participate in systems development. We have a firm belief that this might introduce into the systems design process a higher concern for social values. Such schemes are at least in accordance with democratic values. Data agreements are now found in Scandinavia in individual companies. Here management and the employees (represented by their trade union) have signed agreements securing the employees the right to education in data issues, a high level of information about all systems development, and participation. On the national level a general agreement has been signed in Norway between the federation of trade unions and the employers association securing the employees the same rights. In Sweden a law has been passed securing the participation and co-determination of the employees on all issues of major importance to the work situation. This will include most cases of computer systems development.

Secondly, it seems necessary to influence the *knowledge and attitudes of the participants* in the systems design process. The computer experts' level of consciousness about the aspects of systems design over and above the technical/economic issues must be raised , and their attitudes changed to understand and appreciate the democratic values underlying a true involvement of the users. The traditional expert strategy for systems design, with or without a hostage from the user department, is not going to work in the long run. But users must also be given a proper training, i.e. training and courses provided by their own trade union or outside experts, and not computer manufacturers or the internal systems department. Only then is it possible to make sure that the users obtain a background which will help them form their own attitudes and demands to a new system.

Thirdly, it seems necessary to improve the methods by which systems are designed today. Far too many people are still advocating general methods for doing systems analysis. Here, as in other types of organizational change, a contingency approach is needed; the actual methods used, the way of organizing the systems development, the level of documentation used etc. must be made to fit the particular environment of the system and organization. Furthermore, improvements are needed in the methods for systems

Finally, it is our impression that integrated and highly complex systems serve to decrease democratization and humanization. The greater need—as we see it—is for incremental strategies with fairly loosely coupled subsystems, where the scope for experiments and changes is greater. These suggestions have already been followed in a few organizations. Other organizations would consider them unthinkable. It is, however, rewarding to note the increased awareness of the problems outlined in this chapter. Most of these problems might be avoided, but the technical specialists will have to change their perception of their function. This increased level of consciousness is but the first step.

References

Bjørn-Andersen, N. (ed.) (1980). *The Human Side of Information Processing.* North-Holland, Amsterdam.
Bjørn-Andersen, N. & Hedberg, B. (1977). Designing Information Systems in an Organizational Perspective. In *Prescriptive Models of Organizations* (Ed.) Nystrom, P.C. & Starbuck, W.H., TIMS Studies in the Management Sciences, **5**, 125-142, North-Holland, Amsterdam.
Bjørn-Andersen, N. & Pedersen, P.H. (1977). Computer Systems as a Vehicle for Changes in the Management Structure. *ISRG Working paper No. 77-3*, Copenhagen.
Bjørn-Andersen, N. & Borum, F. (1979). Demokratisering der Gestaltung von Informationssystems. In *Mensch and Computer* (Eds.) Hansen, H.R., Schroder K.T., Weihe, H.J. Oldenbourg, Munich.
Bjørn-Andersen, N., Hedberg, B., Mercer, D., Mumford, E. & Sole, A. (1980). *The Impact of Systems Change in Organizations.* Sythoff and Noordhoff
Blauner, R. (1964). *Alienation and Freedom: The Factory Worker and His Industry.* University of Chicago Press, Chicago.
Eason, K.D., Damodaran, L. & Stewart, T.F.M. (1974). *Report of a Survey of Man-Computer Interaction in Commercial Applications.* Loughborough: Department of Human Sciences, University of Loughborough.
Fromm, E. (1955). *The Sane Society.* Rhinehart and Winston, New York.
Gilchrist, B. & Schiller , C. (1971). *A National Survey of the Public's Attitudes Toward Computers,* AFIPS Press, Montvale.
Gotlieb, C.C. & Borodin, A. (1973). *Social Issues in Computing.* Academic Press, New York.
Hedberg, B. (1970). *On Man-Computer Interaction in Organizational Decision-Making.* Gothenburg: Business Administration Studies.
Hedberg, B. (1977). *Information Systems for Alternative Organizations: Using Information Technology to Facilitate Industrial Democracy and Organizational Learning.* CREST Course, Stafford.
Hoos, I. (1960). Impact of Automation in the Office. *International Labour Review,* **82**, 363-368.
Jaffe, A.J. & Froomkin, J. (1968). *Technology and Jobs.* Praeger, New York.
Jangård, H. (1974). Plan og virkelighet. In Høyer, R. : ...*over til EDB,* Oslo.
Kjaer, J. (1977). *On-Line Sagsekspedition,* Topsikring G/S, Nyt fra Samfundsvidenskaberne, Copenhagen.
Leavitt, H.J. & Whisler, T.L. (1958). Management in the 1980s, *Harvard Business Review,* Nov-Dec., **36**, 6, 41-48.
Mann, F.C. & Williams, L.K. (1962). Some effects of the Changing Work Environment in the Office. *Journal of Social Issues,* **18**, 3, 90-101.
Mason, R.O. & Mitroff, I.I. (1973). A program for Research on Management Information Systems. *Management Science,* **19**, 5.

Morton, M.S.S. (1971). *Management Decision Systems.* Harvard Business Press, Boston.

Mowshowitz, A. (1976). *The Conquest of Will, Information Processing In Human Affairs.* Addison-Wesley, Reading, Mass.

Mumford, E. & Banks, O. (1967). *The Computer and the Clerk.* Longman, London.

Mumford, E. (1972). *Job Satisfaction, A Study of Computer Specialists.* Longman, London.

Nygård, K. & Bergo, O.T. (1973). The Trade Unions—New Users of Research. *Personnel Review*, **4**, 2, 5-10.

Pedersen, E.R. (1977). Systemarbejde og Databehandling på Faeroerne. *DAIMI TR-1 Report,* Århus University.

Pugh, D.S. et. al. (1963). A Conceptual Scheme for Organizational Analysis. *Administrative Science Quarterly*, **8**, 289-315.

Schultz, G.P. & Whisler, T.L. (1960). *Management Organization and the Computer.* Free Press, Glencoe, Illinois.

Simon, H.A.(1960). *The Shape of Automation for Men and Management.* Harper and Row, New York.

SOU (Statens Offentliga Utredningar). (1974). *Datateknikens arbetsmarknads— effekter,* Stockholm.

Stewart, R. (1971). *How Computers Affect Management.* MacMillan, London.

Stymne, B. (1966). EDP and Organizational Structure: A Case Study of an Insurance Company. *Swedish Journal of Economics*, **68**, 4.

Weizenbaum, J. (1976). *Computer Power and Human Reason.* W.H. Freeman and Co., San Francisco.

Westin, A.F. (1967). *Privacy and Freedom.* Atheneum, New York.

Westin, A.F. & Baker, M.A. (1972). *Databanks in a Free Society.* Quadrangle Books, New York.

Whisler, T.L. (1970). *Information Technology and Organizational Change.* Wadsworth,Belmont, California.

Wiener, N. (1950). *The Human Use of Human Beings.* Houghton, Boston.

Wiener, N. (1960). Some Moral and Technical Consequences of Automation. *Science*, **131**, May 6th, 1355-1358.

Wiener, N. (1964). *God and Golem Inc.* MIT Press, Cambridge, Mass.

PART 2

APPLICATION RESEARCH

INTRODUCTION

Five application research areas are referenced in this part of the book: education, information retrieval, management planning, architectural design and medicine. Although these areas are considerably different, there is a broad correspondence in the way that the computer is being employed. For example, the last three chapters have a common goal—to use the computer as an aid in complex human decision making. These three chapters have a similar format: a discussion of the particular characteristics of the environment, a description of the formalisms that have been developed for representing the environment in terms of computer procedures and an evaluation of their success. The first chapter is quite similar to the others in format, but it deals with perhaps the most difficult application of all, the use of computers for teaching. Unlike the other three areas, the aim in teaching is to transmit knowledge to someone who will not be an expert in the application but will be just the opposite—a student. The problems of encapsulating course material and successful teaching principles and of understanding student errors and lack of comprehension are formidable. The second chapter (Chapter 6) deals with the rather narrower subject of information retrieval. However, some form of information retrieval is required in all the above applications, and this chapter provides a good understanding of the problems.

Part two begins with a review of progress in computer assisted learning (CAL). Roger Hartley describes how CAL should be viewed as an adjunct to more conventional teaching methods, its success depending upon such factors as careful integration with existing teaching systems, the capability of the teacher to modify it, and the constraints imposed upon the student. A teaching classification scheme is used to discuss the large number of studies in this area. The classification focusses on three teaching paradigms: behavioural control, discovery learning, and the so-called 'rational' models. Hartley discusses the nature of each before proceeding to examine different applications. These applications range from mastery learning of course material to the teaching of problem-solving skills. The importance of student control of learning progress and the degree of responsiveness that can be built into the communication interface are investigated. The final section discusses the development of more complex systems which embody representations of the task environment, the student's strategies and teaching principles. The chapter concludes with an evaluation of CAL research and its impact on education.

Chapter 6 is concerned with the information retrieval process. Tom Martin reviews what has been learned from the implementation of specialist data base systems over the last few years. These lessons are important because we are about to witness the advent of much larger systems designed for access by the ordinary citizen (e.g., teletext type services). The chapter begins with a categorization of the types of query that are encountered in information retrieval systems. This is followed by a discussion of performance criteria. How should retrieval systems be evaluated? Actual evaluation procedures seldom take into account the user's perspective, being directed almost solely to the technical characteristics of the data base. Martin states that although data bases have continued to increase in size and number, the *quality* of the search process has probably not improved correspondingly. One important factor that affects search quality is the degree of user support. The end-user has typically preferred to make use of an intermediary to perform the search process. The reason that the intermediary has become a vital part of the search process is because of the difficulty of the task. There are often several data bases specializing in different aspects of the same concern that may need to be searched for a particular enquiry. Each requires different access procedures and command languages. The next section describes some of the different forms this interactive search process can take in terms of user query languages. The chapter concludes with a review of the contributions from human factors literature.

In Chapter 7 Michael Scott Morton and Sid Huff consider the subject of planning and decision making in organisations. They point out that while computers have been very successful in automating the more clerical applications in organisations, there are still considerable difficulties with less well-structured, fuzzy decision making problems. The need is seen for computer packages that *assist* managers in solving these problems, rather than replacing them. This concept they call a decision support system. Systems are required that can support the user in all aspects of the corporate planning process. The authors describe an eight-stage model of this process which covers setting objectives, analysing environmental forces, forecasting the future environment, establishing future objectives, setting out alternatives for achieving these objectives, developing action programs and finally implementing the plan. The authors describe the procedures that have been followed under each of these stages. These include such techniques as simulation models, decision theory techniques, and cost-benefit procedures. The last section of the chapter considers an example of a strategic planning system which is used to illustrate the decision support system concept.

Tom Maver looks at the use of computers in the design process in Chapter 8 with specific reference to the architectural design process. He stresses the importance of a systems view of the design activity and in particular the issues of problem representation, measurement criteria, the nature of evaluation, and the modification of the design hypotheses. The complexity of the systems design viewpoint is illustrated with a consideration of two components: the process and energy sub-systems. The above issues are examined for both of these building sub-systems with examples of resource utilization and thermal efficiency. Maver then turns to the problem of 'total' systems design which may involve the handling and integration of several conflicting types of sub-system. This process is explored in some detail using examples drawn from a hospital design package.

In the last chapter Tom Taylor considers the impact of computers in one particular area of medicine—clinical decision making. Although widely used in medical record keeping and instrumentation, computers have so far had little direct impact on the clinician's diagnostic processes. Taylor outlines a model of the clinical decision process at the beginning of the chapter which emphasises its sequential nature, the hypothesis-test-treatment cycle. The initial stage in this procedure is that of patient history taking. Although very important, this is frequently time-consuming and unstructured. Accordingly, there have been attempts to automate the pre-examination questioning of the patient. Taylor reviews these attempts in terms of their justification, the form of the human-computer interface, and the evaluation of results. He then turns to attempts to bring computers into the later stages of the diagnostic process, as decision support aids. There are two basic types of applications based on different formalizations: those based on normative decision theory (i.e., mathematical methods of reducing data) and descriptive models. The latter models usually represent collections of rules that have been elicited from expert clinicians. These descriptive procedures have been implemented in either a very simple form as automated flowcharts, or as knowledge-based systems using artificial intelligence techniques. In concluding, Taylor stresses how the success or failure of such technological aids is heavily influenced by the degree of support given by the medical profession.

Chapter 5

COMPUTER ASSISTED LEARNING

Roger Hartley

Contents

1.0 Introduction

Using the electronic computer as a teaching machine is an intriguing development. On the one hand there is considerable promise in the wider range of educational activities which are potentially available, on the other there are obvious difficulties before these benefits can be realized. For example, the computer can carry out arithmetic and logical operations quickly. By using models expressed as sets of quantitative relations or equations, simulation programs can provide illustrations which are not possible by other means. The student may alter the input values used by these equations, observe differences in the output data, and so explore the characteristics of the model. Through the medium of graphics terminals, the data can be displayed in ways which are informative and visually attractive. Furthermore, in these, and in tutorial programs which teach the material through question-answer sequences, the student is active in his learning. Indeed, the instruction is driven by the responses which he gives at the terminal. The computer programs can evaluate these responses, provide feedback, and use the learner's performance-data to make decisions which are suited to his competence. Through class records the teacher can observe progress, determine which topics are difficult, and arrange tutorials with students whose response patterns show conceptual misunderstandings or unexpected lines of argument.

These are some of the expected benefits, but there are considerable difficulties in realising their full potential, principally because the modes of communication from the student to the computer are limited. The point is not just that typing responses at a keyboard is slow and laborious, but that in most tutorial programs material has to be pre-stored, and the range of student responses anticipated by the author. Therefore the teaching steps must be relatively small, the approach directed, and the types of dialogue restricted. Again, in simulation programs an elementary command language has to be designed for the student. Typically, this only allows the nomination of variables and the alteration of their values—so the response set is limited. Even when the student answers a problem by writing and running a computer program which will carry out the task, the syntax of the language has to be rigidly adhered to. Any discussion of the problem itself, or its formulation, has to be provided by other means.

1.1 Integrating Conventional Teaching and Computer Assisted Learning Schemes

The respective strengths of the human teacher and machine-based programs can often be considered complementary. The teacher has good general knowledge of the topic area and easy modes of communication with the students. Problems are often resource based; he/she must work with groups and cannot easily keep detailed records or summaries of individual performances to closely guide decisions. So Computer Assisted Learning (CAL) can be a useful support when the teacher has neither the time nor the resources to give adequate illustration or small group teaching. However, the practical development of computer learning aids which are realistic in scale, depends upon CAL techniques being able to engage in wide ranging activities such as tutoring, simulation, and the teaching of problem-solving skills. Integrating these methods within normal teaching schemes is not easy. The computer based techniques emphasize individualization and the adaptive nature of teaching, whereas conventional methods tend to favour minimal variation in the conditions under which students are expected to learn.

In order to cope with these problems, the teacher/author can be provided with a variety of techniques and types of languages. *Firstly*, in Computer Assisted Learning, student and teacher communicate indirectly through the machine administration of teaching programs. The author has to interpret objectives (whether expressed in behavioural or cognitive terms) into a sequence of tasks. Thus techniques of analysis and ways of representing knowledge structures are required. Then program designs must be specified: these include, the student commands and permitted types of response, the rules governing the initiatives which are taken by program and learner, and the actual teaching material. For tutorial work, this specification is coded using an author language (i.e., a series of command words and syntax rules interpretable by the computer which are suited to response matching and character/word manipulation). In the case of simulation, the packages are usually written in computer languages such as FORTRAN or BASIC, which are convenient for carrying out more complex calculations.

Secondly, the teacher must manage a class of students who will use the computer based materials individually. Their performance-data must be stored and used by the programs in adaptive decision-making, and in printing study guidelines for the learner. The records must also show the teacher the rates of progress and particular difficulties of students. So the teacher must be able to set up evaluative functions and process class records in order to answer enquiries. In other words, CAL applications require a supporting class management and record creation/processing system.

Thirdly, it is necessary to integrate computer based materials within conventional teaching schemes. The programs are likely to enlarge the educational objectives and stimulate the teacher to undertake curriculum innovations. So he/she must be able to manage, adapt, or re-assemble CAL modules or packages to suit the differing needs of classes or the teacher's own inclinations when redesigning teaching courses. Further, CAL projects are likely to involve groups of cooperating teachers (perhaps in different institutions), so the materials must be adequately documented and be capable of adjusting to these varied settings. In practice, this requires a structured and modular design of programs, and the development of a simple control language which teachers can easily use to select and sequence modules, and connect them together with their own comments and decision rules.

Fourthly, the student has to learn the command language and response conventions, and how to use the instructional material at the terminal. In addition to CAL training programs, it is useful to have some on-line message facility. This enables the student to comment on the teaching materials, ask further questions, or arrange meetings with his tutors. In order to provide a linking framework between the programs and conventional modes of teaching, Student Guides, worksheets and other resource materials are likely to be needed.

1.2 Factors Influencing Learning and Computer Assisted Learning

There are a considerable number of psychological and educational studies which are of interest to the teacher/author since they relate to the design of CAL materials. Much of this work emphasizes the following points:

- The need to provide the learner with informational feedback and the precise conditions under which it is most effective.
- The influence of the relational structures within the teaching material, and its sequencing.
- The importance of encouraging active learner control—i.e. giving the learner some control over the direction and pace of teaching.

However there is, as yet, no agreed overall learning scheme which adequately copes with, and suggests teaching designs for, the many diverse situations in which CAL methods have been applied. The CAL literature reflects this absence in that no adequate taxonomy of tasks and teaching procedures has been defined, and the result is a fragmented body of knowledge comprising the case reports of individual studies. In order to be able to describe this work and the different categories of CAL systems in a coherent fashion, the teaching classification scheme of Nuthall & Snook (1973) will be used. They identify the following types of teaching:

- Behavioural control models
- Discovery learning models
- Rational models (i.e., those which stress the place of reasoning and dialogue in teaching).

In what follows, these distinctions are used to provide a framework for reviewing progress and research in CAL in which the division of control between learner and teacher is particularly emphasized. After this we turn to knowledgeable CAL systems which contain and apply general teaching principles based on explicit representations of the learner's strategy and the tasks he undertakes.

2.0 Behavioural Control Models

2.1 *Underlying Principles*

According to Nuthall & Snook (op cit), behavioural control types of teaching stress complete control over student behaviour and over the conditions of learning. The teacher is a manager who seeks to accomplish specific objectives as quickly and as efficiently as possible. Within CAL the emphasis is on programs which are directive in style, and on adaptive decision-making based on performance records of individual students. The program designs relate to an associationistic view of Learning Psychology of the sort advocated, for example by Skinner (Skinner, 1953). According to this view, complex learning behaviours are seen as a network of stimulus response associations. These bonds are established by providing reinforcing stimuli, such as knowledge of results, directly the learner has given an active and appropriate response to the stimulus material. Thus the teacher must control the selection and arrangement of content and task so that the required responses are elicited. He also controls the type of feedback and other reinforcing stimuli which are used to maintain and regulate effort, and to shape more complex learning behaviours by building up response chains composed of small steps.

The psychological origins of such reinforcement models come from studies of animal learning, and need qualification when applied analogously to the human situation. For example, it is now recognized that feedback, i.e. the message or compound statement which follows the response made by the learner, should not be regarded solely as a reinforcing stimulus, but as information which will locate error and inform the student how to put it right (Anderson et al., 1971; 1972). Thus tutorial programs should not necessarily be small-step, but have tasks large enough to expose the student's misunderstandings and provide feedback to enable him to correct them. Anderson also demonstrated the importance of control over the learning sequence by forcing students to look ahead to the right answers before typing their responses (a cheat condition); their post-tests results were significantly worse than all other groups, even one that was not given feedback at all! Whereas in textbooks and programmed texts students can short-circuit the instruction and look ahead to the right answers, presentation by computer can ensure that feedback is not available until after the student responds.

As well as showing the informational role of feedback, and the benefits of control over learning activity, a third research theme has been that of sequencing learning material, particularly in subject areas which can be arranged in a hierarchical fashion. Typically, decision rules are constructed which only allow the learner to proceed to further sections of the material in the hierarchy after competance has been demonstrated within lower-level modules (mastery learning). As long ago as 1961, Gagne & Paradise, and Gagne et al. (1962), reported studies which showed the value of such decision rules. The experiments were set in Mathematics, and one result was that the best predictor of performance on the higher-level tasks was the degree of mastery shown by the individual learners at the lower levels of the task hierarchy. Note that all these research themes argue for decision rules based on specific information about the individual learner's knowledge and performance. For this reason, adaptive CAL programs should in principle be efficient aids to learning.

2.2 Some CAL Applications

Some of the early attempts to develop behavioural control programs were aimed at a major replacement of the teacher. This was not wholly successful, and the teaching functions now given to the computer are more limited and more precisely defined. This is shown by an example taken from one of the largest centres engaged in Computer Assisted Learning, namely the PLATO Project at the University of Illinois. Several hundred terminals are available for departments to use in interactive teaching, and a library of over four-thousand hours of programmed material has been developed in a wide range of subjects (Lyman, 1974). In the Department of Physics the organization of the introductory courses assumed that students attended lectures, read from specified textbooks, and worked through assigned problems both before and during example classes. However, reality differed from these expectations. For example, 30% of the Science and Engineering students attending the course did not attempt any of the problems before coming to the example class, and an additional 30% failed to master even one problem of these given assignments (Sherwood et al., 1971). Since the Physics course, in common with most teaching in the Sciences, was hierarchical in structure, a lack of mastery of one topic hindered subsequent learning and the progress of weaker students continued to deteriorate. Therefore, instead of totally replacing the conventional teaching, the computer based instruction system was given the managerial task of checking the student's understanding and providing sufficient teaching to ensure that specified performance levels were met. The course was divided into weekly topics, and the tutorial program tested and taught the students and evaluated performances. Each student had to register satisfactory standards before moving on to other course material. Although no independent evaluation of the test-teach project has been published, the observable evidence was that students took a much more active part in the example classes and examination performances improved.

In behavioural control situations, this management of learning is an important aspect of CAL programs. In the Leeds Applied Statistics Project (Hartley, 1976), the initial teaching is not provided by computer programs, but by lectures, textbooks, and/or Student Guides. The Guides summarize the main teaching points within a topic, have illustrations and give references to further reading. The individual teacher can use these in ways which suit—either as an introduction or as a summary of lectures. Following this the objectives of the CAL materials are to check and consolidate the student's understanding of the concepts and to allow the elaboration of knowledge through practice examples. About two-hundred small test-teach modules are provided which lecturers adapt to their own use by specifying control programs. These select and sequence the modules, make decisions, or give some control to the student using performance and time-data, and link sections using the teacher's own comments. Thus a coherent curriculum may be designed for each class.

One aspect of computer managed systems, that of testing, is relatively simple to implement. As well as helping the teacher administratively, computer based tests can permit a wider variety of objective type questions to be used. For example, Dirkzwager (1975) allows the student to state subjective possibilities for all alternatives on each multiple choice test item. By using visual display terminals the input and, if necessary, the changing of a response probability set is easily accomplished. Computer programs can then quickly carry out appropriate rescaling and calculate results in the form of student uncertainty measures. Such procedures can result in more reliable tests and, for judgmental items, a student's probability distributions can be compared with those of the teacher or with other groups of students.

Although many projects employ tutorial programs which favour performance based decision-making, the program designs vary both in style and in the degree of control they exercise over the learner. For example, in the Glasgow Mathematics Project (Daly et al., 1977), the student can tackle his examples in one of three different modes. The first is tutorial in style and, depending on a student's response, provides prompting and feedback. Another mode permits the student to type one basic response to the Mathematics practice task, and the rest of the solution is then displayed. A third mode enables good students to attempt the answer to the problem in one step. In general, the student will follow the modes which are recommended by the program, but he can diverge from this route if he wishes.

Where the teaching objectives require judgement on the part of the learner, e.g., in clinical decision-making, different program styles are necessary. In the Glasgow-based Medical Project (Murray et al., 1976), the student is presented with a case-study and has to decide which management options to prescribe. In fact the student is asked to rate each one of them and, if these disagree with the ratings of the course authors, feedback is given, corrections made, and the case-study proceeds. In a transferred version of the program implemented at Leeds, the student can also be challenged and, through a question-and-answer technique, be asked to justify decisions. The chances of being challenged are probabilistically related to the student's performance levels.

2.3 A Brief Appraisal of Program Designs

In summary, tutorial projects have produced an interesting variety of materials which differ in the design styles which they employ and the controls they assign to the learner, the program, and to the human teacher. Unfortunately, there is little recorded experience of the ways in which these tutorial schemes and programs have been designed. The material is based on teaching practices, and the programs tend to evolve in ways which owe more to pragmatics than to principles of Educational Technology. Typically a representative set of tasks and problems is chosen, and feedback produced by considering their detailed step-by-step solutions.

However, these analyses are often carried out at a logical level rather than considering the psychological processes which are involved. So it is not surprising that the materials do not systematically exploit those principles which have been shown to be effective in controlling learning. The records which they keep of student performance are frequently sparse, and there is little attempt to build up a representation of his/her knowledge and skills. Therefore the programs are content centred: in consequence the teaching is primitive in accommodating individual differences for, to a large extent, decision rules are based solely on the previous response of the student. Mastery level criteria are rarely used, and usually the number of tasks is either specified by the teacher, follows student preference, or terminates when no further material remains.

The types of dialogues which are used in these programs demands comprehension on the part of the learner, but, in general, the type of feedback refers to the worth of the response which has been made, and only seldom engages the student in explanation or attempts a general conceptualisation of the problem. To a large extent these restrictions are imposed on the author, since responses have to be anticipated and identified through pre-stored keyword matching schemes. To make the program writing exercise practical, the question-answer sequences must proceed in relatively small steps. So the responses themselves are small constructed responses, sometimes multiple choices, numbers or a limited set of command words. The opportunities for a student to take initiatives are extremely limited. Of course these deficiencies can be reduced by other supporting methods which usually employ the human teacher.

3.0 Learner Control

3.1 Discovery Learning

In contrast to the previous teaching mode, discovery learning techniques, though not aptly named, place emphasis on the control which the learner has in building up his/her own knowledge structures. The teacher is not the primary source of information, but acts to stimulate and monitor the learner and reveal the inadequacies of generalisations by producing counter examples. It is maintained that such methods allow the student not only to arrive at more general conclusions, but to learn about the process of generalisation itself. The student learns to explore the educational context and, using Bruner's phrase, goes "beyond the information given" in seeking to apply rules or general principles to unfamiliar examples.

In Computer Assisted Learning, simulation programs attempt to realise these aims by allowing the student to test hypotheses held about the underlying model. Typically, variables are denoted, input values specified, and the resulting output displayed. Within these limits few restrictions are placed on the user who has to evaluate the output to guide further decisions. Therefore such packages are best used when the student has sufficient knowledge to provide a coherent framework for such an exploration. For programs which are factually based, elementary command languages are designed so that the student can select and sequence material. In this way the student guides the direction and type of instruction, and builds up his/her own performances.

These teaching modes are loosely related to some of the ideas put forward by Cognitive Psychologists. For them learning objectives are not expressed as behaviours constructed through elementary stimulus-response associations, but as mental procedures and knowledge structures which are developed and used by the learner. Questions of interest include: how information is stored, organised and retrieved, and how new knowledge is integrated within existing cognitive structures. The more fundamental research which addresses these questions has established the importance of the type of representation given to the task, the type of coding activity, and processes of organisation and structuring.

Some studies with a more direct practical application have used organising schemas of the sort suggested by Ausubel (eg., Ausubel, 1968). He states that the degree of meaningful, as opposed to rote, learning of new material depends on its interaction with the cognitive structures held by the student. Learning is helped if the student's existing knowledge can be used to provide ideational scaffolding or anchorage for new material. To help this process, Ausubel suggests that, prior to the instruction, organising material of greater generality or inclusiveness should be studied by the learner.

Although the characteristics of good organisers have not been thoroughly worked out (Graber et al., 1972), there are several plausible arguments for incorporating them within computer based teaching programs. Not only can the organiser be given prior to the instruction, but it can serve as an on-line teaching framework for the interactive programs. Pask has provided evidence that the type of organisation of the material interacts with individual differences in students (Pask & Scott, 1972; Pask, 1976).

Although discovery learning modes must give considerable initiative to the learner, several experiments have been carried out which suggest that students in a free learning situation do not make an accurate appraisal of their abilities, or requirements, and so do not make effective decisions. For example, Pask (1975) reached such conclusions after studies which used a variety of tracking and concept learning tasks. However, he noted that a compromise strategy in which control programs allowed student decisions where they were judged reasonable, maintained motivation and produced good results.

3.2 Learner Control Schemes

In spite of the interest in these ideas, techniques for designing CAL materials which are factual in nature and which allow a considerable degree of learner control are not well advanced. Designing such systems is complex and involves three levels of discourse. First, there is the answering of test-teach questions of tutorial modules and, as before, these responses are matched against keyword pre-stored alternatives supplied by the author. Second, there is dialogue on the instructional process together with a learner control language which allows the student to survey the course of materials required. Third, there is advice and discussion through which control decisions can be modified.

The most extensive learner control system, and one which is also theoretically sophisticated (the TICCIT system), has been designed by Bunderson and Merrill (Merrill, 1973; Merrill & Wood, 1974; O'Neal, 1973). Merrill has implemented a control language which, through function keys, allows students to regulate both content and teaching strategy. (See Figure 1). The subject matter is divided into concepts, operations and rules which can be presented at two levels (either as generalisations or instances) and in two modes ASKING or TELLING. In order to help the student choose a particular lesson unit a diagram showing a map of the course is displayed. The student can obtain a more detailed view of the content and the pre-requisites of each unit, and use response buttons to ask for rules, examples and practice tasks which make up the instructional material. As well as controlling mode, the level of difficulty of the material on a concrete-abstract axis is chosen by pressing a HARD or EASY key. A HELP button

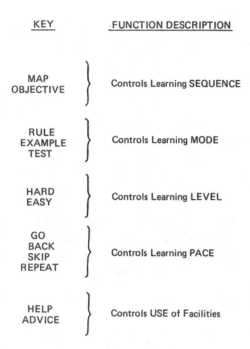

KEY	FUNCTION DESCRIPTION
MAP OBJECTIVE	Controls Learning SEQUENCE
RULE EXAMPLE TEST	Controls Learning MODE
HARD EASY	Controls Learning LEVEL
GO BACK SKIP REPEAT	Controls Learning PACE
HELP ADVICE	Controls USE of Facilities

Fig. 1. The TICCIT System Function Keys.

gives cues which fix attention, for example, on the main attributes of concepts. To help the student acquire more adequate learning strategies, an
ADVISER function is incorporated in the system. This is probably the most
difficult and least effective part of the scheme for there is little stored
information of the student's intentions and knowledge state, yet the AD-
VISER has to give suggestions when choices appear non-productive. This
help is somewhat limited, but the student may be advised on the amount
of practice, the difficulties of examples to be chosen, or be given some help
on methods of organising the material. However, although the rationale
underlying the design of these programs has been thoroughly worked out,
there needs to be further experience and evaluation of the scheme in practice, particularly as this is a tutorial method which proposes a large-scale
replacement of the human teacher.

There is supporting evidence which underlines the importance of the
advisory function which must be supplied by the program or by the human
teacher. In learner control the choices might not lead to the desired objectives or the student may not be aware that his/her understanding is deficient. On the other hand, a directed teaching scheme assumes that the
approach which is imposed can be readily assimilated by the learner. Hart-

ley et al. (1972) studied subjects learning to plan laboratory experiments; one group of subjects had both to determine their own learning sequence and discover for themselves the correct answer after a mistake. This learner control group performed less well than two other groups whose sequence was directed, or who were given active feedback in which further responses had to be made to sub-questions which located and corrected errors. Thus, in the initial stages of learning a complex skill, the teaching treatment which required decision-making and information-collection was not used efficiently, particularly by the less competent students. However, in a further experiment over an extended series of planning trials, the performances of the learner control group improved so that eventually the method produced equivalent learning gains and took a shorter time. Questionnaire data showed it was the method which most students preferred. Similar results were also obtained in teaching the planning of statistical investigations with Psychology students (Abbatt, 1972). Again the evidence argues for adaptive decision rules in which more responsibility is given to the student to direct his own learning as he becomes more competent.

3.3   Learning from Simulation Programs

One of the features of Computer Assisted Learning projects has been the variety of simulation programs which they have produced and used in the Physical Sciences, Engineering, Mathematics, Medicine, and Social Studies. Many of the concepts in these subjects are difficult to illustrate, either because data cannot be produced readily in the lecture room, or because the concepts themselves and the relations between them are represented in formal and symbolic terms which seem remote from everyday experience. However, computer programs which use these equations or quantitative data-bases to provide a model of the system can help to build up a student's knowledge structures. In general, the student cannot edit or amend the programs themselves but can manipulate input values of variables which describe the system and observe their effects on output displays. In this way the properties of the underlying model can be appreciated and hypotheses and ideas about them tested. Thus the student's understanding can be elaborated.

For these reasons, providing simulation exercises through computer programs has proved a popular and useful development in Science Teaching. For example, Roos (1973) has a series of programs which simulate the human menstrual cycle. The output shows the time of ovulation and the time and duration of menstruation. The user can substitute hormone treatments and observe the suppression effects on ovulation, uterine development and/or menstruation. Hormone concentrations and cyclical events are related by a series of simultaneous equations, and randomisation ensures that each cycle is uniquely determined. Again, Dehner & Norcross (1971) have developed a simple program which allows students to simulate acid-base titrations for a variety of weak acids and turbidimetric titrations to obtain solubility product information for a number of slightly soluble salts. Although this type of program does not provide experience with the laboratory technique, the student can perform his titrations more cheaply and quickly than might be possible in the laboratory, and these illustrations will help him to grasp the basic concepts which are involved in titrimetric analysis. Stannard (1972) has also developed a dry Physics laboratory in which the user chooses apparatus and programs allow him to perform experiments with it. For example, in dynamics the student can operate masses at speeds beyond anything that could reasonably be achieved in the laboratory. Engineering is another useful area for simulation, particularly as many real systems, e.g., nuclear reactors, are too expensive or dangerous to be made available to the student. A multi-institutional Engineering Project directed from Queen Mary College, London, has devised over seventy packages in Electrical, Nuclear, Aeronautical, and Mechanical Engineering (Smith, 1977). Almost all of these Science-based simulations translate the output into visual displays so that the student can more easily see the effects of decisions.

An example of teaching through simulation, which shows many of the advantages and difficulties of the technique, is the emergency patient program which has been implemented by Taylor and Scott (1975) of the Glasgow-based Medical Project. The patient is represented at any current time as the state values of a set of vital signs, such as temperature, pulse rate, respiration, coma and cyanosis, which are appropriate to the working context. Functions act on these values and so govern their change through time. At the terminal, details of the situation are printed out, e.g., a car-accident victim with fractures and airway blockage. The student can ask for investigations and tests to be made and treatments to be carried out. In general the tests do not affect the patient's state directly, but they have a time penalty and during this time a condition could deteriorate. The user can monitor changes and the rates of change in the values of the vital signs, and the results are shown graphically. To improve the patient's condition, the student can propose treatments. To each of these a time increment simulates its administration, after which functions attached to that treatment alter the patient's condition values. (See Figure 2). If threshold values are exceeded, the patient dies. The treatments can be classified into those which have good or bad effects in the short and in the long term. The aim, of course, is to hasten the patient's improvement and achieve a stable condition, and this is the sole feedback given to the user through the changing sign-values.

The objectives are to ensure that the student realises the need for com-

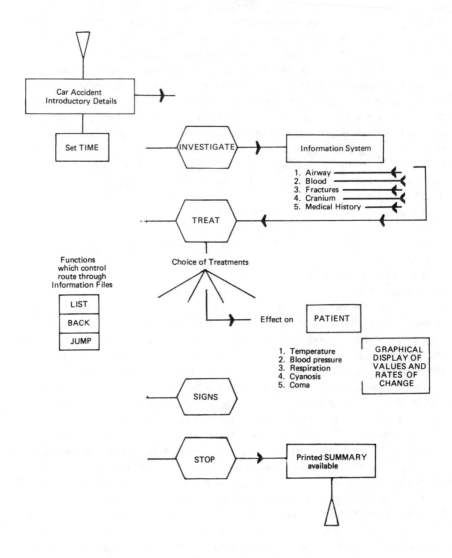

Fig. 2. Commands used in the Medical Simulation program.

prehensive monitoring and for having several ongoing treatments. (Thus, in the particular example given above, cortisone will resolve the problem of falling blood pressure, but unless the airway is cleared in some way, the cyanosis will be fatal.) The student must also learn to evaluate the various effects of the treatments. (For example, although phenobarbitone has a bad effect on respiration, coma, and cyanosis, in the long term it has a good effect on pulse.) An advantage of using this simulation exercise is that the learner can operate with a simpler system than would be encountered in reality. Greater control is possible and so it is easier to appreciate the relationships, i.e., the patient's requirements and the effects of treatments. Further, the student can see the effects of his/her decisions without detrimental consequences, and the real time-scale is compressed so that many exercises can be worked through in a relatively short period of time. However, there are some difficulties in design and in enabling students to derive the most benefit from the exercises. Building simulators to serve as teaching devices is not an easy task and requires careful analysis. Even when the equations or the data-bases which describe the system are known, it is not always easy to decide the task which should be given to the learner, i.e., what combinations of variables should be manipulated, or what types of instructions should be allowed at the terminal. The feedback messages and the form of the output displays are also important influences on learning, and should derive from the educational objectives.

Bearing in mind the initiatives which are required of the learner, it is not surprising that the preparation and background knowledge of the student are strongly related to the insights received from using the packages. In the Medical program, unless the investigation and treatment options engage a student's knowledge so that hypotheses of their possible effect on the patient's state vector can be generated, decisions will not be made systemically. So the student will be unable to draw any consistent interpretations from the exercise. Also the dialogue that can be employed (simple commands and numbers) is limited, and operates within the tree structure of the investigation and treatment files. The student can merely select the test or treatment; he/she cannot discuss decisions, nor ask how or why the treatments have their various effects. There is no discussion of methods of handling such emergency patient situations, and no general teaching guidance is supplied directly by the program. Further, no records are kept of the learner's protocol and so the program is unable to be adaptive on subsequent runs of the simulation exercise. Of course, some of this supporting teaching can be provided by other means. For example, in the Leeds version of the program the student can save the dialogue traces; these are then printed so that decisions can be discussed with a tutor.

So, at present the general designs of simulation programs are limited and the role of the computer is largely that of calculation and display. Although the student has control over the input values selected, and can see their effects, he/she is unable to inspect, to amend or recode, or to discover (because of its complexity) the inner structure of the program which produces the results. Thus, its function is limited to illustration for the naive student and elaboration of knowledge for the student who understands the underlying principles.

For more complex packages the commands (which are the student's tools for obtaining a perception of the underlying model), and the supporting worksheets, should evolve from evaluation studies which observe, question, and test the student's conceptualisations. However, few projects have been able to carry out and document such work, and none have conducted studies which make links to the psychological framework outlined earlier in the chapter.

4.0 Teaching Problem-Solving Skills

Problem-solving is a term which is even more loosely defined and ill-used than simulation. A technical definition will not be attempted, but the interpretation should be clear from the specific contexts. Essentially, problem-solving implies a novel situation for the student; he/she has the requisite knowledge and sub-skills to solve the problem, but has to sequence reasoning and/or develop heuristics which enable movement from the initial to the goal state. By presenting varieties of related tasks, the student can learn to pick out those characteristics which point towards economic methods of solution.

The limitations in teaching dialogue which are brought about by pre-stored response matching in tutorial programs, and by a limited command vocabulary in learner controlled and simulation packages, have been noted. In teaching problem-solving skills by computer these difficulties must be overcome, for the learner must be able to set out methods and discuss steps in the working. Two approaches have been used to extend student initiative and dialogue. Some projects have enabled simulation modules to be used within author language tutorial programs. Others have extended simulation programs to include dialogue facilities, or have developed types of programming languages through which students can express and demonstrate their solutions by designing, debugging, and running their own computer programs.

4.1 Extending Author Language Programs

An example of bringing simulation facilities within an author language program comes from the CALCHEM Project based at Leeds University. The problem context is the analysis of Nuclear Magnetic Resonance

(NMR) spectra. The student is presented with a molecular formula and a diagram of its spectrum; the task is to decide the structure of the molecule. First, the student has to read the spectral diagram and identify peak positions, the multiplicity of each peak and its integrated intensity, i.e., the area under the curve. The program gives any tutorial guidance and feedback which the student's responses require. After this the learner has to suggest a chemical group which will account for a given part of the spectrum. In order to evaluate any suggestions in terms of peak position, multiplicity and intensity, the program works out and compares the spectral characteristics of the group suggested by the student with those of the given diagram. Following feedback, the student can modify responses, if necessary, and so the exercise continues until the complete structural formula has been derived (Ayscough, 1977). An extract from a student printout is shown in Figure 3.

WHAT ARRANGEMENT OF PROTONS IS RESPONSIBLE FOR
    THE SIGNAL AT 1.17 DELTA?
>>**CH3**   *Student—refers to diagram of NMR spectrum*
A CH3 GROUP WOULD EXPLAIN THE INTEGRATED SPEC-
    TRUM.
WHAT ATOM(S) OR GROUP(S) WOULD HAVE TO BE ADJA-
    CENT TO THE CH3 GROUP TO GIVE RISE TO A
    SIGNAL AT 1.17 DELTA?
>>**CO**
CH3.CO WOULD GIVE A SIGNAL AT ABOUT 1.9 DELTA NOT
    1.7 DELTA.
IT WOULD GIVE RISE TO A SIGNAL WITH A MULTIPLICITY
    OF 1 NOT 3.
PLEASE TRY AGAIN.
>>**CH2**
CH3.CH2 WOULD EXPLAIN THE CHEMICAL SHIFT OF 1.17
    DELTA.
THE CHEMICAL SHIFT OF THE CH2 GROUP IS 4.1 DELTA:
WHAT OTHER GROUP MUST BE ATTACHED TO THE CH2
    GROUP (OTHER THAN THE CH3 GROUP) TO GIVE
    A SIGNAL AT 4.1 DELTA?
>>**O**
CH3.CH2.O WOULD EXPLAIN THE CHEMICAL SHIFT OF 4.1
    DELTA.
THIS LEAVES: 8*C 7*H 1*O
TO BE ACCOUNTED FOR.
. . . .
. . . .
. . . .

Fig. 3. An extract from a student printout showing partial analysis of a Nuclear Magnetic Resonance (NMR) spectrum.

The importance of the supporting tutorial dialogue in problem-solving exercises is demonstrated in an experiment reported by Bork & Robson (1972). The computer program simulated an experimental investigation of a pulse in a rope. For example, the student could enter time and position of a rope element, and be told the displacement. From this data the student had to discover enough about the disturbance to be able to undertake numerical problems about the behaviour of the rope. In order to help those students who were working unsystematically and to little effect, Bork and Robson extended the program to retain the student's requests for measurements, make certain checks on them, and print advice based on these evaluations. For example, in contrast to the usual simulation programs, the program could check if the student had encountered non-zero values; if not, comments would suggest where they might be found. If data-collection was haphazard, some hints on techniques of investigation would be given. The program might advise that time should be fixed and the detailed behaviour of the rope studied at a number of different places, or that measurements should be gathered at a particular position for different intervals of time. These hints become progressively stronger, so that if the student was performing poorly, the program almost instructed the correct proceedure on a step-by-step basis.

Ratings showed that half the students liked the program, half did not. It became clear that, for the weaker students, the program didn't sustain interest long enough for them to make sufficient discoveries about the behaviour of the rope. When more advanced students used the program (many of whom understood the basic Physics, and so had a frame of reference) they became more involved, were more successful with the program, and the ratings of this group were enthusiastic.

Such programs are not easy to design and have to evolve from a close examination of their use with students. As Bork & Robson state (op cit), a learning environment is much more difficult to produce than a stimulating environment. Although the teaching dialogue of the rope simulation enhanced the program, what it can accomplish is necessarily limited. This is because the commands are pre-stored and cannot respond to any sequence or type of data-collection which has not been anticipated. The teaching sub-program has not the capability of using or directing the simulation routines to discover the wave characteristic, hence it cannot evaluate student strategies or respond to suggestions.

4.2 Using Programming Languages

A second approach to teaching problem-solving skills is to have students put their solutions in the form of computer programs. The supposed advantage of solving problems algorithmically is that it requires a clear understanding of what is needed, for the student has to give a precise statement in a step-by-step solution. Perhaps one of the first and most important developments in designing programming languages for teaching is that of LOGO, which can be learnt by schoolchildren and which has suggested interesting developments in the curriculum and methods of teaching Mathematics (Papert & Solomon, 1972). Broadly, the teacher follows a problem-solving approach and encourages the pupil to set out solutions in the form of computer programs. These are coded and run at the terminal. For example, programs might be devised to draw geometric shapes on a graphics terminal. One procedure is to instruct the cursor to move forward n steps, rotate through an angle, and repeat these instructions recursively. By labelling the variables and altering their values, the pupil can study the shapes produced. Simple additions of an extra step length will cause spiralling; putting in tests to control the sequence of commands will allow shapes to roll along or move around. Such programs can be extended and generalised so that a child can develop notions of the properties of shapes and symmetry. The structure of LOGO provides a convenient grammar for representing mathematical processes, and its programs are built up from small procedures which contain a limited number of commands. So the learner has to analyse the problem into its component parts, to consider the inputs required by the commands and the outputs they will produce. This activity and the structure of the procedures themselves form convenient discussion points between teacher and pupil, and it has been argued that the exercise of constructing such programs and correcting their faults aids general thinking skills. (Papert, 1971a; 1971b.)

At the university level Brown & Rubenstein (1973) have used LOGO with Psychology undergraduates for teaching topics in Linguistics. The language APL has also been used in Higher Education for developing problem-solving skills (Bork, 1971; 1973; Berry et al., 1973). Again the primitive procedures of APL closely correspond to the idea of a function, so it is possible for the user in Science disciplines to develop procedures which not only calculate, but reflect the conceptual structure of the subject area. These properties, and the ways they are used in teaching, make it a completely different educational exercise from teaching students a language such as BASIC for use as a computational tool. Berry et al. (1973) have set out some examples of applying APL in teaching topics in Mechanics and in Computer Science. However, at present, experience in using these techniques is largely undeveloped and there has been little evaluation of their effects. As these languages become more widespread, their educational potential should become apparent.

5.0 Knowledgeable Teaching

In their classification system, Nuthall & Snook (1973) consider that rational models of teaching emphasize a process of discourse between teacher and pupil as they seek to acquire knowledge. Language is given a central role in the process, as teacher and learner pursue their arguments and explain and defend them. So far we have only been dealing with very rudimentary systems from a language and knowledge point of view. We now consider rather more complex systems.

Ideally, when such knowledgeable teaching programs are implemented on a computer, three data-structures are required. The first is a representation of the task, if possible in terms which will allow the programs to generate problems and undertake their solution. The second is a representation of the student. This should include not only hypotheses which are held about the student's competence, but computer programs which can replicate to some extent his/her information processing. A statement of general teaching principles is the third data structure. This is probably best represented as control programs which are ordered sets of condition-action statements. The conditions relate to characteristics of the task and to programs which model the student's working methods and performances. The teaching actions can select teaching mode, task complexity, facilities of help and type of feedback. The conditions which are met determine which of the actions are applied.

The capabilities of teaching-programs which have these data structures are much increased, but it must be admitted that, at present, they can only be designed in a small number of well-structured subject areas, and that their development costs are large. Some examples will be considered which illustrate both behavioural and learner control. These programs are limited in application but show how design features, based on data structures representing *task, student competence*, and *teaching control*, enlarge the types of instruction which are given and the dialogue which can be used by the student.

5.1 Learning Algorithmic Tasks

A simple application is the learning of algorithmic tasks where both procedures and their sequence are well defined. For example, in a study of arithmetic addition by young children, the numbers were printed in vertical format and it was assumed that the pupil undertook a mental ordering corresponding to the natural number sequence as the task was worked out. This detailed counting model of addition, and its validation, has been described by Woods & Hartley (1971). It identified operations of, (i) moving a hypothetical pointer one position, and (ii) reading each number to be added whilst storing the present (cumulative total) pointer position. The model was used to represent a pupil's performances and methods of processing. As well as noting overall success rate, the computer programs made estimates of success values on the individual operations, and, as a pupil showed increasing competence, the difficulty level was stepped-up. Also, the ability of the program to generate different types of solutions enabled it to test hypotheses about patterns of error (e.g., carrying or transposition of numbers). The results became part of the pupil representation and indicated appropriate types of remedial exercises to be given.

These data structures allow means-ends guidance rules to direct the teaching. First the quantity of feedback is controlled by generating problems which guarantee a specified working level of success, and empirical studies were made to determine the best value. A second type of adaptation is in the type of feedback, "active" (i.e., requiring a response from the pupil to ensure that the feedback message has been correctly processed) or "passive" (where the feedback comment is merely printed). Children who are less able benefit from the active form of feedback (Tait et al., 1973), and the program employed this performance-related decision rule. Further experiments showed that persistent process errors could be eradicated by generating remedial exercises of simpler examples made up from the actual number bonds with which the pupil had made mistakes.

Thus, an adaptive teaching package for arithmetic practice tasks was implemented which followed a behavioural control model. The system could be put under the control of the teacher who could type in the task difficulty parameters, whether or not remedial questions are to be given, the type of feedback to be used, and the criteria for moving between lesson types. Alternatively, these decisions could be determined by the computer programs. The system has been in day-to-day use within a Leeds School for a number of years, and the teachers are well pleased with the adaptive control. They have evolved a library of task specifications from which they make up curricula of examples which suit their classes. Three evaluative studies have all shown significant and beneficial effects.

5.2 *Learner Control in Acquiring Problem-Solving Skills*

In teaching modes which emphasize learner control, and allow choice of the type and sequence of instruction, a formal description of the knowledge area is again needed. In order to permit more realistic types of dialogue, the program should be able to perform a rigorous syntactic analysis of the student response and re-express this in terms which make direct links to the knowledge representation. If this can be done, then answers to student questions, for example, can be retrieved without the author anticipating and pre-storing specific enquiries. The techniques are difficult; the dialogue sequence has to be controlled and the program has to determine when initiative should pass to and be returned from the student.

For programs which teach problem-solving skills, giving a formal representation to the problem and its associated knowledge is equally difficult. The knowledge elements and operations which act on them must be clearly defined; so must heuristics and strategies which are used in problem solutions. Newell & Simon (1972) have suggested a production-system method of representing such knowledge, and demonstrated ways of collecting and analysing student's protocols. The student information which the program holds must be expressed in terms which make easy links to its formal representation of the problem. Then a suitable language interface for use by the student must be constructed. With these data structures the program can solve the problem task in general ways. Therefore the student can construct a solution, have it evaluated, and ask for help and explanations. The program can handle these general types of questions and give specific answers by using particular (stored) context information.

An example is taken from Brown et al. (1974) and Brown & Burton (1975) who have developed a program, SOPHIE, to teach fault-finding in electronic circuitry. SOPHIE works with specific prestored circuits, but the routines which control the fault diagnosis and the help which is given to students are designed to operate over a variety of electronic circuits. When the student comes to the terminal, he/she is presented with a circuit diagram and the program automatically selects and inserts a fault of some specified degree of difficulty. The student can then ask for specific circuit readings, for components to be replaced, for hypotheses to be evaluated, and for help. In this case the system suggests plausible hypotheses which are consistent with the readings the student has taken. When ready, the user can specify the nature of the fault. The system is fully operational and is an intelligent teacher in the sense that it can generate hypotheses about malfunctioning circuits, evaluate the student's hypotheses during fault-finding, and allow communication with the system in relatively unconstrained English (See Figure 4).

THE INSTRUMENT HAS A FAULT AND ITS PRESENT CON-
TROL SETTINGS ARE:
CC   1.0   (CURRENT CONTROL—FROM 0.0 (MIN) TO 1.0)
CR   HIGH   (CURRENT RANGE SWITCH, HIGH=1 AMP,
    LOW=0.1 AMP)
LOAD   20   (LOAD RESISTANCE IN OHMS)
VC   1.0   (VOLTAGE CONTROL—FROM 0.0 (MIN) TO 1.0)
VR   HIGH   (VOLTAGE RANGE SWITCH, HIGH=30 VOLTS,
    LOW=10 VOLTS)

>>**WHAT IS THE OUTPUT VOLTAGE?** *Student—refers to circuit diagram*
THE OUTPUT VOLTAGE IS 11.7 VOLTS.
>>**IS THAT VALUE CORRECT?**
IN A WORKING CIRCUIT THE OUTPUT VOLTAGE IS 19.9 VOLTS.
THAT VALUE IS INCORRECT.
>>**WHAT IS THE VOLTAGE BETWEEN R8 AND Q1?**
THE VOLTAGE AT N1 is 47.6 VOLTS.
. . . .
. . . . *Other questions are put about voltage*
. . . .
>>**WHAT IS THE VBE OF THE CURRENT LIMITING TRANSIS-TOR?**
THE BASE EMITTER VOLTAGE OF Q6 IS 0.349 VOLTS.
>>**WHAT SHOULD IT BE?**
IN A WORKING CIRCUIT THE BASE EMITTER VOLTAGE OF Q6 IS 0.593 VOLTS.
>>**REPLACE Q6**
I AM GOING TO ASK YOU SOME QUESTIONS ABOUT HOW Q6 IS FAULTED.
. . . .
. . . . *The computer questions the student showing*
. . . . *how Q6 is not faulted in that manner.*
. . . .
>>**HELP**
HERE ARE SOME FAULTS WHICH EXPLAIN THE MEASURE-MENTS YOU OBSERVED:
THE BETA OF Q3 IS LOW   *Program suggests some hypotheses*
THE BETA OF Q4 is LOW
OR R22 HAS THE WRONG RESISTANCE
>>**IS THE EMITTER CURRENT OF Q4 CORRECT?**
THE EMITTER CURRENT OF Q4 IS −61 MILLIAMPS.
IN A WORKING CIRCUIT THE EMITTER CURRENT OF Q4 IS −49 MILLIAMPS.
THAT VALUE SEEMS TO BE INCORRECT.
>>**WHAT IS THE CURRENT THRU R22?**
THE CURRENT THRU R22 IS 35 MILLIAMPS.
>>**COULD R22 BE LOW?**
IS IT OK IF I USE 25 OHMS   *Program runs simulated experiment*
FOR THE RESISTANCE OF R22?
>>**YES**
THAT FAULT IS CONSISTENT WITH ALL OF THE MEASURE-MENTS YOU HAVE MADE.

Fig. 4. A sample of a student printout taken when using the SOPHIE system.

Much of the logical and inferencing capabilities of the program are derived from using simulation models of the circuit. For example, in fault evaluation the programs modify the circuit to contain the fault suggested by the student's hypothesis. This model is run to repeat the readings gathered by the student. These values of the faulty circuit are compared with the values of the unmodified circuit, and the program decides if the readings are sufficiently close to be considered equivalent. If the hypothesis is not acceptable, the student is given the reasons for its decision. The system is also capable of generating hypotheses about faults. From output voltage measurements taken by the student, possible hypotheses are generated which are capable of explaining these measurements. Then each hypothesis is evaluated in turn by using the simulation programs in the manner outlined above. Note the interesting feature that the program answers the student after running an experiment with the program model on-line.

Although SOPHIE does not produce or store an adequate representation of student performance, it does provide a framework from which such models can be developed. The student has to use a language to request help and to state hypotheses and lines of reasoning. An examination of the printout will show the various reasoning operations which were employed and the knowledge that was used. When supplemented with individual interviews, the programs become a research tool for investigating problem-solving.

5.3 Program Designs for Teaching Medical Diagnostic Skills

A further example is taken from programs which have been designed for the learning of diagnostic skills of the sort which are encountered in Medicine. Typically, information is collected sequentially from a patient by interview, examination and medical tests, and these symptoms and signs have to be summarised so that a course of treatment can be given. Preparatory to this a diagnosis is usually made in which the patient is assigned with some probability to a limited disease set. Several simulation and tutorial programs have been written (e.g., Weber & Hagamen, 1972; Harless et al., 1971). A diagnosis program has also been developed at Leeds, and the data-base includes six diseases and some seventy attributes or symptoms. The data includes the relative frequencies of the diseases, and for each disease the probability of occurrence of each symptom state. Provided certain mathematical assumptions of independence are met, probability theorems can be used as a basis for diagnosis. In addition, anticipated questions and the patient's comments which are appropriate for each of the symptoms have to be stored. This is the underlying knowledge/data-base which is used by the teaching programs.

The program can easily restrict or expand the disease set so that suitable and individual curricula can be built up on-line for students. A plausible teaching strategy would be to start with a number of well discriminated diseases and add to them as the student improves in performance. Since material is generated by the program when it is needed by the student at the terminal, it makes economic use of computer storage resources and an unlimited number of patients is potentially available.

A second advantage is the variety of teaching modes and types of feedback which can be developed. Examples of specific diseases can be generated and printed on request, or the student can be asked to diagnose the complete case history, or be required to collect the information sequentially by conducting his interview at the terminal. Alternatively, the student can specify a disease set and symptoms. The computer replies by calculating the disease probabilities for that symptom set. By allowing the student to backtrack, and alter symptoms previously typed, their effects on the disease probabilities can be explored.

Of course, these programs have their limitations. They are specialised, can only be used in classification tasks which have probabilistic data-bases, and the effort which is needed to provide such data is considerable. There are also educational difficulties. Although the programs can use the different facilities of teaching mode, help and feedback to maximise learning, such decision rules are pragmatically stated. Also, the representation of the student is extremely limited. It consists of a record of the facilities which are used and the overall performance levels of correct diagnosis. This lack of knowledge is being remedied by studying the methods and strategies individual students use in selecting the patient information and processing it. Models, i.e., programs which distinguish between groups of students on the basis of these skills and which give significant predictions, have been developed (Woods et al., 1972). This knowledge of the student can be stored as procedures and run on the teaching tasks to test hypotheses about the likely ways he/she would perform. This information can then be used to decide on the task and type of feedback which should be given.

A more serious criticism of the diagnosis program is that it uses mathematical methods for diagnosis which the student or physician does not replicate and perhaps does not understand. Thus the dialogue is limited because the computer program cannot explain its decisions or recommendations; the student must accept or reject the mathematical conclusions. However, an interactive program, MYCIN, has been designed which uses the clinical decision rules and methods of experts. It advises physicians in selecting appropriate anti-microbial therapy for hospital patients with bacterial infections (Shortliffe et al., 1975). The aim of the program is not to teach students, but, since the system has to explain its recommendations when queried and in terms which the physician can understand, the dialogue itself is educational. The knowledge-base is a set of approximately two-hundred decision rules (if-then statements) which permit an action to be taken (e.g., a drug treatment) or a conclusion drawn if the set of pre-conditions of characteristics of organisms taken from the patient is met.

After being given some patient-data the consultation program has to select those decision rules which apply to the patient. If, during the search, a condition (i.e., a clinical variable) is not known, a subprogram attempts to find it. If it is not in the records, the user is asked to supply this data. In order to discuss the decisions which are made by the consultation program, an interactive explanation program has been developed. The initiative is taken by the physician who can ask various types of questions. For example, if, during the consultation, the program asks the user for certain data, the user can ask WHY it is necessary to obtain this. In reply the explanation program has to state its goals, and show how the current decision rule set is to be used to establish that conclusion. Thus, statements are printed which show how the data will satisfy the preconditions of those rules and so enable the conclusion to be drawn. The question WHY can be repeated during this line of reasoning so that further enquiries can be made into the subgoals. (See chapter 2 for another discussion of MYCIN).

The teaching potential of MYCIN would be increased if a similar language were devised so that the student could set out his/her own goals, lines of reasoning, and conclusions. The computer programs would need to evaluate this information, ask questions if the steps were too large or incomplete, and provide feedback. The implementation of these teaching dialogues will be difficult to achieve, but this is now being considered. Providing and using student models which can control and co-ordinate such dialogues is a distant but necessary objective. However, Self (1974) has provided a small but useful illustration and Sleeman (1978) is implementing models based on production systems which have these particular aims in mind.

Even in so-called adaptive programs, the decision rules are followed in a fixed way. Although the estimates of student's performances can be improved as more work through the material, this only enables decision rules to be applied more accurately. The programs must operate in the same way and continue to apply the same rules for a student, even if they are not proving satisfactory. In other words, the programs are not self-critical and cannot alter their teaching strategies at run time. To accomplish this, programs need to be able to make assertions which relate student performances to teaching variables in order that larger-scale goals will be attained. These might be to maximise performance objectives or to minimise time at the terminal. The programs then need to be capable of running experiments which test these assertions. This work is still in its infancy, but such a system has been implemented for teaching the solution of quadratic equations by the discovery method (O'Shea & Sleeman, 1973).

The researches of learning theorists and the techniques of Artificial Intelligence, which have been outlined in this chapter, might appear somewhat remote from practical problems of writing CAL programs which are to be used regularly by students. In these circumstances, the work of the program designer is shaped by practical considerations of computing facilities and development costs. However, the suggestions which have been made could be profitably taken into account and at least partially implemented within many of the present designs of CAL materials.

6.0 Some Conclusions

Since the early 1960's there has been an increasing commitment to developing the educational potential of the electronic computer. While most of this activity has taken place in the USA, there have been significant projects in Canada and Western Europe, and in 1972 the British Government allocated 2.5-million for a five-year National Development Programme in Computer Assisted Learning.

What has this work in CAL accomplished? It has enabled the computer to become established as a teaching instrument, and has produced a wide variety of materials which are used for day-to-day learning by a considerable (and increasing) number of students. The most comprehensive program catalogues and indexes are provided by Hickey (1968), Brigham et al. (1972), and annually by Wang (1972-78). The most interesting accounts of their application are contained in the published proceedings of annual conferences on Computers in the Undergraduate Curricula which have been held in the USA since 1969. In the UK, the large projects which were part of the National Development Programme are documented through reports (e.g., Hooper, 1977), and through specialised journal issues (e.g., British Journal of Educational Technology, 1977; Programmed Learning and Educational Technology, 1978). In general, satisfactory standards of documentation have been achieved: in the USA, CONDUIT (University of Iowa), [1] and in the UK, the Council for Educational Technology, [2] will help with the wider dissemination of material. However it is necessary to build on this experience and to maintain momentum with more experienced institutions providing inter-subject links and taking some regional responsibility for helping new participants to establish CAL techniques.

The developments outlined in this chapter have taken place in a relatively few years, so it might be considered unjust to criticise the design of materials and the lack of evaluative evidence on their efficiency. But many of the programs are simplistic and have an inadequate learning rationale.

---

[1] CONDUIT, University of Iowa, 100 LCM, Iowa City, Iowa 52242, USA.
[2] Council for Educational Technology (CET), 3 Devonshire Street, London W1B 2AA.

The techniques of developing the materials seem to have been ad hoc, so the experience is difficult to generalise. For these reasons, and to prepare for future developments, it is important to carry out research projects. To take advantage of progress in Computing, there is a need for studies into highly interactive systems in order to meet the differing processing demands of problem-solving, simulation and tutoring programs. Methods of improving educational programming languages and authoring systems need to be sought, together with designs of teaching programs which more effectively utilise graphics terminals with local storage. More detailed evaluative studies of the way learners use the materials and how differing styles of programs affect their conceptualisations are necessary, and some of this information could be gathered by using the programs already written.

At a more fundamental level, it is important to devise styles of programs which allow the students more initiative in decision-making and take on a wider range of dialogue. So the research must involve studies in Cognitive Psychology and Artificial Intelligence in order that more knowledgeable teaching programs can be designed. The response which CAL developments could make to the stimulus of such research should ensure continuing progress and increase the range and significance of its contributions to student learning.

Acknowledgments

The author acknowledges helpful discussions with colleagues in the Computer Based Learning Project, and is grateful for permission from Drs J.S. Brown and H. Morris to reproduce student printouts from their programs.

References

Abbatt, F.R. (1972). *Preliminary experience in using a computer to teach the planning of experiments in the Social Sciences.* Internal Report P1, Computer Based Learning Project, University of Leeds, Leeds 2.

Anderson, R.C., Kulhavy, R.W., & Andre, T. (1971). Feedback procedures in programed instruction, *Journal of Educational Psychology, 62*, 148-156.

Anderson, R.C., Kulhavy, R.W., & Andre, T. (1972). Conditions under which feedback facilitates learning from programed lessons, *Journal of Educational Psychology, 63*, 186-188.

Ausubel, D.P. (1968). *Educational Psychology: A Cognitive View.* Holt, Rinehart & Winston, New York.

Ayscough, P.B. (1977). CALCHEMistry. *British Journal of Educational Technology, 8*, 201-213.

Berry, P.C., Bartoli, G., Del'Aquila, C., & Spadavecchia, V (1973). *APL and insight: the use of programs to represent concepts in teaching.* IBM Bari Scientific Centre Technical Report, No. CRB-002/513-5302, Italy.

Bork, A.M. (1971). Learning to program for the Science student. *Journal of Educational Data Processing*, **8**, 5.

Bork, A.M. (1973). *Science teaching and computer languages.* Internal Report, Physics Computer Development Project, University of California, Irvine 92717.

Bork, A.M., & Robson, J. (1972). A computer simulation for the study of waves. *American Journal of Physics*, **40**, 1288-1294.

Brigham, C.R., Kemp, M., & Cross, R.J. (1972). *A Guide to Computer Assisted Instruction in the Health Sciences.* Department of Community Medicine, Rutgers Medical School, New Jersey.

Brown, J.S., Burton, R.R., & Bell, A.G. (1974). *A Sophisticated Instructional Environment for Teaching Electronic Trouble-shooting.* Report 2790, Bolt Beranek & Newman Incorporated, Cambridge, Massachusetts 02138.

Brown, J.S., & Burton, R.R. (1975). Multiple representations of knowledge for tutorial reasoning. In *Representation and Understanding* (Eds.) D.G. Bobrow & A. Collins , 311-349. Academic Press, New York.

Brown, J.S., & Rubenstein, R. (1973). *Recursive functional programming for students in the Humanities and Social Sciences.* Technical Report 27, Department of Information and Computer Science, University of California, Irvine 92717.

Daly, D.W., Dunn, W., & Hunter, J. (1977). The Computer-Assisted Learning (CAL) Project in Mathematics at the University of Glasgow. *International Journal of Mathematical Education in Science and Technology*, **8**, 145-156.

Dehner, T.R., & Norcross, B.E. (1971). The use of APL in the Undergraduate Chemistry Curricula. *Proceedings of Second Conference on Computers in the Undergraduate Curricula*, 117-129. Dartmouth College , USA.

Dirkzwager, A. (1975). Computer based testing with automatic scoring based on subjective probabilities. In *Computers in Education* (Eds.) O. Lecarme & R. Lewis, 305-311. North Holland Publishing Company.

Gagne, R.M., Mayer, J.R., Garstens, H.L., & Paradise, N.E. (1962). Factors in acquiring knowledge of a Mathematics task. *Psychological Monographs*, **526**.

Gagne, R.M., & Paradise, N.E. (1961). Abilities and learning sets in knowledge acquisition. *Psychological Monographs*, 518.

Graber, R.A., Means, R.S., & Johnsten, T.D. (1972). The effect of subsuming concepts on student achievement on unfamiliar Science learning material. *Journal of Research in Science Teaching*, **9**, 3, 277.

Harless, W.G., Drennon, G.G., Root, G.A., & Mills, G.E. (1971). CASE: A Computer Aided Simulation of the Clinical Encounter. *Journal of Medical Education*, **46**, 443.

Hartley, J.R. (1976). *NDPCAL: A Summary Report of the Applied Statistics Project.* Computer Based Learning Project, University of Leeds, Leeds 2.

Hartley, J.R., Lovell, K., & Sleeman, D.H. (1972). *The Use of the Computer as an Adaptive Teaching System.* Final Report to the Social Science Research Council. Computer Based Learning Project, University of Leeds, Leeds 2.

Hickey, A.E. (Ed). (1968). *Computer Assisted Instruction: A Survey of the Literature.* (Third edition). Entelek, New York.

Hinton, T. (1977). CAL in Physics—other approaches. *Physics Education*, **12**, 83-87.

Hooper, R. (1977). *National Development Programme in Computer Assisted Learning: Final Report of the Director.* Council for Educational Technology , London

Lyman, E.R. (1974). *PLATO Highlights.* Computer Based Education Research Laboratory, University of Illinois, Urbana 61801.

158   J.R. Hartley

Merrill, D.M. (1973). *Premises, propositions and research underlying the design of a learner controlled Computer Assisted Instruction System: A Summary of the TICCIT System.* Working Paper No. 44, Division of Instructional Sciences, Brigham Young University, Provo, Utah 84602.

Merrill, D.M., & Wood, N.D. (1974). *Instructional strategies: a preliminary taxonomy.* Mathematics Education Report. ERIC Information Analysis Center for Science, Mathematics and Environmental Education, Ohio State University, Columbus, Ohio 43210.

Murray, T.S., Cupples, R.W., Barber, J.H., Hannay, D.R., & Scott, D.D. (1976). Computer Assisted Learning in Undergraduate Medical Teaching. *The Lancet*, 1, 474-476.

Newell, A. & Simon, H.A. (1972). *Human Problem Solving.* Prentice Hall, New Jersey.

Nuthall, G.& Snook, I. (1973). Contemporary models of teaching. In *Second Handbook of Research on Teaching* (Ed.) R.M.W. Travers. Rand McNally, Chicago.

O'Neal, F. (1973). *Learner control of instruction: requirements and potential.* Technical Report No. 2, Institute for Computer Uses in Education, Brigham Young University, Provo, Utah 84602.

O'Shea, T., & Sleeman, D.H. (1973). A design for an adaptive self-improving teaching system. In *Advances in Cybernetics and Systems* (Ed.) J. Rose. Gordon and Breach, London.

Papert, S. (1971a). *Teaching children thinking.* LOGO Memo No. 2, Artificial Intelligence Laboratory, Massachusetts Institute of Technology, Cambridge, Mass, 02139.

Papert, S. (1971b). *Teaching children to be mathematicians v. teaching about mathematics.* LOGO Memo No. 4, Artificial Intelligence Laboratory, Massachusetts Institute of Technology, Cambridge, Mass. 02139.

Papert, S., & Solomon, C. (1972). Twenty things to do with a computer. *Educational Technology*, 12, 9-18.

Pask, G. (1975). *The Cybernetics of Human Learning and Performance.* Hutchinson, London.

Pask, G. (1976). Styles and strategies of learning. *British Journal of Educational Psychology*, 46, 128-148.

Pask, G., & Scott, B.C.E. (1972). Learning strategies and individual competence. *International Journal of Man-Machine Studies*, 4, 217-253.

Roos, T.B. (1973). Computer models in an introductory course in Biology. *Proceedings of the Fourth Conference on Computers in the Undergraduate Curricula*, 60-73. Claremont Colleges, USA.

Self, J.A. (1974). Student models in Computer-Aided Instruction. *International Journal of Man-Machine Studies*, 6, 2, 261-276.

Sherwood, B.A., Bennett, C., Mitchell, J. & Tenczar, C. (1971). Experience with a PLATO mechanics course. *Proceedings of the Second Conference on Computers in the Undergraduate Curricula*, 463-468. Dartmouth College, USA.

Shortliffe, E.H., Davis, R., Axline, S.G., Buchanan, B.G., Green, C., & Cohen, S.N. (1975). Computer-based consultations in clinical therapeutics: explanation and rule acquisition capabilities of the MYCIN system. *Computers and Biomedical Research*, 8, 303-319.

Skinner, B.F. (1953). *Science and Human Behaviour.* Macmillan, London.

Sleeman, D.H. (1978). *Some current topics on Intelligent Teaching Systems.* Computer Based Learning Project, University of Leeds, Leeds 2.

Smith, P. (1977). A UK project in Computer Assisted Learning in Engineering Science. *Computing and Graphics,* **2,** 151-154.

Stannard, C.R. (1972). *The use of the digital computer in Introductory General Physics.* IBM Corporation Report, GC-20-1746.

Tait, K., Hartley, J.R., & Anderson, R.C. (1973). Feedback procedures in Computer-Assisted Arithmetic Instruction. *British Journal of Educational Psychology,* **43,** 161-171.

Taylor, T.R., & Scott, B. (1975). *Emergency patient simulation program.* Internal Report, Department of Computing Science, University of Glasgow, Glasgow W2.

Wang, A. (Ed) (1978). *Index to Computer Based Learning* Instructional Media Laboratory, University of Wisconsin, Milwaukee, Wisconsin 53201.

Weber, J.C., & Hagamen, W.D. (1972). ATS: A new system for computer mediated tutorials in Medical Education. *Journal of Medical Education,* **47,** 637.

Woods, P., & Hartley, J.R. (1971). Some learning models for arithmetic tasks and their use in computer-based learning. *British Journal of Educational Psychology,* **41,** 1, 35-48.

Woods, P., Hartley, J.R., & Sleeman, D.H. (1972). Controlling the learning of diagnostic tasks. *International Journal of Man-Machine Studies,* **4,** 319-340.

Chapter 6

INFORMATION RETRIEVAL

Tom Martin

Contents

1.0 Introduction

During the 1970's a great deal has been learned about the role of computers and the role of people in many task areas. The task discussed in this chapter is that of information retrieval, i.e., the accessing of facts and records from computerized data banks. Until recently these systems were primarily designed for the specialist or professional user, but now, with the advent of widespread data networks, information utilities are being designed that will be accessed by the ordinary citizen. The chapter is devoted to an examination of experience with the specialist systems and the implication of this experience for the design of public utilities. It is divided into five parts: a discussion of the information retrieval task, criteria for assessing performance, the role of the intermediary, interactive search negotiation, and the contribution from human factors research. Throughout the discussion, relevant research findings are mentioned and topics deserving further investigation are pointed out.

2.0 The Information Retrieval Task

Perhaps the best way of thinking about information retrieval is to consider retrieval systems as communication systems. Unlike television, which is

	TASK	CODING	MESSAGE	PROCESS
TABLE LOOKUP	What is the telephone number for the Golden Bull restaurant?	The name Golden Bull serves as a relatively unique identifier	A single record --- name, address, and number --- is desired	The record retrieved is the record contributed
DOCUMENT RETRIEVAL	What reports deal with higher education in Australia?	Descriptors like universities and Australia narrow the description	A number of records --title, author, book location-- are desired	The record retrieved is the record contributed
DECISION SUPPORT	What percentage of students have grade point averages above 3.0?	The category grade point average is used to order student records	An answer is constructed from information in the record	Information from the data base is retrieved
QUESTION ANSWERING	What route do I take from my hotel to the restaurant?	Knowledge about the situation is used to determine which hotel, which restaurant, and which means of travel are implied	An answer is constructed from a map of the city	Many different types of information from multiple data bases are combined

Fig. 1. Retrieval tasks ranked by complexity.

one-to-many, or the telephone, which is one-to-one, retrieval systems are few-to-few. The contributor to a data base knows that he/she is addressing some set of people, but does not know who they are. The user suspects that in the gigantic mass of irrelevant data base records, there are a few which meet his/her interests. Both the contributor and user must share some coding scheme that allows the user to find the contributor's record.

There are many forms that the coding schemes can take, ranging from relatively unique identifiers, to predefined categories, to naturally occurring terms. In addition, records may pass from contribution to retrieval unchanged or may go through substantial conversion. A possible ranking of tasks according to complexity is shown in Figure 1.

Of all the tasks, the one that has been most intractable has been the final one. Artificial intelligence researchers have developed vast numbers of data representations for capturing and storing knowledge about the world so that questions posed in close-to-natural language can be answered (Winograd, 1972; Norman et al., 1975; Schank & Colby, 1973; Waltz, 1978). They have discovered even in the most limited domains that the quantities of information necessary for answering questions are vast and that putting this information into data bases is intellectually uninteresting. It is hard to anticipate the variety of ways in which things can be said or implied. The full power of context, goals, and assumptions has to be brought to bear upon the task of deducing what is being asked and why. The more well-structured the topic, the easier it is for meaningful retrieval to take place.

The query in Figure 1 about student grades is an example of a well-structured task. The categories of information (grades, students, classes) are known beforehand so data can be gathered and organized in advance. These systems have been called decision support systems, management information systems, and data base management systems. Users typically are expected to express categories, values, and relationships in formal notation rather than in natural language. Items entered into the data base are also specified using category names and values. As items are entered they can be split up and merged with other items so that storage responds to query patterns rather than contribution patterns. Decision support systems are successful to the extent that the structure inherent in the system matches the structure inherent in the minds of users (Stabell, 1975).

Document retrieval systems require less shared understanding. There are few categories, and relationships are limited to co-occurence and sometimes word proximity. Users specify sets of words or phrases that characterize concepts. Concepts can be combined or intersected. The query in Figure 2 about higher education illustrates both combining (universities, colleges, higher education) and intersecting (in Australia). Yet words and phrases often have multiple meanings, and can lead to lack of communication. For example, a person interested in how nurses deal with patients from other cultures is likely to find out that in most medical data bases, culture means tissue growth in the laboratory. Correspondingly, in a data base about constitutional law, one may find nothing about citizenship because all contributions talk about nationality (see Lancaster & Fayen, 1973).

The most simple type of retrieval is table lookup. Since identifiers are relatively unique and single items require no specification of relationships, the potential for misunderstanding is minimized. It is likely that initially most data bases offered for public use will be of this form.

In the information retrieval literature there has been a tendency not to distinguish between the various types of retrieval, and this has led to great confusion. We shall primarily discuss document retrieval because a great

```
Adapted from Battelle Memorial Institute's
BASIS System and the ERIC (Educational
Resources Information Clearinghouse)
Data Base

ENTER NAME OF DATA BASE TO BE SEARCHED
    /eric
ENTER  YOU  SEARCH  REQUEST  (ONE TERM AT A TIME)
    1/higher education
        12156 ITEMS
    2/university
        8856 ITEMS
    3/college
        11856 ITEMS
    4/ (1 or 2 or 3)
        19181 ITEMS
    5/australia
        758 ITEMS
    6/ (4 and 5)
        149 ITEMS
    7/ (display 6)

THE DATA ELEMENTS FOR  THE ERIC DATA BASE  ARE
    1-ERIC NUMBER
    2-AUTHOR (S)
    3-TITLE
    4-BIBLIOGRAPHIC DATA
    5-INDEX TERMS

ENTER ELEMENT NUMBERS SEPARATED BY COMMAS OR ALL
    /1,2,3
ITEMS FOR THE ERIC DATA BASE ARE
    ITEM 1
        ED 202 321
        AU: W.R.  RAITHE
        TI: QUEEN'S COLLEGE IN THE OUTBACK
    ITEM  2 ...
```

Fig. 2. A typical Query adapted from Battelle Memorial Institute's BASIS System and the ERIC (Educational Resources Information Clearinghouse) Data Base.

deal of work has been done both in implementing systems and in carrying on research regarding their human computer interfaces. Major systems like Lockheed's DIALOG, the National Library of Medicine's ELHILL, the Mead Corporation's LEXIS, the BRS system, and System Development Corporation's ORBIT in combination contain more than one hundred data bases involving tens of millions of documents and/or citations used by thousands of researchers around the world (see Figure 3). These systems have caught on because they can easily store computer-readable versions of existing data bases and can be used by librarians who have previously carried out manual searches. The systems are viewed by specialists as fast, not too expensive, and as good or better than manual searching (Wanger et al., 1976). In terms of the criteria that Rogers & Shoemaker (1971) identify as indicators of successful innovations, document retrieval systems are clearly compatible with existing practices, are trialable, and have perceived utility.

3.0 Criteria for Assessing Performance

The way in which performance is assessed varies depending upon the

MEDICAL
   MEDLINE (BRS and Nat'l Lib of Med only)
   Pharmaceutical News Index
   TOXLINE (BRS and Nat'l Lib of Med only)

EDUCATIONAL
   Dissertation Index
   ERIC

SCIENTIFIC
   Biological Abstracts
   Chemical Abstracts
   INSPEC (Physics)

BUSINESS
   INFORM (Business Information)
   Management Contents
   Information Bank (N.Y. Times only)

LEGAL
   Supreme Court Reports
   Tax Court Reports
   N.Y. Reports
   California Reports

GOVERNMENTAL
   Government Reports Announcements
   Pollution Abstracts
   Environmental Abstracts
   (Lockheed and SPC only)

   AGRICOLA (Agriculture)
   COMPENDEX (Engineering)
   Science Citation Index (Lockheed only)

Fig. 3. Representative Data Bases that can be accessed by a designated retrieval system or by the Lockheed, System Development Corporation, and Bibliographic Retrieval Systems.

nature of the task. For example, with table lookup one is primarily concerned with how long it takes to locate the desired item (or to determine that it is not in the table). With question answering systems, where the potential for misunderstanding is great, the most common criterion is whether or not the question was answered correctly. In the case of document retrieval systems, the traditional criteria for assessing performance have been recall and precision, often lumped together under the more general term relevance. Assuming that each document in a collection can be rated as relevant or not with respect to a query, recall is the percentage of all relevant documents retrieved, while precision is the percentage of retrieved documents that are relevant. For many years information scientists have used these concepts (see Saracevic, 1975) for a definitive discussion of relevance. Salton (1971) in a number of studies has shown the relationship between various information retrieval system characteristics and relevance. In particular, he has shown that feedback from the user regarding documents retrieved can be used to revise the query and, thereby, improve retrieval. No operational retrieval systems take advantage of relevance feedback. The reason is not that it is impossible to incorporate relevance feedback into existing systems, for Williams (1971) has shown how this can be done; the problem is that to do so would significantly increase the cost of searching. Cooper (1973) has suggested that recall and precision are only one aspect of overall retrieval system performance. What appears more critical is benefit/cost. Many users would rather have an inexpensive, fairly reliable search than an expensive, more reliable one. Cost involves more than charges; it includes delay, inconvenience, and investment of mental effort. One of the major benefits of interactive retrieval is that one can get results within minutes instead of waiting for days for batch retrieval results to return in the mail. The advent of interactive retrieval and the need to charge for searching has made charges and time considerations more salient than recall and precision considerations. Users tend to be quite satisfied with results even though recall is low.

In the first half of the 1970's, as retrieval systems have shifted from being prototypes to being large-scale operational networks, tremendous effort has gone into increasing the size and numbers of data bases, and the numbers of users who can be served. From the point of view of the user, availability has increased while costs have gone down. Quality of searching has most likely not increased. As costs of storage and processing continue to drop, it will be interesting to see whether any attempt is made to enhance the quality of searching.

4.0 The Role of the Intermediary

When retrieval systems were being developed, it was assumed that end users would search for themselves. This has not happened in practice. Over seventy-five percent of all searches carried out as of 1975, were carried out by information specialists (Wanger et al., 1976). Once again cost may be of primary concern. An end user is unlikely to purchase a terminal, subscribe to a search service, and go through training unless he is a frequent searcher. Statistics indicate that most end users need searching done less than once a month (Carmon, 1975). By aggregating usage, it is possible to spread fixed costs and the cost of training intermediaries over many users. Users interact with an information specialist who develops a profile, and who then, usually alone but occasionally with the end user, interacts with the search service. Barber et al. (1973) have shown that when end user and searcher work together, recall and precision are enhanced.

Early blindness to the fact that online searching would become a specialization led to many adverse consequences. Little or no effort was made to develop job descriptions laying out necessary skills. Training of intermediaries came as an after-thought rather than as a central system component. Yet Bailey et al. (1973) point out that personnel factors typically account for fifty percent of reliability problems in computer-based information systems. Nearly half of all searchers in 1975 had had no formal training in computerized searching (Wanger et al., 1976). Since the great majority of searchers come from library schools, it is likely that pressure will be applied to library schools to train their students for interactive searching. In the early stages of system usage, managers felt the productivity of employees was improved by computerized searching and employees felt the searching was new and fun, but with the passage of time, both are likely to demand systematic training.

Perhaps one reason why human-computer researchers and designers felt that end users would search for themselves was that they tended to view the task as one of human-computer communication. Instead the task is one of utilizing data bases and the searching aids associated with those data bases. The typical information specialist uses from three to ten data bases covering topics as diverse as chemistry, engineering, medicine, education, and government publications. Learning how to use the document retrieval system is easy compared to learning how to effectively use some data bases. For example, a few data bases have controlled indexing vocabularies requiring use of exact terminology, while others rely upon terms in abstracts, leaving it to the searcher to request all imaginable variants. For each data base the searcher must learn the indexing policy, whether or not to search for strings of words in text, the coverage of topics and currency of the data base, and the relative availability of documents once retrieved. Data base suppliers are now heavily engaged in training intermediaries.

While the discussion has focused on training, the need has been for continuing support. About seventy percent of all searchers rate telephone contact with online retrieval system suppliers as essential (Wanger et al., 1976). The ability to send messages online to the supplier is rated as important by over half of the searchers. Recently, user forums have emerged in various localities so that intermediaries can swap experiences and essentially support each other. It would be interesting to know the extent to which contact with fellow searchers is related to job satisfaction and effective searching.

5.0 Interactive Search Negotiation

When considering usage of interactive computer systems in general, one of the apparent paradoxes has been that users do not think creatively at the terminal (see Sackman, 1969). Instead, the interactive system is used like a fast batch system. When considering interactive searching, the same pattern has emerged. Intermediaries are trained to work out the searching decisions before sitting down at the terminal. This involves explaining costs and other administrative policies to the end user; attempting to clarify the nature of the question and literature needed; choosing data bases that might contain relevant documents; determining which terms and searching techniques are appropriate with each data base; explaining indexing policies, holdings, and data base coverage to the user; typing the selected vocabulary together with connectors that are appropriate for the query, determining how far back to search; and deciding when to go to the terminal. Carmon (1975) found that transitions among these steps vary from user to user, with intermediaries providing instruction or personal support for new or unsure users.

While a great deal of preparation takes place away from the terminal, it is not correct to say that the interaction at the terminal is equivalent to straight data entry. The online system provides feedback at every stage and searchers find this quite valuable. For example, when selecting or entering search vocabulary, the searcher is informed of the number of hits for each term. The searcher then is likely to add synonyms or variations for each term until the count is large enough. When combining terms with logical AND's and OR's, hit counts are given for the results. If the hit count is too high, additional restrictions are likely to be imposed on the search, and if the count is too low, restrictions are likely to be removed. Before printing search results offline, the searcher is likely to look at a few items to see if they look right. This may suggest negative restrictions and/or additional search terms. Thus, preparation for searching establishes the basic profile until the desired number of apparently relevant items have been located.

Penniman (1975) monitored usage of the Battelle Memorial Institute's BASIS system for a wide range of searchers and data bases. The most heavily used data base during the study was the Transportation Research Information Service operated by the U.S. Department of Transportation containing over 20,000 records of transportation research and development. It was accessed by government, industrial, and university researchers. He started out grouping commands into eleven categories, but upon examining data found that three categories—selecting search terms, combining terms with logical connectors, and displaying results online—accounted on the average for 46%, 18%, and 14% of all commands used. Average transition probabilities from these states to other states were as shown in Figure 4. What is important to note is the strong tendency to revert to selecting new terms.

Penniman's categories combine use of many different command language features. For example, selecting terms may involve entering word stems, entering data element delimiters, viewing alphabetically adjacent terms, or viewing semantically related terms—all of which Wanger found most (40% or more) searchers rated as very useful. Martin (1974) compared commands across eleven different interactive retrieval systems and found not only a great deal of commonality but also over fifty distinct features. Of these some of the most important were availability of a users guide, live help, suffix

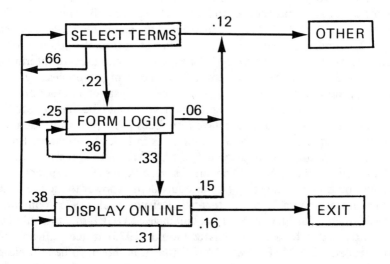

Fig. 4. Probabilities (as found by Penniman, 1975) of transition from three search categories. (Figure 2 illustrates one example of the use of these commands).

removal, control over category to be searched, vocabulary access, relational operators, boolean operators, request fragment numbering, ability to review request fragments, predefined display formats, ability to format online, and printing offline. The commonality was functional rather than syntactic, with lack of agreement even regarding the use of logical connectors.

One of the challenges for human-computer researchers is to assess the impact of system diversity brought on by market place competition. Wanger found that a majority of users believed that dealing with more than one system was sometimes confusing, but neither insurmountable nor efficiency-degrading. The three greatest difficulties were relating capabilities or features with the correct system, remembering the proper procedures for issuing print instructions, and remembering the proper procedures for entering searches.

One approach to reducing cross-system confusion is to design pre-processors that take commands in a single language and re-express them to each system in its own language. Marcus et al. (1977) at M.I.T. have proceeded to develop such a pre-processor. It has taken a number of years and has necessitated the development of extensive translation rules. Perhaps it will be easier to train intermediaries in the use of multiple systems than it will be to program computers to carry out the translation. Anderson & Gillogly (1976) have developed a fairly natural language for instructing a pre-processor about procedures to follow. Using a rule-directed interactive transaction agent (RITA), it can be instructed to call up the retrieval system overnight, connect to the data base and carry out the search without further human interventions. It remains to be seen whether end users or intermediaries will find that the benefits outweigh the costs of pre-processing.

It is appropriate that at this point in the analysis of interaction at a terminal the issue of language representation should be raised. Studies involving different command language interfaces for carrying out identical decision support tasks have shown differences in task performance. Boyce et al. (1974) developed a language called SQUARE for expressing queries involving relational data bases. The queries were expressed in a superscript/subscript notation that they argued was equivalent in power to the predicate calculus and considerably easier to read. Reisner et al. (1975) compared SQUARE to an equivalent procedural language SEQUEL that proved to be significantly easier to use. Thomas & Gould (1975) tested still another method called QUERY BY EXAMPLE that was shown to be still easier to use than SEQUEL. It is similar to filling out a form. McDonald (1975) has developed still another method called CUPID that relies upon putting together components of a diagram and it also is easier to use than SEQUEL and preferred by most users. To illustrate the various query formats, if the query is to "Find the names of those employees who work for departments located in Stockton," and there are two data bases, one containing names and department numbers for employees, and the other containing department numbers and locations for departments, then the query would look as shown in Figure 5.

None of these comparisons of languages appears to be scientifically rigorous. Proper procedures would involve randomly assigning subjects to one of the four languages to receive training and to carry out a large set of tasks. The variations in the languages may make one or another easy to learn, but hard to use rapidly. One would prefer to have information about learning effort involved, and error, time, and motivation measures *after* mastery over the language had been acquired.

Research of this nature is quite important in the long run, for it will have an impact on the types of systems that will be designed for intelligent terminal pre-processors. Currently, the issue is unimportant because overloaded systems and low data rate channels make interaction slow regardless of the command language representation. The issue may always be unimportant with respect to bibliographic data bases because only the simplest types of relationships are needed for document retrieval. However, in the future, users may be able to select formats for representing queries to

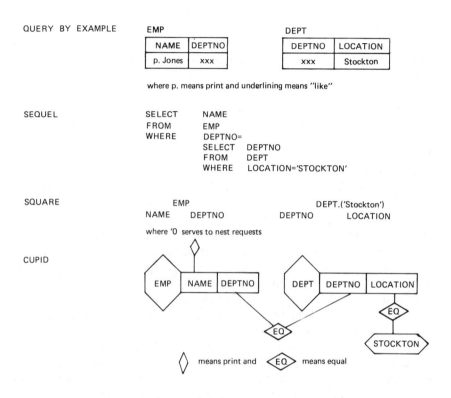

Fig. 5. Alternate ways of requesting "Print names of employees whose departments are in Stockton" in four different languages.

relational data bases just as they now select formats for printing search results.

6.0 The Contribution from Human Factors Research

In the development of existing information retrieval systems, human factors considerations have played a role. Katter (1970) studiously reviewed the literature regarding user acceptance factors before designing ORBIT. He adopted a number of ideas including one that there should be a clear indication to the user when the system was awaiting input. He also decided that there should be verbose, normal, and terse command modes under the user's control. Lockheed's DIALOG system was pretested at Stanford and was modified to reflect user reactions (Timbie & Coombs, 1969). One modification was to automatically number lines of search logic by mentioning the line number (Summit, 1971). At M.I.T. the Intrex project team gathered and published the results of experiments with online searching (Marcus et al., 1971). Systems at Stanford (Martin & Parker, 1971; Thompson, 1971), and at I.B.M. (McAllister & Bell, 1971) referenced either human factors findings or else indicated how user input might help shape system design. Designers, information scientists, and social scientists got together to discuss the human-computer interface (Walker, 1971) while systems were still in their infancy. For an excellent summary of this period, see Bennet (1972).

Since that time the human factors contribution has been present but has not materially altered system design. Treu (1972) proposed a transparent monitor-stimulator that could be used to try out alternate interfaces and to gather usage data. Martin et al. (1973) indicated how features common to many systems related to human factors needs. Some of the needs responded to by systems involved (a) allowing searchers to rely on recognition rather than recall vocabulary (via search vocabulary displays), (b) allowing parts to be developed and put together into a large whole (via logic segment numbering), (c) allowing users with different degrees of experience to interact successfully via verbose or terse modes, and (d) allowing for multimedia training and support via manuals and human trouble-shooters. Bennet (1975) highlighted the need for training and for human support, i.e. an integrating agent, during the system adoption process. Other studies have been mentioned throughout the chapter. The reason the studies have not altered system design is that through good relations with users, vendors have both shaped their users and been shaped by them. The systems and expectations are now well formed, and outside research is likely to have little effect.

In the future human factors research is likely to have its biggest impact in new application areas where expectations are still being shaped. The lessons learned from the document retrieval history should be applied, namely:

- The tasks that will be most successfully automated are those well defined tasks where automation offers a clear benefit, the new way of conducting the task is compatible with the old way, and where the solution is visible and trialable;
- The criteria for assessing performance are more likely to involve reduced cost or more rapid turnabout rather than wholly new results or improved quality;
- The system is likely to spawn new or improved jobs requiring training and support;

- The creative portion of the task is likely to be done away from the terminal with refinements added at the terminal;
- Behavior at the terminal is likely to follow no set pattern and users are likely to find system incompatibilities a nuisance but manageable;
- The system must interface with all types of users, terminals, and data bases; and
- If all goes well, users will not be concerned with the human-computer interface.

7.0 Conclusion

Now that public information utilities like the British Prestel (formerly Viewdata) and Japanese CCIS (coaxial cable information system) are being developed, it is useful to consider the experience gained with the document retrieval systems. The promise that bench scientists would do their own searching never proved true. Is it likely that the public will also delegate their searching? Searching in these systems is carried out by branching through a hierarchical tree of pages (by punching buttons on a ten button keypad) until the right page is located. Admittedly, the types of table lookup tasks for which the systems will be used initially are not difficult. People can easily transfer skills acquired using catalogs, telephone directories, and library catalogs. There will be a definite advantage to searching at home, and the technologies—telephone and television sets—are quite familiar. However, as data bases grow in size, it will become harder to locate specific items. Just as people get disoriented in a new city they are likely to get lost in the hundreds of interconnected pages. Demand is likely to increase for ways to search for generic categories of information, such as which furniture stores carry love seats. Simple interfaces lacking capability for intersecting and combining categories may make searching in large data bases quite difficult. Waiting to assist the public will be specialists like travel agents, real estate agents, insurance agents, investment counselors, and tax advisers. They, and a new breed of specialists, may find it profitable to help the public deal with complex questions which occur infrequently in a person's life. However, for simple everyday tasks like locating a restaurant, finding out weather conditions, or checking grocery prices, the public may become used to do-it-yourself searching.

References

Andersen, R.H. & Gillogly, J.J. (1976). The Rand Intelligent Terminal Agent (RI-TA) as a Network Access Aid. *National Computer Conference Proceedings*, AFIPS Press, Montvale, New Jersey. 501-505.

174   T. Martin

Bailey, R.W., Demers, S.T., & Lebowitz, A.I. (1973). Human Reliability in Computer-Based Business Information Systems. *IEEE Transactions on Reliability*, **R-22**, 3, 140-148.

Barber, A.S., Barraclough, E.D., Gray, W.A. (1973). Online Information Retrieval as a Scientist's Tool. *Information Storage and Retrieval* 9, 9, 429-440.

Bennett, J.L. (1972). The User Interface in Interactive Systems. In *Annual Review of Information Science and Technology*, 7, 159-196, American Society for Information Science, Washington, D. C.

Boyce, R.F., Chamberlin, D.D., Hammer, M.M., & King, W.F. (1974). Specifying Queries as Relational Expressions. In *Proceedings of the ACM SIGPLAN-SIGIR Interface Meeting: Programming Languages—Information Retrieval* (Ed.) R. Nance. 31-38, Association for Computing Machinery, New York.

Carmon, J.L. (1975). *Modelling the User Interface for a Multidisciplinary Bibliographic Information Network*. Georgia University (PB 242-964)

Coles, L.A. (1972). *Techniques for Information Retrieval Using an Inferential Question-Answering System with Natural-Language Input*. Stanford Research Institute, Menlo Park, California. (PB 228 182).

Cooper, W.S. (1973). On Selecting a Measure of Retrieval Effectiveness, Part 1. *Journal of the American Society for Information Science*, **24**, 2, 87-100.

Katter, R.V. (1970). *On-Line User of Remote-Access Citation Retrieval Services*. System Development Corporation, Santa Monica, California. TM (L)-4494/000/00.

Lancaster, F.W. & Fayen, E.G. (1973). *Information Retrieval On-Line*. Wiley-Interscience, New York.

McAllister, C. & Bell, J.M. (1971). Human Factors in the Design of an Interactive Library System. *Journal of the American Society for Information Science*, **22**, 2, 96-104.

McDonald, N.H. (1975). *CUPID: A Graphics Oriented Facility for Support of Non-Programmer Interactions with a Data Base*. Ph.D. Dissertation, University of California at Berkeley.

Marcus, R.S., Benenfeld, A.R., Kugel, P. (1971). The User Interface for the IN-TREX Retrieval System. In *Interactive Bibliographic Search: the User/Computer Interface* (Ed.) D. Walker. AFIPS Press, Montvale, New Jersey.

Marcus, R.S., Reintjes, J.F. (1977). *Computer Interfaces for Access to Heterogeneous Information-Retrieval Systems*. M.I.T. Electronic Systems Laboratory (ESL-R-739).

Martin, T.H. (1974). *A Feature Analysis of Interactive Information Retrieval Systems*. Stanford University, Institute for Communication Research (PB-235-952)

Martin, T.H. & Parker, E.B. (1971). Designing for User Acceptance of an Interactive Bibliographic Search Facility. In *Interactive Bibliographic Search: User/Computer Interface*. D. Walker (Ed.) AFIPS Press, Montvale, New Jersey.

Martin, T.H., Carlisle, J.H., & Treu, S. (1973) The User Interface for Interactive Bibliographic Searching: An Analysis of the Attitudes of Nineteen Information Scientists. *Journal of the American Society for Information Science*, **24**, 2, 142-147.

Norman, D.A. & Rumelhart, D.E. (1975). *Explorations in Cognition*. W.H. Freeman & Co., San Francisco.

Penniman, W.D. (1975). *Rhythms of Dialogue in Human-Computer Conversation*. Ph.D. Dissertation, Ohio State University.

Reisner, P., Boyce, R.F., & ChamberlinN, D.D. (1975). Human Factors Evaluation of Two Data Base Query Languages—Square and Sequel. *National Computer Conference Proceedings*, AFIPS Press,Montvale, New Jersey. 447-452.

Rogers, E.M. & Shoemaker, F.F. (1971). *Communication of Innovations*. The Free Press, New York.

Sackman, H. (1970). *Man-Computer Problem Solving: Experimental Evaluation of Time-Sharing and Batch Processing*. Auerbach, New York. Publishers.

Salton, G. (1971). *The Smart Retrieval System: Experiments in Automatic Document Processing*. Prentice-Hall, New Jersey.

Saracevic, T. (1975). Relevance: A Review of and a Framework for the Thinking on the Notion in Information Science. *Journal of the American Society for Information Science*, **26**, 6, 321-343.

Schank R.C. & Colby, K.M. (1973). *Computer Models of Thought and Language*. W.H. Freeman & Co., San Francisco.

Stabell, C.B. (1975). *Individual Differences in Managerial Decision Making Processes: A Study of Conversational Computer System Usage*. Ph.D. Dissertation, Sloan School of Management, M.I.T.

Summitt R.K. (1971). Dialog and the User: An Evaluation of the User Interface with a Major Online Retrieval System. In *Interactive Bibliographic Search: the User/Computer Interface* (Ed.) D. Walker. AFIPS Press, Montvale, New Jersey.

Thomas, J.C. & Gould, J.D. (1975). A Psychological Study of Query by Example. *National Computer Conference Proceedings* AFIPS Press, Montvale, New Jersey. 439-446.

Thompson, D.A. (1971). Interface Design for an Interactive Retrieval System: a Literature Survey and a Research Description. *Journal of the American Society for Information Science*, **22**, 6, 363-373.

Timbie, M. & Coombs, D.H. (1969). *An Interactive Information Retrieval System: Case Studies on the Use of DIALOG to search the ERIC Document File*. Stanford University (ED 034 431).

Treu, S. (1972). *A Computer Terminal Network for Transparent Stimulation of the User of an Online Retrieval System*. National Bureau of Standards, Washington, D.C.. (Technical Note 732).

Walker, D.E. (1971). *Interactive Bibliographic Search: the User/Computer Interface*. AFIPS Press, Montvale, New Jersey.

Waltz, D.L. (1978). An English Language Question Answering System for a Large Relational Database. *Communications of the Association of Computing Machinery*, **21**, 7, 526-539

Wanger, J., Cuadra C., & Fishbein, M. (1976). *Impact of Online Retrieval Services: A Survey of Users, 1974-1975*. System Development Corporation, Santa Monica, California.

Williams, J.H. (1971). Functions of a Man-machine Interactive Information Retrieval System. *Journal of the American Society for Information Science*, **22**, 5, 311-317.

Winograd, T. (1972). *Understanding Natural Language*. Academic Press, New York.

Woods, W.A., Kaplan, R.M., Nash-Webber, B. (1972). *The Lunar Sciences Natural Language Information System* Bolt, Beranek and Newman, Inc., Cambridge, Mass. (BBN 2378).

Chapter 7

THE IMPACT OF COMPUTERS ON PLANNING AND DECISION-MAKING

Michael Scott Morton & Sidney Huff

Contents

1.0 Background

This chapter is concerned with the impact of computers on the planning process in business organizations. Substantial effort has been directed over the past few years toward bringing computer techniques to bear on organizational planning systems. Unfortunately, planners and computer system designers have encountered myriad difficulties in this work, stemming in part from the undeniable complexity of the planning process itself, and partly from a lack of effective computer-based tools and techniques for assisting managers in their planning activities. Early attempts to "solve" the planning problem, using computers to implement simulation models, discounted cash flow analyses, and the like, generally fell short of the mark. More recently, decision support approaches have been used successfully to turn computers into more effective planning tools. The central focus of this chapter is this widening spectrum of effective computer-based planning techniques.

We begin with an overview of recent trends in the use of computers in organizations. Then we narrow our attention to discuss the organizational planning process and the use of computer-based methods to support that process. Finally, we conclude with a brief case study of a computer-assisted planning system that illustrates many of the concepts discussed.

2.0 Computers In Organizations

The use of computers in organizations around the world has grown to the point where a great many social, business, and government functions are heavily dependent on it. To get a flavor for the extent of this dependence, we need only consider the fact that the order to reduce power consumption in Japan during the 1974 energy crisis specifically exempted computers! Given this widespread dependence on computers and data processing functions, one might imagine that their presence and impact would be felt at all levels of organizations today, from president or director to secretary or file clerk. This is far from the case.

Most organizational computer usage falls into one of three categories. First is information handling, or using the computer to transmit and process information in a variety of ways. Second is transaction processing, where the computer is used much like a machine on the factory floor, to gather, transmit, store and retrieve the detailed transaction data of the organization. The third area is data-base applications, where computers are used (often as extensions of the transaction processing applications) to maintain and access various data files. All of these application areas are basically aimed at clerical replacement: the computer is used either because it is a very fast arithmetic device, or because it is an extremely efficient file cabinet. Applications such as these are frequently referred to as Management Information Systems (MIS).

Generally these applications have been worthwhile. It is even difficult to imagine how certain industries—for example, the airline industry—could function today without computers. However, in nearly all these cases the primary thrust has been improving organizational *efficiency*, through performing very well structured, well understood tasks faster and at lower cost. More and more today, computing departments are becoming concerned with the *effectiveness*, as well as the efficiency, of the services they provide. This change is much more than a play on words; it represents a major process of re-thinking the priorities, goals, capabilities and limitations of computers in organizations. To make the difference clearer, we could easily imagine a computer center that is extremely efficient, one which manages to produce more pounds of printed reports per dollar than any other computer center known. If it happens that every manager in the firm keeps a standing order with his or her secretary to deposit the reports directly into the wastepaper basket, we would conclude that the computer center is not very effective. Efficiency, the engineering concept, is high, but the computer center is not meeting the needs of the organization, and hence is totally ineffective. [1]

In addition to well-structured, efficiency oriented applications, we are beginning to witness the use of computers in a different form, namely, to

[1] This shift to effectiveness is discussed in greater depth in (Scott Morton, 1975).

assist (as opposed to replace) managers in their decision-making activity with respect to less well structured, or fuzzy problems. Such problems possess sufficient structure that computer techniques and analytical methods may be of significant value, but managerial judgment is also *essential*. Neither the manager nor the computer can do as effective a job as the two together. We have come to call these types of applications Decision Support Systems, or DSS.

It turns out that the nature of computer technology, and the design and implementation process, required for Decision Support Systems is quite different from that required for classical management information systems. These differences, while interesting in their own right, are taken up elsewhere (McCosh and Scott Morton, 1978) and will not be discussed in detail here. However, in order to informally convey a feeling for the differences between MIS and DSS (somewhat more formal distinctions are given shortly) consider a simple analogy with games. The game called tic-tac-toe (sometimes called "noughts and crosses") is a well-structured one. Specifically, rules can be defined that permit computers to play humans or other computers with completely predictable results. In fact, it is a fairly straightforward task to write a computer program that will at worst draw against any opponent.

Now, consider the game of checkers (called "draughts" in some countries). While this game has fairly simple rules and a finite number of possible states, it possesses less structure than tic-tac-toe. Indeed, there are many successful checkers-playing computer programs, one of which managed to win the Connecticut state checkers championship. However, these programs do not solve the checkers problem—this would require prediction of the *optimum* move at each turn—but rather employ heuristics, or rules of thumb, similar to those used by the best human checkers players. Since the heuristics themselves are generally fairly simple, it is the computer's tremendous information storage and manipulation capabilities that occasionally allow it to "beat the master at his own game".

Finally, consider the game of chess. The heuristics-based approach described above has also been followed in the construction of chess-playing computer programs. Many of these programs are now at the stage where they can do a good job during the opening moves because of the computer's information retrieval capacity (a large number of textbook opening sequences can be stored), and during the end-game because with reduced dimensionality they can exhaustively calculate all possible moves many steps ahead. However, in the mid-game, chess-playing programs are not yet able to come close to matching the best players. The heuristics used by chess masters are much more complex and difficult to capture than those in checkers. Put differently, chess is inherently a less structured game than checkers. Also, the high level of dimensionality in chess, especially during mid-game play, precludes exhaustive search techniques for more than a few moves ahead. We expect that chess-playing programs rivalling the best human players are likely to make very slow improvements during the foreseeable future.

In developing this analogy, we have cast it in terms of human-against-machine. However, suppose we re-cast it by considering the possibility of a human chess player being provided with computer support and the goal of improving his game. This support might take the form of one of the currently successful chess-playing programs (see Levy, 1976), converted so as to be able to respond to queries concerning the implications of various moves. In this case the human chess player could use his mental powers of pattern recognition, together with the computer's capability for exploring a few options in great depth, resulting in a more powerful chess-playing system than either computer or human taken separately. This is exactly the objective of Decision Support Systems: to improve a given decision-maker's ability to deal with semi-structured problems by judiciously coupling human skill and judgement with the data manipulation and numerical power of computer systems, but *not* to replace the decision maker altogether with a computer system that would make the decision for him. This objective is much easier to state than to actually achieve, but recent technological improvements, plus the results of both commercial and academic work, have shown that the Decision Support System concept is both practicable and very powerful (Keen and Scott Morton, 1978).

Organizational planning is one area where the use of such systems has been investigated. Planning is an information intensive activity. Evidently, if formal planning is to be undertaken at all, some mechanism is necessary to support the information requirements. We take as a point of departure for what follows *a three-way distinction* among various approaches for meeting these needs for information gathering, storage, analysis, and display. The three classes of mechanisms are: (1) manual, (2) Management Information Systems (MIS), and (3) Decision Support Systems (DSS).

The first of these encompasses all non-computer methods of formal information handling, including such things as clerical assistance, libraries, other organized repositories of hard-copy material, and many types of informal information handling activities (talking to people, going to committee meetings, reading newspapers, and, of course, thinking).

MIS and DSS are both types of computer-based support. We can expand on the earlier informally stated differences between MIS and DSS as follows:

- DSS's are oriented toward supporting a manager in some decision-oriented process, but not replacing him; the "system" very much includes both the computer and the manager. MIS's tend to be more independent of particular managers and decision processes. Also, DSS's by definition are constructed with a particular type of decision clearly in mind; MIS's generally are less closely connected with specific decisions, but tend to deal with functions.

- DSS's serve to bring computer support to semi-structured tasks—tasks such that portions of the required analysis have sufficient potential for systematization for the computer to be of value, but where the insight and judgement of a manager is also essential. MIS's on the other hand, have been developed and employed in task environments possessing a sufficiently high degree of structure that human insight and judgement are not required (e.g., payroll, inventory control).
- DSS-supported problem solving is essentially inter-active, and is dependent for much of its power and usefulness on a capability for dialogue between a manager and the computer. Problem exploration is accomplished through a synergism of the intuition, experience and insight of the manager, with the analytical and data-handling power of a computer. MIS's by contrast, are generally not interactive in operation and do not seek the extent of human-machine synergism described above. (Keen and Scott Morton, 1978.)

Of course, to some extent these are distinctions that are less than totally clear in practice; there is some middle ground. We have found that these distinctions are meaningful to many managers and computer system designers however, and they allow us to provide some useful differentiations in what follows without becoming bogged down in specifics of design or implementation detail. Also, the above distinctions are intended to be free of value judgement. We do not mean to imply that DSS's are good, while MIS's or manual methods are bad; such would certainly be naive. Nonetheless, as we said earlier, the DSS approach has been exploited very little compared to other modes of computer support. DSS's have much potential for improving analysis and decision-making in unstructured problem environments such as that of organizational planning, and a substantial share of the discussion to follow focuses on this as yet largely unfulfilled potential (some recent efforts are described in Carlson, 1977).

3.0 Corporate Planning

Formal planning in corporations is a relatively young, evolving field. Nonetheless, we can already distinguish some clear patterns of usage, and change, in American corporations over the past fifteen years.

One of the earliest acknowledged authorities in the field of corporate planning was George Steiner. His philosophy, which was widely adopted in the fifties and early sixties, was that planning should be functionally organized and carried out. That is, one should lay out corporate plans on a functional basis, developing plans for production, marketing, finance, etc., and that these plans, taken together, represent a plan for the organization. This approach is developed in depth in his widely read book, *Top Management Planning* (Steiner, 1969).

As the world changed, the goals of the planning function within organizations have shifted, and Steiner's approach has lost some of its early popularity. The greater complexity and scope of crucial organizational issues today means these issues are less likely to come neatly packaged in a functional format. Nonetheless, a number of firms still use Steiner's basic approach as their guideline for planning.

A second discernible trend has been bottom-up planning, espoused in particular by the Stanford Research Institute. The bottom-up philosophy suggests that planning should begin at the lowest levels of the organization. Successive levels of consolidation cause the plan to bubble its way up the organization (with possible intermediate cycles back through lower levels), eventually to be presented as a unified package to senior management.

The first significant attempts to use computers in the planning process followed a bottom-up approach. The timing was right, since computers first "caught hold" in many organizations when bottom-up planning was in vogue. Also, bottom-up planning begins with operating data, which is usually in computer-readable form, so the idea of combining together all this data (often in the form of a "total systems" model) seemed natural.

Partly in reaction to the bottom-up trend, and partly because of some colossal failures of attempts to use computers in support of this approach, a third trend appeared: top-down planning, as championed by McKinsey & Co. among others. The basic philosophy underlying this approach is that it is senior management's job to lay out the broad objectives and targets for the firm. Once that is done it is up to the rest of the organization to rally around the plan and fill in the missing details.

One of the most recent trends to be identified is something of a combination of top-down and bottom-up, occasionally referred to as top-down guidance/bottom-up planning. The focus of this approach is the nature of the iterations required as hierarchical organizations seek to fine-tune and juggle the components of a plan to make it feasible, acceptable, and goal-directed. The planning model set forth by Lorange and Vancil (Lorange and Vancil, 1977) characterizes this approach nicely.

If we analyze the general nature of each of the four basic approaches discussed above, it is evident that in each case there are some fundamental generic steps which must always be accomplished if an organization is to do formal planning. Since it is our intention to examine the state of the art in planning and the way in which computers are, or may be, effectively utilized in this process, it makes sense to examine the set of fundamental underlying steps that must be accomplished rather than focus on any particular organizational form in which planning process might take place.

We begin the following section with a brief discussion of previous attempts at developing computer-based planning systems. Then we describe such an eight-step model of the planning process, which we use as a framework for assessing alternative methods (manual, MIS, DSS) for supporting planning activity.

4.0 The Role Of The Computer In The Planning Process

Much effort has been directed toward using computer techniques in the planning process (Naylor and Schauland, 1976; Schrieber, 1970). Success has been anything but uniform, however. Many of the grand designs, while successful in terms of employing programmers, systems analysts and planners for relatively long periods, producing many widely read academic papers and articles, and bringing considerable fame and glory to their sponsoring firms for being at the forefront of modern management, nonetheless must be judged as failures in terms of improvement in the effectiveness of the overall planning process. (Bucatinsky, 1973; Hall, 1973).

Many reasons have been suggested to explain the manifest difficulties that planners and computer system designers have faced in the past in trying to effectively couple the computer to the planning process. Foremost is the fact that few of the pioneers in this area clearly realized how complex and ill-understood the planning process really was (see, for example, Hall, 1973). It has been all too common for management scientists and planning analysts to equate planning with simulation, exponential smoothing, discounted cash flow models, and the like, where computers can be used to "solve" the problem. The *real* planning problem, however, simply cannot be solved by computers alone.

During the last few years, the published literature has mirrored the general re-thinking process taking place in the field of computer-aided planning. A number of "factor studies" have emerged; these reports attempts to isolate a reasonably parsimonious list of things, culled from other published studies plus the experience of the authors, that ought to be done (or avoided) if a computer-aided planning system is to be successful (Grinyer and Wooller, 1975; Hammond, 1974). Another set of studies report on modest successes of particular systems (Canning, 1971; Champine, 1977). It seems that what leads to success is not so much the level of sophistication of the management science models used, nor the speed with which the computer executes the program, nor the grand scale of the development project itself. What appears to matter is the provision of computer support for a small, clearly identified and reasonably well understood component of the overall planning process; the simplicity and relatively low cost of the related computer systems development; and the extent to which managers (not staff analysts) actually used the system, and felt they had improved their decisions by so doing. Finally, there have been a few studies, including this one, aimed at synthesizing the current level of understanding by developing general frameworks that serve to codify and interrelate various phenomena that have been identified (see also Lorange and Rockart, 1976; Malm, 1974).

The first important efforts aimed at developing computer-based planning support systems took place in the mid-1960's, during the "total system" era. Not surprisingly, these early systems were huge, monolithic, and very expensive. One well known example is described in (Gershefski, 1969). The last few years have witnessed an unmistakable trend away from the large-scale, total systems approach to planning models, towards smaller, more specialized models. (Hayes and Nolan, 1974). While generally leading to a wider variety of models and a broader spectrum of support, this specialization is bought at a price. As McInnes points out,

"Thus, the problem is both one of truncating a particular aspect of the total enterprise for special attention, and one of re-integrating the two in a satisfactory way." (McInnes, 1977).

The trend toward more specialized models should not be confused with the complexity level of these models. One rather surprising early finding that has emerged in an ongoing M.I.T. field study of computerized planning systems in large U.S. corporations is that it is not necessarily true that a model must be simple in order to gain acceptance by planners and line managers. Both parties recognize that the activities for which they are planning are complex, and therefore an overly simple model is unlikely to be plausible.

In order to provide a framework for an analysis of the computer's role in planning, we present an eight-step model of the planning process (see Figure 1). This model is a drastic over-simplification of the actual process in any real organization. For instance, one has to deal as a practical matter with various levels in an organization and the fact that planning must go on not only at the corporate level but also at divisional and group levels. Nevertheless, there does exist such a discernible generic set of steps that must somehow be accomplished when formal planning is actually carried out, although the specific implementation of these steps may vary from one organization to the next.

Let us now describe in more detail each of the planning steps identified in Figure 1, and assess alternative possible modes of computer-based support for each.

Step 1: Set Out Existing Objectives

The first step in this simplified view of the planning process is to deter-

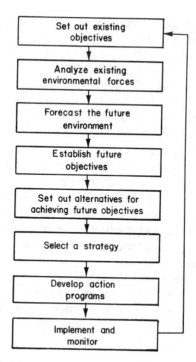

Fig. 1. An Eight Step Model of the Organizational Planning Process.

mine and set out the existing objectives of the firm (i.e., of the top managers) in an explicit form. Each objective or goal should also be accompanied with a statement of how it is to be measured, and what target level the firm would like to achieve.

Generally, organizational goals are multiple and often in conflict. For example, a company might have a profit goal of a certain dollar level, a return on assets objective, and perhaps a market share objective. To increase the market share objective may very well draw down the profits that are available for the year, and hence impact the profit objective.

This step, which of course only involves substantial work the first time planning is undertaken, is generally carried out by a management team operating primarily with manual support mechanisms. Informal information exchanges, small group discussion activity, and personal reflection characterize this step. Computer-based support may play a minor role in certain situations, but generally computers have not been used to much advantage here.

There are certain novel techniques that have potential for supporting this and other similar activities that require a convergence of the ideas and opinions of different individuals. Chief among these is computer-supported

Delphi analysis. Delphi techniques have gained considerable popularity during the last few years, primarily as a mechanism for aiding convergence of expert opinion on some fuzzy subject matter (Sackman, 1974). A good example of the use of Delphi methods is the study of future computer technology, architecture, and applications sponsored by GUIDE (Wylie, 1971). The technique itself is quite simple. The opinions of a panel of experts are sought through sequential individual interrogations, and an effort is made to achieve consensus of convergence of opinion by the feedback of the results to the participants.

Some experimental attempts have been undertaken to speed up the Delphi feedback cycle by having the participants give their responses on computer terminals (Sackman and Citrenbaum, 1972). In this way, a group's responses can be processed automatically, and the information and instructions that make up the next questionnaire can be fed directly back to them. It is also possible to extend the technique by providing easy access to data bases and models, if so desired.

While larger firms would be the most likely candidates for using relatively sophisticated approaches such as interactive Delphi to support the clarification of planning objectives, these techniques hold considerable promise for a wide variety of unstructured expert opinion-elicitation tasks with groups of all sizes.

Step 2: Analyze Existing Environmental Forces

A second early step in the planning process is to understand the major existing environmental forces faced by the organization. Obviously the nature and strength of forces an organization faces will determine in part the objectives that organization currently has, and will explain in some measure its aspiration for each objective.

The assessment of environmental forces requires two distinct phases. One phase involves identifying the types of forces that exist and that have an impact on the organization. The second phase involves trying to understand how those forces impact the organization—in what "direction" they force the organization, how strong they are, what their temporal pattern is, etc.. For example, one obvious environmental force is the strength of the economy in the country in which the company is operating. The target levels that ought to be set for objectives such as profits, or return on assets, in light of a recession economy versus a booming economy, call for some judgement on the part of senior management.

The activity is carried out in most organizations with manual support mechanisms. Management experience and judgement are crucial in this stage, as are a sound grasp of general economic, political and social trends.

MIS-like support systems occasionally play a minor role during this step, by providing periodic or ad hoc reports drawn from the organization's basic computerized database. Also, improved understanding of key environmental forces and their impact often results as a by-product from developing a computer model for the firm. (More will be said about such computer models later.)

Before one can identify points of impact between the environment and the firm, a manager must learn "what's going on out there". Since answering this question requires access to large amounts of diverse information, most of which is independent of any particular firm, opportunities for general purpose database-type services present themselves. In fact, some companies in the U.S., for example Lockheed Corp., have undertaken to provide just such a service to both themselves, and to other, contracting, firms. The Lockheed system allows users to interrogate a large economic database in order to extract trend and profile data series, perform projections, and apply certain econometric models (regression, smoothing, etc.), thereby helping them define more clearly the shape of the economic environment and its interface with their organization.

As business environments become more complex, the ability to provide rapid access to economic and other information about those environments should continue to develop as a specialized industry. The market for Lockheed-style "information utilities" should exhibit continued growth in the future.

Step 3: Forecast the Future Environment

The next stage in the planning process that must take place involves forecasting the future environment over the time period that matters for the organization concerned. If one is dealing with a five-year planning horizon it is necessary to forecast what the relevant components of the organization's environment will look like five years hence.

This forecasting task has two phases. First, changes in the existing environmental forces must be considered—for instance, what the Gross National Product is likely to be five years from now. In addition, it is important to assess what new kinds of forces are going to affect the firm over the coming years. A considerable number of companies were hurt in the recent past because they failed to recognize important new environmental forces such as energy shortages and pollution control.

The first type of forecasting involves concept association and inference-drawing activity based on widely scattered, fragmented sources of data. To date, computers have played only a minor role in supporting this activity. Examples include automatic literature search facilities, and the general-purpose information utilities and Delphi methods discussed above. The System Dynamics modelling work pioneered by Jay Forrester (Forrester,

1975) also attempts to address this problem by trying to capture the essential elements of a system—a firm, a city or even a world economy (Forrester, 1961; Meadows et al., 1972)—in a special kind of simulation model. The emphasis in System Dynamics is not so much on accurate prediction of the future, but rather identification and adjustment of key control points within a system so as to improve the system's behavior and stability in the face of environmental "shocks" (quadrupling of oil prices, for example).

In the case of the second subtask, extensive research in the area of forecasting has produced a wide variety of computer-aided techniques, some MIS-oriented and others DSS-like. Commonly used techniques range in complexity from simple curve-fitting algorithms, to linear and non-linear regression methods, to spectral and Fourier analysis of the type pioneered by Box and Jenkins (Box and Jenkins, 1976).

Corporate Simulation Models. Particular forecasting techniques are usually imbedded, either as modular selectable components or else as an integral mechanism, within larger analytical systems, notably corporate simulation models. Corporate simulation models are quite widely used today, and in many large companies a major proportion of the effort of the corporate planning staff is directed toward the development, improvement and maintenance of these models. In the past, most efforts led to MIS-type models, which tended to be large, complex, batch-oriented programs that were run periodically by the planning group, ostensibly for top management. More often than not, the voluminous reports and tables were scarcely looked at before being filed or disposed of (Gershefski, 1969).

One of their most serious drawbacks has been that these models have allowed only *parameter* exploration, not *structural* exploration. It is easy to change an input parameter of an industry model—say, the inflation rate— and rerun the model to observe effects on, say, industry demand. It is quite another matter to ask what the industry demand would be in the face of various types of governmental interference, or mergers between certain firms, or specific technological breakthroughs. Other problems that have been observed with such models are well documented elsewhere (for example, Hall, 1973).

However, recently attempts have been made to remove some of these drawbacks to simulation models. For example, Keen (Keen, 1976) reports on the effectiveness of the interactive computer language APL in constructing simple models "from scratch" very rapidly, given an adequate data base. Boulden (Boulden, 1975) and others have developed modelling packages, complete with specialized computer languages, to speed up the simulation task and thereby improve the flexibility of this approach. Many of the newer corporate modelling systems are interactive rather than batch, and most allow a model designer to select modules from a library for inclusion or not, as he sees fit. These changes are indicative of a broad swing from MIS to DSS approaches in provision of simulation support for assessment of the impact of changes in the environment.

Effective corporate simulation systems provide users with choices among forecasting methods, both in terms of the models used and the choices of exogenous variables and their values. We will have more to say regarding these models in a moment.

Econometric Models. Another popular type of computer-based forecasting support mechanism is the national econometric model. The best known examples in the U.S.A. include models of the U.S. economy such as those developed by the Wharton School, Chase Econometrics, and Data Resources Inc.. Each such model is embodied in a set of computer programs, containing thousands of variables and equations. Each equation is supposed to faithfully represent some small part of the economy being modelled. When supplied with certain outside data (so-called "exogenous" variables) the equations are all solved simultaneously to provide projections of the economy into the future. Naturally, the accuracy of the projections decreases quite rapidly as one looks further into the future.

The three cases cited are examples of the most common format these models assume—large, periodically-run batch programs. Nor are these the only examples of econometric models. Many large firms have developed their own such models, usually tailored more or less to their particular industry. Sometimes these industry models actually take as input the output (i.e., predictions) of one of the larger models. In some cases, there are three levels to the hierarchy of models: broad econometric models interface with smaller and narrower industry models, which in turn interface with corporate models of individual firms (see Figure 2).

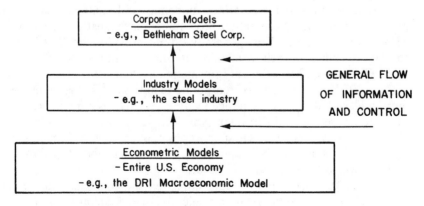

Fig. 2. A Hierarchy of Simulation Models.

On the whole, econometric models of the national economy are MIS-type models, and appropriately so. Their problem environment is not one of human-machine problem-space exploration and decision-making, but rather one of solving a large system of equations. While some econometric models allow parameter adjustment in order to test sensitivity to various assumptions regarding exogenous variables, even these facilities are usually implemented in an offline fashion. Part of the difficulty with making such large complex models function in an interactive mode is that the straight computer time for solution is often on the order of tens of minutes—too long for effective human-computer interaction in the DSS sense. Furthermore, the complexity of the models themselves—the large number of variables and constraints contained, the depth and detail of the reports generated, etc.—serves to make manager-model interaction all but impossible.

It is worth noting that exceptionally powerful systems are available that provide languages, tools and other support for building one's own econometric models—for example, the TROLL system developed by the National Bureau of Economic Research (NBER 1975).

Data Base Management Systems. A third class of mechanism that frequently may be employed in this step is modern data base management systems. While DBM's (or their predecessors, file systems) have been around for fifteen years or more, they have only become widely used in the last few years (Palmer, 1975). The main contribution of DBM's is that they have made it possible, from a cost/benefit standpoint, for planners to carry out particular investigations, using computer-based data, that have always been feasible, but usually not economically justifiable because of the extensive programming effort that was previously required.

Most DBM's, in and of themselves, simply provide planners with a convenient software interface between the myriad data files maintained by most organizations and the various modelling and analytical capabilities provided in high-level general-purpose computer languages such as FORTRAN, PL/1 or APL. They generally do not provide modelling or other special capabilities of their own, although some recent research efforts such as the Generalized Management Information System at MIT (Donovan and Jacoby, 1977) have sought to incorporate facilities along these lines. Also, most modern DBM's come equipped with interactive user interfaces. While they are not really DSS's in their own right, their interactive orientation, plus their ability to enhance the support power of computers through simplifying the development and application of planning models, makes them more DSS-like than MIS-like in nature.

While DBM's have undoubtedly improved the ability of planners and modellers to access corporate data efficiently, these systems are still in their infancy in terms of potential. For example, little work has been done on interfacing DBM's themselves to other software systems such as corporate simulation models. Since major planning efforts in large organizations may require that various planning models draw upon hundreds of different corporate data files, DBM's support is clearly needed.

In summary, there are numerous ways in which computers are being, or may be, used in support of the environmental projection function. Major classes include specialized forecasting techniques, (usually imbedded within general simulation models), econometric models, and database management systems. Both DSS and MIS-based approaches are represented, and both can be of considerable help in this stage of the planning process.

Step 4: Establish Future Objectives

The step that follows the forecasting of the future environment is that of establishing what the future objectives ought to be. The necessity for management to decide, as part of the planning process, what the firm's future objectives ought to be highlights a crucial difference between planning, and extrapolation or forecasting. Planning has a decision orientation, forecasting does not. In effect, forecasting is a complement of planning.

As in Step 1 (the original definition of the firm's objectives) this task must be executed by top management with little in the way of computer support. Again as in Step 1, there are a few circumscribed or novel roles that computers may play, e.g., to support an interactive Delphi study among top managers. In a parallel vein, a few management consulting firms, such as Strategic Planning Associates, have developed their own particular, and highly effective, approaches to corporate planning which they package and sell as a product together with their services (Lewis, 1977). Since these systems often make heavy use of graphical and diagrammatic aids, various computer-based manipulation and calculation modules may be developed and made available by the firm that developed the package. These support modules are usually interactive, and often involve special techniques such as color displays or on-line graph plotting.

The possibilities for effective computer support in Steps 1 and 4 are not yet very well understood. More research and experience will be required before we can fully appreciate the value of these and other possible types of computer support for this phase of the planning process.

Step 5: Set Out Alternatives For Achieving Future Objectives

With the future objectives established, the next stage of the planning process is to set out alternatives by which these objectives could be accomplished. For example, if a company has set a target of a certain profit objective five years out, that objective could be accomplished by sharply reducing the price, driving the competition out of business, and then raising the price substantially during the last two years! A second alternative would be simply to reduce costs now while maintaining price and strive for greater productive efficiency over the five years in an effort to accomplish the profit goal.

During this step, executives and staff planners attempt to answer the question "now that we know the direction in which we want to move, *how* should we do it?" This step is not concerned with evaluating alternatives, nor with selecting the best one; the emphasis here is on creative and uninhibited idea generation.

Computers, on the whole, are not very adept at helping people generate new ideas within a very broad, unstructured problem space. This task, like the previous one, must be accomplished largely, though not entirely, without computer support.

A role in this process may be played by the same corporate simulation models discussed previously, with a slightly different orientation. It has been observed by various investigators in the DSS field (Gerrity, 1970; Scott Morton, 1971) that, in the course of using interactive models of real systems, managers are able to deepen their insight into the operation being modelled. This improved understanding often allows managers to see the organization from new vantage points, and to think about it, ask questions about it, in ways not before considered. The argument here, then, is not that managers can purposefully sit down with an interactive simulation model and generate effective strategy alternatives. Rather, in the process of using such models, the manager's *own* understanding is increased—they come to understand the system at a deeper level—and through this enriched insight come new strategies.

There is an allied body of techniques in the field of corporate modelling often brought into play at this stage. Optimization models. The fundamental difference between optimization techniques and simulation centers around the notion of an objective function. Roughly speaking, a simulation model attempts to represent a system *as it is*; whether one state of the system (as portrayed by the model) is better or worse than another is a value judgement that can only be made by the user of the model, not by the model itself.

In contrast, an optimization model usually seeks to locate the *best possible* system state, as represented by the value of its objective function. When characterized this way, optimization models seem clearly preferable. However, there are important trade-offs to be made. Usually, numerous approximations and simplifications must be made in order to "fit" a real system into an optimizing framework. The requisite mathematical and technical skill required to effectively employ optimizing techniques is high. Also, it is quite possible to create a fine optimization model on paper, but not be able to actually solve it because to do so would require, say, hundreds of hours of computer time (integer programming models often run into barriers of this kind). Optimization techniques have been very successful in certain situations that have a natural structure well suited to a particular approach (e.g., linear programming and oil refinery operations, or decision analysis and resource exploration). However, in the area of organizational modelling for planning purposes, their use has not been widespread (Hayes and Nolan, 1974).

An additional role for computers in this step follows from the use of the graphical/diagrammatical planning packages mentioned in the context of the previous step. Once a manager is accustomed to thinking in terms of colored schematics or shapes on a grid as a representation of the organization within the overall economic environment, he/she or their staff is then faced with the tedious problem of actually supporting this scheme by keeping track of the data, drawing the color diagrams, etc.. On-line computer systems that do the dirty work for this manager provide valuable assistance in the strategy generation process. By greatly reducing the delay in the creation of new graphs, diagrams, or tables of data, a planner can have his ideas reflected back at him by the computer essentially as they occur, rather than having to wait a few hours or days to have the data restructured on paper. By keeping the planning process fluid, with fewer interruptions, the overall quality of the alternative generated ideas and plans will generally be improved. Lewis has recently developed innovative techniques to perform these functions (Lewis, 1977).

Step 6: Select a Strategy

Having laid out alternative strategies and portfolios of action plans, the next stage of planning is that of selecting a strategy and a set of action plans that seem to be best for the organization. This activity involves aspects of the classical costs/benefit analysis in its broadest sense. The central task is to determine which strategy has the best chance of allowing the organization to accomplish its objective.

Computer-based techniques applicable to this step include the following:

Simulation Models. One of the most widely used strategy evaluation devices is, once again, the corporate simulation model. Most corporate modelling activities are geared toward being able to cope with relatively simple "what if" questions, and they are well suited to this task. This is especially true in cases where the alternative strategies being evaluated are characterizable as different parameter sets. However, if some of the strategies demand major structural alterations to the model (for example, acquisitions or divestitures, introduction or deletion of product lines, or major changes in the accounting methods), a considerable amount of staff time may be involved in re-writing the parts of the firm's simulation model that are affected by the new proposals. The time and cost required in making these changes may well over-ride the value of the simulations (Grinyer and Wooller, 1975).

As mentioned earlier, recent improvements in modelling methodology such as the use of APL, special modelling languages, and "instant modelling" packages, are simplifying the task of making structural alterations to simulation models. However, there is some inherent upper bound to these improvements, simply the time it takes for a person to comprehend the changes involved. The fact that it takes one hour, rather than one day, to re-program a particular model to reflect structural changes is not much help if it takes the planning analysts one month to come to comprehend the changes sufficiently well to be able to specify the necessary re-programming.

Graph-Based Techniques. Graph-based techniques form an important class of computerized support mechanisms in the alternative evaluation phase. The most common example is that of event graphs, or decision trees. The usual approach involves breaking each strategic option down into a sequence of managerially directed actions interspersed with event outcomes: "we can take one of these actions, then for each action, these are the possible things that can happen, following which we can take other actions," etc.. When displayed on paper, or on a visual display, the layout forms a tree, the leaves of which correspond to the various possible action-event combinations.

There have been only a few attempts in business organizations to use computers to support strategy evaluation via formal decision analysis. Most of these schemes have simply used the computer to perform housekeeping tasks (maintenance of the tree structures) and calculations (expectations, Bayesian probability revisions, etc.). However, DSS techniques appear to offer much wider scope for effective human-machine interaction in this area. Additional research may well advance this methodology in the future.

Cost Effectiveness Analysis. Finally, there is a "mixed bag" of methods falling under the general heading of cost/benefit or cost/effectiveness analysis. To a large extent, computers are used in these activities as replacements for clerical personnel; in other words, the techniques are themselves not new, and the computer's role is simply one of making the whole process more efficient. Some types of cost/benefit analysis, while not strictly infeasible using manual methods, were sufficiently time consuming that they were used only sparingly. Examples include Net Present Value (NPV) calculations (usually in the context of capital budgeting), and Program Evaluation and Review Techniques (PERT). The former tool is a widely used means of deciding among various investment alternatives on the basis of discounted cash flow; the latter a popular project scheduling technique. Perhaps the most significant advantage that computers have brought to these kinds of techniques is that it is now possible for a planner to examine many more alternatives than he could if he were forced to perform the various calculations manually, thereby giving him a greater opportunity for determining further improvements in the approach used.

Step 7: Develop Action Programs

The next step, having selected a strategy by which the organization hopes to accomplish its objectives, is to set out on a year-by-year basis specific action programs that are needed to implement the strategy. For each of the objectives established previously, targets of achievement must be set for each year, and programs developed that management believes will meet those targets.

The process of mapping a strategy into a reasonably detailed set of plans often requires large amounts of calculation, primarily involving data laid out in an accounting format. Facilities for both bottom-up calculations (consolidating divisional data) as well as top-down ("spreading" corporate directives to sub-units) have served to bring computers into prominence as a crucial support mechanism in this step.

The key resources required to perform this step are computing power, and data. Corporate and divisional databases are intensively assessed. This heavy demand for access to a wide variety of data files, plus the extensive CPU time required for calculations, suggests that conventional MIS-like support is usually most effective during this stage.

Step 8: Implement and Monitor

The final step in the planning process is really an ongoing process— actually executing the detailed programs, and controlling deviations from the plan. This usually takes the form of comparisons between the performance levels achieved during a period, and the levels set out by the plan. This comparison is the most important input into the planning process for the subsequent year.

This step brings to light an important, but often overlooked point; the difference between control of the planning process, and control of the firm's ongoing operations. Control of the planning process is frequently neglected. In an organization that has a planning system without adequate mechanisms to control that system, managers quickly learn to generate planning documents that satisfy the planners, but pay little attention to the content of those documents because they know that it is unlikely that their own performance will be related to their input to the plan. Similarly, it is possible to have an operational control system (a yearly budgetary control system, for example) and yet walk one pace at a time into a major disaster, a disaster that probably would have been foreseen with effective, controlled, strategic planning. Thus, this last step in the planning process is in many ways the most crucial of all.

This step also sharply illustrates the difference between planning and forecasting. It is not the intent of the planning process to produce precisely accurate snapshots of where the firm will be at the end of the year, or five years hence. Rather, the intent is to set out realistic objectives for where the firm would *like* to be. An examination of actual performance this year against the plans established one year ago, two, three, four, and five years ago for this year, is usually informative about the nature of the forces that have been overestimated or underestimated during the intervening years. This analysis of reasons for failure to meet the planning objectives provides initial input into planning for the following year.

Effective planning is a continuing, evolutionary process. Step 8 really ties back to, and often overlaps, Step 1. Formal strategic planning systems frequently follow a rolling five-year format, whereby the year just completed is dropped, a new year added at the end of the horizon, and the entire process repeated.

Monitoring the plan essentially involves capturing from the general corporate data base the data necessary to determine status of the key strategic variables. These key variables include standard accounting data, and usually other information as well (market share, consumer identity, etc.). The support system typically provides, at this stage, a set of reports that identify the degree of success the organization has experienced in achieving its objectives, and information to help understand reasons behind any significant failures to do so.

Exception reports are widely used during the monitoring phase. The guiding philosophy is that line managers are generally overburdened with data (usually in the form of computer reports), most of which is of marginal value at best. It is crucial to devise schemes for informing a manager when outcomes are significantly different from expectations, but at the same time avoiding simply generating reports that have no surprise content. To do this effectively requires that the manager's logic be incorporated into the report generating mechanism. This logic most often takes the form of performance standards for certain key indices, together with levels of tolerance relative to each standard. Other forms are also possible: for example, any change of more than 10% relative to the previous period should be reported.

In many organizations today, nearly all the computer-based support for the entire planning and control process is conventional MIS-like report generation in this final step. For example, Grinyer (Grinyer and Wooller, 1975) has developed an entire typology of planning models based on the level of data aggregation in this context. One theme of the present article is that there is much scope for additional support, of various kinds, in earlier steps within the planning process. Human-computer approaches to the various stages of the planning process offer important opportunities for its improvement and correspondingly improve the economic competitiveness of the user organization.

5.0 A Strategic Planning System

In the previous section, we suggested that provision of computer support for organizational planning ought to be structured around the stages of the planning process itself. While we have illustrated possible types of computer support for each stage, we know of no single corporation today that is attempting to use computers in all, or even most, of the ways we described. In fact, recent documentation of the role of computers in the planning process is surprisingly sparse. Professor Morris McInnes, of the MIT Sloan School, is currently completing a project that will provide concrete examples of the use of financial models as part of the planning process in some 16 companies (see McInnes, 1978).

In order to illustrate ways in which some firms are attempting to extend or enhance the level of computer support provided for planners and managers, we have abstracted elements of an interesting system originally developed by William F. Hamilton and Michael Moses for a large U.S. firm with multiple, independent operating divisions (see Hamilton & Moses, 1974). It includes a number of unique features, and serves to illustrate some of the decision support concepts discussed in the previous section. Their system

"has been designed to operate as an integral part of the strategic planning process. Emphasis is placed on providing useful decision-aiding information within the practical limitations of available computational capabilities and established planning practice. Experience to date has demonstrated that an integrated system is both operationally feasible and appropriate for strategic financial planning."

This system is not just a single model, but in fact a number of different models and data bases coordinated by the computer. Its major components (see Figure 3) include a deterministic simulation modelling capability, econometric modelling and analysis subsystems, risk analysis subsystems, and, at the system's heart, a multi-period mixed integer programming model. The system is easily accessible through interactive terminals as well as batch mode.

Most designers of corporate models decide early in the game whether they intend to develop a simulation ("case study") model or an optimizing model. In this case, both alternatives are provided as separate modules within the overall system. The modularity in the overall system design, and the resulting flexibility provided its users, contribute greatly to the utility of this system.

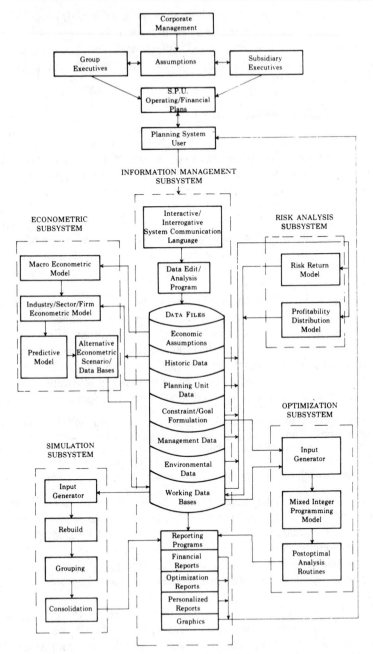

Fig. 3. The Computer-based Planning System developed by Hamilton and Moses.
ⓒ 1974, Institute of Management Science, with permission.

Use of the planning support system begins with corporate management communicating its basic assumptions for guiding sub-unit planning activities to the various strategic planning units (SPU's). Each SPU then submits as a minimum: (a) strategic planning unit data, including Profit and Loss statements, a balance sheet, and a statement of sources and applications of funds for cases where all proposed marketing, development, acquisition and financing strategies were accepted; (b) abbreviated Profit and Loss, and source/application-of-funds statements for each acquisition, development, and momentum strategy being proposed; (c) financial data for each existing or proposed financing instrument.

The data from each SPU, together with other data regarding management assumptions and restrictions, goals, business mix attitudes, etc., are entered, edited and stored in appropriate databases under the control of the information management subsystem (in effect, a special purpose database management system tailored to the requirements of this application).

A second subsystem, the consolidated simulation subsystem, allows the user to conduct deterministic financial simulations for predetermined sets of strategies. This module is based largely on standard accounting variables and relationships. This module includes a rebuilding facility, which allows the user to consolidate or define new SPU's. This facility represents an attempt to solve the structural modification problem discussed in the previous section.

The optimization subsystem maximizes corporate performance over the multi-period planning horizon. Alternative objective functions may be formulated, but the most effective planning objective found to date is a linear approximation to undiscounted earnings per share over the planning horizon. Given an objective function, the optimizing facility selects the best set of sources and uses of funds, subject to various financial, legal, and operating constraints imposed at both corporate and SPU levels. One version of the optimizing model contains about 1,000 variables and 700 constraints, including 250 binary (zero-one) variables. Such a formulation is well within the capabilities of currently available mathematical programming codes, such as IBM's MPSX system.

The econometric subsystem allows the user to develop projections for the economy and industry where the firm is operating or planning to operate. This subsystem draws upon commercially available national—and industry-level forecasting models (see, for example, Hilmire & Smith, 1978). Another part of the econometric subsystem uses computerized financial information from proprietary sources to generate financial planning data about other companies being considered for acquisition.

The risk analysis subsystem is used to generate alternative data bases to provide insights into the possible effects of the inherent variability in the planning data that reaches the corporate planners as point estimates.

Managers provide subjective evaluations of possible future conditions, then these estimates are combined with historical information and used by a profitability profile model to derive artificial probability distributions of performance for the SPU's. These distributions may be used to determine confidence limits for various profit levels.

A number of authors have commented on the inadequacy of management scientist's abilities to succinctly and effectively model the uncertainty aspects of complex systems (see Carleton et al., 1973). Neither the financial theoretical basis, nor our ability to implement uncertainty mechanisms is very well developed yet. While the risk analysis approach taken here is a step in the direction of better modelling of uncertainty elements, additional work is needed.

Operational use of the planning support system takes one of two forms: periodic, or ad hoc. During the annual planning cycle, use of the planning system focuses on the optimizing subsystem. Inputs are both gathered from external sources and generated within the system. Typical results of the optimization and post-optimality analysis routines indicate the financing and investment strategies that produce the best corporate performance over the planning horizon. Particular features of the optimizing subsystem include its capability to consider simultaneously the financing, operating, and investment decision variables, and to evaluate acquisitions and divestitures as part of the total corporate picture.

In contrast to periodic use, ad hoc use of the system primarily involves its simulation modelling capabilities. Typical applications include evaluation of the impact of unanticipated changes in key economic or operational variables such as interest rates or material supplies, and analysis of the advisability of purchasing or selling corporate holdings under favorable terms that may come available at any time during the planning period. Also, the information management facilities of the system may be used directly, much like a high-level data base query language, without involving any of the system's models or other analysis capabilities.

This example is given here merely to illustrate a prototype package of support systems currently being developed and used as part of one organization's attempt to improve their planning process.

6.0 Conclusion

In this chapter we have discussed both the impact, and the potential, of computers in one area of central and increasing importance to management —organizational planning. Progress in this area is occuring partly because pressure is on organizations today to perform well in increasingly complex and difficult environments. Continued progress is made possible by the twin factors of (1) improvements in our understanding of the nature of the planning process, and (2) improvements in our ability to harness recent technological changes in ways that are directly useful to management. We have focused mainly on those areas of planning in which there has been substantial progress. Much of this has occured in the past few years, and with the trend toward giving users more direct access to computer power firmly set in many organizations, we expect to see at least as much progress in the next few years.

It is fashionable to assert that computers have had little impact on management. We would maintain, however, that in the relatively few years computers have been on the scene, their impact has been far from trivial. Furthermore, there is a growing body of hard evidence of new and even more powerful applications of computers by managers, and we fully expect this trend to continue and expand over the coming decade.

References

Alter, S. (1976). How Effective Managers Use Information Systems. *Harvard Business Review*, **54**, 6, Nov.-Dec.

Anthony, R. (1965). *Planning and Control Systems: A Framework for Analysis.* Harvard Business School Division of Research.

Boulden, J. (1975). *Computer-Aided Planning Systems.* McGraw-Hill, New York.

Boulden, J. & Elwood, B. (1970). Corporate Models: On-line, Real-time Systems. *Harvard Business Review*, **48**, 4, July-August.

Box, G. & Jenkins, G. (1976). *Time Series Analysis.* Holden-Day, San Francisco.

Bucatinsky, J. (1973). Unsuccessful Planning Models I Have Known. *The Institute of Management Sciences T.I.M.S. Interfaces*, **2**, February.

Camillus, J.C. (1975). Evaluating the Benefits of Formal Planning Systems. *Long Range Planning*, **8**, 3, June.

Canning, R. (1971). Using Corporate Models. *E.D.P. Analyzer*, **9**, 1, January.

Carlson, E. (Ed.) (1977). Proceedings of a Conference on Decision Support Systems. *Data Base*, **8**, 3.

Champine, G.A. (1977). Univac's Financial Model for Computer Development. *Datamation*, **23**, 2.

Dolotta, T.A., et al. (1976). *Data Processing in 1980-1985.* Wiley, New York.

Donovan, J.G., & Jacoby, H.D. (1977). *GMIS: An Experimental System for Data Management and Analysis.* Center for Information Systems Research, M.I.T., Working Paper no. CISR-16.

Editors Of Business Week (1972). G.E's New Strategy for Faster Growth. *Business Week*, July 8.

Forrester, J.W. (1961). *Industrial Dynamics.* MIT Press, Cambridge, Mass.

Forrester,J.W. (1975). *Collected Papers of Jay W. Forrester.* Wright-Allen Press, Cambridge, Mass.

Gerrity, T.P. (1970). *The Design of Man-Machine Decision Systems.* Unpublished Ph.D. Thesis, Massachusetts Institute of Technology.

Gershefski, G. (1969). Building a Corporate Financial Model. *Harvard Business Review*, **47**, 4, July-August.

Grinyer, P.H. & Wooller, J. (1975). Computer Models for Corporate Planning. *Long Range Planning*, **8**, 1, February.

Hall, W. (1973). Strategic Planning Models: Are Top Managers Really Finding Them Useful? *Journal of Business Policy*, **3**, 2.

Hamilton, W.F. & Moses, M.A. (1974). A computer-based corporate planning system. *Management Science*, 21, 2, 148-159.

Hammond, J.S. (1974) Do's and Don'ts of Corporate Models for Planning. *Harvard Business Review*, **52**, 2, March-April.

Hayes, R. & Nolan, R. (1974). What Kind of Corporate Modelling Functions Best? *Harvard Business Review*, **52**, 3, May-June.

Keen, P.G.W. (1976). 'Interactive' Computer Systems for Managers: A Modest Proposal. *Sloan Management Review*, Fall.

Keen, P.G.W. & Scott Morton, M.S. (1978). *Decision Support Systems: An Organizational Perspective*. Addison-Wesley, Reading, Mass.

Lande, F. (1969). *How to Use the Computer in Business Planning*. Prentice-Hall, New Jersey.

Levy, D. (1976). *Chess and Computers*. Prentice-Hall, New Jersey.

Lewis, W. (1977). *Planning By Exception*. Strategic Planning Associates, Washington, D.C.

Lorange, P. & Vancil, R. (1977). *Strategic Planning Systems*. Prentice-Hall, New Jersey.

Lorange, P. & Rockart, J.F. (1977). A Framework for the Use of Computer-based Models in the Planning Process. In Lorange and Vancil, 1977.

Malm, A. (1975). *A Framework for the Design of Planning Systems*. Lund, Sweden.

McCosh, A.M. & Scott Morton, M.S. (1978). *Management Decision Support Systems*. MacMillan Press, London.

McInnes, J.M. (1977). An Organizational Perspective on the Use of Simulation Models in the Planning and Control Process, *Proceedings of the Summer Computer Simulation Conference*, Chicago, Illinois. July.

Meadows, D. et al. (1972). *The Limits to Growth*. Universe Books, New York.

Naylor, T. & Schauland, H. (1976). A Survey of Users of Corporate Planning Models. *Management Science*, **22**, 9, May.

Palmer, I. (1975). *Data Base Systems: A Practical Reference*. Q.E.D. Information Sciences.

Sackman, H. & Citrenbaum, R. (Eds.) (1972). *On-line Planning—Towards Creative Problem Solving*, Prentice-Hall, New Jersey.

Sackman, H. (1974). *Delphi Critique: Expert Opinion, Forecasting, and Group processes*. Lexington Books, Arlington, Mass.

Schrieber, A. (Ed.) (1970). *Corporate Simulation Models*. Graduate School of Business Administration, University of Washington, Seattle.

Scott Morton, M.S. (1975). Organizing the Information Systems Function for Effectiveness as Well as Efficiency. *Proceedings of Society for Management of Information Systems*. Ann Arbour, University of Michigan. 1976.

Steiner, G.W. (1969). *Top Management Planning*. MacMillan, London.

Wylie, K. (1971). *Summary of Results: GUIDE/IBM Study of Advance Applications*. Guide International, Chicago, Illinois.

Chapter 8

COMPUTER AIDED DESIGN: APPLICATIONS IN
ARCHITECTURE

Tom Maver

Contents

1.0 Design Concepts

Design is the activity of making explicit proposals for a change from
some existing state to some future state which more closely approximates
to a concept of the ideal. As such it embraces a wide spectrum of human
endeavour; the outcomes of the design activity are part and parcel of our
everyday life and are determinants, for better or worse, of our human-made
future. In common with all complex human functions the activity of design
is ill-understood: it involves the most rational and systematic processes of
human thought and also the most intuitive and conjectural leaps within the
mind.

The design professions are many and varied; they include the engineering
professions—mechanical, civil, electrical, electronic, aeronautical, nuclear,
naval architecture, chemical, environmental—the architecture profession
and the industrial design profession. The educational systems from which
these professionals emerge, and the institutes of which they are members
are unique, disparate and, sadly, often competitive. Design then, unlike
medicine, has no unifying educational or professional corpus; the Design

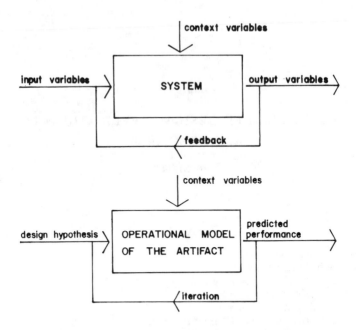

Fig. 1. An operational model of a designed artifact seen in system terms.

Research Society is a modest but important force in identifying the intellectual core of the design discipline and as the impact of the outcomes of design decision-making impinges more and more on our daily lives it is likely that the educational implications will be more responsively recognized.

More than anything else the application of the computer to design is drawing together the endeavours of designers from a host of professional spheres. Central to the activity of Computer Aided Design (CAD) is the concept of developing, within the computer, a model of the operational behaviour of the proposed artifact. The behavioural model can be thought of as a system: the system inputs are in effect the design hypotheses and the system outputs are predictions of the performance characteristics of the design under a particular set of context variables (Figure 1).

This systems view of design recognizes that the activity of design decision-making is not wholly contained within the technological sphere but may well have implications—functional, economic, social and aesthetic—for society at large. Successful computer applications to limited technical problems abound, of course: it is very useful to input to the computer a set of beam loadings and to have it output a minimum depth of beam. The pressing problems facing society today—ecological pollution, dwindling

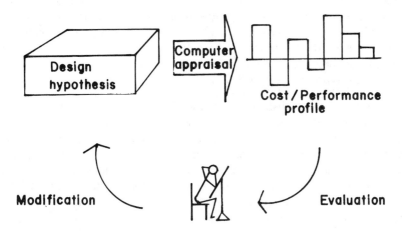

Fig. 2. A systems representation of the design activity.

energy and material resources, urban deprivation, etc.—demand a more systemic view of design; a view that will recognize the aspirations and value judgements of all those who will be affected by the design decisions.

The development of systemic computer-based design models is in its infancy but advancing rapidly in most fields of design endeavour. Nowhere more so than in the field of architecture, building science and urban planning. In the course of designing a building the architect is concerned to satisfy, as best he/she can, a wide range of disparate and sometimes conflicting objectives: the building must be structurally sound, environmentally comfortable, efficient for its purpose, aesthetically pleasing and economical to acquire and run. The brief the architect is given is unlikely to be explicit as to the acceptable level of any of these criteria (except perhaps to impose an upper limit on capital cost). The architect engages, then, in an iterative, open ended, multi-variate search process during which the directions of search and the final outcome depend in large measure on implicit and subjective value judgements.

The philosophy underlying the current generation of Computer Aided Architectural Design (CAAD) models is not one of simplifying the problem in order to make it uni-variate and free of subjective value judgement; rather it is one of recognizing the complexity of the problem—the fact that it *is* multi-variate (and multi-person)—and of providing as rich an information base as possible about the predicted performance of the hypothesised solution on which *explicit* value judgements can be justifiably made.

Developing the systems model of Figure 1, the CAD activity can be represented as in Figure 2. The designer generates a design hypothesis which is input into the computer (*representation*); the computer software models the behaviour of the hypothesised design and outputs measures of cost and performance on a number of relevant criteria (*measurement*); the designer (perhaps in conjunction with the client body) exercises his/her (or their) value judgement (*evaluation*) and decides on appropriate changes to the design hypothesis (*modification*).

Representation. As subsequent examples will illustrate, the representation of the design hypothesis will be required to take a form appropriate to the appraisal measures which the software is designed to carry out. The representation may be simply alpha-numeric, or increasingly commonly, topographic (e.g., a building plan, a bridge elevation, a printed circuit layout, a mechanical linkage, etc.); it is the interface between the designer's mental model and the computer based model and, as such, is the focus of the human-machine exchange.

Measurement. The software model of the behavioural characteristics of the design artifact which exists within the computer must be capable of interpreting the input representation and of applying known algorithms which model aspects of the design's character and behaviour. The output measures of cost and performance may be wholly descriptive (e.g., building plan area, maximum bridge span, number of circuit nodes, lengths of linkage arms, etc.), wholly predictive (e.g., the capital cost of the plan layout, the deflection profile of the bridge span, the resistance between two circuit nodes, the angular velocity of a linkage arm, etc.) or an appropriate mix of descriptive and predictive measures. Additionally, it may be advantageous to have the software effect a visual transformation on the input representation, to output additional views of the design hypothesis (e.g., a 3-D perspective of the building plan or bridge).

Evaluation. The profile of the cost and performance characteristics which are output by the computer—supplemented by perspective or other views—form the information base on which the designer acts. Evaluation of a profile of measures on disparate and possibly conflicting criteria can be undertaken only by the application of value judgements relating to the perceived needs of the client/user body and of society at large. The introduction of CAD models does not obviate the need for evaluative decisions; indeed, by making the information base explicit, CAD models throw into sharp focus the subjective aspects of the design decision-making activity. In some instances, the brief for the design problem may express upper and lower limits of acceptability for some or all of the cost/performance characteristics, against which the profile may be judged. Increasingly, however, it is recognized that such *a priori* constraints cannot be set sensibly in ignorance of the causal inter-relationships between the elements of the cost/performance profile: for example, the requirement to achieve a minimum of 2% daylight factor in a school plan may result in an unacceptably high energy cost for heating. In effect, if *a priori* cost/performance specification is a meaningful concept, agreement on its form is likely only to emerge from extensive and controlled explorations using the CAD model.

Modification. Any design hypothesis embodies a unique set of design variables. For example, a particular plan layout has a particular floor area, shape of envelope, topological relation of spaces, etc.. Each design variable contributes, to a greater or lesser extent, to the behaviour of the design as a whole and hence to the cost/performance profile. If, from the evaluation of the profile it is considered that, for example, the level of daylighting in some rooms is unacceptably low, the designer must decide in respect to which design variable the overall design hypothesis must be modified. Improvement in this aspect of performance may be achieved by modification of any one of several design variables; moreover, a change in any particular design variable is likely to affect not only daylighting but many (if not all) of the other cost/performance characteristics. The nature of the causal relationships between each and every design variable and each and every cost/performance variable is not, unfortunately, known *a priori*, but must emerge in the process of iterative use of the CAD model.

It will be seen, then, that if the *representation* and *measurement* modules of the design system can be set up and made available, the processes of *evaluation* and *modification* take place dynamically within the design activity as determinants of, and in response to, the pattern of explorative search. This mode of working puts a premium on ease of communication with the computer: current developments are divided roughly equally between bureaux offering remote multi-access to a large processor and in-house dedicated mini-computers.

The claim has been made that the systems view of design developed thus far has applicability to most fields of design endeavour—from the design of a gearbox to the design of a nuclear power station. The evidence needed to justify the claim is more voluminous than could be contained within a single chapter in a book of this type. Instead, the intention is to exemplify, from a single profession—architecture—the application of CAD to a range of problems relating to sub-systems within buildings and to the problem of the systemic design of the building as a whole.

2.0 Sub-System Design

A building can be thought of as comprising a number of interconnected sub-systems—structure, construction, plant and services, etc.—each of

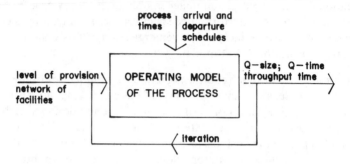

Fig. 3. An operational model of an air terminal seen in systems terms.

which is sufficiently complex to warrant a specific CAD model. In this section two models will be discussed:

- The operation of the facilities within a building in relation to the processing of people and/or materials (the *process* sub-system) and
- The operation of the fabric of the building in relation to environmental control and energy consumption (the *energy* sub-system).

2.1 The Process Sub-System

In a significant number of building types—notably transport termini—the processing of large numbers of people is crucial to the functioning of the building. In an airport, for example, the designer is concerned to incorporate an adequate and economical provision of facilities (check-in desks, ticket desks, baggage reclaim carousels, etc.) to satisfy the demand which will be made on the building. In systems terms, the design problem is as shown in Figure 3.

Representation. In the computer program AIR-Q (Laing, 1975) the designer represents a design hypothesis to the computer by constructing the network of passenger movement on the computer screen, accompanied by suggested levels of facility provision. This mode of representation can be explained by reference to Figure 4.

For each type of process, the designer causes a symbol to be drawn on the computer screen as follows:

☐ Activity Node: e.g., check-in, bank, customs. Associated with each activity node the designer inputs a 'number of servers' and parameters which give the distribution of 'serving time'.

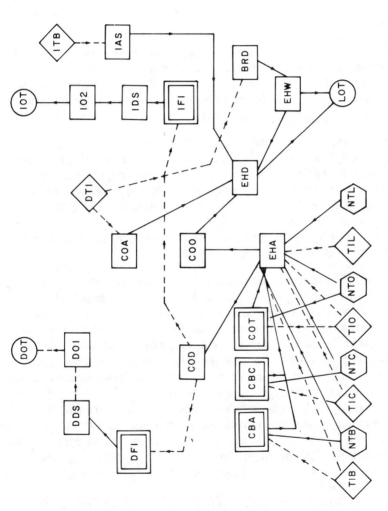

Fig. 4. Mode of representing an air terminal network on the computer screen.

◇ Trigger Input Node: e.g., scheduled bus arrival, scheduled plane arrival. Associated with each trigger input node is an arrival time and passenger complement.
◯ Non-Trigger Input Node: e.g., sporadic car arrivals. Associated with each non-trigger input node are the parameters which give the distribution (perhaps random) of such arrivals.

The symbols are connected on the screen by means of directional links, as follows:

— Open Link: e.g., uncontrolled flow of passengers. Associated with each open link is the proportion of passengers taking this route.
--- Trigger Link: eg., controlled flow of passengers. Associated with each trigger link is the scheduling time of the 'call' for passengers and the numbers of passengers involved.

Measurement. The program models the operation of the air terminal by painstakingly advancing the set of processes by a succession of small time increments. Typically, the time interval chosen might be four minutes. In the first time step, a bus may have arrived and the passengers may have been processed through check-in; meantime, a scheduled aircraft arrival may have taken place. And so on. The program measures and records in a file, the status of the system at each time increment; measures consist of queue sizes, throughput times, idle server times, etc..

Evaluation. A tableau of synoptic output can be obtained from the program: which provides, for each facility, the average passenger 'stay time', the maximum and minimum population at that facility and the time at which the maximum and minimum populations occurred within the whole period simulated. This tableau guides the designer to look in more detail at critical aspects of the system. For example, the variation in population over any chosen time period (in any degree of temporal detail) within any group of facilities can be displayed (see Figure 5).

Even in a CAD model which focusses specifically on a particular building sub-system—in this case movement of airport passengers—there is no obvious single optimizing measure of performance. The designer (perhaps in conjunction with the client) has to consider, evaluatively, the trade-offs between, for example, extra provision (e.g., more check-in desks) and smaller queue sizes.

The evaluation problem is exacerbated by the fact that the system operates stochastically. The time taken to sell one passenger a ticket, or the time taken for a passenger to claim luggage is variable; the program, each time it simulates such an event, samples from the 'serving time' distribution provided as input. As a consequence, even if all design variables are held

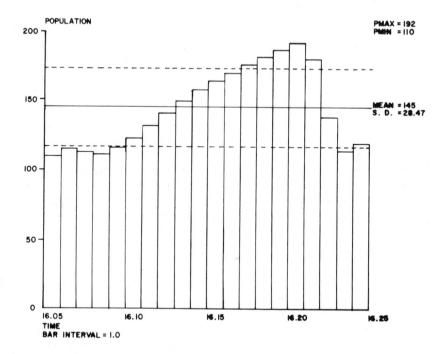

Fig. 5. Computer-drawn histogram of population at a particular facility within the air terminal.

constant, a repeat run of the program will result in the output of different performance measures; thus, letting the program operate iteratively will eventually turn up that particular set of extreme conditions which the building will ultimately have to cope with.

Modification. Based on the evaluation the designer can purposefully explore changes in the design variables and in the context variables. Changes in the design variables would be carried out with the intention of getting the levels of provision into "balance": i.e., increasing the provision where queueing is excessive, reducing the provision where the server idle time is excessive. Balancing the system by iterative modification is a delicate activity as a change in the level of provision within any single facility will affect the loadings experienced by all of the facilities further on in the system.

Changes in the context variables would be made to test the robustness of the design hypothesis under changing operating conditions—the incidence of fog, the introduction of Jumbo Jets, the need for security checking, etc..

Other Applications. The computer program AIR-Q is a sophisticated classic example of the use of simulation to model a dynamic process. The scope for the use of simulation in building design is enormous. Increasingly, it is being used to model the movement of people in transport termini—tube stations, railway stations, ferry terminals—and in other building types—museums, stadia, cafeteria, etc; within any of these (and other) building types, simulation can focus on a particular feature of the process sub-system, for example the behaviour of lifts, escalators, pater nosters, etc..

The application of computer simulation models, however, extends well beyond the field of building design. Programs embodying the same principles of logic as AIR-Q are used by designers of traffic control systems, factory assembly lines, steel production plant, etc.. Hopefully, as the models become more flexible and sophisticated and as access to computers becomes easier and less expensive, the danger of technological advance outstripping our understanding of the systems we create will recede.

2.2 The Energy Sub-System

The 'energy crisis' has focussed attention on the systemic nature of the earth's resources. Increasingly, we are becoming aware of the need for husbandry of exhaustable natural resources, including fossil fuels. In the Western World, a high proportion of our energy consumption is devoted to the heating of buildings—a consumption which is now recognized to be little short of profligate.

The problem of predicting at the design stage the actual energy consumption of a building can be divided into two distinct stages. The first is concerned with the actual energy requirements needed to satisfy the demands of the activities undertaken within the building. This is found through modifying the prevailing climatic conditions by the thermal storage and lag effects of the building. In the second stage these energy requirements are further modified by the part-load inefficiencies and running characteristics of the installed plant to give the energy actually consumed by the building. Thus, the first stage is concerned with the design of the building to reduce the energy requirements (and hence consumption), while the second stage is concerned with the design of the installed plant to best match the building's energy requirements and, at the same time, minimize the consumed energy.

The computer based thermal model ESP (Environmental Systems Performance—Clarke, 1978) addresses the first stage of the design problem and is intended to aid the designer in the prediction of how well alternative design hypotheses will behave thermally. In systems terms, the design problem is as shown in Figure 6.

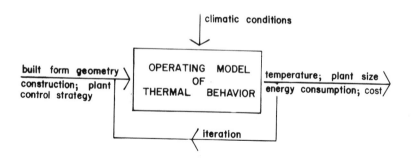

Fig. 6. An operational model of the thermal behaviour of a building seen in system terms.

Representation. In the program ESP, the designer represents a design hypothesis to the computer by inputting the following design variables.

• The building geometry: the shape configuration of the proposed building is input by a system of cartesian coordinates. The general polyhedral case is implemented to allow the representation of complex architectural forms.

• The construction: for all surfaces of the proposed building the thermal properties—conductivity, density, specific heat, thickness, solar heat transmittance, etc.—are input.

The prime context variable is, of course, climate. The program ESP uses annual meteorological tapes on which are recorded the hourly variation of six climatic parameters: dry bulb temperature, direct normal solar radiation, diffuse solar radiation, relative humidity, prevailing wind speed and direction.

Measurement. The model operation is based on an implicit numerical technique which is unconditionally stable for all computational time increments. For any building enclosure under consideration, nodes are automatically placed at appropriate points external and internal to each surface of enclosure and throughout all multilayered constructions. For each node in turn, and in terms of all surrounding nodes which are in thermal contact (by conduction, convection and radiation), an implicit difference heat balance equation is formulated. The resulting set of algebraic equations (one for each node) express all nodal temperatures and energy injections in terms of both future time and present time values. This is achieved by equating the net heat flow to each node, at the start and finish of some finite time-increment, with twice the total change in the heat stored in the region

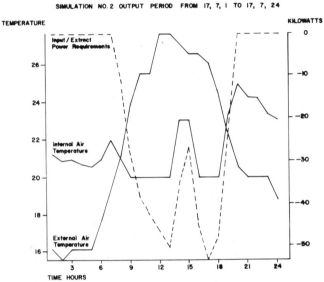

Fig. 7. Computer-drawn graphs of building behaviour during a warm spell.

represented by the node in question.

The model inherently takes account of transient conduction through all multi-layered constructions. In addition, the model takes consideration of: the internal long wave radiation exchange between enclosure surfaces, the casual gains from occupants, lights, machinery, etc., the effects of short wave radiation exchange between enclosure surfaces, the shading of external surfaces, the effects of ventilation and infiltration, and plant characteristics.

For any period of simulation of the thermal behaviour of the building the program computes and transfers into a file the relevant nodal temperatures and energy injections. These filed measurements are accessible to the designer as output.

Evaluation. Six evaluation options are open to the designer, as follows.

- The designer can evaluate the effects of imposing complex plant and/or temperature regimes on the system, for any chosen time period. Figure
- 7 shows the performance of the building in warm weather if internal air temperature is allowed to 'free-float' outside occupied periods, but is held constant at 20 degrees Centigrade between 8 a.m. and noon and between 2 p.m. and 5 p.m. In this regime, an intermittent plant operating strategy is being explored with preheat allowed between 6 a.m. and 8 a.m. The graphs plot the internal air temperature, the plant input/extract requirements and the external air temperature. The next three options are special cases of this one.

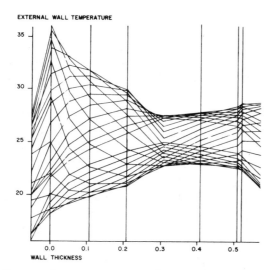

EXTERNAL WALL TEMPERATURE

WALL THICKNESS

Fig. 8. Computer-drawn temperature gradients through a multi-layer wall construction.

- An assumption can be made that no plant capacity is available at any time. This allows the designer to improve adverse environmental conditions by modifying the building design—i.e., the shape and construction —before considering the operation of installed plant.
- The internal air temperature may be held constant at some preselected value by allowing unlimited heating and cooling when available.
- Air temperature, alternatively, may be held within specified upper and lower limits.
- The designer can evaluate the effects of process loads from within the building, e.g., the installation of some heat generating equipment such as a computer.
- The annual energy requirements of the building can be computed and displayed (under any of the above conditions) by simulating 2 days in every month and 'multiplying-up' to obtain an annual figure.

The output formats for evaluations are extremely flexible. The designer can, for example, have displayed—as in Figure 8—the variation in temperature gradient with a south-facing exposed wall over, say, a 20 hour period, in order to evaluate the suitability of the chosen construction.

Modification. Typically, a designer might determine the frequency of occurrence and severity of unacceptable environmental conditions by utilising the second option. An insight into appropriate construction modifications to the design would then be afforded by output such as that in Figure 8. If these modifications alone do not alleviate the conditions, or if the modifications suggested are not economical, the third and fourth options could be used to determine the order of benefits likely to accrue from the adoption of an intermittent plant operating regime. The facility to construct graphical output interactively ensures a solid information base against which modifications to the design hypothesis can be explored and evaluated.

Other Applications. The program ESP is based on a finite difference technique of implicit enumeration. The basic logic, as it relates to thermal response, is applicable to any thermally dynamic system or artifact. Thus, the same design approach could be taken to the design of a wide range of plant items such as boilers, calorifiers, gas or stream turbines, etc..

Under development, is a complementary program which will allow design investigation of complex plant configurations. The intention is to aid the designer in the comparative evaluation between, say, a 'total-energy' building and a conventional building supplied both with fossil fuels and from the national electricity grid. The logic of the systemic appraisal will be as potentially relevant to national decisions on electricity generation, district heating schemes, solar and wind power, etc., as it is to the design issues of a single building.

3.0 Total System Design

Section 2 of this chapter dealt in outline with two specific sub-systems relevant to building design. There are, of course, other sub-systems worthy of special consideration—for example, the structural sub-system. More importantly, as suggested in the section on Design Concepts, is the complex interaction of the individual sub-systems, each with the others, within the systems model of the building as a whole.

The interaction between the two sub-systems already described is fairly obvious. At one level it will be clear that the number of people congregated within any part of the building—for example, the number of passengers queueing in the baggage reclaim area of an air-terminal complex—will significantly affect the thermal conditions within that space; conversely, the environmental conditions within the different parts of the terminal will influence where passengers choose to wait out the time until aircraft departure. Thus we see that the output from one sub-system may form the input to another sub-system, and vice-versa.

At another level, the performance of two or more sub-systems may be affected concomitantly, but diversely, by one or more of the design variables. The obvious example is the effect of the layout hypothesised by the designer on both the process and energy sub-systems: the layout which makes processing of air passengers efficient may be profligate in energy terms, and vice-versa. Thus, (as depicted in Figure 2) the designer in coping with the *total* system must receive feedback of cost/performance measures if he/she is to find that particular solution which is, in some sense, 'best'.

It is, of course, impossible to model the 'total' system; such a model would be as complex and unweildy as the real world itself. The intention in this section is to indicate how the models of individual sub-systems can be 'nested' together to model what we shall *call* a 'total' system. This 'total' system may itself become a sub-system within a more complex schema of design; and so on. Thus, the computer-based model of the operation of a boiler may become part of a computer based model of an energy system within a building, which may in turn become part of a computer-based model of the whole building, which, in its turn, may become part of a computer based model of the urban environment, etc.. Fortunately, as the scale of modelling encompasses larger portions of the real world, the models relating to sub-sub-systems can be proportionally cruder, given that doubts can be allayed by invoking the sophisticated model of the sub-sub-system as an independent design exercise.

To exemplify the concept of nested models, this section will continue to focus on building design, as represented in Figure 9. This figure summarizes the form and content of the computer program called BILD (Building Integrated Layout Design—Gentles and Unsworth, 1978). By means of a series of 'command menus' which appear on the computer screen, the designer can describe the building SITE to the computer and proceed to build up on the site a progressively detailed building design hypothesis. At the outset the designer may hypothesize a BLOCK outline which can then be detailed in terms of ROOMS; STRUCTURE and CLADDING can then be added to the building representation.

In effect, BILD is a set of nested models allowing the designer to obtain the cost/performance characteristics of the design hypothesis at progressively more detailed levels of specification. At any particular level of specification, the program will model the operational behaviour of the building—as best it can be modelled—and output cost and performance attributes. The more detailed the level of specification of the design hypothesis, the more sophisticated the computational model and hence the more reliable the cost/performance output.

Within any level, however, are representational and operational models of separate but related sub-systems. Thus, at the BLOCK outline stage, the program predicts, as best it can from the input, the process implications, the energy implications, the structural implications, the capital cost implications, etc., and provides the designer with a profile of cost/performance. Quite clearly, the accuracy of a capital cost prediction at the BLOCK outline stage in the development of a design hypothesis will be significantly lower than will be possible after the STRUCTURE and CLADDING have

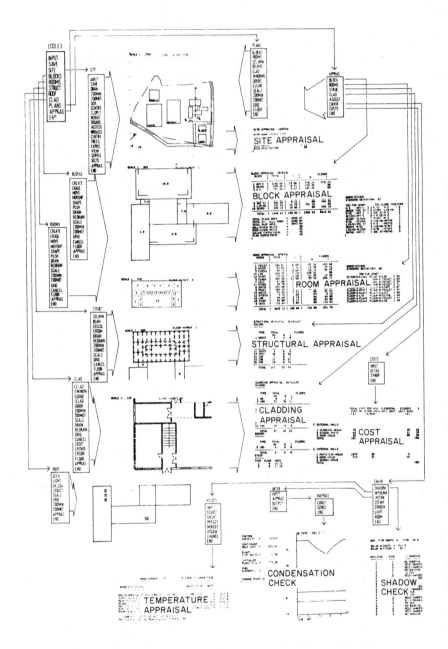

Fig. 9. Representation of the form and content of an integrated and comprehensive computer model for building design.

been specified; equally clearly, however, there is little value in proceeding to a highly detailed specification of the design hypothesis if the basic geometrical form of the building is suspect.

It would be quite wrong of course if a computer aid such as BILD dictated the sequence of design decision-making. There is no suggestion that it should, or does. If the designer wishes to proceed immediately to a high degree of specification, that is quite feasible. More typically, however, he/she will develop the design progressively from a rather symbolic model to a more literal one with occasional 'sorties' forward on one or two important exploratory fronts.

At the time of writing the BILD software is nearing completion. Currently, the various stages exist as separate programs and one of these has been applied to hospital design. This program, which is known as PHASE (Package for Hospital Appraisal, Simulation and Evaluation—Kernohan et al., 1973), will now be described.

3.1 The Form and Content of PHASE

The execution of the program is carried out in two stages. The first stage involves the inspection and upgrading of data files, the second is concerned with the appraisal routines. During the operation of the program a dialogue is maintained with the designer. This controls the sequence of operations and allows the designer to loop-back within the program to a previous operation.

For the appraisal of hospital design, a considerable amount of varied information has to be stored in a databank. For convenience of use this information is structured into four basic data files—a standard data file, solution file, project file and scheme file.

The standard data file: This contains information on environmental conditions, cost and interdepartmental traffic associations. Where relevant, they are stored for each of 40 individual hospital departments. Environmental data include air change rates, occupancy numbers, hours of occupancy, percentage wall glazing, percentage roof glazing, day and night external temperatures, solar heat gains, thermal transmittance values and desired lighting levels. Cost data include elemental capital costs, service running costs and fuel tariffs. Association data are in the form of a matrix reflecting the traffic between each pair of the 40 hospital departments. These data are taken from authoritative sources such as the Department of Health and Social Security's hospital guidance publications, the Scottish Home and Health Department's Hospital Planning Notes and IHVE Guide.

The solution file: The function of the solution file is to store the cost and performance characteristics of previous projects and of earlier schemes relating to the current project. These data are accumulated automatically and are used to provide the basis for a comparative evaluation of the characteristics of one scheme against other similar schemes.

The project file: This file contains information which is likely to remain constant throughout the design project. It includes information relating to the contours and orientation of the site, the building life and interest rates. Site information is formatted by imagining a grid placed over the site. A spot height is entered on each cell of the grid. The spot heights are fed into the project file together with the angle of orientation of the grid.

The scheme file: The scheme file may be created online or, more conventionally, offline by producing a tape and subsequently reading the tape data into a file. This file contains the three dimensional description of the geometry of the proposed scheme.

The block form is subdivided into:

- Components, which correspond to hospital departments and may number up to 40.
- Elements which are used to describe a complex component by the use of rectangular blocks and may number up to six for each component.

The size and shape of each element is described by stating the x, y, and z coordinates of a reference point together with the length, breadth and height of the element and its angle of deviation from the x-axis of the site grid. From this angle the program calculates the angle to true north by accessing the project file to obtain the orientation of the site grid. This specification is compiled for all hospital departments, and when completed, forms the scheme file for the run being undertaken. Because of variations in performance specifications, operational policies, market conditions and so on, a facility for the inspection and alteration of all data prior to the execution of a program run is provided. The designer is able to obtain a printout of the listing of any file or, in a specific case, an edited version containing those lines specified for inspection.

The input check involves the display, on the screen of the graphics terminal, of either the building plan, floor by floor (Figure 10) or of an axonometric view of the whole building. Input errors can thus be detected and altered accordingly and last minute changes in design intention can be incorporated. The method of effecting these modifications is described later.

The program output is at two levels—synoptic and detailed. The synoptic output shown in Figure 11 initially contains a check output for floor areas, wall areas and roof areas. The remaining measurements are produced in

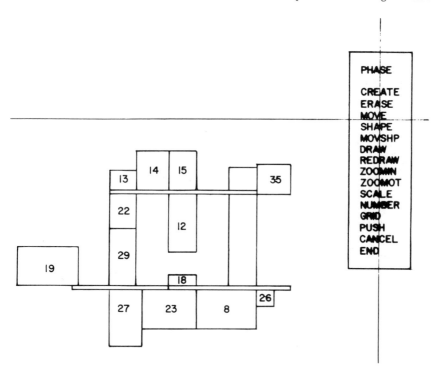

Fig. 10. Plan form of a floor of a hospital drawn on the computer screen by the designer.

tabular form, in which each measure can be compared to a sample of results from existing hospitals with similar characteristics. When a solution has been fully worked out, it can be entered in the table as the most recently attempted project result. If four results are already entered, the first result that had been entered is deleted as the columns are updated with the new result.

The wall/floor ratio and plot ratio are accepted standards, either desirable or mandatory. Site utilization is a measure of the area of site covered by the building and reflects relative density. Plan compactness compares the plan perimeter to the circumference of a circle of equal area. Mass compactness compares the surface area of the solution to that of a hemisphere of equal volume.

Department location is a total travel factor—a figure produced from the sum of all the products of the associations and their respective distances—which reflects the performance of the proposed layout in relation to the conditions imposed by departmental association. The lift dependency factor is produced from the number of vertical journeys used in the calculation factor. From these measures, and by relating performance to the size of the hospital, an index per bed can be produced. This allows meaningful com-

OUTPUT—SYNOPTIC	MWLC4	MWLC2	MWLC3	MWLC1	MWLB4
NUMBER OF BEDS	866	866	866	866	866
AREA—TOTAL FLOOR	62275	62269	61573	61112	59715
AREA—EXTERNAL WALL	28557	25875	22273	26367	28991
AREA—ROOF	30898	25727	28209	26502	24197
WALL/FLOOR RATIO	.46	.42	.36	.43	.49
PLOT RATIO	.39	.39	.39	.38	.37
SITE UTILISATION	.18	.14	.16	.14	.13
PLAN COMPACTNESS.	12.62	15.03	15.98	13.56	11.95
MASS COMPACTNESS	24.90	29.39	28.98	26.96	27.52
LIFT DEPENDENCY FACTOR	518	666	500	668	800
DEPARTMENT LOCATION PER BED	3628	5390	3386	5115	5444
BOILERHOUSE LOCN PER BED	2503	1742	2736	1850	1571
INDIC. CAPITAL COST PER BED	3973	3847	3768	3777	3744
INDIC. ENERGY COST PER BED	366	370	349	362	363

```
> DO YOU WISH A PRINTOUT OF (1) ALL DETAILED OUTPUT,
  (2) PART OF DETAILED OUTPUT, (3) NO DETAILED OUTPUT

>2

> DO YOU WISH A PRINTOUT OF:
  (1) 10% UPPER AND LOWER MATRIX VALUES
  (2) DEPARTMENT LOCATION MATRIX
  (3) BOILERHOUSE LOCATION MATRIX
  (4) ELEMENTAL CAPITAL COSTS
  (5) ENERGY COSTS
  (6) HEAT GAIN/LOSS DIAGNOSTICS

>
```

Fig. 11. Synoptic output from the computer comparing the performance of the current hospital design with earlier designs.

parisons of layout to be made between hospitals of differing size.

The boilerhouse location index is produced from the sum of all the products of the heating loads and their respective distances from the boilerhouse, in a similar manner to department location.

The indicative capital and energy costs are totals produced from the relative cost tables which are presented in the detailed output.

The detailed output consists of:

- Department location.
- Matrix of divergence.
- Boilerhouse location matrix.
- Detailed capital costs.
- Detailed energy costs.
- Heat gain/loss diagnostics for any specified number of components.

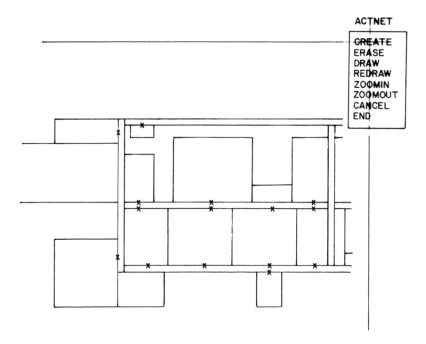

Fig. 12. More detailed descriptive input of the hospital floor plan showing the doors.

Department location: The first section of detailed output consists of a printout of all the departmental activity relationships which have not been satisfactorily met; a list of those relationships which could possibly be sacrificed is also given in order to effect an overall improvements in activity performance. If the designer cares to identify on the computer screen the positions of the doors to each department (Figure 12) the program will simulate the movement patterns over a working day and output critical journey times.

Boilerhouse location: From a knowledge of the department heating loads, the maximum hourly hospital load is calculated. This occurs at a particular time, for example, during a morning in January—and for this period, the product of the loads for each department and the distance from the boiler-house to each department are summed to produce a boiler location factor. In a similar manner to the procedure adopted for department location, a matrix of divergence is produced to illustrate which departments have been located too far from the boilerhouse in relation to the heating load required in the department.

INDICATIVE ENERGY COSTS (DETAILED)

ELEMENT	QUANTITY	RATE	PRESENT WORTH	ANNUAL EQUIVALENT
HEATING (KWDAYS)	1346504	.230		309696
PSALI (M2)	7565	.022		166
CORE VENTILATION (M3/HOUR)	672134	.001		403
AIR CONDITIONING (M3/HOUR)	58800	.004		235
			TOTALS	310501

Fig. 13. Output from the computer predicting energy costs for the hospital.

Detailed Capital Costs: A table is produced of the capital costs for a range of elements. The elements selected are those elements whose quantity significantly varies with changes in building form. The quantity of each element, which is measured from the design proposal being appraised, is multiplied by the appropriate cost taken from the standard data file to produce a present worth for each element. The present worth is then measured over the expected life of the building to produce an annual equivalent cost for a given interest/life factor. The costs measured include the normal building elements of walls, floors, roofs, windows, etc., and in addition certain items of engineering services, including the capital cost of boilers, ventilation and air conditioning plant.

Detailed Energy Costs: In a similar manner to capital costs, a table of basic energy costs is compiled. These costs are produced for heating, lighting, ventilation and air conditioning as a present worth. In addition, an annual equivalent cost is produced over the expected life of the building for a given interest/life factor (See Figure 13).

Heat Gain/Loss Diagnostics: For any specified number of departments, a printout can be obtained of the heating loads (losses) or overloads (gains) for each department in each month of the year, at four points during the day. The loads take into account heat loss through the building fabric and from ventilation, and the heat gain from occupants, lighting and solar radiation. The standard data file is accessed for the required environmental data for each department, which together with a measurement of all the surfaces of the proposed design, are used to automatically produce loads for each

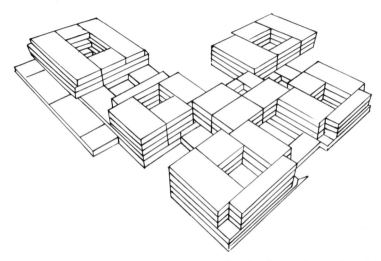

Fig. 14. Computer drawn perspective view of the hospital from a chosen viewpoint.

department. These loads are based on particular departmental character-istics of temperature, number of air changes, hours of occupancy, times of occupancy, number of occupants, lighting levels, etc., in addition to thermal transmittance and percentage glazing values appropriate to each surface of each hospital department.

Following the detailed output, or following the synoptic output if no detailed output is required, a number of options are presented. The first option allows the user to modify the form of the scheme by allowing changes in the geometry; the opportunity therefore exists to converge iteratively on a solution which, on the basis of the output appraisal and other non-quantifi-able design criteria appears to be the most advantageous. The second option simply allows the user to hold the scheme, in its current state of develop-ment until some future occasion. The third option provides the user with the opportunity to add this current scheme into the solution file so that it is reproduced in the synoptic output each time the program is run and can be constantly updated.

If it is decided to change the geometry of the scheme, the program returns the user to the floor plans and provides a menu of commands which, along with the cursor, allows easy manipulation of the geometry (Figure 12). By pointing the cursor at the command menu and at appropriate reference points, the designer can move, reshape, add to, delete from, or change the scale and planning grid of the proposal.

If a perspective view of the scheme is desired, the current geometry can be stored in a file and subsequently accessed by another program which will automatically generate perspective views from any chosen viewpoint (Fig-ure 14).

3.2 Observations on PHASE

Although it may not be clear at first sight, the conceptual approach embodied in the program PHASE is virtually identical to that embodied in the sub-system programs AIR-Q and ESP. In systems terms the inputs consist of all the design variables which specify the design hypothesis (geometry, construction, etc.) and all the context variables which modify the operational behaviour of the model (climatic data, desired environmental conditions, activity relationships, etc.). The output variables are, of course, the predicted cost and performance attributes for the hypothesised design.

PHASE models, as best the input representation will allow, both the *process* and *energy* sub-systems.

Process Sub-Systems. The input and output to the logic which models the process sub-systems are as illustrated in Figure 12. Accessing filed data on the movement pattern of nurses, food trolleys, etc., the program sub-routine simulates, over a day in the life of the hospital, the movement which takes place. For any particular nurse-journey, the program identifies the origin and the destination of the journey, invokes a 'shortest-route' algorithm from the geometrical representation of the building, and traces the route over the journey period. It is thus possible to print out journey lengths and times and the resulting congestion in corridors, and at stairs and lifts. It will be seen that this sub-routine although simpler and somewhat different, is nonetheless, in principle, similar to that in AIR-Q.

Energy Sub-System. The program ESP provides a dynamic model of the thermal behaviour of buildings appropriate to a fairly advanced stage in the development of the design. In PHASE—which is intended to be appropriate at an earlier stage in design—the thermal behaviour is modelled by a simple 'steady-state' algorithm which is capable of running on less detailed constructional data.

Other Sub-Systems. The process sub-system and the energy sub-system are only two of the many program sub-routines within PHASE, all of which operate on the design and context variables which make up the design hypothesis. Any one of them could be developed in more detail as 'free-standing' programs in their own right—in the same manner as AIR-Q and ESP.

Conceptually, the important feature of PHASE is the manner in which the disparate sub-routines are organized to operate on a single representation of the design hypothesis. As argued in the opening section of this Chapter, a comprehensive model such as PHASE is crucial to a systemic view of design decision making.

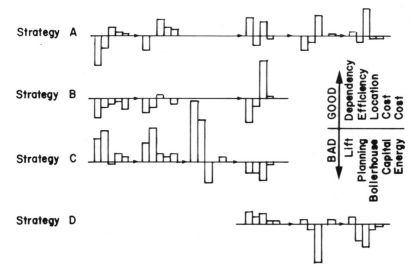

Fig. 15. A sequence of performance profiles generated during the search for the best hospital design.

The program will in fact produce a graphical representation of the balance between synoptic cost and performance attributes. The sequence of profiles obtained from exploration and development of four fundamentally different design strategies is illustrated in Figure 15. When these measurable attributes are considered in conjunction with the aesthetic qualities embodied in the perspective views an opportunity is afforded the designer and client body to base their subjective value judgements on a shared and explicit information set.

PHASE in Relation to BILD. We have seen how PHASE represents, at one level of design detail, the integration of many disparate *aspects* of the design problem. The program BILD is also integrative—this time over disparate *levels* of design detail. By extension of the principle of integration (i.e., the 'nesting' of appropriate models), it will be seen how the designer and others can, progressively, build up an understanding of the natural and human-made world and the complex interactions between them. Equally, it will be seen that a progression based on such an approach depends, not solely but nonetheless certainly, on advances in the science of computing.

4.0 Conclusion

In this chapter, the role of CAD has been exemplified by reference to architecture and building design. It is worth noting that it is some 5,000 years since architectural drawings first made their appearance as models of future reality. Up to about 10 years ago, little or no development had taken place in these modelling techniques. Quite suddenly, with graphical access to powerful computing facilities, vast new modelling possibilities were opened up. In the ten years since, the progress has been rapid, but it would be absurd to imagine that the model developers have done any more than scratch the surface of the modelling potential. Not only is there scope for technological advancement but also for the adoption of these techniques within the profession; who, by and large, have remained sceptical if not downright resistant.

Modelling is not of course a panacea for all problems: the data on which a simulation is based must be accurate, as must the assumptions incorporated in the model, or at least known to some specified degree of accuracy. The need for careful evaluation of options is no less important. Indeed the strength of the computer approach is that it provides the opportunity to examine many more alternatives in greater detail than previously. Thus in principle allowing more consideration of the balance between objective measures (e.g. costs) and subjective factors (e.g., aesthetics). Another potential benefit is that the design process can be "opened up" to involve more participation by those affected by design decisions.

Some glimpses of this potential have already appeared. In one experiment, several hours of TV time in California were given over to computer modelling of highway routes in part of the State. In the studio the operators of the computer model superimposed alternative routes for a proposed highway on a map drawn on the graphics screen; the computer output, for any particular route, information on construction cost, houses lost, agricultural land used, etc.. Viewers at home were able to phone in to suggest alternatives which seemed to them, systematically, to provide a better balance. At a more technologically modest level, work sponsored by the Science Research Council and the Social Science Research Council at Strathclyde (Aish, 1977) has shown that, with access to an appropriate computer based design aid, nursery school teachers can develop outline proposals for the design of a nursery school which are at least equal in 'design quality' (as judged by experienced critics) to those designed professionally.

However it is appropriate to point out in conclusion that we shall approach the 'ideal state' of design only if we consciously *design* our *design methods*, i.e., if we are prepared to model alternatives and exercise our value judgements in deciding between them. The computer is as powerful a tool in reinforcing totalitarianism as it is in emancipating the individual: a conscious and considered choice is required.

Acknowledgments

Advances in CAD are achieved only through the committment and effort of integrated teams of able and far sighted people from a variety of disciplines. The examples used in this Chapter are acknowledged as due to Lamond Laing and Jim Gentles (AIR-Q), Joe Clarke (ESP), Harvey Sussock (BILD), David Kernohan, George Rankin, Graeme Wallace and Roger Walters (PHASE), Robert Aish (PARTIAL) and all other members of ABACUS, past and present.

References

Aish, R. (1977). Prospects for Design Participation. *Design Methods and Theories,* **11**, 2.

Clarke, J.A. (1978). Thermal Simulation in Building Design. *Proceedings of CAD 78.* IPC Science and Technology Press, Guilford, England.

Gentles, J.C. & Unsworth, M. (1978). An Integrated and Comprehensive Database for CAAD Appraisal Packages. *Proceedings of CAD 78.* IPC Science and Technology Press, Guildford, England

Kernohan, D., Rankin, G., Wallace, G. & Walters, R. (1973). PHASE: An Integrated Appraisal Package for Whole Hospital Design. *Computer Aided Design,* **5**, 2.

Laing, L.W. (1975). "AIR-Q: Flexible Computer Simulation Model for Airport Terminal Buildings Design. *Design, Methods and Theory—Design, Research and Methods Journal,* **9**, 2.

Chapter 9

THE ROLE OF COMPUTER SYSTEMS IN MEDICAL DECISION-MAKING

Tom R. Taylor

Contents

1.0 Introduction

While applications of computers in medicine cover a very wide area the number that can be related to a review of human/computer systems is still quite limited. The underlying technical and conceptual problems associated with such systems can be best illustrated if a specific area is highlighted. In this critical review the focus of analysis is clinical decision-making. It is assumed throughout that the term human/computer system implies a sophisticated software and hardware interface and a high level of interaction between the user and the computer system.

We begin with a fairly explicit model of those parts of the clinical decision-making process that are relevant to this review. A model of the "task environment" in which the human/computer system must function is very valuable in evaluating and designing such systems. However, it is important to make a disclaimer at this point. The areas of clinical decision-making covered by the model are those which are, at this stage of understanding, most accessible to observation and measurement. As in all good models its value lies not only in the power of prediction and explanation but also in its ability to highlight our ignorance. In other words the gaps in the model are as important as the formal elements. The more powerful the model, the more fascinating are the gaps.

2.0 A Formal Model of the Clinical Decision-making Process

Clinicians spend their lives making decisions. They have to choose treatments and management policies. They must choose the most appropriate test to clarify their own understanding of a patient's problem. The central process is one of sequential decision-making in the face of uncertainty; but this process is embedded in a series of parallel and closely inter-locking processes each of which will be discussed below.

2.1 Goals, Strategies and Resources

The context in which such decision-making takes place is one where the clinician has certain *goals* set by himself and by the patient, with broader ones set by society at large. In order to reach such goals he must expend *resources* such as his own time and empathy, as well as choosing investigations or treatments which will cost money and involve others in expending their time and energy.

Such resources are always limited and so the clinician operates in a *macro-economic environment* competing with numerous other demands on society's resources. When dealing with the individual patient the clinician is concerned with the *micro-economic environment* of, for example, a clini-

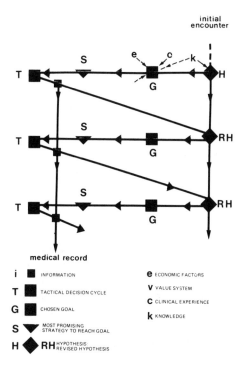

Fig. 1. Schematic representation of some of the principal processes involved in clinical decision-making.

cal ward where an individual patient must compete with (perhaps more acutely ill) patients for the hospital's limited resources.

The clinician, during the management of a case, must set *personal clinical goals* (e.g., "to eliminate the possibility of cancer"). In order to reach any of these goals a clinician must consider a number of possible strategies. Each *strategy* might consist of a series of tests, a sequence of treatments or a combination of both (Figure 1). Each strategy has a probability of achieving the goal and will call for the expenditure of such resources as the physician's time, energy, and empathy, as well as financial and other resources (e.g., nurse's time, patient's time).

The clinician chooses what he/she considers the most appropriate *set of possible strategies* from which he then makes his final selection. Both choices are made by trading-off risk against cost and the chance of reaching a goal. Such decisions are, of course, made in the face of *uncertainty* with no guarantee that a test will yield useful information or that a treatment will be effective.

2.2 Clinical Hypotheses

Along with clinical goals, the most important influence on the choice of strategy is the clinician's current set of working *hypotheses*. These represent the most plausible explanation of the patients's problem. The strategy chosen may be aimed at a short-term goal of eliminating one hypothesis (e.g., cancer) or discriminating between two others. Hypothesis generation may be viewed as a method of coping with the limited capacity of the human nervous system for processing information. Clinicians can usually only entertain four to six hypotheses simultaneously. The hypothetico-deductive process has been shown experimentally to be a critically important feature of clinical decision-making (Elstein, 1976; Norman et al., 1977).

2.3 The Tactical Decision Cycle

The sequence of tests or treatments which make up a strategy can be modified as new information becomes available from the tests or treatment responses in the early part of any strategy. This represents an important *tactical* level of decision-making within any individual strategy. The wording of questions is frequently modified to take account of information already gained in the early segment of a strategy.

At this tactical level a recurrent *decision cycle* occurs with each test or treatment which is performed on a patient. The decision cycle is an integral part of the sequential decision process. A *test* is defined as any procedure which elicits clinical evidence.

As each test or treatment is performed four interlocking processes are carried out. The clinician

- *Performs* a test or treatment (e.g., asks a question);
- *Observes* the outcome (e.g., hears the patient's responses);
- *Categorizes* the outcome (e.g., "positive/negative");
- *Selects* the next most appropriate test or treatment.

This analysis will be used to illustrate the role of the computer in many areas of clinical decision-making. The performance of a test usually involves psycho-motor skills (e.g., using an opthalmoscope). The observation depends on perceptual processes such as sight or hearing. Categorical judgements are a critically important aspect of clinical decision-making being influenced by the goals of the clinician. Thus, criteria for obesity will vary depending on the goals of the clinician (e.g., "ideal" weight for an insurance examination, but a less stringent range of normality in population screening if the resources available for treatment are limited). The selection of test and treatment is made by a process of sequential decision-making and is influenced both by the current hypothesis and by consideration of costs.

2.4 The Role of Decision Theory

The diagnostic process can be viewed as a sequence of decisions in which two types of information are used by the clinician:

- A differential diagnosis or prognosis which represents an assessment by the clinician of the available information about possible diagnoses or response to treatment (i.e., a clinical hypothesis).
- An estimate by the clinician of the cost of each possible test and the likely benefit to the patient of each possible treatment.

The clinician is then assumed to choose the path of minimum cost to select the treatment which is most appropriate to the needs of the patient. These needs include not only the relief of distress and pain but also a return to health which is as rapid and complete as possible. The assessment of such clinical costs pervades the whole of clinical decision-making, both in hospital and in family practice. In arriving at any estimate of such costs a number of factors must be weighed up:

- The advantages of making an immediate and appropriate selection of treatment;
- The consequences of making an overhasty and inappropriate choice of treatment;
- The financial cost, as well as the discomfort, inconvenience and delay due to further tests before treatment is begun.

It must be emphasized that costs and information both feature in the selection of tests, as well as of treatments, even though information appears more dominant in the earlier diagnostic phase and cost in the later therapeutic phase of the clinical decision-making process.

The *principle of rationality* (one of the bases of decision theory) when applied to the clinical situation asserts that any rational decision-maker acts as if he/she is able to measure the advantages and disadvantages of a decision in common units and make decisions (such as to continue testing or to select a treatment) so that the expected net advantage to the patient is as large as possible. In other words, the decision maker attempts to achieve the greatest benefit for the patient at a minimum cost. In decision theory such values are referred to as utilities. This view of the practice of medicine in terms of costs or utilities represents the implicit value system with which clinicians manage their patients.

Since clinicians differ in their judgements of these costs, it can be said that *each state of health, or of illness, has its value* (measured in utilities) for each clinician. Thus, one clinician in a chronic renal dialysis unit, where potential patients greatly outnumber the limited number of kidney machines available, may feel that only young adults should be accepted for

T. Taylor

chronic dialysis. By contrast, another clinician may feel only patients with a criminal record should be excluded and that all others should be put on a waiting list. The importance of such value systems is that they strongly influence the number of investigations and type of treatment chosen (Taylor et al., 1972; Taylor et al., 1975)

2.5 The Sequential Decision Process

Having illustrated the complementary influence of information and costs in any understanding of a decision problem, we must move to a more detailed level of analysis. The process of decision-making can be represented as a sequence of decisions in which the clinician selects a path through a decision tree. Such a tree is seen as consisting of a number of nodes connected to one another by branches. Nodes are of two kinds—a *decision node* where the clinician must choose from a set of actions and a *chance node* where the outcome of the action is not under the clinician's control but is determined by the response of the patient to the chosen action.

The clinician makes a choice of action at each decision node. For example, at the first decision node the choice will be what is regarded as the most appropriate question. This will be selected from a list of possible questions that the working set of hypotheses bring to mind. The order of preference in this list will change as new information from previous tests or observations comes in. The clinician can be seen to choose the tests at the top of the *preference* list as he/she moves through the problem. After hearing the response to the first question, the clinician then moves to the next decision node to choose the next most appropriate question from those remaining. Actions may be chosen singly in this way, or in blocks depending on the strategy.

The response of the patient to any action is not under the clinician's control and thus is designated the chance node. The chance node represents a set of possible outcomes for any action. Each of these possible responses can be assigned a probability of occurence. Probabilistic data of this kind can be collected in surveys (Taylor et al., 1972) or based on subjective estimates provided by experienced clinicians (Ginsberg & Offensend, 1968). Such probabilities can then be used in various forms of computer-assisted decision-making. The up-dating of a hypothesis or diagnosis in the light of new information can be accomplished statistically by Bayes's Theorem whenever such probabilistic information is available. This has been the most commonly used statistical technique in computer-assisted decision-making over the past decade (Taylor, 1967; 1970).

The same probabilistic data can be used not only to up-date a diagnosis but it has also been used to select tests in an optimal sequence (Taylor, 1970). The cheapest route to a diagnosis can also be chosen by the addition of financial costs (Taylor et al., 1972). However (as decision theory makes clear) at each decision node the clinician selects the next test or treatment using not only probabilistic information but combines this with a value judgement about the expected costs or benefit of each possible outcome. The delineation of the probabilities and costs associated with each set of possible tests or treatment outcomes lies at the basis of most forms of decision analysis. The writer has critically reviewed the contribution of many studies of clinical decision analysis to the provision of health care and to medical education (Taylor, 1976).

2.6 Alternative Models of the Decision-making Process

It is important to emphasize here that the sequential decision model used as a basis of this analytic review is very unlikely to be a complete model of all the intellectual proccesses involved in clinical decision-making. It is more likely to represent the most easily accessible cognitive functions of the clinician. Clinicians themselves have always claimed that they frequently use a "spot diagnosis" or "pattern recognition" approach to problems. Thus, a patient may exhibit the typical posture or gait of Parkinsonism allowing a diagnosis to be made "on sight".

Yet, Mintzberg (1973) in his studies of business executive decision-making found that the linear planned approach to decision-making which is widely taught in business schools is seldom followed in practice. Executives tend to make complex "ad hoc" decisions and then find a justification for their choice of action. He strongly suggests that the influence of the intuitive, holistic type of judgement (recently associated with the non-dominant cerebral hemisphere) is very much more frequently used than is admitted (Mintzberg, 1976).

3.0 Computer-based History-taking Systems

In most discussions about human/computer systems, particularly in medicine, the usual assumption is that the "human" in such a system is an expert user or a trained technician. The interface (both hardware and software) is geared to such a level of expertise. However, one interesting application of human/computer systems, *medical history-taking systems*, involves the general public, often elderly, ill-educated and frequently very apprehensive. It is worthwhile examining this group of applications to understand how interfaces have been developed to reconcile the goals of the "naive" user on the one hand and the medical system on the other.

3.1 Clinical Background

If a patient presents himself with the complaint of a pain in his chest the clinician takes a history of this current complaint and tries "to build up a picture" of the evolution of the patient's problem. The taking of a history is one of the most time-consuming and important parts of the assessment of a patient's problem. The history provides subjective information about the time-dependant features of the evolution of the patient's subjective complaints and their relationship to one another over time. The history very often (particularly in neurological diseases) provides the main source of information in the initial assessment of the patient about the pathological nature of the illness, while the physical signs found on examination point to the location of the lesions in the patient's body.

The clinician elicits information from the patient by a process which has been described by Holt (1961) as "Listening to what the patient says, in an inter-active context of participant observation". As well as this verbal communication with the patient however, the clinician gains much non-verbal information based on observation (e.g., facial expressions, mannerisms, posture or gait).

Much of this non-verbal information is not recorded in the case record but will influence the clinician in setting up the initial hypothesis and in choosing a treatment. The building-up of hypotheses about the patient's illness (and in particular about its time-relationships) is absolutely essential to history-taking. The complex interaction between patient and clinician, the intricate interplay between hypotheses and strategies, and the tactical modifications of strategies, cannot as yet be captured by any existing human/computer system. Nevertheless, the "Case" teaching simulations of Harless et al. (1969) are extraordinarily flexible in representing the information gathering inter-action between clinician and patient.

The main role of existing history-taking systems, as Lucas (1976) has argued, lies in the routine questioning aspect of the history. Hence, his preference for the term "computer interrogation". Simborg, Rikli and Hall (1969) have suggested that the different approaches to acquiring medical history data can be classified into:

- *Dialogue:* namely, the traditional patient/clinician interview.
- *Questionnaire:* these have a long history in medicine and can be self-administered by the patient, used to guide paramedical staff and, once completed, can be further annotated by a clinician.
- *Interactive automotive:* this is the on-line computer-based type of history system which is the main concern of this review.

3.2   The Role of Automated Systems

The main justifications which are cited for turning to automated systems for collecting historical information from the patient are:

- History-taking demands a significant portion of the clinician's *time*.
- The personal or *intimate* nature of the information being sought, for example in gynaecology or alcoholism, may lead the patient to prefer a less personal approach (Slack & Van Cura, 1968; Lucas et al., 1977).
- Uniform and consistent wording and selection of *questions* is possible with an automated approach.
- Questions can be repeated and expanded if necessary *without effort*; i.e., "previous night's activities do not impede its functioning the morning after" (Kleinmuntz & McLean, 1968).
- Information gathered in a computer system can be used not only for the patient's immediate needs but also for use in *clinical epidemiology* and for administrative uses such as *scheduling visits* (Rockart et al., 1973).
- The variability of the interviewer is eliminated since the response of the clinician to the patient may influence the whole sequence and content of the interview. Lucas et al. (1976) compared a teletype and a visual display unit with an experienced gastro-enterologist and found the data collected on dyspepsia by computer interrogation to be highly reproducible in its content.
- The information acquired can be used as the basis of administrative *screening* procedures in hospital. Some may simply assign the general outpatient population of hospital referrals to the appropriate *specialists* while others allow the selection of some *preliminary investigations* before being seen by the physician.
- It may produce a *legible case record* in contrast to the quality of many written records (Slack et al., 1967). A Clinician need only annotate the printout to complete the initial record.
- The information collected could form the basis for *diagnosis* of specific problems such as headache (Stead et al., 1972; Freeman, 1968), dysphagia (Edwards, 1970), arthritis (Freis, 1970), hysteria (Woodruff et al., 1973), dyspepsia or alcoholism (Lucas, 1977), or be geared to the needs of special clinics such as thyroid (Taylor et al., 1972) or headache clinics. It can be mailed in advance of attendance at a clinic (Rockart et al., 1973) and used for scheduling first and second visits.

3.3   Approaches to Automated History Systems

Automated techniques for collecting clinical information have their origins in the use of questionnaires. These were seen as having the many benefits of automated history taking systems already discussed. However, time and experience have revealed not only the complexity of the clinical information-gathering process but also the rigidity of the pencil and paper approach.

Many different approaches have been used in automating the accumulation of clinical information. Collen et al. (1969) used a deck of pre-punched question cards which were sorted into "yes" and "no" groups by patients. Slack et al. (1969) developed the first on-line system using a LINC 8 laboratory computer and a branching logical decision tree. A later development by the same group used video tape feedback which encouraged patients to ventilate their problems (Slack & Slack, 1972). This approach to psychotherapy was similar to that of Colby et al. (1975). Mayne et al. (1969) used a sophisticated computer controlled microfilm terminal with coloured pictures (e.g., the patient's abdomen). This involved the use of an interactive display and a light pen and was eventually abandoned because of cost. A modified teaching machine was used by Edwards (1970) in the computer diagnosis and management of dysphagia using a logical decision tree.

There has been a tendency to gravitate back to simpler standard video displays because of the simplicity of their use and transferability of programs.

3.4 The Patient-computer Interface

Lucas (1977) has focused particular interest on evaluating the form that the interface between the patient and computer should take. This analysis of the interface concerns not only the hardware, but also the mode of presentation of questions, the layout of the keyboard to allow simplified answering by the "naive" user, and the selection of the questions themselves. He discusses in detail:

- The relative merits of a *teletype versus a visual display*: 71% of patients preferred the latter. Accuracy was comparable between the two.
- The relative value of *spoken versus written* (or displayed) questions: they were equally acceptable to patients.
- The *speed* of displaying data: the system which he developed is organized to adjust its speed according to the response time of the patient in the early part of the interview.
- *Range of responses*: this is set at three or seven choices depending on the patient's response in the early part of the interview.
- *Wording of questions*: this has been studied in great detail.

The system developed in this way elicited information which was highly reproducible, comparable in accuracy to an experienced specialist and more accurate than physicians in eliciting reliable information on such topics as alcohol intake. Detailed attitude surveys of patients found 82% favourable; especially among younger patients (less than 30 years), in males and in manual rather than non-manual workers.

3.5 Overall Evaluation of History-taking Systems

The general conclusions from the use of several of such systems appear to be that:

- The *time* taken per case is on average about 12-60 minutes (Hassler, 1969). Patients have been found to tolerate well an automated history of up to 60 minutes duration (Mayne et al., 1968). The cost of a history taken on-line is directly related to the time spent on-line to the computer. Older patients, those with many complaints, and those with a poor formal education, predictably enough were found to take the longest (Coombs et al., 1970). The last authors used these findings to select those patients who were suitable for on-line history-taking alone and those who would benefit from the help of an attendant in entering their responses. This selection process was found to reduce time and, therefore, to cut costs. Lucas (1977) found the cost of patient interrogation using a system based on a commercial time-sharing system was only marginally more expensive than that of a specialist in the United Kingdom. Comparable costs for North America are not as yet available.
- The *reaction of patients* of all socio-economic backgrounds to such systems was remarkably favourable (Slack & Van Cura, 1968). Similar findings have been reported by Mayne et al. (1968) and Rockart et al (1973). Lucas (1977) confirmed the above findings with detailed attitude questionnaires. Grossman et al. (1977) who found a 91% positive response has noted, however, it is not known to what extent the patient's response is due to a novelty effect or to a true acceptance of the technique.
- The *clinical usefulness* of the questionnaire has also been analyzed. The pencil-and-paper and the inter-active type compare well with the clinician's notes in the traditional case record. No single technique has yet shown overall superiority (Mayne & Martin, 1970). The same authors showed from a comparative review of the medical records in 500 patients that the chief complaint was picked up in more than 93% of cases by both pencil-and-paper and interactive versions of their systems. Significant omissions by the computer-based systems were found to be negligible (Mayne et al., 1969) but patients tended to be over scrupulous in reporting minor symptoms. The inevitable increase of irrelevant and redundant information was eventually found to be very irritating and a hindrance, rather than a help to clinicians participating in the same study. (This is

similar to the problem of *feature extraction* in image processing systems (see sections 4.4–7). This resulted in those who were initially enthusiastic losing interest. The information was not useful in selecting investigations and it was suggested that if decisions were to be made the questionnaire should be designed with these decisions in mind. In Massachusetts General Hospital, several different language versions of the history-taking system are available and systems in which data are collected in one language and displayed in another are already being used.

- A major consideration as far as practical day-to-day use of such systems is that of *cost*. The most detailed cost evaluation that is generally available is that of Mayne & Martin (1970) when they compared the true cost of both their off-line branching questionnaire and their complex visual display station with a light pen. Their conclusion was that "Such techniques are far too costly for routine medical practice, although they are being tried experimentally. While the questionnaire version, which is much less flexible, is normally cheaper, this is only so if large volumes of histories are processed.". However, as noted earlier, Lucas (1977) using a simpler system is much more optimistic.

- *The reaction of medical staff* is not nearly so clear cut as that of the patients. Slack et al. (1970) have discussed this aspect in some detail. The initial response by clinicians in their study was enthusiastic but was not sustained and may have been a Hawthorne effect. The limitations of the technique when in regular use became irritating since, unlike patients who only interact with the computer on one or two occasions, the clinicians were regular users. The attitudes to their inter-active system were found by Grossman et al. (1971) to be mixed and not as favourable as those of the patients. The impression gained was that the data yielded did not quite fit into the sequence in which clinicians build up a clinical picture (a hypothesis) about their patients. Their normal pattern of history-taking is aimed at collecting evidence for or against such a hypothesis and to aid in selecting an appropriate strategy of management. Data from an automated history tend, in their present form, to disrupt this flow of decisions. The clinician also records much less than is actually collected. He/she chooses to concentrate on those items which are believed to be important, which support the hypothesis or which may be of future medical-legal significance.

- The final consideration is the *practical implementation* of such systems in *routine practice*. This assessment is influenced, above all, by cost and by the health care system in which it will operate. As Mayne & Martin (1970) have emphasised "Until we can define the data base needed for medical decisions in terms of its usefulness, it will be difficult to compare the effectiveness of different techniques for collecting and recording data.". This again alludes to the specific clinical goals for which the system is designed.

It is important to emphasize what an automatic approach *does not do* in contrast to the traditional clinical encounter. Many *visual clues* to the patient's problem, such as signs of tension, apprehension, may belie the answers given by patients. Indeed, as Balint (1957) has shown, a symptom or complaint may serve as a "token" to allow contact with the clinician to take place in a traditional disease-oriented context. This "token symptom" is discarded if the clinician addresses himself to the patient's most compelling problem, which in such cases is a psychological one (Taylor, 1969).

Human/computer applications of this type touch on a number of important *basic issues*. The fact that the general public have direct access to such systems imposes considerable limitations on the type of interface to be used, both in terms of the hardware (video, teletype or audio) and in terms of the software. The software interface allows flexibility in the form of the questions posed, the words used, the speed of presentation and the responses needed to clarify the terms which the patient fails to understand. An important feature of history-taking systems is how clear an understanding of the process of data-acquisition and decision-making is implicit in the design of the system. Most systems merely conduct a process of data-acquisition with or without a logical decision tree to cut down the amount of redundant information recorded. Others imply a more decision-oriented approach to the acquisition of information, i.e., information is collected in order to calculate certain decisions. (Lucas, 1977).

However, when we move to actual interviews involving practising clinicians and patients, the flexibility and strategic adaptability of the clinician cannot as yet be matched in any way by available history-taking systems; although they are obviously moving in this direction.

4.0 Diagnosis Systems

The group of studies most relevant to a survey of human/computer systems in medicine are those where there is "on-line" interaction between clinician and computer and where there is some sharing of the task being performed. Clearly, the better the understanding of the task the more effective will be the system used to perform it. Hence, we will tend to concentrate on those techniques which have been based on some background of understanding of the decision-making process in medicine.

The great majority of studies of computer-assisted decision-making in medicine are of the "single-stage" type where all available data are used simultaneously to calculate a diagnosis or to predict the outcome of treatment. Many other variants of this single stage approach have been used. The brief review of radiological decision-making at the end of this section illustrates the variety of statistical and technical routes taken to reach broadly similar diagnostic goals.

The single stage approach was based on an incorrect understanding of the process of diagnosis. This is the assumption that diagnosis is essentially a classification exercise in which all available evidence is reviewed before placing the patient in a suitable category; for each category there is an appropriate treatment. In using this type of model, data were collected on a series of reference or "training" cases where the diagnosis had already been clearly established. The data consisted of the responses to a series of "tests" such as items of history, physical examination, or laboratory tests. These were used to set up a probabilistic matrix relating disease categories to test outcomes. Then in the majority of cases a diagnosis was calculated using Bayesian or linear discriminant function calculations. The resemblance of each new case to the previously assembled sets of "training" cases was then calculated (Taylor, 1967).

The single stage approach equates clinical decision-making with the statistical technique of class allocation so that a patient is allocated to a class with a calculated level of probability or equivalent weight. In the model of clinical decision-making already described such single stage approaches confine themselves to the hypothesis generation aspect of the total process. However, it soon became clear that such single stage models were of no practical interest to clinicians who, as we have seen earlier, make decisions (about the relevant information to collect) in sequences.

The next stage was the development of multi-stage or sequential models which more closely match the clinician's normal approach to practice (Taylor, 1970). One of these sequential decision models is described by Taylor et al. (1972) dealing with a simple three disease decision problem and is outlined below.

4.1 Sequential Cost-conscious Computer-assisted Decision-making

In patients with enlarged thyroid glands but not thyrotoxicosis the diagnosis usually rests between simple goitre, Hashimoto's disease, and thyroid cancer. Data on thirty diagnostic tests used in this three-disease system were run on two computer programs—one based solely on the discriminating power of the tests, while the second, in addition, took account of the financial cost of tests. Conditional probability theory provides techniques for calculating the differential diagnosis in a test case from data summarising the previous behaviour of the diseases being considered. These data are derived from past surveys and provide information about the incidences of the diseases in the population (prior probabilities) and the pattern of test outcomes in each disease (likelihoods) (Figure 2). From these data the

No	Test	Response	Hashimoto's disease	Simple goitre	Thyroid cancer
25	Consistency	Firm	0.9057	0.5800	0.4600
		Hard	0.0566	0.0400	0.5300
		Soft	0.0377	0.3800	0.0100
27	CF test	+ +	0.8372	0.0100	0.0200
		+	0.0698	0.0513	0.1081
		—	0.0930	0.9387	0.8719
8	Pyramid lobe	Absent	0.8491	0.9608	0.9783
		Present	0.1509	0.0392	0.0217

Fig. 2. Examples of likelihoods of disease by test outcome for selected population.

differential diagnosis (posterior probabilities) can be calculated by Bayes' theorem (Taylor, 1967).

A sequential form of Bayes' theorem was used; instead of all tests being considered at once, they are selected in an "optimal" sequence. This is done in the computer program by using a *test selection function* namely, the "minimal entropy" calculation derived from information theory (Lindley, 1956). This measure makes it possible to calculate from past experience (represented by the likelihoods) the test which is expected to yield the most information at the current stage in the diagnostic process. In an earlier study, this sequential model was found to use less than a third of the available tests to reach a diagnosis. There was no loss of diagnostic accuracy in comparison with a similar model which used all available tests (Taylor, 1970).

The first program in this study selects, by the above technique, the test which is expected to yield most information at each stage in the diagnosis. The outcome on the selected test is observed from the patient's record and a differential diagnosis is calculated by the computer, which then selects the "next best" test from those remaining. The program stops when a final probability of 0.99 has been reached on three successive tests.

The second program is identical except that, by taking account of costs, it selects a test which is expected to yield the most information per pound sterling. This *cost-conscious* model was as accurate as the *cost-free* one and, in a series of 67 cases of thyroid enlargment, was 30% cheaper. The method offers a means of choosing the "best buy" among possible sequences of diagnostic investigations and could be extended to treatment.

The selection of tests by the computer programs used in this study greatly reduced the number of tests needed to make a diagnosis. Some 24 out of 38 cases of Hashimoto's disease and 32 out of the total 67 cases were diagnosed with less than seven tests out of a possible thirty. In the cost-free version a clinical test such as consistency of the thyroid gland (liable to considerable observer error), was consistently better than any of the expensive complex tests.

Finally, a version of the first program (cost-free entropy) was modified to run with four treatment blocks namely, history, physical examination, tests run from a single blood-sample, and other more complex tests (Figure 3). The results showed that 44 out of 67, cases were correctly diagnosed. This experimental program is more appropriate to the organization of an out-patient clinic. The history block could be adapted to a *history-taking computer terminal*, while the examination and blood sample block could be completed by trained *paramedical* personnel in an out-patient screening clinic. This is broadly similar to the approach proposed by Lucas (1977) and by Knill-Jones (1977).

The preliminary data collected in such a screening clinic might allow some laboratory investigations to be selected by the computer-based decision system. The clinician would then first see the patient at a normal out-patient clinic when most of the relevant information had been collected and a diagnosis could be established in most cases. The clinician could then decide on treatment for these routine cases where he agreed with computer diagnosis and reserve much of his time for those difficult cases in which the screening investigations had not led to a diagnosis. The emphasis of such an approach is on a minimum of investigations, at the lowest possible expense, discomfort, and inconvenience, to establish an accurate diagnosis.

There are a number of other approaches which are sequential in type. The essential structure in such sequential systems is a decision tree. Such a tree is seen as comprising of a number of nodes connected to one another by branches. Nodes as we have already seen are of two kinds—a decision node, where the clinician must choose from a set of actions, and a chance node, where the outcome of the action is not under the clinician's control but is determined by the response of the patient to the chosen action.

In understanding sequential decision systems, a key element is the method of selecting the most appropriate route down the decision tree. This is done by a *selection or evaluation function* which operates at each decision

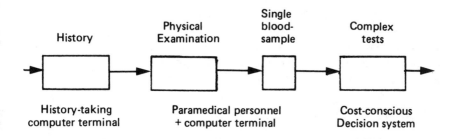

Fig. 3. Suggested organisation for a screening clinic based on cost-concious computer-assisted decision making.

node. In the sequential Bayesian model the function is the "entropy" calculation from information theory. In the cost-conscious version it is the expected information yield per pound calculated by a combination of the entropy calculation and the cost of each test. A broadly similar approach was taken by Gleser & Collen (1972) and by Warner et al. (1972).

A large number of other sequential techniques have been based on logical decision trees (Freis 1970), and a few on probabilistic inference. Many of these are reviewed under *history-taking systems*.

4.2 Limitations of Systems Based on Statistical Decision Models

A multiplicity of statistical techniques have now been used for computer assisted decision-making with Croft (1972) comparing 10 different statistical methods in the same diagnostic problem. Yet, they have had almost no impact on clinical practice. The reasons for this failure are diverse. Most studies of computer-assisted decision-making have concentrated on differential diagnosis despite the fact that diagnosis occupies a subsidiary role in clinical practice to decisions about the selection of investigations and regimes of treatment.

Studies have also been, for the most part, confined to the well-structured areas of medicine, such as thyroid disease (Taylor et al., 1972) or congenital heart disease (Warner et al., 1961). However, the bulk of decisions in clinical practice are much less clearly defined.

The cost and the accessibility of suitable computing facilities have limited the spread of even the successful applications. To justify the need for constantly available computing facilities, one would have to choose a problem which was very frequently encountered, such as acid-base disorders (Bleich 1969) or an area of health care where intensive use of facilities would be likely. Two widely uniform areas which fall into this latter category are the diabetic clinic and the ante-natal clinic. An experimental ante-natal system aimed at avoiding some of these, and other, pitfalls is described below.

4.3 An Ante-natal Clinic System

In an attempt to take account of the limitations of purely statistical types of decision-systems the writer (Taylor et al., 1976) developed a system of computer-based decision-making which would allow nurses to monitor the normal pregnancies in an ante-natal clinic, while the "high risk" cases were detected and directed, after appropriate investigations, to an expert obstetrician. The approach is based on a number of stages of "descriptive decision analysis".

- A list of relevant management and investigative decisions was made covering all decisions made in a typical ante-natal clinic.
- By questioning and by introspection on the part of an obstetrician, a set of decision rules was developed for each decision.
- A computer program was written incorporating all the decision rules so that the input into the program was the data normally collected at the first and follow-up visits of the patient in most ante-natal clinics. The program scans the input data, observes any deviation from a normal pregnancy and chooses the appropriate investigations and management decisions (see Figure 4).
- This program was amended in collaboration with the obstetrician by repeated trials with a number of case records from the ante-natal clinic. All obvious errors and discrepancies in the program were eliminated.

This form of descriptive decision analysis is discussed in detail elsewhere (Taylor et al., 1976; Andersen et al., 1976). The program was validated by randomly selecting some 200 test cases from the previous year and the decisions taken then were compared with those made by the computer. In the 200 test cases, the program successfully detected all "at risk" pregnancies at their first visits to the clinic. Abnormalities appearing at later visits were all detected and appropriate investigations ordered by the program.

Case No. 7 Hospital 85422:
Age 42. Married for 11 years.
Past history medical—anaemia; surgical—none; family—twins.
Obstetric history—2 previous viable pregnancies: 1 abortion.
Obstetric complications—none
Menstrual history: date of last menstrual period is 12/07.
 not known if sure of dates
 length of last period is not known
 length of menstrual cycle is 30 days
History of present pregnancy:
 urinary tract infections
 patient height is 152 cms.
Abnormalities detected in past history:
Elderly patient
Patient with low height—potentially at risk in labour
Urinary tract infections—perform M.S.S.U.
Note history of anaemia.
Follow up of pregnancy:
Visit No. 1 Date 8/02
EF/30 RF/32 PR/VX EN/NR GLY/NO PRT/NO WT/185 SBP/140
 DBP/90 HB/86 OED/NO
High blood pressure
Low haemoglobin level
Check full blood count
Visit No. 2 Date 22/02
EF/32 RF/32 PR/VX EN/NE GLY/NO PRT/NO WT/187 SBP/125
 DBP/80 HB/99 OED/NO
Average weight gain is 1.00 lb/week
Average weight gain since last visit is 1.00 lb/week
Low haemoglobin level. *Check full blood count.*
Visit No. 3 Date 22/03
EF/36 RF/38 PR/VX EN/NE GLY/NO PRT/NO WT/183 SBP/130
 DBP/85 HB/111 OED/NO
Average weight gain to date is 0.33 lb/wek.
Average weight gain since last visit is 1.00 lb/week.
Appoint patient to return in one week.
Visit No. 4 Date 29/03
EF/37 RF/78 PR/VX EN/FR GLY/NO PRT/NO WT/183 SBP/145
 DBP/110 HBP/111 OED/NO
Average weight gain to date is 0.29 lb/week.
Average weight gain since last visit is 0.00 lb/week.
Low weight gain. *Refer to obstretician.* High blood pressure.

Fig. 4. Sample output from computer recording clinical data, noting abnormalities and ordering investigations according to clinic policy. (EF—expected fundal height; RF—recorded fundal height; PR—presentation; EN—engagement; GLY—glycosuria; WT—weight; SBP—systolic blood pressure; DBP—diastolic blood pressure; HB—haemoglobin; OED—oedema; VX—vertex).

The program ordered rather *more* investigations than the obstetricians. Since all the basic data in this clinic would be collected by nurses, *observer error studies* were done which showed no significant differences between obstetricians and nurses.

The decision analysis in this study and its resulting computer program have been confined to a simple set of logical decision rules. The important problem of *risk* is taken into account in the criteria used by the clinician in arriving at the particular set of decision rules. In this case the risk of a wrong decision has been minimised by making the criteria over-sensitive so as to pick up most abnormalities at the cost of an excess of investigations. Future studies might attempt to use a more sensitive approach to costs and risk based more directly on statistical decision theory. This approach has many conceptual similarities to the machine intelligence systems described below (Section 5). The main difference is that the decision rules were elicited by observation, interrogation and introspection, while in the machine intelligence approach, all this is done by the clinician "talking" to the program. (Shortliffe et al., 1973).

There is wide variation in obstetric practice from centre to centre but the basic data routinely collected at every ante-natal clinic is fairly uniform. Different obstetricians will place different emphasis and interpretation on deviations from the normal in certain cases. Since most obstetricians have fairly rigid criteria of abnormality, this makes elementary clinical decision-making simpler and allows easy adaptation of a basic program to suit the needs of the individual consultant.

Here, the critically important factor of *clinical responsibility* was considered from the very beginning. The aim of the decision analysis performed on the three obstetricians was to arrive at an explicit representation of their policy. The outcome of the analysis, observation and interrogation was a "decision module" linking the clinical information to the outcome of each of 17 key management and investigative decisions.

Since all three participating obstetricians agreed that the final version of each decision module did represent their policy for the clinic and since validation with test cases was completely successful, then responsibility for any decision taken by the program lay with the obstetricians. In the previously described statistically-based programs, responsibility is not at all so clearly allocated.

4.4 Computer-assisted Decision-making in Radiology

Radiology is an area of clinical practice where computer-assisted decision-making techniques were developed very early. A wide variety of techniques have been applied to the set of problems concerned with identifying abnormalities on x-rays. Radiology provides an interesting illustration of the diversity of computer-based approaches to similar decision problems.

Normally, the radiologist scans the film and dictates a description in his report of the salient features of the organ or system being examined. He completes this description by indicating the likely diagnosis and perhaps suggesting further investigations. The use of human/computer systems in this process varies in complexity and in the extent of human participation in the observation and interpretation processes.

In the simplest systems (conceptually and technically) the radiologist can scan a radiograph and enter findings at a terminal which will then indicate the likely diagnosis based on a logical decision-tree (Lusted, 1968). A similar approach was made by Wilson et al. (1965), where clinical data was combined with the individual features of the visual radiological examination of the upper gastro-intestinal tract to distinguish between benign and malignant ulcers of the stomach using a probabilistic form of analysis based on Bayes' Theorem. A similar Bayesian approach was made by Lodwick (1966) in the differential diagnosis of 7 different types of bone tumours using radiographic data. Templeton et al. (1967) applied a broadly similar approach to the diagnosis of solitary "shadows" on the x-ray of lung with a diagnostic accuracy of 80%.

Du Boulay et al. (1977) developed a different type of human/computer system by combining probability information from case surveys with probability estimates provided by expert radiologists in the diagnosis of cerebral tumours. Since there are over 100 possible diseases to be considered, their diagnoses were combined into 3 broad groups. The first group of diseases all occur in a very localised area near the base of the brain. The second group are all managed in the same way and so consist of a management grouping. The third group was also an anatomically related group but was more diverse than the first. The Bayesian form of analysis combining survey data and expert opinions was as successful as the expert in group 1, much better in group 2, and not as successful in group 3.

4.5 *The Decision-making Process in Radiology*

In all of these applications the radiologist scans the x-ray film (following the criteria laid down for classifying the visual data) and either enters the data "en bloc" or is interrogated by the computer sequentially.

The processes by which all clinicians appear to process information have already been discussed. In the case of radiologists the major emphasis is on visual information but the same analysis holds. The radiologist has the test *performed* on the patient by having a technician carry out an x-ray. He then *observes* the result of the test by scanning the resulting radiogram and *categorizes* what he sees according to criteria laid down for the system. The scanning process is done by the radiologist selecting a *goal* (e.g., eliminate the possibility of tuberculosis) and then adopting a *visual search strategy* to reach this goal. Such "search strategies" have been studied by Tuddenham (1962) and Kundel & Wright (1969). Both groups have examined practising radiologists by using head-mounted cameras which allow experimental tracking of the radiologist's eye movements as he scans and samples the x-ray film. Radiologists apparently follow no simple search patterns. The initial strategy seems to be chosen on the basis of prior knowledge about the film or patient. The strategy is subsequently modified as unsuspected abnormalities are detected or suspicious areas are found to be normal. This sequence corresponds to the *hypothesis-revision, strategy selection* and *tactical* modification of search strategies which were described earlier. Kundel & Wright (1969) drew the conclusion from their studies that the visual search is a sampling procedure (i.e. strategy) aimed at obtaining information or resolving ambiguity. The goal is to produce an unambiguous perception of the real world. The perception must be consistent with past experience, with memory of similar stimulus patterns and with the information from other sensory systems.

This kind of analysis is useful in relating a model of how the human decision-makers behave (and try to achieve their goals) to the design of the human/computer systems which aim to replace or assist them. Different systems use the computer in different ways. In one, the perception process remains with the radiologist but the search is inherent in the logical decision tree. In another, ambiguity is reduced by the elimination of undiscriminating data or by selecting precise criteria for categorizing visual patterns.

4.6 Computer-assisted Radiological Image Analysis

The most all-encompassing approach to radiological decision-making involves the computer in the observation (perception) phase, as well as in the categorization of the stimulus patterns, the choice of search strategy and the calculation of the diagnostic probabilities. Typical of this type of human/computer system is that developed for computer analysis of routine chest radiographic images by Hall et al. (1971) at the University of Missouri.

In this approach, the radiologist is apparently eliminated; even from the role of a "feature extractor". The most difficult step in any type of image analysis has been acknowledged from its earliest experimental days (Selfridge 1955) as being "the extraction of significant features from a background of irrelevant detail". This is thought by Hall et al. (1971) to be particularly true in radiographic image analysis. An important problem noted by these writers is that the relevance of a feature is dependent on the goal of the system and, hence, the strategy being followed. Thus, a feature is significant if one disease is being eliminated but irrelevant in discriminating between two other diagnoses. In this study (Hall et al., 1971), the particular set of features chosen for extraction were those used by the radiologists: in other words the radiologists *implicitly provided the search strategy*. In this way, the most complex process (feature extraction) is provided by the human expert so that in reality the radiologist is only apparently eliminated in the system.

In this particular form of direct computer diagnosis, the chest x-rays are scanned by an image dissector camera which converts the visual image into numbers. These numbers (the digital image) are stored on magnetic tape. The numbers are obtained by converting the 14 x 17 inch chest radiograph into a grid of points 256 x 256. Each point is converted by the camera into a point on a numerical grey scale of light intensity. This takes about one minute per radiograph. This numerical digitised image is then processed to extract the chosen features such as cardiac outline, as well as several other cardiac parameters. A discriminant function analysis is used on this data to separate normal from abnormal hearts and then to sub-classify into four different types of abnormality. A comparison between this system and ten radiologists gave an overall accuracy of 73% for the computer and 62% for the group of radiologists. All diagnoses were finally established by a more complex investigative procedure (Hall et al., 1971).

The field of radiographic image processing is a rapidly growing one and it has been submitted to an excellent review by one of the most active groups in the field (Harrow, Dwyer and Lodwick 1976). The review covers the strategy of developing a library of reference films, system hardware, as well as image analysis techniques, including preprocessing and feature selection. The areas of application which are reviewed include nuclear medicine, bone disease, lung and heart disease.

4.7 Alternative Approaches to Image Analysis

However, in order to put all this technology in perspective, it is important to realize that the computer-based approach is not the only one. Recent studies have substituted a trained technician for the radiologist without any computer at all. Sheft et al. (1970) have shown that after a training program and guided practical experience the interpretations of chest x-rays by the specially trained radiological assistants compared favourably with staff radiologists in the interpretation of chest radiographs. The rates of false negatives (4-8%) after a total of five months training and five months practical experience were almost identical to senior registrars and staff radiologists (6-8%). The false positive rate (13-19%) was somewhat higher than the radiologists (7-9%). But this was clearly of less clinical significance: it is obviously better that they err on the side of caution (i.e., false positives).

So while many aspects of the radiologist's task can be wholly, or in part, delegated to human/computer systems a specially trained technologist may be even better. Radiologists tend to favour the direct computer diagnosis system rather than those based on technologists since the introduction of a new group of skilled paramedical staff is no longer enthusiastically supported by a medical profession threatened in North America and in the United Kingdom with an excess of doctors. By contrast, the human/computer system will be more directly controlled by the radiologists. This is an important practical consideration if these systems are to be widely used.

4.8 Other Diagnosis Systems

The range of computer-based systems for clinical decision-making already reviewed is by no means exhaustive. However, considerations of space have limited detailed analysis to examples above. Other relevant areas are computer-based patient-monitoring (Shepherd & Kouchoukos, 1976), electro-cardiographic analysis (Pordy, 1977), electro-encephalographic analysis, as well as a wide range of image analysis applications dealing with cervical cytology, chromosomal analysis and blood cell analysis (Preston, 1976).

5.0 Consultation Systems

The technique of descriptive decision analysis of ante-natal care described earlier is based on a computer program which reproduces the management policies of an obstetrician. This behavioural approach which aims to "capture" the wisdom of experts is a prominent trend in the field of artificial intelligence particularly as it is applied to medical problems (Pauker et al., 1976). This parallels a trend in computer-based chess-playing where some systems are based not on statistical evaluation of selection functions, but on techniques for storing the past game behaviour of chess masters and matching this to various stages in new chess games (Zobrist & Carlson 1973).

5.1 The Role of Knowledge Structures and Task Structures in Computer-based Consultation Systems

Much undergraduate teaching is concerned with imparting factual knowledge about physio-pathological processes and about disease and its management. This basis of knowledge can be represented as as set of complex relationships or associations between the features of a patient's problem and its management. This preoccupation with the knowledge base of clinical practice can be designated *clinical epistemology*. Such a knowledge base is represented by statements in lectures, textbooks or scientific papers. Randomised control trials contribute even more precise information about such relationships. All this information (relating procedures to patients) can be viewed as a *knowledge structure*. Many medical examinations are based on assessing fragments of such knowledge structures by the use of multiple choice questions.

However, when confronted with a patient's problem, the student must learn to transform the knowledge structure into a *task structure*. In the task structure, however, although the relationships between the clinical features on the one hand and the investigations and treatment on the other are the same as in the knowledge structure, they are reorganized into a framework suitable for decision-making. The process of transforming a knowledge structure about a problem to a decision or task structure is fundamental to the clinical training of the undergraduate and the post graduate and represents the development of *clinical cognition*. Computer simulations of diagnostic problems (Taylor, 1975) aim to accelerate the development of such task skills by providing the student with the opportunity to manage certain types of clinical problems and to assume responsibility for the consequences of actions.

5.2 Artificial Intelligence Approaches to Computer-based Consultation

Some types of consultation systems are much more closely aligned to a knowledge structure than to a task structure. These applications allow existing knowledge to be reorganized into a form most suitable for guiding decision-making, yet do not actually form a decision policy as such. The relationship between information or knowledge, and the judgements which are made using this knowledge, are one of the central preoccupations in the study of computer-based artificial intelligence systems.

Gorry (1973) dealing with kidney failure initially began by describing a statistical approach to decision analysis (and to computer-based decision—making) which was based on the "lottery" game suggested by Raiffa (1968). He expressed dissatisfaction with the rigidity of this approach as contrasted with the flexibility of clinicians. He then went on to suggest a change in the direction of investigation towards a knowledge/decision rule approach to computer management of clinical problems. His approach towards eliciting knowledge and decision rules was broadly similar to that described above in relation to the ante-natal clinic study. He saw as a critical feature of any system the ability to constantly assimilate new knowledge. This proposed approach would allow the storage in the computer of the expert's knowledge by the use of programming languages which allow concepts to be identified and defined. Thus, in theory, allowing expert clinicians to express their policies and decision rules directly to a computer terminal.

More recently, the same Boston group have used a similar approach to the problem of eliciting information about the present illness in a patient with oedema. The program was tested with a number of prototypical cases and amended to take account of discrepancies until the program's behaviour closely matched the clinician's. The special features of this approach were the use of goal-oriented programming, pattern-matching and a large associative memory. It utilised the CONNIVER suite of programs (Sussman & McDermott, 1972), a development from the MICRO-PLANNER programs used earlier by the same group. This study provides an excellent critical review of the application of artificial intelligence concepts and techniques in medicine (Pauker et al., 1976).

Shortliffe et al. (1972) used the techniques developed by the artificial intelligence group at Stanford University to represent the knowledge of an expert in microbiology so as to provide advice to physicians about appropriate anti-microbial therapy for infections. It uses a limited base of about 100 decision rules and provides explanations for its advice. The program was "primed" with a great deal of fundamental knowledge about most anti-microbial drugs and clinically important bacteria.

The system was then "challenged" with a variety of theraputic problems and modified its decision rules in the light of this experience. The program (MYCIN) utilizes a flexible representation of knowledge which facilitates inter-active advice-giving sessions with physicians. Two key categories of questions can be asked of the MYCIN system; rule-retrieval questions and informational questions (IQ). The rule-retrieval question can either be specific to a given consultation (Figure 5a) or more general in nature (Figure 5b). The informational question (IQ) refers to the current value of a clinical parameter from the dynamic data base (e.g., the final diagnosis—Figure 5c). This system has been described in considerable detail in a recent book (Shortliffe, 1976) which is an excellent reference text to the use of artificial intelligence applications in medicine.

Kulikowski at Rutgers University has developed a decision-rule based physiological model of glaucoma which serves as the basis of computer consultations (Weiss, 1978). The system is implemented as a causal association network model (CASNET) that characterizes the patho-physiological mechanisms and clinical course of treated and untreated cases of glaucoma.

Finally, a much more comprehensive approach is being undertaken at the University of Pittsburgh by Dr. Jack D. Myers, who with a computer scientist (Harry E. Pople), has developed over the past eight years a program called "INTERNIST" based on artificial intelligence techniques developed at Carnegie-Mellon University. This program is described as a "computer-based consultative system for medical diagnosis" and it is at present limited to internal medicine. It is based on the representation within the program of Dr. Myers' 40 years of personal clinical experience as a consulting internist. It contains information on about 400 diseases (Lawrence, 1978).

** WHAT MADE YOU THINK ORGANISM-1 MIGHT BE A PRO-TEUS?

I USED RULE 163 TO CONCLUDE THAT THE IDENTITY OF ORGANISM-1 IS PROTEUS. THIS GAVE A CUMULATIVE CF OF .277. THE LAST QUESTION ASKED BEFORE THE CONCLUSION WAS MADE WAS 26.

I USED RULE 084 TO CONCLUDE THAT THE IDENTITY OF ORGANISM-1 IS PROTEUS. THIS GAVE A CUMULATIVE CF OF .119. THE LAST QUESTION ASKED BEFORE THE CONCLUSION WAS MADE WAS 24.

Fig. 5a. An example of a specific rule retrieval response from the MYCIN program dealing with the diagnosis and treatment of infections. Instead of displaying all the relevant rules, the program mentions what rules were used, when they were invoked during the consultation (i.e., after which question number), and what certainty factor (CF) was associated with the specified conclusion.

** WHAT DO YOU PRESCRIBE FOR ACTINOMYCETES INFEC-TIONS?

RULE 002

IF: THE IDENTITY OF THE ORGANISM IS ACTINOMYCETES
THEN: I RECOMMEND THERAPY CHOSEN FROM AMONG
    THE FOLLOWING DRUGS:
    1—PENICILLIN (0.99)
    2—TETRACYCLINE (0.99)
    3—ERYTHROMYCIN (0.99)

Fig. 5b. A general rule retrieval response. General questions reference the corpus of rules without considering the status of the dynamic data base, i.e., they ask questions about MY-CIN's knowledge rather than about how that knowledge has been applied to the patient under consideration.

** IQ WHAT IS THE FINAL DECISION REGARDING THE IDENTITY OF ORGANISM-1?

THE IDENTITY OF ORGANISM-1 IS PSEUDOMONAS (0.357), KLEBSIELLA (.177), ENTEROBACTER (.166), E.COLI (.137), PROTEUS (.118), SERRATIA (.042).

Fig. 5c. An example of an informational question (IQ). An IQ question requests the current value of some clinical parameter from the dynamic data base. It does not ask how the value was acquired (i.e., whether supplied by the physician or inferred using rules).

The concepts which the clinician uses in dealing with actual cases are incorporated into decision rules. He assigns the weights attached to information within the system so that it represents his view of the problem. The program interrogates the clinician about his views on a particular case and then organises these views into its data base for guidance in similar cases in the future. The approach is broadly similar to the others described above. The program is written in the language INTERLISP and is run on a dedicated medical computer in Stanford University.

In all of these applications, the communication with the user in the consultation program is by *natural language*. It is likely that the approaches which lie at the interface between knowledge representation and task representation will make a major contribution to human/computer systems in the future.

5.3 Computer-selected Digoxin Dosage Regime

Another closely related area of the same interface between clinical knowledge and clinical cognition is where *patho-physiological concepts* and data are organized to provide *advice* about the management of clinical problems.

When a clinician chooses a drug for a patient, he/she calls on knowledge of both the individual patient and of the particular drug. Where there are alternative therapies (e.g., different antibiotics) the pros and cons of each alternative must be familiar to the clinician.

In choosing a drug regime for a patient, the clinician is concerned about psychological, as well as physiological factors. Such psychological factors as compliance in actually taking the prescribed drug, and reliability in attending for regular follow-up visits, must be taken into account. Physiological factors include the ability of the patient's liver to break down the drug and of his/her kidneys to excrete it. Thus, a patient with failing kidneys cannot tolerate certain drugs, since they will tend to accumulate in the blood stream causing toxicity.

An example of such a problem is the use of *digoxin*. Digoxin is a drug which influences the efficiency of heart muscle and is used in the treatment of heart failure; overdosage with this drug (in 20% of patients, particularly the elderly and those with impaired kidney or liver function) is common enough to be the cause of some concern (Bellar et al., 1971). The drug can be administered as unrefined digitalis leaf or as at least three closely related active ingredients (namely, digoxin, digitoxin and deslanoside).

One approach to the management of this problem is to use a computer selected dosage regimen accessible to physicians via a time-sharing terminal (Jelliffe et al., 1970). This particular approach is a direct extension of previous statistically based methods of digitalis therapy which used nomograms and simple arithmetic.

The computer based prescription is based on a number of factors; these include a mathematical analysis of drug kinetics for all four drugs in patients with normal and with reduced kidney function, as well as a similar mathematical analysis of the metabolic breakdown of digitoxin to digoxin.

Ten clearly specified pharmacological assumptions about all four drug preparations are made by the program including their metabolism, relative potency and toxicity. These assumptions are provided for review at the terminal by users and potential users.

The program has three main parts:

- The first part asks for *basic data* such as body weight, age and indices of renal function (normally available from the patient's case record). It complements these with other clinical data to establish a pharmacological dosage base line.
- The next part of the program asks for *previous dosage* of the drugs so as to establish the past input for this particular patient and to calculate the current distribution of the drug within the patient's body. This takes account of the different potencies and metabolic pathways of each of the drugs since patients may have been on more than one of the four drugs in the immediate past.
- Finally, it computes and prints out a *dosage regime* aimed at achieving the goals previously laid down by the clinician. In other words, the clinician specifies the drug blood levels which he would like to achieve in this patient and the program adopts the strategy inherent in its basic assumptions in order to reach these goals. The output usually consists of a 20 day regimen of drug dosage.

This particular application represents an extension of the human/computer interface to take account of some fairly complex calculations which the clinician previously did by hand, by guesswork, or by calculator. The program accepts the *goals* laid down by the clinician while the clinician usually accepts the *strategy* laid down by the designer of the program in reaching his goal. In this way, the clinician and the computer interact and complement one another. The experimental evidence suggests that this system provides much more consistent drug levels in the patient's blood, and the reduction of over-dosage of the drug from 35% to 12% (Jelliffe et al., 1972).

An important general issue for human/computer systems which is specifically dealt with in this application is that of the *sharing of responsibility* for decisions taken using the system. The physician who uses the program is responsible for the accuracy of the clinical data and for his decision about the goal of a specified blood level for the drug. The terminal operator is responsible for the data transmitted and for spotting transmission errors within the system.

The patient's physician is also responsible for integrating the prescribed regime into the total management of the patient and for accepting the pharmacological assumptions on which the program operates (these are specifically listed for the physician).

5.4 Computer-assisted Management of Acid-base Disorders

A closely related application of a similar computer-based consultation program was developed by Bleich (1969) for the management of acid-base disorders. This was the earliest clinical application of computer-based consultation in medicine. The program is now widely available via commercial time-sharing systems in the U.S.A. and Canada costing about $2.00 per usage. It takes about 7 minutes to enter the data and to receive feedback. References to appropriate medical literature are provided.

The structure of the program combines standard calculations in this area of biochemistry with a great deal of branching Boolean logic and logical decision rules. It includes a great deal of software concerned with checking the data entered for proper syntax, for compatibility with life, and for consistencies with previous values. This body of information represents current opinion about the physiology and management of this group of disorders. The program was developed by an acknowledged expert in this area of clinical medicine (Bleich 1972). Broadly similar approaches to the same problem have been developed by Goldberg et al. (1973) and by Suero (1970). The same approach to the closely related problem of *blood-gas analysis* has been described by Cohen (1969) and by Menn et al. (1973).

6.0 Some Critical Issues

A number of basic issues have recurred frequently in this review and merit an attempt to highlight and discuss them briefly. They are important enough to critically influence the chances of any of the above experimental systems surviving into routine clinical practice.

Almost all medical human/computer systems are confined to hospitals. The hospital milieu differs significantly, for example, in North America and in the United Kingdom. In the United Kingdom the *hospital physician* is usually salaried with a full-time hospital appointment and has responsibility for a designated group of patients. The American physician is more likely to have a part-time attachment to hospital with an office practice "downtown". The North American physician is paid a fee for each item of service and many specialists earn a large part of their salaries from the common routine activities (like reading blood smears or electrocardiograms).

Hence, a human/computer system which proposes to relieve a British physician of part of the routine workload without impact on his/her salary has a much better chance of acceptance than a similar system in North America. In the latter, to relieve a physician of routine reading of blood smears by an image analysing computer system or a computer based electro-cardiographic system, will result in a significant drop in income for the physician. This explains some of the difficulties associated with implementing most diagnosis systems in North America, and hence, the emphasis there on "consultation" systems which augment, but do not replace the physician. This effect works both ways. A human/computer system controlled by the physician can appear more attractive than the alternative of training a paramedic to do the same task as a physician. This issue is discussed in the section on radiology (4.4–7).

Another feature of human/computer systems in medicine, is the accusation that they are "technology for technology's sake", i.e. they propose complex expensive solutions to problems which are better tackled by nurses, paramedical, or scientific staff. At a time of considerable unemployment, this argument has many supporters. The contrast between the technological and the human solutions to image analysis problems has already been discussed. There is also now an over-production of doctors in Canada, United States, Great Britain and Australia. Therefore, the medical profession is not taking too kindly to the suggestion that either nurses or computers can effectively replace them. Another important aspect of the debate about technology for technology's sake, is that of *financial evaluation*. The comparison of computer systems with conventional systems is relatively simple in, for example, electro-cardiographic analysis. A detailed comparison between a computer-based system of patient interrogation and a consultant has already been described (3.5). However, in the great majority of medical human/computer systems direct comparisons with conventional systems is fraught with difficulty: frequently, there is a divergence of goals between computer systems and current clinical practice as in the history taking systems. The financial evaluation of many of the postulated benefits of human/computer innovations is very difficult. Cost-effective computer selection of investigations may reduce costs but may be in conflict with well-established routines of investigation which are expensive to disturb.

The way in which an innovation can be inserted into the *existing logistic framework of health care* is an issue of great importance and enormous complexity. It involves the trade-off and balancing of many social, economic, personal and organizational considerations. It is seldom simply a matter of discontinuing the conventional system and inserting the new. The very large number of medical, paramedical and administrative personnel who interact with one another in any area of clinical practice is a critical factor in moulding and distorting important innovations. Thus, despite 15-20 years of research, computer based decision systems have had practically no impact on day-to-day health care. The many reasons for this failure are reviewed in more detail elsewhere (Taylor, 1976).

In such complex systems the issue of *clinical responsibility* is critical especially with the impact of possible *malpractice* litigation in North America on clinician's styles of practice. When we propose to introduce complex human/computer systems we must pay careful attention to the pinpointing and delineation of clinical responsibility in the complex interaction between clinician and machine. This is particularly well illustrated in the computer selected digoxin dosage regime (5.3) already described. This is an issue which has already been faced in other areas of medical technology. For example, if a clinician receives a laboratory result he assumes that the Director of the laboratory is responsible for the accuracy of that measurement. If a computer is interposed into this process, then presumably the computer is seen as an extension of the laboratory and of the Director's responsibility.

Similarly, the policies inherent in advice-giving computer programs are the responsibility of the designer. The clinician, of course, must adopt the same critical approach to advice-giving programs as he would to the reliability of a textbook. If we want to have human/computer systems used routinely, then they must be based on the policies agreed upon by the appropriate clinicians. This approach is illustrated in the ante-natal clinic system described above (4.3). The decision rules which are the basis of the computer based decision system were those extracted (by observation and discussion) from participating clinicians. The decision rules were seen as a formalization of the policy normally followed by these clinicians. The computer-based decision system was, therefore, seen as an extension of their policy and responsibility. In other words, if something goes wrong then you sue the clinicians responsible for the policy and certainly not anyone associated with developing the computer-based decision system. It is extremely important that the basic issues involved in introducing such systems are clearly analyzed and resolved as the problem of clinical responsibility can seriously hamper the practical implementation of even the most successful system.

Lastly, the comparison and analysis of the systems reviewed here is made much easier if a formal model of the task environment and of the clinical decision-making processes is assumed. The model proposed (2.1-2.5) is fairly simple minded but makes the analysis of specific contributions of human and machine much more incisive. Indeed, the most promising feature of the systems in the artificial intelligence field is their relatively sophisticated, computer compatible models of clinical cognition. The future of such medical human/computer systems seems bright, and their contribution to a basic understanding of the intellectual basis of the practice of medicine is likely to be substantial (Kassirer & Gorry, 1978).

References

Anderson, G., Llerenna, C., Davidson, D. & Taylor, T.R. (1976). Practical Application of Computer-Assisted Decision-Making in an Ante-Natal Clinic. *Methods of Information in Medicine (Stuttgart)*, **15**, 224-229.

Balint, M. (1957). *Doctor, His Patient and the Illness*. Pitman, London.

Bellar, G.A., Smith, T.W., Abelman, W.H. et al. (1971). Digitalis Intoxication *New England Journal of Medicine*, **284**, 989-997.

Bleich, H.L. (1969). Computer Evaluation of Acid-Base Disorders. *Journal Clinical Investigation*, **48**, 1689-1696.

Bleich, H.L. (1972). Computer-Based Consultation-Electrolyte and Acid-Base Disorders. *American Journal Medicine*, **53**, 285-291.

Du Boulay, G.H., Teather, D., Harling, D., Clarke, G. (1977). Improvement in the Computer-Assisted Diagnosis of Cerebral Tumours. *British Journal of Radiology*, **50**, 849-854.

Cohen, M.L. (1969). A Computer Program for the Interpretation of Blood-Gas Analysis. *Computers and Biomedical Research*, **2**, 549-557.

Colby, K.M., Watt, J.B., Gilbert, J.P. (1966). A Computer Method of Psychotherapy: Preliminary Communication. *Journal Mental Disorders*, **142**, 148-152.

Collen, M.F., Cutler, J.L., Siegelaub, A.E., & Cella, R.L. (1969). Reliability of a Self-Administered Medical Questionnaire. *Archives Internal Medicine*, **123**, 664.

Coombs, G.J., Murray, W.R. & Krahn, D.W. (1970). Automated Medical Histories: Factors Determining Patient Performance. *Computers and Biomedical Research*, **3**, 178.

Croft, D.J. (1972). Is Computerized Diagnosis Possible? *Computers and Biomedical Research*, **5**, 351.

Edwards, D.A.W. (1970). Flow Charts, Diagnostic Keys and Algorithms in the Diagnosis of Dysphagia. *Scottish Medical Journal*, **15**, 378-385.

Elstein, A.S., Shullman, L.S. & Sprafka, S.A. (1978). *Medical Problem Solving*. Harvard University Press, Cambridge and London.

Freemon, F.R. (1968). Computer Diagnosis of Headache. *Headache*, **8**, 49-55.

Fries, J.F. (1970). Experience Counting in Sequential Computer Diagnosis. *Archives Internal Medicine*, **126**, 647.

Ginsberg, A.S. Offensend, F.L. (1968). An Application of Decision Theory to a Medical Diagnosis-Treatment Problem. *IEEE Trans. Systems Science & Cybernetics*, **SSC-4**, 355-362.

Gleser, M.A. & Collen, M.F. (1972). Towards Automated Medical Decisions. *Computers and Biomedical Research*, **5**, 180-189.

Gorry, G.A. (1973). Computer Assisted Clinical Decision-Making. *Methods of Information in Medicine*, **12**, 45-51.

Goldberg, M., Green, B., Moss, K.L., Marbach, C.B., Garfinkel, D. (1973). Computers and Acid-Base Disorders. *Journal American Medical Association*, **223**, 269.

Grossman, J.H., Barnett, G.O., Mcguire, M.T., & Swedlow, D.B. (1971). Evaluation of Computer Acquired Patient Histories. *Journal American Medical Association*, **215**, 1286-1291.

Hall, E.L., Kruger, R.P., Dwyer, S.J., et al. (1971). A Survey of Preprocessing and Feature Extraction Techniques for Radiographic Images. *IEEE Trans Computers*, **C-20**, 10.

Harless, W.G., Lucas, N.C., Cutter, J.A., Duncan, R.C., White, J.M., Brandt, E.N. (1969). Computer-Assisted Instruction in Continuing Medical Education. *Journal of Medical Education*, **44**.

Harlow, C.A., Dwyer, S.J. & Lodwick, G. (1976). On Radiographic Image Analysis. In *Digital Picture Analysis* A. Rosenfield (Ed.), Springer-Verlag, New York.

Holt, R.R., (1961). Clinical Judgement as a Discipline Inquiry. *Journal Nervous and Mental Disorders*, 133, 369-382.

Jelliffe, R.W., Buell, J., Kalaba, R. (1972). Reduction of Digitalis Toxicity by Computer-Assisted Glycoside Dosage Regimens. *Archives Internal Medicine*, 77, 891-906.

Kassirer, J.P., Gorry, G.A. (1978). Clinical Problem Solving: A Behavioural Analysis. *Archives Internal Medicine*, 89, 245-255.

Kleinmuntz, B. & Mclean, R.S. (1968) Diagnostic Interviewing by Digital Computer. *Behavioral Science*, 13, 75-80.

Knill-Jones, R.P., Stern, R.B., Girmes, D.H., Maxwell, J.D., Thompson, R.P.H. & Williams, R. (1973). Use of Sequential Bayesian Model in Diagnosis of Jaundice by Computer. *British Medical Journal*, 1, 530-533.

Kundel, N.L. & Wright, D.J.L. (1969). The Influence of Prior Knowledge on Visual Search Strategies During the Viewing of Chest Radiograph. *Radiology*, 93, 315-320.

Lawrence, S.V. (1978). Internist. *Forum on Medicine*, 1, 44.

Lindley, D.V. (1956). On a Measure of the Information Provided by an Experiment. *Annuals Mathematics & Statistics*, 7, 986-1005.

Lodwick, G.S. (1966). Computer Aided Diagnosis in Radiology. A Research Plan. *Investigative Radiology*, 1, 72-80.

Lucas, R.W., Knill-Jones, R.P. Watkinson, G. & Cream, G.P. (1976). Computer Interrogation of Patients. *British Medical Journal*, 2, 623.

Lucas, R.W. (1977). Questioning Patients by Computer. *Health Bulletin*, 296-302.

Lucas, R.W., Mullini, P.J., Luna, C.B. & Mcinroy, D.C. (1977). Interrogation of Patients by Computer. *British Journal of Psychiatry*, 131, 160.

Lusted, L.B. (1968). *Introduction to Medical Decision-Making*. Charles C. Thomas, Springfield, Illinois.

Mayne, J.G., Weksel, W. & Sholtz, P.N. (1968). Toward Automating Medical History. *Mayo Clinical Proc.*, 43, 1-25.

Mayne, J.G., Martin, M.J., Morrow, JR., G.W., Turner, R.M., Hisey, B.L. (1969). A Health Questionnaire Based On Paper and Pencil Medium Individualized and Produced by Computer, I and II. *Journal American Medical Association*, 208, 2060-2068.

Mayne, J.G. & Martin, J.M. (1970). Computer-Aided History Acquisition. *Medical Clinics of North America*, 54, 825.

Menn, S.J., Barnett, G.O., Schmechel, D. (1973). A Computer Program to Assist in the Care of Acute Respiratory Failure. *JournalAmericanMedicalAssociation*, 223, 308.

Mintzberg, H. (1973). *The Nature of Managerial Work*. Harper and Row, London

Mintzberg, H. (1976). Planning on the Left Side and Managing on the Right. *Harvard Business Review*, 49-58.

Norman, G.R., Barrows, H.S., Feightner, J.W. & Nuefeld, V.R. (1977). Measuring the Outcome of Clinical Problem Solving. *Proc. 16th R.I.M.E. Conference*, 311-316.

Pauker, S.G., Gorry, G.A., Kassirer, J.P., Schwartz, W.B. (1976). Towards the Simulation of Clinical Cognition. *American Journal of Medicine*, 60, 981.

Pordy, L. (1977). *Computer Electro Cardiography: Present Status and Criteria*. Futura Publishing Company, New York.

Preston, K. (1976). Digital Picture Analysis in Cytology. In *Digital Picture Analysis* (Ed.) A. Rosenfield, Springer-Verlag, New York.

Raiffa, H. (1968). *Decision Analysis: Introductory Lectures on Choices Under Uncertainty*. Addison-Wesley, Reading, Mass.

Rockart, J.F., Mclean, E.R. & Hersberg, P.I. et al. (1973). An Automated Medical History System: Experience of the Lahey Clinic Foundation with Computer-Processed Medical Histories. *Archives of Internal Medicine*, **132**, 348.

Sheppard, L.C. & Kouchoukos, N.T. (1976). Computers as Monitors. *Anesthesiology*, **45**, 250-259.

Simborg, D.W., Rikli, A.E. & Hall, P. (1969). Experimentation in Medical History-Taking. *Journal American Medical Association*, **210**, 1443.

Selfridge, O.G. (1955). Pattern Recognition and Modern Computers. *Proc. Western Joint Computer Conference*, 91-93.

Shortliffe, E.H., Axline, S.G., Buchanan, B.G. et al. (1973). Artificial Intelligence Program to Advise Physicians Regarding Antimicrobial Therapy. *Computers and Biomedical Research*, **7**, 554-560.

Shortliffe, E.H. (1976). *Computer-Based Medical Consultations: MYCIN* Elsevier Inc., New York.

Slack, W.V., Hicks, G.P., Reed, C.E., Van Cura, L.J. (1966). A Computer-Based Medical History System. *New England Journal Medicine*, **274**, 194-198.

Slack, W.V., Hicks, G.P., Reed, C.E., Van Cura, L.J. (1966). A Computer-Based Medical History System. *New England Journal Medicine*, **274**, 194-198.

Slack, W.V., Peckham, B.M., Van Cura, L.J. & Carr, W.F.A. (1967). A Computer Based Physical Examination System. *Journal American Medical Association*, **200**, 224-228.

Slack, W.V., Van Cura, L.J. (1968). Patient Reaction to Computer-Based Medical Interviewing. *Computers and Biomedical Research*, **1**, 527-531.

Slack, W.V., Van Cura, L.J. & Griest, J.H. (1970). Computers and Doctors: Use and Consequences. *Computers and Biomedical Research*, **3**, 521.

Slack, W.V. & Slack, C.W. (1972). Patient-Computer Dialogue. *New England Journal of Medicine*, **1**, 1304.

Sheft, D.J., Jones, M.D., Brown, R.F. et al. (1970). Screening of Chest Roentgenograms by Advanced Roentgen Technologists. *Radiology*, **94**, 427-429.

Stead, W.W., Heyman, A. & Thompson, H,K, et al. (1972). Computer-Assisted Interview of Patients with Functional Headache. *Archives of Internal Medicine*, **129**, 950.

Sussman, G.J., Mcdermott, D.V. (1972). From Planner to Conniver—a Genetic Approach. *Proceedings of the Fall Joint Computer Conference*, Anaheim, California , 1171.

Suero, J.T. (1970). Computer Interpretation of Acid-Base Data. *Clinical Biochemistry*, **3**, 151-156.

Taylor, T.R. (1967). *The Principles of Medical Computing*. Blackwell Scientific Publications, Oxford.

Taylor, T.R. (1969). Psychological Illness in Medical Outpatients. *Post-Graduate Medical Journal*, **45**, 173-179.

Taylor, T.R. (1970). Computer-Guided Diagnosis. *Journal Royal College of Physicians*, **4**, 188-195.

Taylor, T.R., Aitchison, J., Mcgirr, E.M. (1971). Doctors as Decision-Makers: a Computer-Assisted Study of Diagnosis as a Cognitive Skill. *British Medical Journal*, **3**, 35.

Taylor, T.R., Shields, S., Black, R. (1972). Study of Cost-Conscious Computer-Assisted Diagnosis in Thyroid Disease. *Lancet*, **2**, 79-83.

Taylor, T.R., Aitchison, J., Parker, L. & Moore, M. (1975). Individual Differences in Selected Patients for Regular Haemodialysis. *British Medical Journal*, **2**, 380-381.

Taylor, T.R. (1976). Clinical Decision Analysis. *Methods of Information in Medicine* (Stuttgart), **15**, 216-224.

Templeton, A.W., Jansen, C., & Lehr, J.L. (1967). Solitary Pulmonary Lesions. Computer-aided Differential Diagnosis and Evaluation of Mathematical Methods. *Radiology*, **89**, 605-613.

Tuddenham, W.J., (1962). Visual Search, Image Organization and Reader Error in Roentgen Diagnosis. *Radiology*, **78**, 694-704.

Warner, H.R., Toronto, A.F., Veasey, L.G., & Stephenson, R. (1961). A Mathematical Approach to Medical Diagnosis: Application to Congenital Heart Disease. *Journal American Medical Association*, **177**, 177.

Warner, H.R., Rutherford, B.D., & Houtchens, B. (1972). A Sequential Bayesian Approach to Medical History Taking and Diagnosis. *Computers and Biomedical Research*, **5**, 256.

Wilson, W.J., Templeton, A.W., Turner, A.H., JR. et al. (1965). The Computer Analysis and Diagnosis of Gastric Ulcers. *Radiology*, **85**, 1064-1073.

Woodruff, R.A., Robins, L.N., Taibleson, M., Reich, T., Schrin, R., Frost, N. (1973). A Computer Assisted Derivation of a Screening Interview for Hysteria. *Archives General Psychiatry*, **29**, 450.

Weiss, S., Kulikowski, C.A., Safir, A. (1978). Glaucoma Consultation by Computer. *Compters and Biological Medicine*, **8**, 25-40.

Zobrist, A.L. & Carlson, F.R. (1973). Chess by Computer. *Scientific American*, **228**, 93-105.

PART 3

PROGRAMMING RESEARCH

INTRODUCTION

The cabinet maker builds fine tables and chairs, trying to please the public with articles that look attractive and at the same time do a useful job. He spends a good deal of his time pondering how one might design a perfect desk. But his craft has another side: how to sharpen saws and planes, how to choose wood, what kinds of glue are best—the basic skills that he must not just know but master before he can produce presentable furniture. No matter how good his designs are, they cannot be created without the workman's skills.

In computing terms, Section 2 dealt with finished articles, tables and chairs and desks, and they were discussed and criticised by the same lights as finished furniture: does it do a job that is useful? and does it do it well? Here in Section 3 we deal with the underlying skills and techniques, with the craft of programming.

It is nothing new to speak of programming as a craft, and there are many parallels. Much of the environment is essentially arbitrary rather than ordered: one type of glue or one type of machine just happens to have certain properties, and the craftsman learns to know them and get the best from them. From a heap of scrappy notes and a vision in her mind the programmer conjures a program, and from rough wood and some nails come smoothly fluted furniture. But the differences are just as important. The programmer's actions are in her mind, and she does not think with her fingers but fingers with her thoughts, producing an article that inhabits the same intangible plane as a novel, an article that cannot be judged just by looking at it but only by reading with care and attention. The nearest experience in our everyday lives is perhaps trying to write down precise and explicit instructions for playing a card game like bridge, or for operating a domestic machine. What order should we discuss the various points in? Do the instructions deal with unexpected events—or do they do so at the cost of obscuring the main points? Can the user find out what he wants? Are there sudden gaps?

Writing a program that will do exactly what we want, in all possible circumstances, raises all those problems and many others of its own. And so in the first chapter of this section, Green deals with "Programming as a cognitive activity", from an applied psychological viewpoint and asks what makes it so difficult. First he considers programming languages as examples of notations, just like algebraic or musical notations, and discusses what grammatical and perceptual features make some notations more confusing than others. Then he compares programming languages to natural languages, such as English, to see what can be learnt from the extensive research on the psychology of language. Finally he considers programming as problem-solving, describing rather caustically the panaceas offered by the zealots of structured programming and lamenting the inability of cognitive psychology to tell us more about the central problem in his eyes, what it means to understand a program. His conclusions stress the importance of the psychological notion of discriminability—it should be easy to discriminate what a program is from what it isn't, and this discrimimability should be present at every level of the program, from being able to discover the bracketing structure of an expression up through being able to see the program's control structure and finishing at how the algorithm works. His conclusions also stress the need for empirical evaluation of developments in the design of programming languages, rather than mere optimism.

While Green tries to turn programming from a hard craft to an easy one, Jackson has tried to turn it into something different altogether, replacing the mystery of craftwork with straightforward and methodical techniques. His discussion of "The design and use of conventional programming languages" opens with a historical account of programming, describing how its difficulties were recognised. An outstanding early problem was that programmers had to be too close to the machine; they had to know what size its words were, where various constants were stored, and so on. This was resolved by devising languages that were (in theory) machine-independent, and using special systems programs called compilers to turn Fortran programs into machine-code programs. But another difficulty remained: the programs were too complex, it was too hard to understand them. Attempts to reduce their complexity led to the two strands of structured programming, the use of a limited set of conventional patterns of control and 'top-down' design by the technique of stepwise refinement. But top-down design, as Green argues in his chapter, is not a sufficiently powerful precept. Even in the very first step of stepwise refinement the programmer commits himself to the exact sequence of his operations—and yet there is no way, at that point in the process, to know what is the best sequence.

We need, says Jackson, to separate problem-oriented concerns from machine-oriented ones, without losing sight of either: "Any language would then be split into a pair of complementary languages: the Programming Language proper, in which we write our solution to the problem, and the Execution Language, in which we specify how that solution is to be compiled and executed to obtain the necessary efficiency." He illustrates two techniques for avoiding unnecessary specification of execution details. One is to use his technique of 'program inversion' to create coroutine structures inside conventional programming languages, as demonstrated in his approach to the telegrams problem; the other is to use concurrent processes, illustrated through Hammond's sequence problem. Both problems can be solved using conventional techniques alone, of course, but Jackson's claim is that these problems (and, more importantly, much larger versions of the same problems) can be solved more readily by first creating a Programming Language solution and only then working out an Execution Language solution. In his view, much of the difficulty of the craft of programming is unnecessarily built into our programming languages and our programming outlook.

Finally, in "New directions in computing" Arblaster takes on the prophet's daunting mantle. This is of course a lively area of research where predictions could go catastrophically wrong, and one of his points is that while predicting certain hardware or software developments is easy enough, to predict their interactions is quite another matter. Within theoretical computing science he sees likely developments in computer architecture and concurrent processing which will require quite different sorts of programming languages and techniques. Another exciting area, the semantics of computation, is equally likely to generate new styles of programming language, springing perhaps from the ADJ group's work with universal algebra. However, although "the overwhelming trend in theoretical computer science is away from the Von Neumann computer" and its languages, he thinks that the widespread introduction of new kinds of computer is unlikely to be suddenly disruptive. Software development will concentrate more on packages and comparatively less programming in conventional languages will take place. He concludes that while the last thirty years have seen a progressive deskilling of programming in general, making the craft as a whole an easier one, the demand for highly skilled programmers has continued and will continue; although they may be a continually decreasing proportion of all programmers, the highly skilled are in fact increasing in absolute numbers, and "this paradoxical process will continue".

Three views, then, on The Difficult Art of Programming.

Chapter 10

PROGRAMMING AS A COGNITIVE ACTIVITY

Thomas Green

Contents

1.0 Introduction

Everyone knows one fact about computer programs: they never work first time. Very often they go on not working properly for a very long time, while the programmer defensively tells people that "it's *nearly* working"; or they seem to work, and then go and do something awful when an awkward combination of circumstances shows up. The person with the nearly-working program and the computer atrocity story are set fair to become standard comic props, like mothers-in-law and newly-weds. The problem is not in the programmers, who are not stupid; nor in the computers, which are doing exactly what they have been programmed to do; it must be in the activity of programming itself, something to do with the human factors.

Without doubt there are many possible improvements in the human factors of programming: manuals could be made more readable, the script of teleprinters and line printers could be made clear, something could be done about the inability of compilers to correct even the most trivial of spelling mistakes. All these are matters of lesser psychological interest, however. The necessary tools for studying them have already been developed by applied psychologists; reasons why obscure manuals or illegible printing cause trouble are not exactly hard to find; and, as a matter of fact, the techniques for improving matters already exist. All the same, the person whose program is "nearly" working is not in trouble for any of those reasons. He/she knows the programming language, knows what they want done, all the spelling mistakes have been put right, but somewhere the program is not doing what was intended.

What we need to consider, then, is why programming is such a strain on the mind and what can be done about it. I shall discuss psychological contributions that might be useful for the development of programming—more or less immediately, not one-day-if-we're-lucky. I shall particularly avoid as far as I can the two Utopian 'solutions' of either educating everybody quite differently, preferably starting 20 years ago, or else invoking technical wizardry that's said to be just around the corner, such as Jones's Automatic Bug Detector.

1.1 The Role of Applied Psychology

Once psychologists have taken the wrinkles out of a Theory of Thinking, programming can be treated as a special case and it will be obvious how to make it easier. Alas, that is another Utopian solution, and it will come true about the same time as Jones's Automatic Bug Detector. Psychology does *not* have a general Theory of Thinking, and it is not likely to have one in any reasonable time to come.

So much for what the methods of psychology cannot offer; now let's consider what they can. In the first place, they can be used to check the truth of your intuitions, which—however expert—might, just possibly, be wrong. Many psychological experiments meet the brutal response "Oh, I knew *that* all along", and maybe you did; but there's a good chance that if the result had been the other way you'd have "known" that, too. In many different areas, including programming, one expert will declare that it's obviously, patently, self-evidently easiest to do things his way; but on the next page in the same book, another expert will avow that it's plain as a pikestaff you should do things his way. How can we choose which expert we should believe? Principally by recourse to the theories and experiments of psychologists.

In the second place, for practical decision-making we need to know a bit more than that it's obviously better if such-and-such. We need to have some idea of *how much* better. A good example here is the value of mnemonic names for things in programs, so that we can refer to VARIANCE instead of just V, which could mean Variance or Velocity or Value or merely the next letter free working backwards from W. Mnemonics obviously help, but the problem is, how much. When BASIC was designed, its creators decided that the computational overheads of allowing mnemonics were too expensive compared to the gain in human ease, but not everyone agrees, and many implementations of BASIC now allow mnemonics. Sometimes the choice is forced, of course: on a tiny microprocessor there won't be room for mnemonics. But often it is a real and difficult decision. This is an interesting question for applied psychology, because it bangs us straight into the problem that people don't obey simple laws. We shall therefore not find any simple answer to the question of how much help mnemonics give; it will depend on experience, on the size of problem, on whether this and that— and in this respect it is absolutely typical of the questions that applied psychology faces. The sort of answer that can usefully be given is *not* "using mnemonics, programmers always make 53.7% fewer mistakes", but (I don't know if this is true) "the amount of help mnemonics give depends critically on the experience of the programmer, and professionals need them much less than novices; the size of the problem has little effect; even under the worst conditions, i.e. with novices writing big programs, disallowing mnemonics only puts up the error rate by about 20%". The designer can then decide whether to tolerate 20% more mistakes by novices.

Finally, applied psychologists can offer suggestions that clearly were not obvious to the experts in the field. My example here comes from the work of Sime, Arblaster & Green (1977). Briefly, many programming languages include conditional constructions of the form '*if* P *then* do A *else* do B'. What my colleagues and I found was that both novices and professionals found it easier to use the following form, even though it is logically equivalent: '*if* P: do A; *not* P: do B; *end* P'. We found, for instance, that novices corrected mistakes in their programs ten times faster in the second form. We arrived at this idea by following fairly unremarkable psychological thoughts, but there are absolutely no languages in standard use that use such a form.

This view of applied psychology's role is, I hope, becomingly modest. On the one hand it offers a kind of quality control: do experts' good ideas really work, and if so, how much effect do they have? On the other hand, by relating field problems to laboratory phenomena, it can occasionally offer suggestions of its own. It is a view that is being expressed more frequently these days, and in more than one milieu. A most thorough-going review of the relations between pure and applied research on language comprehension (Wright, 1978), considering all the issues in far greater depth and with much more sophistication than I have space or ability for, reaches essentially the same conclusions, although programming and its problems do not figure at all in her work. At the other end of the scale, F.P. Brooks (1977), definitely a computing scientist in outlook rather than a psychologist, reviews the human factors components of several related systems his laboratory has designed, and reaches the conclusion that "principles" of good human factors design are a chimera, that the best one can do is to eliminate misfits: a good design is a design there's nothing wrong with.

I cannot go all the way with Brooks. Certainly applied psychology is rather less than a beacon unto the mind's eye, but at the same time it is rather more than a mere gadget to get stones out of the mind's hooves.

2.0 Programming Languages as Notations

Now let us return to the scenario of the introduction: the person whose program is nearly working. One of the problems is that the notation of programming obscures the information that the person needs.

Notation matters. There are no two ways about that. A few experiments in doing arithmetic using Roman numerals should be enough to persuade anybody. Yet the Roman system had a very long life, and indeed it was a considerable advance over the system used by the Greeks in which each letter of the alphabet denoted a different number. How come all those Romans and early Europeans, right up to the Middle Ages, failed to think of the Arabic system? More urgently, how can we be sure that our programming notations are not just as backward?

2.1 Tractability

Much of the history of mathematics is the story of improvements in notations. The same will probably be true when people look back at programming, but it seems to be happening much faster. The comparison between mathematics and programming notation has been much played on by some writers, notably Hoare (1973), who presents school algebra as a good notation with many virtues that ought to be copied in programming notations. Essentially these are the virtues of *mathematical tractability*, which it is easier to illustrate than to define.

The following passage states the rule for finding the area of an acute-angled triangle, as presented by a leading scholar of his day, which was about 150 AD:

"For example: a triangle with unequal sides and acute angles, 15 from one side, 14 from the other side and 13 from the third side. Whoever wants to measure, let him seize the three of them together, they amount to 42: let him take the half of it and see how much greater it is than the first side, and let him multiply the half upon the difference, this is 21 into 6, which gives 126, and put it on the side; let him again, for the second time take the half and see how much greater it is than the second side, and let him multiply the difference, which is 7, into the first 126, which amounts to 882, and put it on the side; let him again, for the third time, take the half, and see how much greater it is than third side, and let him multiply the difference, which is 8, into the last 882, and this amounts to 7056, and its root is 84, and this is the measure of the area." (R. Nehemiah, in Midonick, 1968, vol. 1, pp. 202-3)

Today a schoolboy would write something like:

$$A = [\, s\, (s - a)\, (s - b)\, (s - c)\,]^{1/2}$$

where $s = \frac{1}{2}(a + b + c)$ and a, b, c are the sides of the triangle.

For communicating information of this kind, school algebra is clearly better than English. The notation is a highly evolved compromise between conciseness and simplicity: it is just powerful enough to do the jobs it is used for, without being too hard to learn. (Although a few quaint idiosyncracies remain; for example, x^{-1} means $1/x$, but $\mathrm{Sin}^{-1} x$ does not mean $1/\mathrm{Sin}\, x$, it means the angle whose Sine is x.)

The tractability of the algebraic notation is shown by a few quick manipulations; we could also write

$$A = \tfrac{1}{4}\, [\, (a + b + c)\, (a + b - c)\, (a + c - b)\, (b + c - a)\,]^{1/2}$$

or

$$A = [\, s^4 - as^3 - bs^3 - cs^3 + abs^2 + acs^2 + bcs^2 - abcs\,]^{1/2}$$

each of which is readily derived from the original statement, and each of which when put into words would look so different from Nehemiah's version that most of us would only with great difficulty work out that they were equivalent. In fact, within its limits school algebra is very tractable indeed, and it is very little effort to dismantle a formula and reassemble it in a different way.

Programs are at present much more like English than like algebra, in that they are relatively intractable. Reassembling them to do the same tasks in a different order, for instance, can often be a major effort. There have been various attempts to improve them; essentially there are two main approaches, either to provide a second notation to accompany the programming notation, or to reform the programming notation itself. To the first approach belongs the method pioneered by Floyd (1967), in which assertions are attached to the program stating the conditions under which each component can be reached, and the axiomatisation developed by Hoare (1969). Because these methods make a program look more like a theorem in formal logic there has been intensive activity in developing techniques for automatic program verification, using the techniques originally developed for automatic theorem proving. At present, however, automatic program verification as a standard technique remains a Utopian solution, something that may be available one day if we're lucky (and very nice it will be too).

Meanwhile the second approach to tractability (developed originally to make the first approach possible, but later taking on a life of its own) has had great success. This is the reform of notation by eliminating arbitrary *goto* statements and by using well-designed data structures. Such a reform is one of the main planks of the structured programming school, along with the top-down approach to programming and the policy of avoiding unnecessary frills in a programming language, each of which will be mentioned below. Elsewhere in this volume (Chapter 11) the *goto* question is discussed in some detail by Michael Jackson: the basic principles apply not only to programming notations but also to flow-charts. In the past, flow-charts were only asked to do the job specified, and no principles or codes governed their construction. By these lights Figure 1 is an adequate flow-chart. The reformers of today would insist that a flow-chart be built from the few components shown in Figure 2, or some very similar set, which would make the process shown in Figure 1 come out as in Figure 3. Figure 3 has more boxes—eight as against five, a 60% increase—but the reformers would say it is better, because it can be understood by the 'divide-and-rule' method (Figure 3b and c). The version shown in Figure 1, in contrast, cannot be split up, so it must be comprehended all at one gulp or else not at all. By the same token Figure 3 is more tractable. Its component parts could be rearranged or made to accomodate some more processes with minimal trouble.

(Any reformer worth his propagandist salt would also point out that I have had to cheat in Figure 1 to achieve such economy. The test "more eggs needed?" means utterly different things at different times. Initially it means 'Are there enough eggs for the amount I wish to make?'; but once the oil is being added, it means 'Has it curdled?' This is a fairly bad case, but in its obscurantism it is typical of what happens when flowcharts or programs are compressed to achieve economy).

By finding ways to make programs more tractable, the reformers have done us all a service. Similar principles have been extended to the design of data structures, where the equivalent of avoiding arbitrary *gotos* is the avoidance of arbitrary pointers (Hoare, 1975).

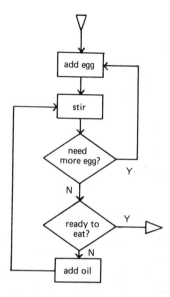

Fig. 1. How to make mayonnaise: take enough egg yolks, stir, then add some oil, stir again, and so on until the right consistency is reached and there is enough for your purposes. But if it starts to curdle, because too much oil was added at once, you will hurriedly need more yolks. The flowchart does the job but it is poorly structured; it cannot be broken in components. Nor can it be modified easily—for instance, if we now desire to add mustard after the eggs and before the oil, there is nowhere to insert the instruction 'add mustard' without it being potentially performed several times not just once; a complete new structure would be necessary. Programs that make free use of *go-to* statements get into this trouble.

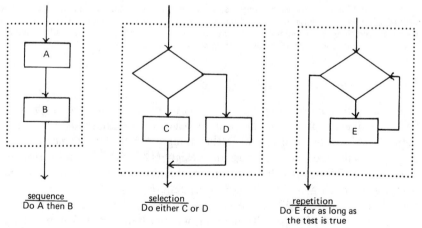

Fig. 2. Three basic components from which flowcharts can be constructed. Using these components avoids the tangles of Figure 1. In practice it is often helpful to introduce a few more components, such as subroutines and other forms of repetition loops.

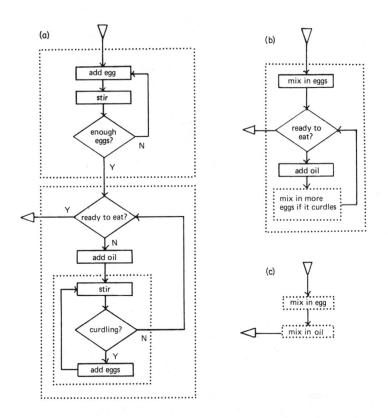

Fig. 3. Making mayonnaise presented as an orderly process using basic components. The process can now be understood by the "divide-and-rule" technique: understand what happens within dotted lines, then understand the interrelations, as in (b) and (c). It would now be a trivial job to put 'add mustard' between the two boxes of (c).

2.2 The Proof-reading Effect

An early discovery about notation was that slips of the pen are hard to find, just like misprints on the printed page. I hope that this 'discovery' seems banal to you, and provokes the thought "Well, I don't need a psychologist to tell me *that!*" Because the designers of FORTRAN overlooked it. (And FORTRAN is still the commonest language, used in 80% of initial teaching according to recent figures: appalling thought.) If you mistype something in FORTRAN there is a good chance that what you produce makes some kind of sense, although not what you intended. The particular horrors of FORTRAN have long been recognised and modern languages avoid them, but there are plenty more. The Statistical Package for the Social Sciences (SPSS), another widely used system, demands that certain input control records start in column 16: God knows how much expensive time is wasted by this unnecessary whimsy, left over from punched cards and the FORTRAN input/output structures.

Somewhat more general is the question of default options, where the programmer can request the computer to use option A or option B and, if neither one is specified, option A is taken by default. Hoare (1973) emphasises the difficulties that default options give to people trying to understand the program, who have to work out that option A is the case by its absence. Thus instead of reading the program and looking up anything that one doesn't understand in the manual, one has to read the manual right through looking for things that might furtively apply to the program.

Hoare does not go far enough, to my mind, and I should like to add my own pet hate, the 'significant omission'. Three people recently spent over an hour looking at an assembly-code program before noticing that at one point the programmer had typed "NAME" instead of "#NAME", giving him something different (a value instead of an address). How easy it would be to change that syntax slightly, so that one didn't use the absence of a hash sign to mean one thing and its presence to mean something else. Curiously enough the PASCAL language, in many respects so well designed, has just the same fault with just the same interpretation attached: in declaring formal parameters for procedures, "NAME" gives a value and "*VAR* NAME" gives an address. The only difference is the change from # to *VAR*. There are many other examples of significant omissions to be found, each of which has no doubt caused fury in its time.

2.3 Perceptual Obviousness

The proof-reading effect is just one example of the problems of making sense of a program. Programming languages are impressively well-equipped with devices to make them hard. Time spent deciphering bad notation is not merely unproductive but actually destroys the thought-process. Here is an example line adapted from a book on programming style (Kernighan & Plauger, 1974a) showing the best style that can be achieved:

$$XNEW = R*(1.0 - COS(A)) + L - L*SQRT(1.0$$
$$- (R*SIN(A)/L)**2)$$

Translated into conventional school algebra style, that reads:

$$Xnew = R(1 - Cos\ A) + L - L\left[\,1 - \frac{(R\ Sin\ A)^2}{L}\,\right]^{\frac{1}{2}}$$

Unfortunately, technical limitations of standard terminal equipment do not yet allow equations to be written on more than one level, but the other notable differences could all be rectified. Some compilers already accept lower-case, which is more legible than upper-case alone. There is no need to make programmers smother their text in round brackets when they could perfectly well use a mixture of round, curly and square; it would cost nothing for the compiler, it would obviously clarify complicated expressions, and it would give a better check on mistypings, since a round bracket would only match with a round, curly with curly, and square with square. Writing 1.0 to mean unity is pointless. Rather more expensive for the compiler to handle would be the avoidance of unnecessary brackets, but it could be done; it knows that "Sin" is a function of one argument, and brackets are only needed when the expression reads "Sin(A+B)". Similarly the multiplication sign, "*", can frequently be omitted without ambiguity.

A different source of perceptual confusions was noted by Atkinson (1978), who pointed out that people frequently ask for a loop to be performed until something (e.g. convergence) has happened by writing

> *while* unconverged *do* . . . .

The catch is that a conditional test inside the loop on 'unconverged' is made mentally hard because of the negative. If the conditional has an *else* arm,

> *if* unconverged *then* . . . . *else* . . .

then one has to cope with a double negative, while if one encounters the form

> *if not* unconverged *then* . . . *else*

one has to handle nothing less than a triple negative. Atkinson recommends that programmers should use positive forms of words, not negative ones, and (a rather fiercer suggestion) that *if-then-else* should be used far more rarely. Instead he advocates case statements in which both alternatives are named explicitly; 'hot' and 'cold', rather than 'hot' and '*not* hot', and so on. This has the added advantage that if it subsequently becomes important to discriminate between hot, cold and warm, the extra case can be slipped in quite readily.

Why are these things not done? Some of them—omitting redundant brackets, for example—would genuinely make compilation more expensive. I suspect others have just not been thought about seriously, or when they have been thought about they have been dismissed because there is no evidence that they would do any good; a perfectly sound but rather saddening appraisal of current knowledge about language design. In general I think it is very likely that the importance of perceptual factors in programming is grossly underestimated. One can see why. Understanding a program is a very cognitive task, something that one goes about slowly and painstakingly

—how on earth can perceptual confusions be important? Yet a moment's reflection will reveal the opposing argument. Understanding a program is a quite hard enough task under the best of conditions. Making it hard to read as well, inviting the reader to miscount the brackets or get tangled up in triple negatives, is the last straw.

When they are well-treated, the perceptual mechanisms of people can become aids to understanding rather than liabilities. Programs can be indented, so that their structure is clearer. Distinct syntactic constructs can be terminated in distinct ways, using *end-if, end-do*, etc., (or *fi, od*, etc., if preferred) to make it more obvious which construct ends where, avoiding the plethora of *ends* that ALGOL 60 and PASCAL generate; a number of examples and several excellent suggestions can be found in Burnett-Hall (1978). When examples of one construction have to be nested, individual ones can be labelled repeatedly, giving nested *if*-statements of the form

> *if* P:
> > *if* Q: . . .
> > *not* Q: . . .
> > *end* Q
> *not* P: . . . .
> *end* P

This device is very effective, as mentioned above (Sime et al., 1977). All these are examples of devices to help get a message across, such as where a conditional starts and ends, by *redundant* recoding. The message can be deduced from the plain text of the program, but to make it clearer it is re-expressed in another form such as indenting. There are two snags to this principle of redundant recoding. The first is that it is only effective when the message being conveyed is one that is actually useful to the programmer; the second is that the more perceptually distinct two programs are, the harder it becomes to change one into the other, and thus the harder it is to revise and modify programs (Fitter and Green, 1978).

2.4 Signalling Syntactic Constructions

One can extend the consideration of perceptual obviousness to a deeper level, the signalling of particular components of patterns. In a series of studies in which people learnt artificial languages by a combination of trial-and-error and case examples, I got subjects to learn how to construct meaningless sentences looking like this:

NAL CLOPE EAG KON LOSYM UST CHOLT

This sentence contains a number of signals, readily spotted because they are the only three letter words. The non-signalling words, CLOPE, LOSYM, and CHOLT, are each drawn from a different class, and the grammar of the language gave rules for the possible combinations of those classes and others. Each class was accompanied by its own signal, so that all words from the LOSYM class were accompanied by KON, and so on, and then particular combinations of phrases also had their own signals: the phrase made by combining a LOSYM-class word with a CHOLT-class word was signalled by the word EAG, for instance.

We have rather similar patterns in English, although both more supple and more subtle; for instance, "the" signals a noun phrase, and "who" signals a question. The signals of English carry meaning, however, and the aim of my experiment was to investigate the learning of grammatical patterns in their own right, so I assigned no meanings whatsoever to the sentences. People seemed to enjoy the task just the same. What I found (Green, 1977a) was that the signals were essential. When I compared the dialect described with other dialects where the signals were degraded, say by using the same signal for two classes of words or for two different phrases, I found that the dialects with degraded signals were consistently harder to learn. When *all* the signals were eliminated performance dropped dramatically—and people hated the task, grumbling to me afterwards about its pointlessness. All in all, this study showed very clearly that when a language is made up of a variety of syntactic constructions, it pays to make it perceptually apparent which construction is being used, by putting in some sort of signal.

A further illustration of the importance of signals in a quite different setting is given by Sloboda's studies of sight-reading by pianists. This work is rather technical unless one can read music, but briefly Sloboda showed that one of the factors that affected sight-reading was whether the printed music was laid out so that musical phrases were signalled by their spacing (Sloboda, 1977). A speed-skill task performed by experienced subjects forms about as complete a contrast to my learning task as one could imagine, showing that the signalling of syntactic phrases is a matter of very wide generality.

At this point it would be instructive to examine Figure 4. Here I have

(a) PASCAL version

```
q := 0;
for j := 1 to 10 do
        begin
        read (p);
        if p > 1 then q := q + 1
        end
write (q);
```

b) FLOWCHART VERSION

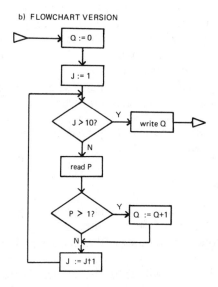

(c) Pseudo-machine code version

```
       load  +0
       store Q
       load  +1
       store J
LA     load  J
       subtract +10
       jumponposve LB    ('go to LB if positive')
       dosubroutine READ
       subtract +2
       jumponnegve LC    ('go to LC if negative')
       load  Q
       add   +1
       store Q
LC     load  J
       add   +1
       store J
       goto LA
LB     load  Q
       dosubroutine WRITE
       stop
```

Fig. 4. The same program in three languages: "Read 10 numbers and count how many are greater than 1". Its structure, a conditional inside a loop with a simple statement at each end, seems to get more obscure as we go from (a) to (c). PASCAL signals the loop and the conditional quite explicitly; in the flowchart, we have to examine the contents of the boxes and how they are linked to determine whether the test boxes control conditionals or loops; and of the pseudo-machine code, the less said the better.

contrasted a short program in PASCAL, which does contain markers to
signal most types of syntactic construction; in a mythical language which
is rather like assembly-code, which does not have any signals at all, but is
widely used; and in a flow-chart, which also has no signals but is even more
widely used. The fact that there is a conditional inside a loop is clearly
apparent in the PASCAL version, rather less clear in the flow-chart, and
totally obscured in the mythical assembly-code.

The moral is easy. A good language signals its syntactic constructions,
using devices that make it perceptually obvious what each construction is
and where it starts and stops.

2.5 How Many Features?

One of the most difficult decisions facing a language designer is when to
stop. The more features put in, the more the language will be able to do with
elegance and economy, which means that harder problems will be soluble
for the same amount of programming effort; but at the same time, the more
features put in, the harder it will be for the learner. There have been various
fashions, languages with many frills and languages with few, and the trend
at the moment is probably towards languages with rather few. (A trend to
some extent nullified by the seemingly unstoppable urge of systems programmers to add their own features to a language. The resulting proletaria-
tion of local dialects causes great confusion. One might cynically suggest
that the cause of the beginner is best served by making the language horribly
complex in the first place, so that at least it is available in the same form
everywhere one goes.) .

A 'feature' of a language is a pretty ill-defined concept, of course. I am
using it here for just that reason, to include everything from what kind of
data types are available to the maximum length of identifiers; everything,
that is, from the most semantic to the most syntactic. Although, in the mind
of the user, feature is as feature does—if something's used to help organize
the reference manual it's a feature, and if it just crops up somewhere in the
manual then it's a quirk.

The trade-off between number of features and ease of learning is a truism.
All the more surprising and regrettable, therefore, that the literature not
only gives us no guidance on where to draw the line, but does not even offer
useful suggestions on how to find out in a particular case whether the line
was drawn well or badly. Common sense tells us that if we are designing
a language for occasional use by people like managers or doctors, who will
not want to spend much time learning the language nor checking through
the manual when they want to use it, there should be rather few features,
while a language for constant use by highly-motivated people can afford to

have a wide variety of different features each tailor-made for one exact task. And that, at present, is all. In fact the idea of a feature is so vague that we cannot even offer a useful way to compare two languages to see which has more features.

With so few facts to go on, it is interesting that such very firm opinions are voiced, declaring that languages should have few features. Wirth remarked in a conference discussion that "I have always maintained that you should have not more than one facility to express each single concept" (Perrot, 1977 p.180); having earlier compared a programming language to a Meccano tool kit containing nuts and bolts, wheels and axles, he went on to say that there should be "only one kind of axle in your tool kit". A level-headed radical, Wirth included three kinds of repetition construction in his language PASCAL, and he "suffered very severe criticism from many distinguished friends and colleagues" as a result.

Why such pressure for a minimum number of features? There seem to be intuitive reasons to suppose that notation will be easier to comprehend if it supplies a healthy range of features, reduplicating each other's function quite merrily. Let me take an extreme example. It is possible to handle all the conventional logical relations, 'and', 'or', and 'not', by a single all-powerful relation 'not-and' or 'is incompatible with'. Thus 'p is incompatible with q', written 'p/q', means that at least one of them must be false. The relations can then be written as follows: 'not-p', or 'p is false', becomes 'p/p'; 'p and q', or 'both p and q are true', becomes '(p/q) / (p/q)'; and 'p or q', or 'at least one of p and q is true', becomes '(p/p) / (q/q)'. So the expression

$$(p \text{ or } q) \text{ and } r$$

meaning at least one of p and q is true and so is r, becomes

$$([(p/p)/(q/q)]/r)/([(p/p)/(q/q)]/r)$$

It will take a lot to convince me that the latter expression is more readable.

This is an important, ill-understood and very pervasive problem, so a second example is called for. Back to flowcharts. We saw above (Section 2.1) that flowcharts could be made more tractable by sticking to certain rules, and using only three types of component in their manufacture. Once we decide to do that, we can go a step further and decide to draw those three components differently (see Figure 5). We can now compare the 'orderly flowchart' of Figure 3, built from the three components, with a 'structure diagram', as it is termed by the inventor of this particular notation (Jackson, 1975), which is logically identical (Figure 6). From the point of view of someone who is handed an orderly flowchart or a structure diagram and told to understand it, which is easier? Well, there are certainly fewer kinds of feature in the conventional flowchart: start/stop boxes, action boxes, and

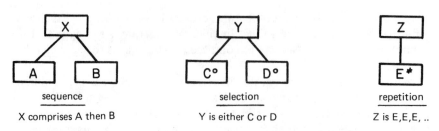

(a) Basic components of Jackson's structure diagram notation

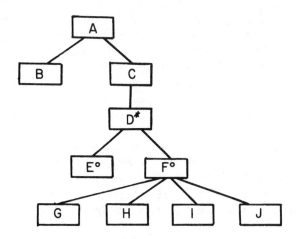

(b) Linking up components into a process.
A is the sequence B,C.
B is primitive; C is a repetition of D.
D is either E or F.
F is the sequence G,H,I, J.

Fig. 5. An alternative to the flowchart notation is to use a structured notation. Several have been devised; this one comes from Jackson (1975). To restrict oneself to the flowchart components of Figure 2 needs self-discipline; structured notations need no self-discipline because the restrictions are built into the notation, making it impossible to produce an unstructured process.

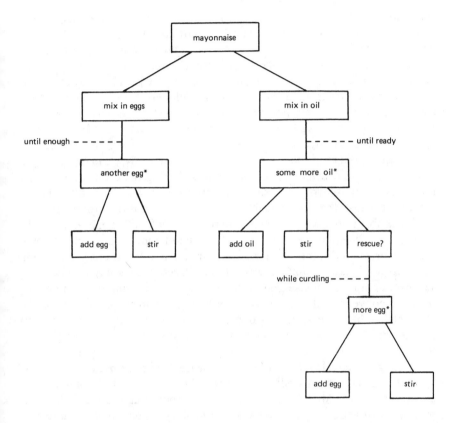

Fig. 6. How to make mayonnaise, represented as a structure diagram.

test boxes—just three. (I am disregarding the other couple of dozen symbols that creep onto flowcharting templates, and considering what you might call domestic flowcharts, for which those three are quite enough.) It undoubtedly takes less time to explain how conventional flowcharts work and less time to become proficient. Nevertheless, after little experience the person who has learnt structure diagramming will be able to give better answers to questions about the behaviour of his/her program. That person will get a deeper understanding in a shorter time. These, it must be stressed, are unsupported statements for which I have only my own experience and intuition to appeal to.

The principles involved seem (still speaking intuitively) to be straightforward but contradictory. First, when a language has few features they can be explained very quickly, and that goes both for the 'not-and' logic and for the flowchart. Second, if the language is dealing with familiar concepts they should be represented as such in the notation. As far as flowcharts are concerned beginners usually have no prior concepts about control structures, but the 'not-and' logic is a different case; here we have familiar concepts of 'and' and 'or', and we lose more than we gain by replacing them with different concepts—even though the number of different concepts is smaller. And third, we come up against the problem of *discriminability*. When the language has a lot of features the learner has trouble keeping them apart in his/her mind, and the more similar they are the more trouble it is. That is an argument for having few features. But once they can be kept apart in the mind, the learner has the problem of sorting them out on the page: it is much harder to work out what happens in a flowchart than in a structure diagram because the higher-level components are not discriminable.

The problem that we are tackling here is a very familiar one to psychologists. It is well-established that people can handle information more easily if they can 'chunk' it into higher-level components. But there is no reliable guide to how many chunks are desirable. Psychologists have made fairly serious attempts to devise good techniques for measuring discriminability of more conventional stimuli, such as figures or noises, and at least one attempt has been made to develop a function to predict discriminability (Crossman, 1955); not surprisingly, it depends on both the number of things to be discriminated and also on how physically distinct they are.

Making our constructions physically distinct takes us back to the use of syntactic signals, discussed above, and Wirth's three kinds of repetitive construction in PASCAL are laudably different. But there has been no proper investigation of syntactic discriminability as such, and so there is no evidence that bears on the fundamental question: how many constructs? Given that PASCAL's three repetition constructs have been made quite sufficiently distinct not to be confusable, is it then true that a program will be easier to understand if it uses all three as appropriate rather than confining itself just to one of them? I personally believe that Wirth was right—indeed, I would like to go farther and use all the typographic devices for discriminability that printers use, such as different sizes, different fonts, and even different colours; but it would be nice to have some hard evidence.

2.6 Are Some Grammars Difficult?

Apart from the number of features in a language and their discriminability, there are some grounds to believe that the way they link together is important. Shipstone (1960) reported a series of studies in which people tried to find out the grammars of various small languages. These languages are so small that they were really patterns made up of nonsense syllables, but they can still tell us about what is hard to learn. Two of her findings are

```
X := 0; Y := 0;
while read = 1 and read = 2 do ;
if read = 3 or read = 4 then else X := 1;
if read = 4 then
else
        if read = 5 then
        else
                if read = 6 then
                else Y := 1;
```

Fig. 7. A program containing numerous null statements. Given that each call of 'read' takes a number from an input stream, what conditions must the sequence of numbers fulfil in order that the final values of X and Y should both be 1?

particularly notable in the present context. People found the 'zero' concept difficult: when a syntactic pattern included an element that could be repeated any number of times but could also be omitted entirely, they found it hard to work out that the omission could be regarded as repetition zero times. In a programming language that would correspond to not realising that a loop or a conditional can control any number of statements *including none*, and therefore finding it obscure and awkward when someone wrote a program in that way. Kernighan & Plauger (1974a) specifically advise one not to do that, but to find a way to rephrase the program (see Figure 7). Shipstone's second finding of interest was that while a formula could be managed when it contained just one repeating element, if it contained two—a 'double loop' in her terminology—it became difficult. That would perhaps correspond in programming to explaining that a procedure heading, in the ALGOL family, can declare as many parameters as desired and then can *also* declare as many local variables as desired. Needless to say, when a double loop also permitted zero repetition, it was extra hard. (Notice that is actually the case in the procedure heading example.)

Shipstone's work dealt with grammars where no phrases were ever hierarchically nested inside others. We also know a little about languages where the patterns are entirely made up of hierarchically-nested phrases, where Restle (1970) showed that errors followed a rather neat law. In his patterns, each 'sentence' consisted of two phrases; each phrase of two sub-phrases; each sub-phrase of two sub-sub-phrases; each sub-sub-phrase of two 'words'. After the second word, therefore, a sub-sub-phrase ends. After the fourth word, both a sub-sub-phrase, and a sub-phrase end; after the eighth word, a sub-sub-phrase, a sub-phrase, and phrase all end. Restle showed that the more units had just ended, the harder it was to get the next word right. So errors were higher on the third word than on the second, higher again on the fifth word, and higher still on the ninth. Now, it has to be admitted that Restle's task was not very similar to programming: subjects saw a display of six lights and had to predict which one would come on next. But at the other end of the scale of complexity there are numerous demonstrations of similar effects in natural language (see Cairns & Cairns, 1976, for a review), all leading to the conclusion that the bigger the syntactic break—i.e., the more phrase units that have just ended—the more processing goes on inside the head.

Restle's work bears on one of the important syntactic options, that of using a tight hierarchic structure with steep nesting or of using a loose concatenated structure. The LISP language is one where programs have steep nesting, since a program consists of a function call and some parameters, and each parameter is either a constant or else a function call and some parameters, and so on down and down until all the parameters are constants. The more usual approach is to construct a program from a string of statements, all at much the same hierarchical level, as in FORTRAN and BASIC or to a slightly lesser extent the ALGOL and PASCAL family. The structure of LISP is like a tree, while the structure of FORTRAN is more like firewood. Which is better?

The popular opinion is that nesting is a Bad Thing. Weinberg, Geller & Plum (1975) say that no construction should *ever* be nested inside itself (or 'self-embedded', in the technical phrase). Kernighan & Plauger (1974b) recommend the programmer to avoid nesting if-statements inside each other, in the form

> *if* A *then*
>   *if* B *then* . . . *else* . . .
> *else if* C *then* . . . *else* . . .

The problem is the statement beginning '*if* B', which is nested between *then* and *else*. Instead, they say, one should reorganise one's code into *else-if* sequences:

> *if* A *then* . . .
> *else if* B *then* . . .
>   . . .
> *else* . . .

Very similar arguments are advanced by Richards (1976). In both cases the reasoning is that the *else-if* organisation will be easier to comprehend, because the self-embedding is avoided; Kernighan and Plauger say that "it seems to more closely reflect how we think", while Richards says (p.338) that self-embedding involves queueing a pending decision, which is "well within the capability of the mind provided that the queue does not grow too large. If the *if* was more complicated, invoking deep nesting of other two-armed *if*-statements, then the mind becomes confused and comprehension is much more difficult". (Sensibly, he continues ". . . unless some pattern or underlying principle can be found.") The result of Restle's work described above would support this view.

There are two studies that deal directly with the organisation of if-statements. Mayer (1976a) found results that supported the claims of Kernighan and Plauger. However, Green & Manton (1978) pointed out that the construction *if* A *then* . . . *else* . . . was not as easy as the construction *if* A: . . . *not* A: . . . *end* A, a finding already mentioned above (Sime et al., 1977). Testing this latter construction, which is logically identical to the standard if-statement and therefore forms just as steep nests, they found that for some tasks it was actually easier to use than the form recommended by Kernighan and Plauger, and for other tasks the two forms were equivalent. It appears therefore that self-embedded constructions do not always create the memory load problems that have been supposed.

Important issues are never decided easily, and the few studies cited are by no means definitive. But they are at least suggestive, and what they suggest is that steep nesting is hard to handle when the boundaries of phrases are not clearly signalled. Hence, the results of Restle and of Mayer. When the boundaries are signalled, however, there are no special difficulties attached to nestings. Popular opinion could very well be simply wrong, and nesting *not* inhuman.

So far this section has succeeded in finding slightly more positive empirical results than average: zero elements and double loops are hard, steep nestings are hard unless their constituents are signalled but are easy enough when the signals are there. At this point, therefore, it is time to cloud the issue by pointing out that the structure of the grammar *in the head* is not likely to be the same as the structure on paper, derived from the definition of the programming language. The reason is that it is convenient to define programming languages in terms of formal grammars which do not do very complex operations. These grammars, usually a particular kind of context-free phrase-structure grammar called Backus-Naur form or BNF, allow one symbol at a time to be rewritten during the derivation of a sentence; no other kinds of operation are possible.

Here is an example of Backus-Naur form, adapted from the ALGOL 60 report:

```
<if clause> ::= if <Boolean expression> then
<if statement> ::= <if clause> <unconditional    statement>
<conditional statement> ::= <if statement>
      | <if statement> else <statement>
      | <if clause> <for statement>
      . . . .
      . . . .
```

It means: if you want to write a conditional statement, you can do so by writing *either* an if statement, *or* an if statement followed by an else branch, *or* an if clause followed by a for statement. Things in diamond brackets are defined by other rules; things outside diamond brackets, like *if,* are to be actually written down. The vertical bar separates alternatives. Nothing need be said, you will observe, about when these rules may be applied, because they are always applicable.

But the programmer's head works in much more powerful ways. Where the BNF form only allows a choice between alternatives, the programmer's head allows for rules that are only applicable in certain contexts. This is quite natural and typical—for instance, "Put I before E, *except* after C"; in fact that rule then has its own exception, "Don't forget please the little word 'seize'".

This ability to use context-sensitive rules makes nonsense of the 'official' grammar of a language as a guide to what the programmer does. An unfortunate fact, that, and one which has not always been appreciated. For example, Reisner (1977) says how nice it would be if we had an index of the structural complexity of a language so that we could avoid creating ones that were too complex—and up to here I am in complete agreement with her; but she suggests (p.227) that "A natural index of the complexity (of a statement) might be the number of rewrite rules . . . used to describe it. . . . By this we mean to suggest that a BNF description of a language, usually intended to describe the set of valid statements, may have *psychological* validity". Finally she proposes experimental investigations seeking "a single, consistent, psychological BNF".

I fear her proposal is doomed before it starts, because BNF just isn't what people use. Although the fragment of ALGOL 60's grammar that appears above does what it is designed to do, namely to prohibit the sequence

> *if . . . then for . . . do . . .*
> *else . . .*

It does so by means that are psychologically bizarre. The import is very straightforward: "If you've written *if. . then for. . do . . .,* and now you want to put an else-branch on the end, you must go back and put *begin-end* round the for-statement". (*Begin* and *end,* like brackets in algebra, turn a complex expression into a single, simple entity, which can then be manipulated like an ordinary unconditional statement. Without them, should the for-statement contain a further if-statement, it can be ambiguous whether the *else* should go with the first *if* or the second.) No problem arises in remembering the rule in that form, which I am sure is how most ALGOL 60 programmers do remember it. But the effect of the BNF grammar is to create two kinds of conditional statement, one with and one without the *begin-end-else,* which have practically nothing in common (Figure 8).

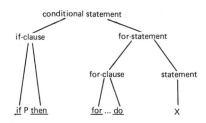

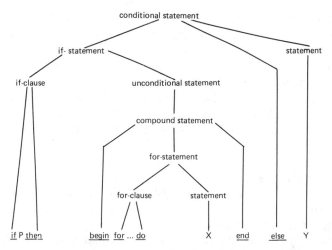

Fig. 8. The derivations of two ALGOL 60 statements, following the 'official' grammar (slightly adapted). Although the statements are very similar in the head, their derivations are different from the second row onwards, which shows that the official grammar has little to do with the grammar in the head.

A psychological index of complexity would be a fine thing, but it cannot be arrived at from BNF. What we need to know is what the grammar might look like in the head; and to get some idea of that, we must turn to what is known about natural language and how we use it.

3.0 Programming Languages and Natural Languages

Although programming languages are very different from natural languages, they have to be handled by the same animals, and it would be surprising if there were not substantial similarities between the ways of doing the handling. Computer scientists have tended to fight shy of evidence from natural language, but opinion is now beginning to change. And so it should; whatever the differences between them, features that make natural language harder or easier to comprehend are certainly worth bearing in mind when we start designing artificial languages.

3.1 How Do We Parse Sentences?

Earlier we put the question of whether some grammars were inherently hard, and met the difficulty that people use more powerful techniques for parsing than the context-free phrase-structure grammars of computing. Just what we do is still a matter of lively conjecture, but there is evidence enough from studies of parsing English to have allowed a broad consensus in present theory. By parsing here I mean decoding the surface structure of the sentence, deciding whether words are nouns or verbs and in what relationship they stand. This is a process in which it is almost certain that we usually make heavy use of semantic cues taken from our knowledge of the meanings of words and how they interrelate, but it is also a process that we can manage, when we have to, without any such help. Inserting unfamiliar nonsense words into otherwise well-formed sentences ("Twas brillig, and the slithy toves did gyre and gimble in the wabe") shows that we can still parse the sentence into nouns and verbs, subjects and objects, with not much extra trouble by and large.

Ideas about how people parse sentences depend rather heavily on whether one believes that the famous transformational theory of grammar does or does not have any psychological reality (as opposed to linguistic power). One very influential paper by Bever (1970) starts from the premise that standard transformational grammar is basically correct, and that the parsing problem is that of discovering the deep structure underlying the surface structure—or in other words, working out who did what to whom and how, or actor, action, object, and modifier. He distinguished three different kinds of mechanism, the basic perceptual mechanisms, perceptual strategies for guessing the deep structure from the given words, and an internalisation of the rules of grammar which will supply the meaning. It is the middle level that concerns us here. While Bever's particular strategies are, naturally, aimed at parsing English, his basic assumption is that strategies of a similar type would be used for parsing any natural language and indeed any kind of patterned structure, which would evidently include programming languages.

A typical Bever strategy is his Strategy B: "The first N ... V ... (N) ... clause is the main clause, unless the verb is marked as subordinate." We can make several observations about this. It is a heuristic, a rule of thumb, a way to make an imperfect guess that will usually be right; when we meet

S1: The horse raced past the barn.

it works perfectly, but it goes wrong when we meet

S2: The horse raced past the barn fell.

(i.e., The horse *that was* raced past the barn fell). When a strategy goes wrong we have to think again. Secondly, its essential nature is to make the shortest, simplest hypothesis. Gaps are left for intervening material that cannot be fitted in, which will be sorted out later in the parsing, but the rule is to close off the gap as soon as possible. By implication, the more ways there are to close the gap off too soon, the harder the sentences will be to parse; S2 is hard to parse because we initially treat 'raced' as the main verb we are looking for. Strategy B is also, we see, a context-sensitive rule. It is to be applied *unless* we meet a certain context: 'because', 'the fact that', or a similar indication that the subsequent verb is not the main verb. Finally, the context-sensitive part relies on the presence or absences of markers to signal the syntactic construction, and that is a theme that runs right through Bever's strategies.

Is Bever's theory broadly correct? Yes, I believe it is. For one thing very similar inferences can be drawn from other recent theories of parsing, even ones that explicitly reject the transformational theory of grammar on which Bever's is based, such as Johnson-Laird (1977). For another, it fits well with a broad range of evidence from many different kinds of study (see Fodor, Bever & Garrett, 1974). Much of the evidence, of course, is drawn from studies comparing sentences that have no equivalent in programming terms, such as active versus passive. To get as close a check as possible on whether the theories about English are likely to apply to programming languages, Simpson and I studied the comprehension of a fragment of English grammar that has similar properties to a programming language, the relative clause. Relative clauses can be discontinuous, and their components can be separated widely or only slightly, and they can be nested.

Because there are two types of relative clause there are two ways to form nests, a property we took advantage of. In S3 a subject relative, "the clerk that warned the soldier", has been nested inside an object relative, "the butler that the clerk ... admired"; but in S5 one object relative, "the clerk that the soldier warned", has been nested inside another object relative, which is once again "the butler that the clerk ... admired". Sentences like S5 where a construction is nested inside itself are known technically as self-embedded.

S3: The butler that the clerk that warned the soldier
      admired rebuked the nurse.
S4: The butler warned the clerk that admired the
      soldier that rebuked the nurse.
S5: The butler that the clerk that the soldier warned
      admired rebuked the nurse.

We compared S3, S4 and S5, and all the other variations—27 in all, counting ones where 'that' is omitted; and we found that Bever's principle of parsing by the shortest simplest hypothesis gave a good approximation to our results (Green & Simpson, 1979). When that hypothesis worked, the sentence was easy (S4); when it did not work, the sentence was very hard (S5); when it partially worked, the sentence was fairly hard (S3)—and that last result, by the way, disposes of the frequently expressed but false belief that sentences are only hard when they are self-embedded. There is an exact parallel with the nested if-statement described above; here, as there, it is claimed that self-embedding is hard, and that the reason must be memory limitations (Miller & Isard, 1964; Blaubergs & Braine, 1974), and yet in both cases it turns out that self-embedding is not the source of difficulty. So support for Bever's view comes not only from its good predictions, but also from rivals' poor predictions.

Supposing, for the sake of argument, that Bever has correctly divined not only how people parse English but also how they parse programs, what have we learned? Of course, his detailed strategies would not apply unchanged; and the internalised rules that discover the meaning would have to describe data operations and flow of control, rather than actors and actions; but the essence has two parts. We look for markers to help us parse by making the simplest, shortest guess. The need for markers ties up nicely with the requirement that syntactic constructions should be signalled, discussed above, but the simplest-guess principle is more disturbing. In fact it runs counter to the whole philosophy of modern programming language design.

In a modern language, programs are made up of many discontinuous constructions nested inside each other, in a manner that is extremely hard to parse by using the 'simplest hypothesis' method because it will constantly be trying to close off a construction too soon. If people are forced to construct a tree of the complexity of Figure 8 it will be rough going for them, unless they can find markers, semantic cues (see below), or some other contextual features that will help. It is very easy to think of how markers could help, and some ways have already been discussed. The simplest way is to use indenting; alas, many editing systems for rewriting your program do not make the slightest effort to be helpful by automatically correcting your indenting after a program change, so it turns out to be quite difficult and expensive to indent a program correctly through all its various growths. Another way is to go beyond the uninformative *begin-end* and to use a closing symbol that is expressly tied to its opening, such as the *fi* and *od* of ALGOL 68 (meaning end-if and end-do). Better still to tie the ending symbol uniquely, using some developed form of the "*if* juicy: . . . *not* juicy: . . ." syntax mentioned before.

I am emphasizing the closing-off of constructions because modern languages are already very good at signalling the beginning of constructions.

There is a good reason for that, but it has nothing to do with human convenience. It is simply that modern compilers using high-performance parsing techniques work much better if each construction can be identified very early, preferably by its first symbol. The closings-off are another affair entirely. The computer, with its enviable ability to nest and de-nest without getting confused, needs nothing to tell it which syntactic construction has just ended, when it meets an *end*; so the designers of languages don't bother to put anything in. If humans have trouble they'll just have to learn to do better. We are, in short, back at the level of putting in round brackets only, and not allowing humans to use square ones as well because the machine can manage fine without.

3.2 Aids from Semantics

If what people are bad at is handling complicated context-free structures, what they are good at—superb, even—is using semantic cues to help. The pronouns we use so freely would be unintelligible without semantic cues. "I threw a brick at the window and broke it" may seem unambiguous, but we soon run into "I threw a soap-bubble at the window and broke it", where 'it' refers more easily to the bubble than the window, and then "I threw a glance at the window and beat it", where 'it' has no physical reference at all. There is brisk activity at present in the investigation of semantic aids to comprehension of language, from the viewpoints of both artificial intelligence (Wilks, 1976) and psychologists (Clark, 1976). The best attempt to date at a unified global view of what people are doing (Miller & Johnson-Laird, 1976) gives the overwhelming impression that whatever it is, it's difficult.

Nevertheless, difficult or not, people do it and it helps them. Would it be possible to gain any mileage for programming languages in this way? At first sight it might seem not. But in fact there are some interesting possibilities.

One idea is to introduce semantic categories into the programming language. To some extent they are already there, because in many languages identifiers are declared with a particular type, such as Real or Integer or String or Boolean, and there is evidence that programmers, especially the less experienced, find it helpful to have typed identifiers (Gannon, 1977—but as he himself points out, there are some confounding factors in his study that make it necessary to hedge his conclusion slightly). Within a restricted application area one can go farther and categorise objects not just by their type but also by their meaning. Programs dealing with physical magnitude, for instance, might profitably utilise the simple but powerful idea of dimensional analysis. Physical magnitudes are measurements upon a small number of dimensions, such as mass, length and time. Velocity is, say, miles per hour, or length per time, written L/T; acceleration is an increase in velocity over time, or length per time per time, written L/T²; mass is simply M, but 'putting on weight' (i.e. getting fat) would be mass per time, or M/T, while doing physical work, or moving a given mass through a given distance, is ML²/T². And so on. Now it is evident that if an equation is a true statement, the magnitudes on each side of the equals sign must be equal, and *a fortiori* their dimensions must be equal. The programmer need only specify the dimensions of each data object as he declares it, and the compiler can then check for him that in each assignment statement the dimensions match on both sides. Better still, perhaps, would be to specify the units of measurement of numbers found in the program, whether miles per hour or metres per second, since that would not only indicate the dimensions but also prevent confusions about conversions between units. Karr & Loveman (1978) have explored the idea quite convincingly but it has not been tried in practice.

Similar schemes could be devised for statistical programming, which is another large area, and no doubt for other major types of computer usage; but if every application produced its own semantic scheme there could be a rather tiresome proliferation, and Cleaveland (1975) proposes a mechanism for the programmer to create his/her own scheme for each program. To generalise the concept of dimension Cleaveland uses the term 'pouch', and suggests how programmers can not only create their own pouches, such as 'rate', 'time' and 'pay', but can also define the relations between pouches, such as 'pay = rate * time'.

The full possibilities of such a scheme would need careful working out. In Figure 9 I have sketched out how a program might look, using the pouch scheme, but one would clearly need to decide what to do about loops, how to represent the pouches of arrays and their indexes, whether every statement needed to be pouched or some could be omitted, and other practical details. Compiling would be harder, of course, but more errors would be detected and the probable increase in program legibility makes this a proposal that really ought to be tried.

Hobbs (1977) has gone rather farther, having extracted some characteristics of coherent English text and worked out how they could be incorporated into programming languages. Some of his particularly interesting suggestions are how to decode such 'anaphoric' references as "Link through list L, printing out *the value fields*", where it must be deduced that 'the value fields' are contained in the nodes making up list L; and how to use spatial metaphors, such as "the value fields are *contained* in the nodes", or "P *moves along* the list one node *behind* Q". These ideas take us considerably nearer to the Utopian, however; although present knowledge is probably adequate to try them, they are not at all likely to reach the level of routine practice in the near future.

(a) Sample program without pouches.

```
begin
        integer age, birth, death;
        integer population, workers;
        . . . .
        integer year := 1902;
        if year > birth and year death then
            begin
            population := population + 1;
            age := year − birth;
            if age > 17 and age < 60 then workers := workers
                + 1
            end;
        . . . .
end
```

(b) Sample program with pouches

```
begin
        pouch years integer age, birth, death;
        pouch people integer population, workers;
        . . . .
        pouch years integer year := 1902 years;
            if year > birth and year < death then
            begin
            population := population + 1 people;
            age := year − birth;
            if age > 17 years and age < 60 years then
            workers := workers + 1 people
            end;
        . . . .
end
```

Fig. 9. Sample programs illustrating how 'pouches' might be used to convey semantic information about a program. (Adapted from Cleaveland, 1975).

3.3 How People Use English

In contrast to thoughts about the structure of language, whether at the level of syntax or semantics, we can also consider the manner in which it is used. A number of papers on 'programming' in natural English have appeared, principally from the IBM Thomas J. Watson laboratories in New York. One aim may very well be to identify problems that need solving before we can routinely address computers in natural English, and it can truly be said that the problems are formidable; the entertaining paper by Hill (1972), "Wouldn't it be nice if we could talk to computers in English—or would it?" gives many examples of the illogicalities that we often don't notice. One of my favourites from his paper is "Dogs must be carried", an innocent-looking sign found by most escalators. Only the similar command "Crash helmets must be worn" makes one wonder if doglessness is an offence.

Although the routine use of English will not be with us for a long time, there have been investigations and experimental systems using various amounts of reduced English, and these appear to have uniformly run into the same two difficulties, described by Plum (1977) as fooling the user. One difficulty is that the system cannot handle constructions that the user reasonably expects it to handle, on the basis of its other abilities, and the other difficulty is that the system and the user do not interpret the same sentence in the same way. (Incidentally, Plum also shows how these problems occur when attempts are made to utilise the full power of mathematical notations.) Even the 'Lifer' system, which its creators believe to be "one of the most robust computerised natural language systems ever developed" (Hendrix et al., 1977), runs into these difficulties. For instance, if a user knows that the system accepts the question about shipping "Who commands the Kennedy?", and that it also accepts "The Kennedy is owned by whom?", he/she may be surprised and upset to find that it will *not* accept "The Kennedy is commanded by whom?". An irregular coverage like that would be caused by the difference in the semantically-oriented syntactic categories for 'command' and 'own'; all designers can do is to try to minimise the irregularities. The Lifer system does on the other hand introduce a way to cope with disagreement about interpretation. The user can ask about the interpretation used and can direct Lifer to modify it. This kind of escape into a meta-language is familiar enough in everyday discourse and is probably an essential if we are going to use a woolly natural language: "Well, what exactly do you mean?", "Oh, I thought you meant ... " and so on are phrases that every traveller should learn by heart.

Supposing that English, possibly in a restricted form, were available, what can we learn from the studies on the use of English as a 'programming' medium? The picture that emerges is not too encouraging. People find it very hard to make their instructions unambiguous, a finding that showed up strongly in experiments on quite different tasks, both in simple file manipulations (Miller & Becker, 1974) and in writing about patterns of children's blocks or of typed characters (Gould, Lewis & Becker, 1976). When a restricted form of syntax was used, with a slight flavour of programming, the amount of ambiguity dropped considerably in Gould et al.'s study, but even with a restricted syntax Miller (1974) found that conditionals were difficult, especially when negatives were involved. When the syntax was unrestricted, Miller & Becker found that the problems with transfer of control, specification of conditionals and failure to cope with unused data were quite striking, and that their subjects would give them such instructions as

1. See if the person is over 50;
2. Write his name down on a list.

Thomas (1976) reports a whole variety of problems with expressing quantification, 'all' versus 'some' and allied distinctions.

On the other hand, these studies also show something of people's marvellous adaptability. Gould et al. found that their subjects could follow each other's instructions, even when ambiguous, which presumably indicates that they have some common sense knowlege of what to do. They also found that although there was a slight tendency for subjects to write procedures for constructing a figure rather than descriptions of figures, quite mild suggestions in the experimental instructions readily reversed that tendency. Finally, Gould et al. also showed that when subjects started off doing their descriptions in natural English, ambiguities and all, and then gave another description in a restricted syntax, they readily switched to using a more restricted and less ambiguous style thereafter, even though the instructions made no such suggestion. They conclude that "In designing a hypothetical computer system dealing with blocks figures, for example, one could not just find the 'natural' way of referring to them and implement it, since there is not a single natural way."

The problems of transfer of control that these experiments have reported do quite possibly exceed people's ability to adapt. The designers of BDL, IBM's business definition language, took Miller's results to heart, and to get round the difficulties faced by naive programmers they eliminated normal concepts of transfer of control. They produced instead a data flow language, where instructions are executed whenever their input data has been computed and is available (Goldberg, 1976). Information on user performance is not yet available, but the approach is promising.

Taking a deep breath one might risk the following conclusions from the flimsy evidence. First, full English is out; we can choose between restricted English and a programming notation. What is difficult about a programming notation is not its formality, because people can and do readily pick up a restricted style in natural language, according to Gould et al. The difficulties come from negations, conditionals, and transfer of control, problems that arise in natural as well as artificial language as soon as precise descriptions of processes are attempted. The problems of misinterpretation and ambiguity are real but acceptable and computer scientists, rather than seek ways to prevent programmers from saying ambiguous things, should put more effort into making sure that reasonable interpretations are made (preferably based on semantic cues such as pouches) and into giving the programmer the means to check on interpretations. Similarly the syntax of the language should not aim solely at slick context-free parsing by the compiler, but also at the messy context-sensitive methods which humans find much easier. Let me repeat that all this has the user's interest at heart, not the systems programmer's; it would be quite rational to decide it was too expensive. But it is *not* rational to continue designing languages and saying they are easy for humans when they clearly are not.

4.0 Programming as Problem-solving

The previous section ended with a discussion of how people go about writing 'programs' in natural English. There is little difference, except in the point of view, between these studies and more traditional studies of problem-solving. The generality of the findings, such as the difficulty of negation, is illustrated by work in related areas that has not sprung from a programming motivation, such as Wason's work on plausible denial (Wason & Johnson-Laird, 1972). In this section, therefore, we shall consider what can be learnt by concentrating on the problem and its solution.

4.1 The Mental Picture

One of the hardest questions in cognitive psychology is what we have in our heads when we think about problems. It is all too easy to slip into assumptions that our heads only hold propositions—"the cat is on the mat"—or, contrariwise, pictures—"(picture of cat on mat)". Put baldly both views are ludicrous, for although good work has been based on each as a simplifying model it is patent to anyone that each has some truth.

Attempts are being made to find more general models that are workable (Kieras, 1978a; Anderson, 1978); until these attempts meet some measure of success and acceptance we shall have to wave our hands around. Yet it can certainly be demonstrated that it matters a great deal what we think about when attacking problems. Choose a good mental representation and the chances of getting a solution are at once much better. One can persuade oneself by following the try-it-yourself books of de Bono (1969) and Wickelgren (1974) or by looking at laboratory evidence (e.g. Schwarz, 1971). It is just like choosing a good notation, except that the notation is in the head rather than on the page. Evidence of this in a programming milieu has been found by Mayer (1976b), who showed that children learnt programming better when given a simple concrete model of the computer than when given rules about the behaviour of a black box.

Despite its obvious importance, both theoretical and practical, this area has not received much help from applied cognitive psychology. Perhaps that is because our natural tendency to look for short, snappy answers is quite out of place here, as has been well demonstrated by Durding, Becker &

Gould (1977). Much of Gould's work has gone to show that hunting for a single 'best' way of doing something, such as debugging, is a waste of time. In the case of debugging, it seems that programmers can adapt their strategies so successfully to the tools at hand that their performance is very similar whether the debugging aids are powerful or primitive (Gould, 1975). Similarly, what Durding et al. showed was that there is no single 'best' data organisation. Comparing data that fell naturally into various predefined organizations, such as hierarchy, network, list, or table, they showed that US liberal arts college students had all these structures available for use and preferred to organize data in a manner consistent with its internal relationships. When they were required to organize the sets of words that were the data into inappropriate structures, they had considerable difficulty, spending longer on the task and failing to preserve the semantic relations.

Although large numbers of data structures have been devised and reported, the standard languages until very recently constrained users to fit everything into one or two rather simple structures, such as arrays, files, or strings. To this rule COBOL provided an honorable exception, since it allowed the user to create a tailor-made structure appropriate to the data, and other languages are now following. Yet even so, the structures that can be made are usually restricted to more or less ornate systems of cells containing values and cells containing pointers. This works very well for family trees, where value cells contain people's names and pointer cells show marriages and offspring, but it is still a long way from what people have in their heads. The visual element, in particular, is spectacularly absent, so that computations on pictures, graphs, or board games are made quite difficult. To discuss how it might be brought in would take us into that Utopian land I want to avoid, but we should at least observe that the present state of affairs is so bad that posterity will surely see it as the Stone Age of data representation.

4.2 Planning a Program

The most important advance that computer science has ever made, if it is really true, is the elimination of all mistakes. In his assertively-titled paper 'How to write correct programs and know it', Mills (1975) declares that "The new reality is that professional programmers, with professional care, can learn to consistently write programs which are error-free from their inception—programs of twenty, fifty, two hundred, five hundred lines, and up. . . . The professional programmer of tomorrow will remember, more or less vividly, every error in his career."

Mills offers us the 'top-down' method of programming. Once trained in the technique it seems that programming becomes a routine, automatic, almost de-skilled business. Training was certainly pretty casual in the good old days, which in most places are still with us: you were simply introduced one by one to each syntactic construction in the language. All the worked examples were small, so small that it was easy to see how to solve them, and you only had to turn the solution-in-the-head into a program. After a five-day course you went off and tackled real problems by the same method; start at the top and sort out the problems as they occured to you.

That old-fashioned and totally undisciplined method gave poor results. Looking after snags as they occur quickly turns the code into intractable spaghetti, the stuff mentioned in Section 2.1. For the same reason the load on working memory gets out of hand and the programmer makes many mistakes that could be called oversights. When a programmer has an oversight it is shrugged off, but an architect would probably be sued; one of the goals of the new 'software engineering' movement is to make programmers less irresponsible (see Hoare's prologue to Perrot, 1977). Finally, the failure to think about likely modifications in advance, or even to think through the basic design properly, makes the program overcommitted to the first way of doing things the programmer happens to think of. All too often, as Jackson (chapter 11) shows, programmers will find themselves trapped between the alternatives of completely rewriting the program or putting in frig after frig to prop up what was the wrong method to start with. I still blush to remember some of my own work, captured so well by Brown's cartoon (Figure 10).

Here, then, is Mills' recipe.

"The task of the programmer begins with a functional specification which describes what the program-to-be is to do. In the traditional process, the programmer somehow converts that specification into program statements and then verifies that the statements created in fact do what the program was intended to do. In structured programming there is a precise description of the results of this mental activity. It begins with the functional specification and repeatedly divides it, a step at a time, into new functional subspecifications, connected by program statements, until the program is complete. It does not consist of a large leap in faith and hope from a functional specification to a loose collection of program statements which are fitted piece-by-piece into a program. The structured programming process analyzes functional specifications rather than synthesizing program statements." (p.366)

The steps are simple. (a) Every functional specification can be regarded as a box mapping inputs into outputs. (b) Every such box can be realized using just the three components of Section 2: sequence, selection, and repetition; so the process proceeds by deciding how to expand one box into several boxes connected in one of those three ways. (c) "At each expansion step, the correctness of that step can be decided by answering a standard question that goes with that type of expansion"—e.g. for a repetition we ask whether it is guaranteed to terminate, etc.. (d) "When steps b and c are carried out to the point where no subspecifications remain, the result is a complete

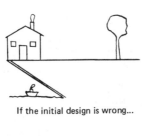

If the initial design is wrong...

...it can always be frigged...

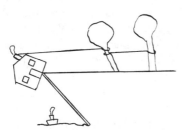

...though this may lead to further difficulties

Fig. 10. Design and fall. (From Brown, 1974.)

program and the proof of its correctness has been completed as well."

So much for top-down working. 'Stepwise refinement', introduced by Wirth (1971, 1974), is similar, except that Wirth brings in a notation for 'program invariants' to keep track of what the program's effect is. But Wirth does *not* make claims as strong as Mills. Not that Mills is alone: one can hear similar enthusiastic homilies about top down programming delivered in many computer centre coffee-rooms.

We are being offered by Mills a model of how problem-solving *could* work, and a recommendation that that is how it *should* work for best results; and if he is correct, it is a remarkable achievement. Yet one cannot help feeling sceptical. The work of the great mathematician Polya comes to mind. He points out that the formal mathematical proof may be what you end up with, but how you get there is something else entirely, and he describes a whole bag of tricks. The formal exposition, he says, is perfect for checking the argument in detail; but it "fairly often proceeds in an order exactly opposite to the natural order of invention" (Polya, 1971, p.70). Nor is Polya afraid of reasoning that is merely plausible, rather than checked scrupulously at each step; sometimes intuition will rush ahead of formal reasoning, sometimes the opposite.

I suggest that good programmers work the same way. They leap intuitively ahead, from stepping stone to stepping stone, following a vision of the final program; and then they solidify, check, and construct a proper path. That proper path from first move to last move, in the correct order, is the program, their equivalent of the formal proof.

Mills recipe contains a very important truth, that wherever possible a problem that is uncomfortably large to handle should be split into smaller subproblems *that do not interact.* This principle of divide and rule, or the 'separation of concerns' as Dijkstra (1976) calls it, is obviously valuable as a technique to keep complexity in check. But I question the wisdom of propounding it as the single vital principle that allows a program to be produced mechanically and errorlessly. Wirth (1974) is quite explicit; having described his stepwise refinement, he says "I should like to stress that we should not be led to infer that the actual program development proceeds in such a well organized, straightforward, top-down manner. Later refinement steps may show that earlier ones are inappropriate and must be reconsidered."

The top-down theory is equivalent to the simple form of a theory of problem-solving that has become known as GPS, for 'General Problem Solver', from the name of a program written to demonstrate it (Newell & Simon, 1963). GPS in its simplest form is not a very good model of how people solve problems; and indeed Newell and his followers have now moved on to much more sophisticated techniques making use of production systems that have a great deal of power. GPS does not, for example, allow for anything corresponding to the two levels of planning, local and remote, demonstrated in human problem-solving by Hayes (1965) and Greeno (1974). Remote-level planning could be identified with Polya's account of how plausible reckoning can rush ahead of formal proof, or my metaphor of leaping across stepping stones leaving gaps to be filled in later by local planning. Nor can GPS, nor any other strictly top-down model, deal with interdependent subgoals. When people plan menus for dinner parties they cope with many kinds of interdependency, for dishes must be chosen to complement each other and to contrast with previous meals, so that there is no possible way to achieve a complete 'separation of concerns'. How they do it is quite interesting (Byrne, 1977); they can put aside one subgoal temporarily before they get overcommitted to details that may have to be abandoned, they can choose to attack first the subgoal that will most closely restrict the other subgoals, and insert what Byrne calls 'need slots' into the mental program, reminders that certain choices will need special examination ("Are the vegetables in season? Does anyone refuse curry?") which ought to be carried out early in the planning process. People are evidently habitual and skilful problem-solvers by techniques considerably more powerful than simple top-down working.

Writers like Mills have got hold of the wrong end of the stick. Good programs are not necessarily written top-down, but they *look* as though they are. The technique is certainly a useful discipline, one that will help to stop the program getting too complex for the programmer, but it is no more a mechanical recipe for fine programming than using a good notation is. Denning (1976) sums up a most sensible paper by comparing books and programs: "The good writer uses identifiable, controlled patterns of prose, producing a book whose nested modularization is elegantly displayed in its table of contents. Yet the process of creating, of evolving, that structure can be characterised neither as a top-down process nor as any other well structured process; it is a matter of individual creativity." In short, neither psychologists nor programmers have a sure-fire recipe.

It is somewhat depressing to reach such a negative conclusion. Far from finding a way to eradicate every single programing error, we seem to have arrived at the opinion that no such way is possible at all. But surely it would have been a miracle if we could have reduced programming to a mechanical process? A good experienced programmer knows a large number of outline programs, some of them as small as finding the biggest number in an array and some of them as large as the last project. Similarities will be recognised between one process and another and will be exploited whenever possible, so that a new program will often be based on an existing one. He/she will notice when the work is getting harder than expected, will step back and reconsider the approach; will be able to find the core problem quickly, and use judgement to find a plausible solution. There is no escape from the need for good judgement, nor from the costs of misjudgement. If one has to choose how to represent reasonably complex data in some way that allows two or three quite different processes to obtain the information they need without inconvenience, all one can produce is a solution that looks plausible. One cannot *know* that the suggestion is adequate until the processes have been programmed—and if it becomes clear in doing so that the data representation is not adequate, the cost of reprogramming can be embarrassingly high.

4.3 Understanding a Program

The surest way to make programs easier to write is to make them easier to read. Everyone needs to check their working as they go along; there is a dual process, in which the mental specification is programmed and the program is then de-programmed to see if it re-creates the original specification. Making programs more understandable is the nub of the problem.

Unfortunately, we have not yet brought into being very good ways to find out how much people understand about a program, nor do we have very good metaphors to describe their understanding. Research must at present perforce be largely methodological, leaving something of a gap between the complexity of the questions we can answer and the complexity of the questions computer scientists would like answers for. I shall look at the former first.

If, as I argue above, a good programmer knows a large number of outline programs to refer to, then it will hardly be surprising if he/she goes about trying to understand a given program by attempting to make it fit with one of the outlines. Sooner or later, the programmer hopes to say "Oh, it's a program of *that* kind!" Naturally, sometimes the program is not one of a class that has been met before—perhaps this is the first program that has been seen for string manipulation—and then the programmer will have to work from first principles, which is much harder. Whether or not the type of program is recognised, the job will be made much easier if the notation is good, as discussed in Section 2. All this has been captured in the 'syntactic/semantic' model first proposed by Shneiderman and Mayer (1977).

"The syntactic/semantic model of programmer behaviour suggests that programming experience and education build two kinds of knowledge structures (see Figure 11). *Syntactic knowledge* is language dependent, acquired through meaningful learning and hierarchically organized from low level constructs such as the meaning of an assignment statement or an arithmetic expression, to intermediate program structures such as the sequence for clearing or sorting an array, to higher level problem domain issues such as the computation of a matrix inverse or a correlation coefficient."

Shneiderman cites studies of the comprehension of English sentences to show that methods involving recall and memorization can offer good demonstrations of internal recoding, the process by which people go from a verbatim memory of the sentences to a higher level representation of their gist, and he has worked on the development of a similar methodology for studying program comprehension. Results have been encouraging, suggesting both that the basic model is right and that memorization studies can be fruitful; for example, he found that programs that were easier to memorize were also easier to modify. But the memorization and recall of English sentences has turned out to be a highly complex affair, in which what people do depends very much on fine details of the situation (Fillenbaum, 1974; Aaronson, 1976), and we can probably expect similar complexities in the memorization of programs.

The main alternative at present is the direct attack: hand the subject a

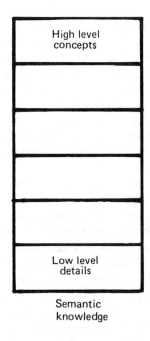
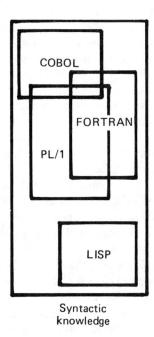

Fig. 11. Long-term memory structure in Shneiderman & Mayer's syntactic/semantic model (from Shneiderman, 1977).

program and ask questions. This too has its drawbacks. For one thing, the type of information that has to be extracted from the program is critical. Differences between notations can show up clearly when one type of information is tested and not when a different type is (Green, 1977b). For another thing, it is extremely difficult to devise questions that can be answered succinctly while giving any adequate test of comprehension at a deep level.

Hoc (1977) has reported on extremely detailed observations as novice programmers attempted to make a flowchart simulation of a slot machine for giving change. While a good deal of further work may be necessary before readily-interpretable results arrive, Hoc's work has already pointed up the need to keep some easily-forgotten precepts constantly in mind. One can comprehend the operation of a program most readily in terms of known outline programs, or 'Systemes de representation et de traitement' in Hoc's terminology. Novices, with an impoverished stock of these, will obviously find it hard to understand a program, but they will also find it hard to talk about it or to reason about it even when they do understand it—because these activities, also, depend on a vocabulary of known outlines and terms. Thus, there may be rather more comprehended by a novice than can be discovered using direct-attack methods like questioning. (And if a novice, why not all of us?) Another finding, perhaps more specific to novices, was the failure to generalise: the simulated slot machine would only work in rather particular circumstances. That suggests that a useful comprehension question would aim at finding out *exactly* what circumstances were required to make a program behave in a given way, but unfortunately that is just the sort of question that is hard to answer succinctly, which makes empirical work difficult.

At present none of these techniques has been used to make proper tests of existing ideas about comprehensible and incomprehensible programs. Here are some possibilities. First is the use of large-scale production systems for programs that may be required to "explain their reasoning", if the anthropomorphic phrase is acceptable. Fitter and Sime, in this volume (Chapter 2), have described the need for explanations when large systems are developed to help people make decisions, and they suggest that it may be easier for non-specialist users to obtain the information they want from a production system than from a conventional program. Are they right?

A second problem is the programming of parallel processes. Developments on various fronts make it seem very likely that we shall see the idea of computers doing several things at once creeping down into everyday programming, either in the form of genuinely simultaneous operations by several different micro-processors, or else as an apparently simultaneous operation by a single processor sharing its time out between different jobs. The associated software developments look very promising: for the multiple processor several forms of dataflow languages are being developed, and as mentioned in Section 3.3 there is some hope that by eliminating the explicit statement of the order in which operations are to be performed some of the problems of novice programmers may be eased. (In this respect dataflow languages have affinities with production systems.) For the single large processor there are languages like MODULA, a descendant of PASCAL, where there are ways to specify which parts of a job may go ahead independently. The different parts of a job need to communicate with each other from time to time, and special techniques have been developed to deal with the problems created when one process wants to take a piece of data just when another process wants to change it. Such techniques were intended in the first place to improve tractability; the degree to which they can also improve comprehensibility has not yet received much attention.

Communication between parts of an ordinary, conventional program is a third area to investigate. Programs are frequently broken up into subroutines, and one reason is to achieve an automatic 'separation of concerns': having written one subroutine for one task we can then write a second subroutine for a second task without fear of using the same name twice for different things, or of inadvertently altering something in one subroutine that the other is about to use. Hoare (1973) lays great stress on how subroutines should communicate with each other and with the main program, but current languages show great diversity, from the labyrinthine complexities that can be achieved in ALGOL 68 through PL/I to the comparative simplicity of PASCAL. The BASIC language, in fact, retains immense popularity without any provision for genuine subroutines at all, and I suspect that one reason is that novice programmers find subroutines hard to understand. An object referred to by one name in the main program can be passed to a subroutine by another name, and can then be passed to a sub-subroutine by another name again, and so on. To discover what objects a subroutine is handling, the trail has to be worked out backwards. Is this really necessary? (Notice the interesting parallel with the problems of the *goto* notation: after a series of jumps to labels, it is only possible to discover how the program reached a certain point by searching backwards through the text looking for jumps.)

Subroutines are also used as a way to condense the program. If the same sequence is to be performed more than once, it can be parcelled up as a subroutine and called wherever it is needed. This raises a further question, since even when we know how the data objects are being passed along the program from subroutine to subroutine, we still have to deal with a fragmented flow of control. Without subroutines, the simple perceptual code of textual propinquity can be used. If two lines are close together, they have a good chance of being performed close together in sequence. Loops and jumps break up the contiguity of sequence, but subroutines dislocate it still more. Although I know of no direct work on program texts, related studies suggest that dislocations of sequence cause difficulty. Green & Jackson (1976) defined a coefficient of 'harkback' based on the number of steps in a sequence before an earlier step was revisited, and Jackson (1977) showed that it was hard to reconstruct interviews with high harkback values (i.e. big jumps back to earlier points); Kieras (1978b) found similar results with the comprehension of paragraphs of English text. It seems quite likely, therefore, that it is hard to understand the trajectory of programs divided into many subroutines, and that improved notations might be desirable.

5.0 Conclusions

Here are five questions about the cognitive aspects of programming.

- How can we decide, as a quality control test, whether a given language in a given application has too many features?
- What makes context-free grammars hard or easy?
- When should context-sensitive grammars be used?
- What help could we get from semantic aids, e.g., units of measurement, in our programs?
- Programs are full of one-way pointers, e.g., *gotos*, passing data objects into subroutines, flow of control in nested subroutines. Does it matter?

There are no firm answers yet. What, then, is the future of the person whose program is nearly working? I think his/her problems could be made much easier if we had at least rough answers, and I think all those questions are roughly answerable; some of the issues lead off into unknown seas, but many just require better charting of waters already familiar.

The material represented has deliberately been selected rather narrowly. For example, there has been no mention of 'software physics', which attempts to develop equations relating the time to write a program to many other variables, often making extensive use of multiple regression techniques (Halstead, 1977); nor of attempts within artificial intelligence to develop a theory of program understanding (Waters, 1976; R. Brooks, 1977). I hope we shall hear more from both these schools, but I believe that in the near future they will only have indirect influence on making programming easier. Sensible questions and answers about the details of language design cannot emerge without thinking about what goes on in the programmer's head and reasoning carefully about it; multiple regression might tell us that programs take longer to write in language X, but it cannot tell us why—and hence, it cannot tell us how to improve language X. In contrast, a genuine AI theory of program understanding would tell us a great deal, of course, but what it told us would only be useful if it were the true theory, the one that described what people actually do: we have a long way to go before arriving at that point.

Nor have I made any attempt to describe alternatives to conventional languages, not even recent developments towards 'descriptive' languages. In these languages a program specifies the characteristics of the required answer, whereas in conventional language what is specified is the procedure for a constructing the answer. A program in a conventional, 'procedural' language produces answers that have the required characteristics because they have been constructed by means of a particular procedure. The argument in favour of descriptive languages is that it is much easier just to specify the required characteristics than to show that a given procedure will produce an answer that has those characteristics. Nevertheless, they seem unlikely to have a large impact in the near future, although I may be proved profoundly wrong by a recent paper of Backus (1978) arguing that many of their problems can be overcome in ways comprehensible to the average programmer, as well as to the specialist. Backus calls conventional languages "fat and flabby" and presents a carefully worked out alternative for an 'applicative' language that eliminates many of their hardest features. If it proves workable it will be a classic contribution. Yet even so the same psychological questions will arise: when unnecessary details are omitted, what remains can still be expressed comprehensibly or not. These developments should not, therefore, be viewed as likely to make the nearly-working program extinct.

Concentrating, therefore, on the more available parts of the head of the person with the nearly-working program, we have looked at the basic perception of program notations, at how the grammars of programming languages might be parsed, and at how the program might be written and comprehended; echoing, not entirely by coincidence, the tripartite division made by Bever (1970) in his work on language comprehension cited above. Needless to say, as we have gone from discussing shallower to deeper levels of thought the contributions present-day psychology can offer have become more sparse, and regrettably that situation will probably not change for many years. Nevertheless, there is plenty to be done right now, working with evidence already available or easily obtained, in the way of improving languages.

Discriminability is one key issue. Does this test here take part in a conditional or a loop? Easy to tell in a high-level language, hard in a flowchart or an assembly language. Is this loop event-driven or count-driven? Easy to tell in modern languages, hard to tell in some older ones. Under what conditions can this action occur? Easy to tell in decision tables, also easy with Sime et al.'s if-P, not-P, end-P notation, hard with conventional languages. Discriminability can be increased by introducing synonyms, so that the text is not full of repetitions: synonyms are unnecessary for objects like plus signs, but would be a great help with discontinuous constructions such as pairs of brackets, where each bracket's partner has to be discriminated from the heap of candidates and the use of square and round brackets as synonyms would make it that much easier. Discriminability can be increased by clear signalling to identify each syntactic construction distinctively. Under the influence of the modern high-speed parser, today's programming languages identify the beginnings of constructions very clearly, but the endings are another matter. Discriminability can also be increased by having fewer constructions to identify, but the evidence suggests—at least to my eye—that people can cope with as many constructions as desired, as long as they are well signalled; what people need to do is to determine each contruction's role in the behaviour of the program, which they may do better if there are many different constructions each identified with only a few possible roles, rather than one or two incredibly general-purpose constructions. Finally, at the semantic level the role of an identifier and the structure of an expression could be made more discriminable by putting explicit units of measurement into programs, or using the pouches illustrated in Figure 9.

A special aspect of discriminability is redundant recoding, where some important aspect of the message is presented twice by the text in different ways. Indenting programs is one way to redundantly recode information about where control statements start and stop; using two kinds of synonymous brackets would be another kind of redundant recoding; yet another kind would be to print each subroutine in a different colour or type-font and each line where that subroutine was called in the same colour or font. These are all instances of *perceptual* recoding, making them very easy to detect. Adding comments to programs is a way to give *symbolic* recoding; so is the if-P, not-P, end-P notation. Standard computer hardware makes it rather difficult to do much perceptual recoding, but even symbolic recoding is quite helpful; however, it is probably more helpful when it is forced by the language to be always present in a consistent form, unlike most people's haphazard use of comments. The point of recoding part of the information in a program is to make it easier to extract that information, and it ought to go without saying that if the information recoded is never wanted by the programmer there's no point whatsoever in wasting time or effort recoding it. So, before taking up my colourful subroutines or any similar idea, make sure that it would supply information that programmers do actually want and find it hard to get out of a program.

The other key issue is learning. Because there is less to be said it has been touched on rather lightly; what we have at present consists mainly of questions. How many features can we afford to have in a language? What kinds of grammar are hard and easy to learn? Where we can make guesses from studies on related areas, they tend to be disturbing: context-free grammars, the darlings of computer science, may have feet of clay; optional elements that can occur once, several times, or not at all may be awkward.

Superordinate to both discrimination and learning is understanding. This, I maintain, is what it's all about. The message is not new, it has been repeated again and again in the computing literature that programs should be understandable—but it has not been accompanied by much effort to work out what prevents understanding. In particular, computer science has been slow to recognise the importance of perceptual factors in understanding a program. The idea of perceptually recoding some aspect of a program may seem trivial; the recoded information can by definition be obtained from the program without having to mess around with perceptual codes, and it wouldn't take a skilled programmer long, so why bother? Whether we actually want to have *skilled* programmers is a question to return to. But even granting that we do, we still need perceptual recoding. When a train of thought is broken again and again by the need to find something out the hard way, it is difficult to piece thoughts together into inspirations; it is difficult enough even to finish a simple train of thought without making a mistake, simply because of having to get the information in some tedious and error-prone way.

When a language is being designed, I recommend that the questions of understanding be frequently returned to. When the design is completed, try a simple quality control test: give some people a description of the language, a few programs, and some questions to answer. See if they can answer quickly and accurately. If not, more sophisticated methods may reveal how to improve the trouble spots.

At this point, since computing science is collectively being urged to mend its ways, it is only fair to allow its collective voice to express an unease that I hear very often. What is the status of the evidence cited? Is it really good enough—collected from small experiments, usually in laboratory conditions, sometimes not even connected with programming—to be used in designing something like a computer language, since mistakes are so costly? My candid answer is that it's still pretty dubious. Single experiments are not good enough, they need to be supported by similar experiments using varied materials or techniques. But it's better than nothing, and rapidly improving. One point needs special mention, and that is the desire of active programmers to see results taken from studies on life-size programs; the literature contains few of these, because they are incredibly expensive. Imagine a sample of say 50 professional programmers for a fortnight each—who foots the bill for a total of two years' salary? But in any case I have never seen the point. If it is shown that people read one page faster if, say, the print is improved, what is to stop them reading the whole book faster?

Programs are not chunks of natural language. They have formal properties that admit of formal proofs. They are created artefacts that have to be shaped and reshaped till they fit their purpose, and then may be modified extensively to fit another purpose. We have reached some of our conclusions by looking at those aspects of programs that most closely resemble natural language, but there is more to a good programming language than that; it must be tractable. We must be able to find out how one part relates to another and what happens if we change it. Tractability is a formal property rather than a psychological one and so it has been treated lightly above; even so, the section on problem-solving ended with it. In between it has pervaded the field, reappearing tirelessly in new guises: hierarchical decomposition, separation of concerns, stepwise refinement, top-down programming, divide-and-rule, information hiding, and so on. Computer scientists have done well in improving the tractability of programming languages, and that is one component of making them understandable. The work of men like Hoare, Dijkstra and Wirth has revolutionised programming. A similar effort applied to other components might and should take us still farther. An interesting paper by Embley (1978) proposes a new construct and then subjects it to both empirical evaluation and formal analysis before reaching a final version; I hope that is a sign of things to come.

Finally, let me welcome the change of attitude visible throughout every computing circle in recent years, the change from a basic belief that programmmers ought to be more skilful to a basic belief that programming should be easier. At one time, if programmers couldn't manage we said they weren't gifted enough, and tried to develop selection tests; or else we said they weren't trained well enough, and yet another FORTRAN primer got written. The cost of selecting and training all those skilled programmers—and then retraining them, for another machine or a new language—is ludicrous. In other circles the incomprehensibility and remoteness of computing systems is injecting an unnecessary animosity towards computers into basically sensible debate about alternative technology. By making programming easier we shall cut down on training and retraining, and we shall make it more accessible to more people, easing the tensions caused by its past elitism. When algebra was so hard that it was the property of the intellectual elite you could be burned for knowing too much about it; today we teach it in school. Programming could be easier than algebra if we tried. Let's.

References

Aaronson, D. (1976). Performance theories for sentence coding: some qualitative observations. *Journal of Experimental Psychology: Human Perception and Performance, 2,* 42-55

Anderson, J.R. (1978). Arguments concerning representations for mental imagery. *Psychological Review,* **85,** 249-277.

Atkinson, L.V. (1978). Should if-then-else follow the dodo? To appear in *Software – Practice and Experience.*

Backus, J. (1978). Can programming be liberated from the von Neumann style? A functional style and its algebra of programs. *Communications of the Association for Computing Machinery,* **21,** 613-641.

Bever, T.G. (1970). The cognitive basis for linguistic structures. In *Cognition and the Development of Language* (Ed.) J. Hayes. Wiley,New York.

Blaubergs, M.S. & Braine, M.D.S. (1974). Short-term memory limitations on decoding self-embedded sentences. *Journal of Experimental Psychology,* **102,** 745-748.

Brooks, F.P. Jnr. (1977). The computer 'scientist' as toolsmith—studies in interactive computer graphics. In *Information Processing 77* (Ed.) P. Gilchrist. North Holland.

Brooks, R. (1977). Towards a theory of the cognitive processes in computer programming. *International Journal of Man-Machine Studies,* **9,** 737-751.

Brown, P.J. (1974). Programming and documenting software projects. *Computing Surveys,* **6,** 213-220. © 1974, ACM, Inc., with permission.

Burnett-Hall, D.G. (1978). *Explicit terminators for language constructs.* Unpublished MS, Department of Computer Science, University of York, UK.

Byrne, R. (1977). Planning meals: problem-solving on a real data-base. *Cognition*, **5**, 287-232.

Cairns, H.S. & Cairns, C.E. (1976). *Psycholinguistics: a cognitive view of language.* New York, Holt, Rinehart & Winston.

Clark, H.H. (1976). *Semantics and comprehension.* The Hague, Mouton.

Cleaveland, J.C. (1975). Meaning and syntactic redundancy. In *New Directions in Algorithmic Languages* (Ed.) S. Schuman. Rocquencourt, France, Institut de Recherche d'Informatique et d'Automatique.

Crossman, E.R.F.W. (1955). The measurement of discriminability. *Quarterly Journal of Experimental Psychology*, **7**, 176-195.

De Bono, E. (1969). *The Mechanism of Mind.* Jonathan Cape, London.

Denning, P.J. (1976). A hard look at structural programming. In *Structured Programming.* Infotech International, Maidenhead.

Dijkstra, E.W. (1976). *A Discipline of Programming.* Prentice-Hall, Englewood Cliffs, N.J..

Durding, B.M., Becker, C.A. & Goulds, J.D. (1977). Data organization. *Human Factors*, **19**, 1-14.

Embley, D.W. (1978). Empirical and formal language design applied to a unified control construct for interactive computing. *International Journal of Man-Machine Studies*, **10**, 197-216.

Fillenbaum, S. (1974). Syntactic factors in memory. In *Current Trends in Linguistics* (Ed.) T.A. Sebeok. Mouton, The Hague.

Fitter, M.J. & Green, T.R.G. (1978). *When do diagrams make good computer languages?* Memo No: 210, MRC Social & Applied Psychology Unit, University of Sheffield. (In press, Intl. Journal Man-Machine Studies.)

Floyd, R.W. (1967). Assigning meanings to programs. *Mathematical Aspects of Computer Science*, **19**, 19-32.

Fodor, J.A., Bever, T.G. & Garrett, M.F. (1974). *The Psychology of Language.* McGraw-Hill, New York.

Gannon, J.D. (1977). An experimental evaluation of data type conventions. *Communications of the Association for Computing Machinery*, **20**, 584-595.

Goldberg, P.C. (1976). Structured programming for non-programmers. In *Structured Programming.* Infotech International, Maidenhead.

Gould, J.D. (1975). Some psychological evidence on how people debug computer programs. *International Journal of Man-Machine Studies*, **7**, 151-182.

Gould, J.D., Lewis, C. & Becker, C.A. (1976). *Writing and instructions.* Memo No: RC 5943, IBM Thomas J. Watson Research Center, New York.

Green, T.R.G. (1977a). *The necessity of syntax markers: two experiments with artificial languages.* Memo No: 145, MRC Social & Applied Psychology Unit, University of Sheffield. To appear in *Journal of Verbal Learning and Verbal Behavior.*

Green, T.R.G. (1977b). Conditional program statements and their comprehensibility to professional programmers. *Journal of Occupational Psychology*, **50**, 93-109.

Green T.R.G. & Jackson, P.R. (1976). 'Hark-back': a simple measure of search patterns. *British Journal of Mathematical and Statistical Psychology*, **29**, 103-113.

Green, T.R.G. & Simpson, A.J. (1979). The relative difficulty of relative clauses. (In preparation).

Green, T.R.G. & Manton, J. (1978). *What does problem representation affect: chunk size, memory load, or mental process?* Memo No. 243, MRC Social and Applied Psychology Unit, Sheffield University, UK.

318   T.R.G. Green

Greeno, J.G. (1974). Hobbits and orcs: acquisition of a sequential concept. *Cognitive Psychology*, **6**, 270-292.
Halstead, M.H. (1977). *Elements of software science.* Elsevier Computer Science Library, New York.
Hayes, J.R. (1965). Problem topology and the solution process. *Journal of Verbal Learning and Verbal Behavior*, **4**, 371-379.
Hendrix, G.G., Sacerdoti, E.D., Sagalowicz, D. & Slocum, J. (1977). *Developing a natural language interface to complex data.* Technical Note 152, Stanford Research Institute Artificial Intelligence Center.
Hill, I.D. (1972). Wouldn't it be nice if we could write programs in ordinary English —or would it? *Computer Bulletin*, **16**, 306-312.
Hoare, C.A.R. (1969). An axiomatic basis for computer programming. *Communications of the Association for Computing Machinery*, **12**, 576-583
Hoare, C.A.R. (1973). *Hints for programming language design.* Computer Science Report STAN-CS-73-403, Stanford University. Invited address at 1973 SIGACT/sigplan Symposium on Principles of Programming Languages. ACM, New York.
Hoare, C.A.R. (1975). Data reliability. In *Proceedings of the ACM/IEEE Conference on Reliable Software*, Los Angeles, 1975. ACM, New York.
Hobbs, J.R. (1977). What the nature of natural language tells us about how to make natural-language-like programming language more natural. Association for Computing Machinery, *Proceedings of symposium on artificial intelligence and programming languages*, SIGPLAN **12** (8). 1977/SIGART No. 64.
Hoc, J.M. (1977). Role of mental representations in learning a programming language. *International Journal of Man-Machine Studies*, **9**, 87-105.
Jackson, M.A. (1975). *Principles of Program Design.* Academic Press, London.
Jackson, P.R. (1977). *Reconstructing interviews as a function of hark-back.* Memo 235, MRC Social & Applied Psychology Unit, University of Sheffield.
Johnson-Laird, P.N. (1977). Psycholinguistics without linguistics. In *Tutorial Essays in Psychology, Vol I* (Ed.) N.S. Sutherland, Lawrence Erlbaum Associates, Hillsdale, N. J..
Karr, M. & Loveman, D.B. III (1978). Incorporation of units into programming languages. *Communications of the Association for Computing Machinery*, **21**, 385-391.
Kernighan, B.W. & Plauger, P.J. (1974a). *The Elements of Programming Style.* McGraw-Hill, New York.
Kernighan, B.W. & Plauger, P.J. (1974b). Programming style: examples and counterexamples. *Computing Surveys*, **6**, 303-319.
Kieras, D.E. (1978a). Beyond pictures and words: alternative information-processing models for imagery effects in verbal memory. *Psychological Bulletin*, **85**, 532-554.
Kieras, D.E. (1978b). Good and bad structure in simple paragraphs: effects on apparent theme, reading time, and recall. *Journal of Verbal Learning and Verbal Behavior*, **17**, 13-28.
Mayer, R.E. (1976a). Comprehension as affected by structure of problem representation. *Memory & Cognition*, **4**, 249-255.
Mayer, R.E. (1976b). Some conditions of meaningful learning for computer programming: advance organizers and subject control of frame order. *Journal of Educational Psychology*, **68**, 143-150
Midonick, H. (1968). *The Treasury of Mathematics.* Harmondsworth, Penguin Books. (Two Vols.)

Miller, G.A. & Isard, S. (1964). Free recall of self-embedded English sentences. *Information & Control*, 1, 370-398.

Miller, G.A. & Johnson-Laird, P.N. (1976). *Language and Perception.* Cambridge University Press.

Miller, L.A. (1974). Programming by non-programmers. *International Journal of Man-Machine Studies*, 6, 237-260.

Miller, L.A. & Becker, C.A. (1974). *Programming in natural English.* Memo No. RC 5137, IBM Thomas J. Watson Research Center, New York.

Mills, H.D. (1975). How to write correct programs and know it. *Proceedings of the International Conference on Reliable Software*, IEEE and Association for Computing Machinery, Los Angeles. ACM, New York.

Newell, A. & Simon, H.A. (1963). GPS, a program that simulates human thought.In *Computers & Thought* (Eds.) E.A. Feigenbaum & J. Feldman. McGraw-Hill, New York.

Perrot, R.H. (1977). *Software Engineering.* Academic Press, London.

Plum, T. W-S. (1977). Fooling the user of a programming language. *Software— Practice and Experience*, 7, 215-221.

Polya, G. (1971). *How to Solve It.* Princeton University Press.

Reisner, P. (1977). Use of psychological experimentation as an aid to development of a query language. *IEEE Transactions on Software Engineering SE-3*, 218-229.

Restle, F. (1970). Theory of serial pattern learning: structural trees. *Psychological Review*, 77, 481-495.

Richards, M. (1976). Programming structure, style, and efficiency. In *Structured Programming.* Infotech, Maidenhead.

Schwartz, S.H. (1971). Modes of representation and problem representation: well evolved is half solved. *Journal of Experimental Psychology*, 91, 347-350.

Shipstone, E.I. (1960). Some variables affecting pattern conception. *Psychological Monographs*, 74, 17.

Shneiderman, B. (1977). Measuring computer program quality and comprehension. *International Journal of Man-Machine Studies*, 9, 465-478

Shneiderman, B. & Mayer, R.E. (1977). *Syntactic/semantic interaction in programmer behavior: a model and experimental results.* Unpublished MS, Department of Information Systems Management, University of Maryland, USA.

Sime, M.E., Arblaster, A.T. & Green, T.R.G. (1977). Structuring the programmer's task. *Journal of Occupational Psychology*, 50, 205-216.

Sloboda, J.A. (1977). Phrase units as determinants of visual processing in music reading. *British Journal of Psychology*, 68, 117-124.

Thomas, J.C. (1976). *Quantifiers and question-asking.* Memo No RC 5866, IBM Thomas J. Watson Research Center, New York.

Wason, P.C. & Johnson-Laird, P.M. (1972). *Psychology of Reasoning.* Batsford, London.

Waters, R.C. (1976). *A system for understanding mathematical Fortran programs.* AI Memo 368, MIT Artificial Intelligence Laboratory, Cambridge, Mass., USA.

Weinberg, G.M., Gellar, D.P. & Plum, T. W-S (1975). IF-THEN-ELSE considered harmful. Association for Computing Machinery, *SIGPLAN NOTICES*, 10 8, 34-44.

Wickelgren, W.A. (1974). *How to Solve Problems.* Freeman, San Francisco.

Wilks, Y. Parsing English, I and II. In *Computational Semantics* (Eds.) E. Charniak & Y. Wilks. North-Holland.

Wirth, N. (1971). Program development by stepwise refinement. *Communications of the Association for Computing Machinery*, 14, 221-227.

Wirth, N. (1974). On the composition of well-structured programs. *Computing Surveys*, **6**, 247-259.

Wright, P. (1978). Feeding the information eaters. *Instructional Science*. (In press).

Chapter 11

THE DESIGN AND USE OF CONVENTIONAL PROGRAMMING LANGUAGES

Michael Jackson

Contents

1.0 Introduction

Jean Sammet's Roster of Programming Languages for 1974-75 (Sammet 1976) includes 167 different programming languages which were in use in the United States at the end of 1975: a full list, including languages used chiefly outside the United States and languages which had fallen into disuse by the end of 1975, would perhaps have run to 500 languages. There are languages for special purposes: APT is for programming numerical control of machine tools; SIMSCRIPT is for discrete simulation; COGO is for civil engineering; CONNIVER is for artificial intelligence studies; COBOL is for administrative and business data processing. There are languages intended for general-purpose use: ALGOL 60, ALGOL 68, PASCAL, PL/I and SIMULA 67 are perhaps the best known of these.

The proliferation of programming languages has been an important factor in the spiralling costs of programming: just as most people speak only one natural language, so most programmers have learnt to use only one programming language; as a result, similar or even identical problems have been programmed many times in many places by many programmers. Even where two programmers use what is nominally the same language—say, FORTRAN—they are likely to use slightly different dialects of the language; the differences are often enough to prevent one programmer from using a program written by the other.

From time to time, efforts are made to devise a language which can be standardised and applied to a wide variety of problems in its standard form. PL/I is such a language: in its original conception it was to combine the best features of COBOL and FORTRAN, and would thus be well suited to both numerical scientific computation and business data processing; it was also to draw on the widely acknowledged elegance and power of ALGOL 60. PL/I was conceived in the early 1960s; in 1979, at the time of writing, the United States Department of Defense has placed contracts for the development of a new programming language (the "Ironman" project) appropriate for a wide range of applications in which the computer is an integral part of a complete military system.

Such efforts have not, in the past, met with any notable success. Opinions vary widely on the merits of PL/I; in spite of the high hopes at its conception, and the continued energetic support of IBM, few people today would regard PL/I as a definitive answer, even in the broadest terms, to the question of what a good general-purpose programming language should be. Informed opinion on the Ironman project is no more optimistic.

Numerical scientific computation and business data processing account for a very large proportion of all the programming work done in the past and being done today. Most of that programming is done in FORTRAN or COBOL, languages which are about 25 and 20 years old respectively. At least two reasons may be discerned for this apparent conservatism. First, and this is especially true of COBOL programs, a program is a capital asset; it is expensive to build, and the cost of building must be recouped over an extended period of years. An organisation which owns a million COBOL statements—say, 1000 programs of an average size of 1000 statements—can no more think of abandoning that investment than a nation can think of abandoning its road network or its telephone system. The resources required to replace it are simply not available, and even if they were, the cost replacement could hardly be justified. Second, it is becoming more widely recognised that a change of programming language can bring only very limited benefits. The defects which have been identified in existing programs and systems of programs will not be cured by rewriting them in a new language: they are defects of underlying structure attributable to the way the languages have been used rather than to the characteristics of the languages themselves.

In this chapter I would like to suggest that programming languages of the kind which are in wide general use today—and especially COBOL, FOR-TRAN and PL/I—suffer from a fundamental difficulty; they are trying to do two incompatible things at once. They are trying to allow the programmer to express what he wants the machine to do, and, at the same time, what order he thinks the machine should do it in. I am suggesting that both of these are necessary, but they cannot coexist in one language in the way they have done in the past. We need to separate the two concerns, forming two language classes, which we may call the Programming Languages and the Execution Languages. Only if this is done will we be able to rise above the difficulties which have been apparent, but apparently insoluble, for the past fifteen years.

2.0 Beginnings

Early computer programmers conceived of their task as one of directing the operation of the machine; indeed, in the incunabula of computer literature (for example, Mauchly (1947) and Alt (1948)) we usually find the programmer referred to as 'the operator'. Given a problem, and some prior mathematical analysis, the programmer's task was to devise a sequence of machine operations which would solve that problem, encode the sequence of operations onto a tape, and present the tape as input to the machine. The program thus encoded was, in essence, the expression of the operator's instructions to the machine: instead of pressing buttons, setting dials or pulling levers, the programmer wrote 'commands', 'instructions' or 'orders', which the machine then 'obeyed'.

Since the programmer was concerned to direct the operation of the machine, step by step, he/she was required to understand and to take account of the detailed manner in which the machine worked. The exact representation of data, the use of the various machine registers, the absolute location of the program in core storage, the placing of subsequences of instructions on a drum to minimise rotational delays during execution, ordering instructions to take advantage of any available parallelism in the machine—all these were the programmer's responsibility.

Later, symbolic assemblers and simple autocodes relieved the programmer of some of the more irritating clerical parts of the task; commands could be issued to the machine in a more palatable form than the machine's own order code, but they were essentially the same commands and the programmer had essentially the same control over, and responsibility for, the action of the machine.

The development of 'high-level programming languages' such as FOR-

TRAN and COBOL and their predecessors, was largely motivated by a recognition that the hardware machine, even when approached through the medium of a symbolic assembler, was not really suitable for solving either mathematical or data processing problems. The new languages transformed the machine, as it appeared to the programmer, into one with a more directly useful set of data types and operations. The hardware machine, with its highly specialised registers, accumulators and stores, and a wide repertoire of similarly specialised operations, was to be replaced by a software machine offering a smaller but more general repertoire better suited to the problems to be programmed. Programs in these high-level languages, while their texts might contain no fewer characters than the machine-language programs they replaced, consisted of fewer distinct statements and commands, more directly identifiable with steps in solving the problems as originally posed to the programmer. At the same time, structural mechanisms were formalised as declarations and calls of procedures, subroutines and functions, encouraging the programmer to abstract and generalise; it was hoped that large libraries of general-purpose procedures could be developed and used to good effect.

Of course, the underlying concept was still that of a machine to be instructed by the programmer. To be sure, the FORTRAN machine and the COBOL machine were more accessible and less esoteric than the 7090 and the 1401, but they were still definitely machines, and it was still the programmer's role to instruct them, to guide them step by step through the desired computation. The compilers were essentially translators, producing machine-code programs which followed very closely the pattern of the COBOL or FORTRAN program text. The declaration of an *INTEGER* in FORTRAN or a *PICTURE S9(8) COMPUTATIONAL* in COBOL produced something specific and predictable in the machine-code program, just as the declaration of a binary full word had done in the symbolic assembly language; each executable statement in the FORTRAN or COBOL text produced manifestly equivalent machine instructions in the corresponding place in the machine-code program.

2.1 Difficulties

In the early and middle 1960's, with the increasing availability of larger core stores and a consequent growth in the size of programs, a number of difficulties became apparent which were more fundamental than the unsuitability of the hardware data formats and instruction sets.

The foremost difficulty was complexity. The potential complexity of a program with an arbitrary control structure increases geometrically with the size of the program text; inevitably, most programmers found that they could not ensure the correctness of a program of 500 executable statements in which branching was permitted without constraint. Some programmers developed informal intuitive methods which allowed them, as individuals, to work effectively; some exercised capacious and surprisingly accurate memories in a triumph of brainpower over lack of method; others comforted themselves with the reflection that the inevitability of error was a delightful and impressive evidence of the sophisticated nature of their vocation.

The difficulties of complexity were exacerbated by the demands of program maintenance. The typical program was no longer an isolated object, to be run from time to time in response to ad hoc demands; it was a part of a system, to be run regularly in careful co-ordination with other programs of the system. The system itself was expected to have a lifetime of several years, and during that life-time its programs were subject to a succession of modifications as the system's specifications changed. A large data processing system, of 100,000 statements or more, is effectively a giant program running continuously for several years; not surprisingly, changing one of the constituent programs of such a system is difficult and error-prone. As more such systems came into existence, the ratio of program maintenance to original programming work rose steadily; today the ratio in data processing is commonly quoted as 2:1, 3:1 or even 4:1. The cost of program maintenance is determined largely by the quality of the original work done in the design and programming of the system, but in ways that are not well understood.

The difficulties of complexity and of program maintenance may be attributed, at least in part, to the unusual nature of programming languages as a construction medium. Programs are essentially homogeneous: the basic stuff of which they are built is provided by a relatively small set of elementary statements in the programming language, and this same stuff is used everywhere in the program to the exclusion of all else. Thus, a constraint which promotes modularity in physical artefacts such as motor cars and aeroplanes is absent. The programmer, unlike the mechanical engineer, is free to weld any part of a program to any other part, or, indeed, to mix up the parts in any desired way. It need not be considered that this part is made from steel, that from glass and a third from plastic—all can be merged and partitioned without constraint. Nor does the stuff of programs provide any constraint, such as the strength of physical materials or a required power-weight ratio. Any program, however poorly conceived, can be made to work by ad hoc expedients and patches. Since the structural form of the program is largely invisible to its buyers and users it is horribly easy—and tempting—to allow the quality of the design to sink to a standard which would not pass muster for a moment in a motor car or a bridge.

The ideas of modular programming emerged in response to these difficulties. The function of a program was to be decomposed into subfunctions, which in turn could be further decomposed, and so on for as many levels as necessary. For example, the function 'Compute Pay' could be decomposed into 'Compute Gross' and 'Compute Net'; 'Compute Gross' into 'Compute Basic Pay' and 'Compute Overtime Pay'; 'Compute Net' into 'Compute Deductions' and 'Subtract Deductions from Gross'; 'Compute Deductions' into 'Compute Tax' and 'Compute Other Deductions'; and so on. Each subfunction could then be programmed as a closed subroutine, preferably separately compiled, and the resulting program would be a hierarchical structure of these subroutines. By limiting the size of the individual module or subroutine complexity would be brought under control; by ensuring that each subfunction was programmed in a separate module maintenance would be localised; by recognising, at the design stage, generally useful subfunctions, a library of modules would be created which could reduce the amount of new work required for each successive program.

These high hopes were not realised except to a very limited extent. It became clear that the task of the designer, the decomposition into subfunctions, was crucial to the success of the program: if it was done poorly, the mechanics of modularisation would actually make the program worse rather than better, separating what should have been together and incurring large overhead costs in the space and time needed for the program's execution.

The chief residual effects of modular programming were a widespread acknowledgement of the importance of program design as a subject in itself, and an almost universal conviction that the subroutine call was the primary, or even the only, structural device. There was some debate about the value of separate compilation, and some COBOL compilers were slow to acquire *CALL* and *ENTRY* statements; but it was clear that the subroutine call was the natural and obvious means of connection between a function and its subfunctions.

This emphasis on the subroutine call, like functional decomposition itself, was also an organic development of the earliest view of the programmer's task. The program was a sequence of instructions to the machine; if a particular instruction, such as 'divide', was not in the machine's repertoire, it could be readily simulated by a subroutine call. In the same way, more elaborate instructions, such as 'calculate gross pay', or 'update master record from transaction record', could be simulated too. The programmer would still instruct the machine exactly: but he/she was not able to provide themselves with a variety of machines at various levels of the subroutine hierarchy, each machine having a carefully crafted instruction repertoire of their own devising.

2.2 The GO-TO Controversy

The next substantial contribution to the conceptual basis of conventional programming was provided by the seminal work of Dijkstra (1968; 1970;

1972) on Structured Programming. However, before continuing with that theme, a major digression is necessary. Structured Programming contains two main strands: one is the adoption of an explicit design concept, stepwise refinement; the other, which gave rise to the celebrated *GO-TO* controversy and thus makes our digression necessary, is the strong recommendation of a sequencing discipline to limit patterns of control flow.

A programmer who makes free use of *GO-TO* statements, permitting a jump from any point to any other point in a program, is in serious danger of constructing programs whose action he/she cannot predict. Such a free use of *GO-TO* statements was a usual ingredient of programming technique, and a major contributor to the complexity and obscurity of the resulting programs. Dijkstra (1968) recommended that control flow patterns should be limited to the three, now classical, constructs of 'concatenation', 'repetition' and 'selection'; in this way the dynamic behaviour of a program (that is, the computations it can evoke) is simply and readily deducible from the static text. These points are illustrated by Figures 1 & 3 of Green's chapter in this volume. It had been shown by Bohm and Jacopini (1966) that any proper flowchart (that is, a flowchart with one entry and one exit and all connected) could be decomposed into a hierarchy of these constructs, although in general the decomposition would require duplication of some parts of the flowchart and the introduction of some new Boolean variables: the limitation on control flow patterns recommended by Dijkstra was not therefore a limitation on the programs that could be written.

Unfortunately, a catchy and easily remembered headline "*GO-TO* Statement Considered Harmful" was added to Dijkstra's letter to the Communications of the ACM (1968). As his ideas spread, they became diluted and oversimplified; it seemed attractive to encapsulate the whole matter in a single-minded ban on the *GO-TO* statement, presenting a complex intellectual issue as a readily understood slogan. Control flow is a complex issue for at least two reasons. First, because it is possible to conceal sequencing by implementing it in program variables instead of in the explicitly sequenced executable text: at the limit, any program can be expressed by the interpretive scheme:

```
begin instructioncounter := 1;
    do while instruction (instructioncounter) ≠ 'halt'
        execute instruction (instructioncounter);
        set next value of instructioncounter;
    od
    halt;
end
```

The true control flow of a program is not therefore always evident. Second, because it is not clear that concatenation, repetition and selection are an entirely adequate set of constructs: several writers, including Zahn (1974) and Jackson (1975), have proposed further constructs.

To identify Structured Programming with the avoidance of the GO-TO statement is simplistic, and traduces the depth and importance of the ideas involved. But such an identification has been widely made, and has had an eccentric effect on the comparative evaluation of programming languages. Attention has been concentrated on a minor issue of superficial syntax, on whether a particular language allows repetition and selection to be expressed without resorting to the condemned GO-TO, and has thus been drawn away from more significant questions. The point is well illustrated by the widely held opinion that FORTRAN is a very bad language for Structured Programming, while ALGOL 60 is very good for the same purpose. FORTRAN provides anomalous and idiosyncratic constructs for repetition and selection; so anomalous are they that it is generally held, with considerable justification, that the only practicable way of writing 'structured programs' in FORTRAN is to simulate the repetition and selection constructs by the use of GO-TO statements and labels. ALGOL 60, on the other hand, provides something more appropriate. Ergo, ALGOL 60 is good, and FORTRAN is bad. But neither of these languages provides for any kind of non-elementary data construct than the homogeneous array, all of whose elements are of the same type. This is a much more serious defect, which both languages exhibit: whereas the lack of repetition and selection in logic flow can be readily overcome by simulation of the constructs with GO-TO statements and labels, the lack of data structures cannot be overcome at all easily. FORTRAN programmers are well accustomed to the unpleasant dilemma between passing a large number of parameters to a subroutine, each referring to a single variable or array, and placing the variables in COMMON storage, thus bypassing the parameterisation mechanism with a consequent vulnerability to many types of error. The better solution would be to form the variables into one or more data structures, of the kind provided in COBOL and PL/I, and also in later ALGOL-derived languages such as PASCAL, and to pass references to those data structures as parameters to the subroutine. But neither FORTRAN nor ALGOL 60 provide such data structures.

In a similar vein, and for similar reasons, PL/I is judged better than COBOL. Proponents of COBOL and FORTRAN rush to equip their favoured languages with 'structured programming facilities' which will allow textual nesting of reasonably sanitary repetition and selection constructs. It is interesting to observe that the new facilities are often to be provided by precompilers and preprocessors which detect the new constructs and translate them into the standard language which the standard compiler can handle. Such precompilers and preprocessors are relatively simple and cheap to build, allowing experiments in programming languages to be made without incurring the cost of a full compiler and a full language definition. In programming language design, the age of optimism has passed away.

2.3 Levels of Abstraction

The other strand of Structured Programming is an explicit concept of program design: design by stepwise refinement. (The same notion, in a slightly coarsened form, is often known as 'top-down design'.) Using stepwise refinement, the programmer starts with a very simple statement of the algorithm in terms of very high-level actions and data objects; at each step the actions and data objects are refined until eventually they are expressed in terms of actions and data objects which are available in the repertoire of the programming language being used. The progress from step to step may be considered to be a progress from the more abstract to the more concrete, from the programming of an idealised conceptual machine to the programming of the machine which is actually available. In this way, the programmer is encouraged to see a relation between an abstract conception of the problem at the first step, and the concrete implementation of its solution at the last: the purpose of the later steps is to give effect to the earlier. The point is well expressed in a remark by Dijkstra in a recent book (1976):

"It used to be the program's purpose to instruct our computers; it became the computer's purpose to execute our programs."

In the first steps of stepwise refinement, the programmer was to become free of the task of instructing the computer; only in the last step need that responsibility be considered directly.

The change of viewpoint implied is of fundamental significance; but the new freedom for the programmer, the freedom from the responsibility to direct the step-by-step operation of the machine, is more apparent than real. The programmer is free to postpone questions of representation, both of data objects and of operations on those data objects; but is not free to avoid them altogether, since in the final step of stepwise refinement he/she must choose representations in the programming language being used. More important, the programmer is not freed at all from the need to decide the exact sequencing of the machine operations. Even in the very first step he/she commits themself to the exact sequencing of the high-level or abstract operations. For example, in solving the problem of printing the prime numbers less than 1000, the programmer must choose whether the first step is to be

> *begin* create table of primes;
>   print table of primes
> *end*

or

> *for* n := 1 *step* 1 *until* 1000
>   *if* n is prime *then* print n
>   *fi*

or

> *begin* n := 2;
>   *while* n < 1000
>   *do* print n; generate next prime n
>   *od*

or some other possible sequence. Evidently, this choice at the first step predetermines the sequencing of the final program to a large extent; further, it affects the representation of the primes themselves; the table of primes used in the first choice could be conveniently represented by a string of 1000 bits, but such a representation would hardly come naturally to a programmer who had chosen the second or third possibility.

3.0 Freedom from the Machine

Freeing the programmer from the tyranny of the machine had been a recognised objective from the earliest days of symbolic assemblers. The machine dealt in absolute storage addresses, but the users of a symbolic assember were free to deal in names of their own choosing for both data and instructions. The user of a language like COBOL or FORTRAN was invited to think in terms of data types judged suitable to the problem, and appropriate operations on objects of those types. The generated machine instructions were not, in principle, of concern, although he/she could, and often would, make it their business to know what they were: the action of the compiler in generating the object machine program was entirely predictable.

More significantly, the programmer was invited to give up control of certain aspects of the generated object program which then became effectively unpredictable. In machines which used program-addressable registers for arithmetic or for addressing core storage, the allocation and use of the registers was left to the compiler, and the programmer could do nothing to affect it. In IBM Virtual Storage systems the pagination of the program was outside the programmer's control.

The justification for removing these matters from the scope of the programmer's consideration was, of course, that this thereby enabled attention to be concentrated on the problem rather than on the details of the machine's execution of the program. The programmer was using a 'problem-oriented' language rather than a 'machine-oriented' language. Correct and clear solution of the problem was more important than extreme efficiency in the use of the machine.

Many programmers, with varying degrees of justification, fought against this trend. Unwilling to abandon control over the machine, they resorted to a number of expedients. One expedient was to discover the rules by which the compiler generates machine instructions from statements of the programming language, and then to choose programming language statements with a view to efficiency of the generated machine instructions.

For example, a compiler might generate a call to an exponentiation subroutine when it encounters a statement such as

    x := y ** z ;

aware of this, and of the relative inefficiency of such a call, a programmer wanting to write

    x := y ** 2

might instead choose to write

    x := y * y

which would generate a simple multiplication instruction instead of the subroutine call. In the same vein he/she might write

    x := y + y

in place of

    x := 2 * y

in order to generate an addition instead of a multiplication instruction. Obviously, such an expedient depends heavily on an accurate knowledge of the code generation part of the compiler, including any optimisation; it is easy to imagine perfectly sensible compilers for which the preferred statements shown above would give rise to less efficient, rather than more efficient, machine code.

On a grander scale, we see the same technique advocated for efficient use of IBM Virtual Storage systems. A virtual storage system is intended to permit the programmer to write programs whose instructions and internal variables occupy more main storage than is physically availble in the machine; the virtual storage system allows some of the instructions and internal variables to be held in secondary storage, such as disk or drum, and to be brought into main storage when they are required. It is intended that this swapping of 'pages' between main and secondary storage should be invisible to the programmer, and that he/she should be able to program as if the machine's main storage were as large as desired. Obviously, a program which requires many pages to be swapped during execution will be less efficient than one which requires fewer; the programmer is therefore tempted to discover how the compiler allocates storage in a machine code program and how the paging system operates, so that advantage can be taken of this knowledge in planning the program. Rogers (1975) suggests such guidelines as:

- Separate unused code and data space from code that is frequently used.
- Seek algorithms or techniques that use small data areas.
- Store data as closely as possible to other data that are to be used at the same time.
- Data should be referenced in the order in which they are stored, if possible, especially for large data aggregates occupying several pages.
- If possible, separate read-only data from areas that are to be changed.
- Avoid implied FORTRAN *DO* loops in I/O statements because they cause repeated return to the calling program.

Some of these guidelines require the programmer to make a particular choice between apparently equivalent alternatives in the programming language; some (such as the second and fourth) will affect his program substantially. Essentially, the programmer is invited to circumvent the efforts of the language designer and of the virtual storage system designer to relieve him of the need to consider storage allocation at the machine level.

Even more determined unwillingness to lose control over the machine is shown by anotherr widely used expedient. In IBM S/370 COBOL, the machine format of a *COMPUTATIONAL—3* item is packed decimal, in which two decimal digits are encoded in each byte, except for the rightmost byte which contains the least significant digit and the sign. Where the sign is not required, and the variable has an even number of digits, some space can be saved by creating a new variable type: unsigned packed decimal. The following illustration shows the technique:

```
02  TEN—TIMES—AND—SIGN PICTURES S9 (5)
        COMPUTATIONAL—3.
02  FILLER REDEFINES TEN—TIMES—AND—SIGN.
    03  UNSIGNED—PACKED—DECIMAL PICTURE  XX.
    03  FILLER PICTURE X.
```

The technique depends, of course, on adding 10 to the item TEN-TIMES-

AND-SIGN whenever 1 is to be added to the item UNSIGNED-PACKED-DECIMAL. The resulting program will be obscure to the point of opacity: the inevitable disadvantages should be regarded as a measure, not of the programmer's folly, but of the importance in the eyes of the individual of retaining control over the machine code program.

3.1 Embracing the Machine

A more simple and direct approach to the problem of obtaining efficient machine code from programs written in high-level languages is to introduce overtly machine-oriented elements into the languages themselves. This approach is, of course, in conflict with the trend towards problem-oriented programming; it is an avowed reversion to the idea, at least in part, that the purpose of the program is to instruct the machine; but it has been widely adopted.

An obvious example is the provision, in the programming language, for explicit specification of machine representation of variables. COBOL permits the programmer to specify *COMPUTATIONAL, COMPUTATIONAL-1, COMPUTATIONAL-2, COMPUTATIONAL-3*, etc., for numeric variables: these are specifications of 'implementor-defined meaning', giving in the case of IBM S/370 COBOL, binary half-word or full-word, floating-point, double-precision floating-point, packed decimal, etc., representations. PL/I provides purely machine-oriented types for numeric variables, in the form *FIXED* and *FLOAT, BINARY* and *DECIMAL*: no nonsense here about problem-oriented data types.

Another example, showing a regression from problem-oriented to machine-oriented language, is the *INDEX* feature of COBOL. Originally, COBOL provided subscripting, much after the manner of FORTRAN, although subcripts could not be expressions. The compilers commonly available tended to generate very inefficient machine code for subscripted references; the inefficiency was worse in COBOL, where subscripted variables were likely to be of arbitrary size, than in FORTRAN, where they were likely to be represented by single machine words. The *INDEX* feature was introduced to make it easier for the compiler to generate acceptably efficient machine code; the price paid by the programmer was a new set of operations and declarations for *INDEX* variables themselves, and the arbitrary restriction that an *INDEX* variable, unlike a subscript, may refer to the elements of only one array.

The most dramatic example, however, of machine-orientation in programming languages is so deeply embedded in much of our thinking that it goes largely unnoticed. The machine conventionally presented to the programmer is a single processor: there is only one processing unit, and only one instruction address register. Since it follows that the machine can be doing only one thing at one time, the instructions of the program must be executed in some sequence or other. Conventional programming languages, as commonly used, require the programmer to specify the exact sequence of instruction execution, whether or not he/she wishes to do so.

I will argue below that this over-specification of sequencing is harmful. It necessitates a multiplicity of sequencing mechanisms; it burdens the programmer with a task which often need not be carried out to solve the problem; it is a fruitful source of error; and it obscures the simplicity of some problems by confusing the problem itself with the mechanics of executing its solution.

3.2 Resolving the Conflict

There are thus two conflicting pressures in programming language design. On the one hand, there is the recognition that the ideal programming language would be oriented towards the problems which the programmer is trying to solve, and would not require the burden of considering too closely the characteristics and operation of the machine. On the other hand, we cannot afford to abandon our concern with the machine. Neither the general-purpose compiler nor the general-purpose operating system is capable of producing the efficient execution we desire and need; we must still issue explicit instructions about the representation of data, the sequencing of machine operations, and other characteristics of program execution.

The only resolution of the conflict must lie in ceasing to demand these conflicting services from our porgramming languages; we should recognise the need for a clear separation of the problem-oriented from the machine-oriented concerns, and we should make exactly that separation in our languages. Any language would be split into a pair of complementary languages: the Programming Language proper, in which we write our solution to the problem, and the Execution Language, in which we specify how that solution is to be compiled and executed to obtain the necessary efficiency.

The vestiges of such a separation are already visible in COBOL: the COBOL Environment Division was intended to provide a separate place for the programmer to specify certain machine-oriented requirements, especially in the matter of physical file formats. The idea is that machine-oriented characteristics are to be specified in the Environment Division, while problem-oriented characteristics are to be specified in the Data Division. Thus, to define a serial file of 80-character card images, the programmer writes

```
...
DATA DIVISION.
FILE SECTION.
FD  CDFILE, DATA RECORDS ARE CARD-IMAGE.
01  CARD-IMAGE PICTURE X(80).
```

and to specify that the file is to be physically held on magnetic tape the following is written, separately,

```
...
ENVIRONMENT DIVISION.
...
  SELECT CDFILE, ASSIGN TO
    MAGNETIC-TAPE-UNIT.
```

in which the *SELECT* sentence specifies the machine-oriented characteristics, while the *FD* (File Definition) entry in the Data Division specifies the problem-oriented structure of the data records. Unfortunately, the allocation of further specifications to the SELECT sentence or FD is bizarre: for example, physical blocking of the file, which is invisible to the program, is specified in the *FD* entry; the name of the record-key item, for a file to be accessed by key, is specified in the *SELECT* sentence. A decision has recently been taken to reallocate these and other specifications to their proper place.

The pattern of programming activity which would emerge from such a separation between the Programming Language and the Execution Language is clearly one of two ordered steps:

1: The problem is solved in the Programming Language, without consideration of the execution characteristics of the solution.
2: The Execution Language is used to specify the execution characteristics, indicating how the Programming Language program should be compiled and executed to obtain acceptable efficiency.

The statements in the Execution Language would refer to the Programming Language program text, but would not modify it in any way: they would only direct the operation of the compiler and, perhaps, of the operating system.

Such a scheme could be considered a full satisfaction of P. Landin's prescription: 'most programmers start by writing a program which they know to be efficient, and then transform it during debugging by transformations which they hope will make it correct while preserving efficiency; they ought instead to start by writing a program which they know to be correct, and then transform it by transformations which they know will preserve correctness and hope will make it efficient.'

4.0 Separating the Problem from the Machine

4.1 Process Scheduling

One of the aspects of excessive machine-orientation mentioned above (in section 2.2) is the requirement that the programmer specify, in the program, the exact sequence of machine operations to be executed by the single processor which the programming language assumes. In this section, we will illustrate how that machine-oriented concern may be isolated from the problem solution and relegated to the Execution Language.

As illustration, we take the following example problem, derived from a problem originally posed by Henderson & Snowdon (1972) and further treated by Ledgard (1973) and by Gerhart & Yelowitz (1976).

"An input file on paper tape contains the texts of a number of telegrams. The tape is accessed by a 'read block' operation, which reads a variable-length character string delimited by a terminal EOB character; the size of a block cannot exceed 100 characters, exluding the EOB character. Each block contains a number of words, separated by space characters; there may be one or more spaces between adjacent words, and at the beginning and end of a block there may (but need not) be one or more additional spaces. Each telegram consists of a number of words followed by the word 'ZZZZ'; the set of telegrams is followed by a null telegram, consisting only of the 'ZZZZ' word. There is no special relationship between telegrams and blocks: a telegram may begin and end anywhere in a block, and may span several blocks; several telegrams may share a block. There is a special end-of-file block, recognisable as producing the result EOF from a 'read block' operation; no word can occur after the 'ZZZZ' word of the null telegram and before the EOF marker block. The telegrams are to be analyzed, and a report printed showing for each telegram the number of words it contains and the ordinal number of the telegram. 'ZZZZ' does not count as a word for purposes of the analysis, nor does the null telegram count as a telegram."

An approach to this problem, as given in Jackson (1975), may be based on a consideration of the data structures of the input and output files, seen essentially as grammars of regular expressions. (Figure 1 illustrates this approach.) It is then clear that there is a 'structure clash', and that the solution to the problem must be constructed in two parts: one part dissects the paper tape file into a stream of words, while the other reconstructs the stream of words into a file of telegrams. We are thus led to view the program not as one process, but as two: not as

but as

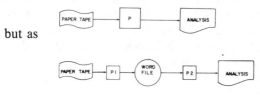

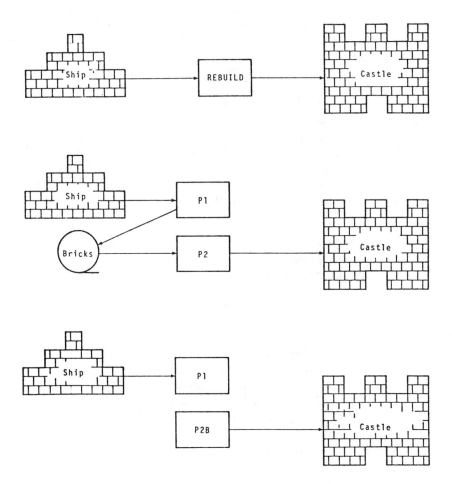

Fig. 1. A structure clash and its resolution. A Lego model of a ship is to be rebuilt as a castle, but while the ship consists of a hull, a superstructure and a funnel, the castle has a very different structure. Obviously the solution is to create two different programs, one to deal with each structure. These are written in the Programming Language; how are they to be expressed in the Execution Language? One way would be to use P1 to dismantle the ship into a pile of bricks and then use P2 to build a castle from the pile, but in real terms this would be very inefficient because the 'bricks file' would have to be completely written before the first record could be read. But instead we could 'invert' one program, say P2, into a subroutine of the other, say P1. We will call the new program P2B. P1 calls P2B to dispose of a brick of the brick file, which it does by adding it to the castle. It turns out that P2B is effectively identical to P2, except for a minor mechanical transformation at the coding level. There is no difficulty in devising suitable implementations in languages like COBOL and PL/I. Moreover there is no reason why a compiler should not be capable of compiling P2 or P2B indifferently from the same source text.

This decomposition into two processes can also be justified by the need to build a correct model of the reality which is the subject matter of the computation. In the problem environment, there are evidently two distinct and independent processes: on the one hand, there is the process of receiving telegram texts from customers and counting the words in order to make a correct charge; on the other hand, there is the process of punching these texts into paper tape, block by block. The telegram process is iterative by telegrams, while the punching process is iterative by paper tape blocks; the only connection between them is that the punch operator is required to punch into paper tape the words of the telegrams in the order in which they occur in the telegram texts. It is therefore not merely appropriate but necessary for correct design that the solution should consist of two processes mediated by a serial stream of words.

The program texts for the resulting programs, P1 and P2, are as follows:

```
P1:   begin open ptape; read ptape;
        open wordfile;
        do while not EOF
          ps := 1;
          do while ptch(ps) ≠ EOB
            if ptch(ps) = space
            then ps := ps + 1
            else begin ws := 1;
                do while ptch(ps) ≠ EOB
                  and ptch(ps) ≠ space
                  wch (ws) := ptch(ps);
                  ps := ps + 1; ws := ws + 1
                od
                write word
              end
            fi
          od
          read ptape
        od
        close ptape; close wordfile
      end

P2:   begin open wordfile; read wordfile;
        open analysis;
        print 'TELEGRAMS ANALYSIS';
        tn := 0;
```

```
    do while word ≠ 'ZZZZ'
        nw := 0; tn := tn + 1;
        nw := nw + 1;
        read wordfile;
        do while word = 'ZZZZ'
            nw := nw + 1;
            read wordfile
        od
        print 'TELEGRAM NO', tn,
                'CONTAINS' nw, 'WORDS';
        read wordfile
    od
    read wordfile;
    print 'END ANALYSIS';
    close wordfile;
    close analysis
end
```

The problem solution is now effectively complete in the Programming Language. However, it still remains to specify in the Execution Language the scheduling of the two processes so that they may share a single CPU.

There are, of course, several choices available to us. We could run P1 to completion before starting P2; the controlling algorithm within the operating system would then have the simple form:

```
begin execute P1 to completion;
      execute P2 to completion
end
```

and the 'read' and 'write' operations in P2 and P1 respectively would refer to a sequential file on backing store such as magnetic disk or tape. Or we could swap between P1 and P2 on each word, when there would be a controlling algorithm of the form:

```
do while not finished
    execute P1 until it produces a word;
    execute P2 until it needs the next word
od
```

and the 'write' and 'read' operations would merely be suspensions of the active process and resumptions of its partner.

These are not the only two available choices; but they are noteworthy because they allow the scheduling to be fully determined at compile time.

The first choice can be implemented by the compilation of the 'read' and 'write' operations into appropriate invocations of input-output procedures, together with the generation of a suitable declaration of the wordfile and the ordered invocation of P1 and P2. The second choice can be implemented by the compilation of P1 and P2 as coroutines, with the 'read' and 'write' operations generated as 'resume P1' and 'resume P2' respectively; or by 'program inversion' of either P1 of P2 (Jackson 1975) making one of the pair into a subroutine of the other (a semi-coroutine).

There are other, more elaborate choices, such as the introduction of a bounded set of buffers between P1 and P2, which leave the scheduling to be partly determined at execution time.

Now, whichever choice we make, and express in the Execution Language, we are surely entitled to expect that the program texts will remain unchanged in the Programming Language: the computation carried out by each of the two processes is unchanged, and the results of the two processes taken together are unchanged. There seems to be no good reason why our choice of scheduling should affect the texts of the scheduled processes, P1 and P2. To put the same point the other way round, there is no good reason why the texts should determine the process scheduling.

Unfortunately, however, in the commonly used programming languages the scheduling of the two processes is expressed directly by the way their texts are written. The variety of the possible program texts that can result is a serious barrier to simplicity and understanding in programming. The fundamental communication between the two processes, the writing and reading of the serial file wordfile, is obscured by the specification of a scheduling scheme which is entirely irrelevant to either process taken alone. It is as if we were required to use completely different syntax for the same program according to whether it is run under a multi-programming or a uni-programming operating system. In effect, the programmer is forced to overspecify the sequencing of the program: a program has been designed consisting of two processes; the communication between them has been specified by means of the wordfile; the programming language forces the specification, in the most obscure and inconvenient way, of the scheduling of the two processes on a single-processor machine.

4.2 Procedures and Processes

In the preceding example, the fundamental structuring device is decomposition into processes communicating by serial file operations, by passing streams of records. The procedure invocation plays no part at all, except that we may, under duress, press it into service as an implementation of a particular scheduling scheme. But we would prefer to use a programming language which did not place us under such duress, and to relegate the scheduling concerns to the Execution Language.

The process, rather than the procedure, is appropriate as a fundamental structural component because of its suitability as a modelling medium. In a very large class of problem we are concerned with a reality, as the subject matter of the computation, which can usefully be regarded as peopled by individual, independently active, entities. For example, in business data processing we may be concerned with customers, with suppliers, with employees, with products; in operating systems we are concerned with user jobs, with files, with hardware devices, with periods of usage of resources such as main storage or input-output channels; in airline reservations systems we are concerned with flights, with seats, with airports, with customers and journeys. It is attractive to model such realities in terms of processes, using one process for each individual entity: one process for each employee, one process for each hardware device, one process for each journey, and so on. (This kind of modelling is very closely akin to the ideas underlying the SIMULA *class* concept (Dahl, 1972) and more recent work on abstract data types (Guttag, 1976): an individual object in the program is present for each individual entity in the modelled reality.)

To illustrate the point from the preceding example, the essential sequentiality of the paper tape is represented by the text of P1, while the essential sequentiality of the telegrams is represented by the text of P2: we may, as it were, follow the lifetime of the paper tape punch operator by followng the text pointer of P1, and the lifetime of the telegram clerk by the text pointer of P2. The text pointer of a single process, being unique, is a satisfactory representation of the progress through time of the individual entity. That is, if we know where the text pointer of P2 is currently pointing, then we know where the telegram clerk has reached in the supposed lifetime. We are easily able in the process text to direct that sequentiality which belongs to the reality we are modelling.

Another Example. The telegrams analysis example is particularly simple because its network of processes is linear. A slightly more complex kind of network is needed to handle a problem such as the following. The problem is taken from Dijkstra (1976), who in turn attributes it to R. W. Hamming.

The problem is to generate a sequence of numbers in increasing order. The values in the sequence are defined by three axioms:

1. The value 1 is in the sequence.
2. If x is in the sequence, so are $2*x$, $3*x$ and $5*x$.
3. The sequence contains no other values than those which belong to it by virtue of axioms 1 and 2.

We may embody axiom 1 in a process P which produces the sequence S from the unique value 1:

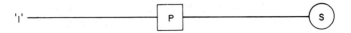

We may embody axiom 2 by adding three further processes P2, P3 and P5, which generate respectively the values 2*x, 3*x and 5*x for each value in S:

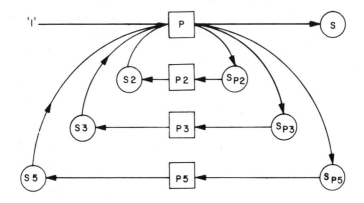

SP2, SP3 and SP5 are simply copies of S: we prefer to avoid at this stage the difficulties of having one file input to (or output from) more than one process. P is now responsible for co-ordinating the files S2, S3 and S5 correctly, as well as for making the three copies of S.

Axiom 3, of course, we embody by refraining from adding further inputs to P.

The text of P is:

```
P:    begin open, S, SP2, SP3, SP5;
          write 1 to S, SP2, SP3, SP5;
          open S2, S3, S5; read S2, S3, S5;
          n := min(S2, S3, S5);
          do while true
              write n to S, SP2, SP3, SP5;
              if S2 = n then read S2 fi;
              if S3 = n then read S3 fi;
              if S5 = n then read S5 fi;
              n := min(S2, S3, S5)
          od
      end
```

while the text of each of the Pi is:

Pi: *begin* open Si; open SPi; read SPi;
      do while true
         write i*SPi to Si;
         read SPi
      od
   end

The solution in the Programming Language may now be considered complete. It remains to determine, and to express in the Execution Language, the desired scheduling of the four processes.

The scheduling considerations are reasonably clear. First, the network contains cycles (P—SP2—P2—S2—P, etc.) and it therefore not possible to run each process to completion (even if we had written terminal conditions for the do-loops) before starting another: we may not choose to run P first, producing SP2, and then, when P is complete, to run P2. Second, although the processes P, P2, P3 and P5 will necessarily be run with some degree of parallelism, it will not be possible to avoid buffering records. Clearly, P5 is producing its output file S5 'faster' than P3 is producing S3—that is, from a given value x of S P5 produces 5*x, which will occur later in S than the value 3*x produced by P3; similarly, P3 produces S3 faster than P2 produces S2. At a general point in the execution of the whole program, therefore, there must be either records of SP5 which have been produced by P but not yet consumed by P5 or else records of S5 which have been produced by P5 but not yet consumed by P; and similar considerations apply to P3.

Scheduling of the network of processes is constrained, therefore, by more complex interconnections than we saw in the telegrams analysis problem; but it is still, in principle, possible to leave the scheduling to some suitable general-purpose operating system. In practice, such an operating system is unlikely to be available, and we are forced to consider explicitly questions of the scheduling of the processes and the associated buffering of records.

A reasonably simple implementation may be obtained by the following choices, to be expressed in the Execution Language:

- Only the first 1000 values of the sequence S are to be generated;
- The files SP2, SP3, SP5 are to be represented by arrays of integers, the writing and reading operations for those files being therefore represented by assignments to subscript variables and assignments to and from elements of the arrays;
- The same array will be used for all of the files SP2, SP3, SP5;
- P3 and P5 are to be activated only when P requires to read from S3 and S5 respectively: that is, only records of SP3 and SP5 need be buffered, not records of S3 and S5.

344   M. Jackson

The reader may be sufficiently interested to work out the resulting program for himself, and to compare it with the program given in Dijkstra (1976). The same problem is also treated in Kahn & McQueen (1976), where there is a very illuminating discussion of the programming of process networks.

4.3 Microscopic Sequentiality

If, in the preceding example, we had been a little more careless (or a little less lucky), we could have created a deadlock. Suppose that we had written P as:

P: *begin* open S, SP2, SP3, SP5;
        open S2, S3, S5;
        read S2, S3, S5;
        write 1 to S, SP2, SP3, SP5;
        . . .

This would have been perfectly satisfactory from the point of view of P alone. However, the system would have been deadlocked: P cannot proceed beyond the 'read S2' operation until P2 writes the first record of S2; but, as inspection of the text of P2 clearly shows, P2 cannot write the first record of S2 until it has read the first record of SP2, which P in turn cannot yet write.

The deadlock thus arising would be a sequence of the overspecification of sequentiality in P. The initial operations of P are only partially ordered: we may represent the partial ordering by the precedence graph:

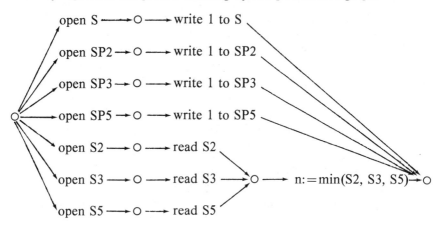

It appears at first sight desirable to equip the Programming Language with a means for expressing such partial orderings, to avoid the danger of over-specifying sequentiality; but the means would apparently be cumbersome and difficult to use.

The deadlock threatened in the preceding example can be avoided by a relatively simple rule for ordering operations within a process: the rule is to execute all 'write' operations as early as possible, and to postpone all 'read' operations to as late as possible. It may be practicable for the compiler to reorder operations automatically to satisfy this rule, or it may require some interactive involvement on the part of the programmer, using the Execution Language.

5.0 Summary

Evidently, the two examples given have done little more than break the ice: we have aimed only to use the notion of a system as a network of processes to illustrate the separation of sequencing which is essential to solve the problem, from sequencing which is convenient or necessary for efficient execution of that solution. And this separation, in turn, is only one illustration—although arguably the most important—of the separation of problem-oriented from machine-oriented concerns.

The idea of the programmer's task as control of the detailed operation of the machine is deeply ingrained in today's conventional programming languages, and in the way we have become accustomed to think about programming. Indeed, a programmer internationally renowned for his skill, asked at a conference on Structured Programming to explain his success, began his reply with the words

"When I am programming, I carry in my mind a picture of the machine registers, the storage areas I have declared, and the values they currently hold..." (Baker, 1974).

Also deeply ingrained is the idea that the Programming Language is the medium for the exercise of that detailed control Knuth (1974) quotes with approval a remark of C.A.R. Hoare to the effect that "an optimising compiler should be able to explain its optimisations in the source language". Some interesting work on control structures (de Millo & Eisenstadt, 1976) has been published under the title "Can structured programs efficiently simulate GO-TO programs?". Should we not similarly ask whether ALGOL 68 can efficiently simulate the IBM System/370?

I have argued that these deeply ingrained ideas are harmful to the development of programming languages, and that the time has come for us to consider relegating to a separate Execution Language those concerns which are fundamentally related not to the correctness of a solution but to the characteristics of its execution. We can already see, in some of the work which has been done in program transformation, an explicit recognition of the harm which execution considerations can do to the practice of programming. For example, Burstall & Darlington (1975) write:

"It is perhaps surprising to notice that even in the rarified language of purely recursive programs there is a sharp contrast between those written for maximal clarity and those written for tolerable efficiency. . . . We are interested in starting with programs having an extremely simple structure and only later introducing the complications which we usually take for granted even in high level language programs."

But Burstall and Darlington are considering transformations of programs into different programs written in the same language; so too are some other researchers in the same field, such Arsac (1978). They, therefore, leave open the possibility of the programmer exerting himself to produce the transformed program directly in the first stage of his programming activity: by contrast, I have argued that the Programming Language should be purged of those elements which make such an exertion necessary today and would otherwise continue to make it possible tomorrow. This, perhaps, is the ultimate realisation of that separation of concerns which lies behind many, if not most, of the major advances already made in conventional programming technique and language.

References

Alt, F.L. (1948). *A Bell Telephone Laboratories computing machine.* MTAC 3, 1-13, 69-84. Reprinted in *The Origins of Digital Computers* (Ed.) B. Randell. Springer Verlag, New York. 1975. (2nd Edition.)

Arsac, J. (1978). *An Interactive Program Manipulation System for Non-naive Users.* Report No. 78-10, Laboratoire Informatique Theorique et Programmation, University of Paris, 2, Place Jussieu, 75221 Paris Cedex 05.

Baker, F.T. (1974). Infotech Conference on Structured Programming. London 1974 (quoted from memory).

Bohm, C. & Jacopini, G. (1966). Flow Diagrams, Turing machines, and languages with only two formation rules. *Comm. ACM 9*, **5**, 366-371.

Burstall, R.M. & Darlington, J. (1975). Some Transformations for Developing Recursive Programs. *Proc International Conference on Reliable Software.* Sigplan Notices **10**, 6, 465-472.

Dahl, O.J. (1972). Hierarchical Program Structures. In *Structured Programming* (Eds.) O-J Dahl, E.W. Dijkstra and C.A.R. Hoare. Academic Press, New York.

Dijkstra, E.W. (1968). Go-To statement considered harmful. *Comm. ACM* **11**, 3, 147-148, 538, 541.

Dijkstra, E.W. (1970). Structured Programming. In *Software Engineering Techniques* (Ed.) J.N. Buxton, & B. Randell. NATO Scientific Affairs.

Dijkstra, E.W. (1972). Notes on Structured Programming. In *Structured Programming.* O-J Dahl, E.W. Dijkstra & C.A.R. Hoare. Academic Press, New York.

Dijkstra, E.W. (1976). *A Discipline of Programming.* Prentice-Hall, New Jersey. 201.

Gerhart, S. & Yelowitz, L. (1976). Observations of Fallibility in Applications of Modern Programming Methodologies; *IEEE Trans. on Software Engineering SE-2*, **3**, 195-207.

Guttag, J.V., Horowitz, E., & Musser, D.R. (1976). *Abstract Data Types and Software Validation.* University of Southern California, Los Angeles. ISI/RR-76-48.

Henderson, P. & Snowdon, R. (1972). An Experiment in Structured Programming. *Bit*, **12**, 38-53.

Hoare, C.A.R. (1974). *Hints for Programming Language Design.* Computer Science Report STAN-CS-74-403; Stanford University.

Jackson, M.A. (1975). *Principles of Program Design.* Academic Press, London.

Kahn, G. & MacQueen, R. (1976). *Coroutines and Networks of Parallel Processes.* IRIA Rapport de Recherche 202.

Knuth, D.E. (1974). Structured Programming with Go-To Statements. *ACM Comp. Surveys*, **6**, 4, 261-301.

Ledgard, H.F. (1973). The Case of Structured Programming. *Bit*, **13**, 45-57.

Mauchly, J.W. (1947). Preparation of problems for EDVAC-type machines In *Annals of the Computation Laboratory of Harvard University*, **16**, 203-207. Reprinted in *The Origins of Digital Computers* (Ed.) B. Randell. Springer Verlag, New York. 2nd Edition.

Milo, R.A. de, Eisenstadt, S.C. & Lipton, R.J. (1976). Can Structured Programs be Efficient? *Sigplan Notices*, **11**, 10, 10-18.

Rogers, J.G. (1975). Structured Programming for Virtual Storage Systems. *IBM Systems Journal*, **14**, 4, 385-406.

Sammet, J.E. (1976). Roster of Programming Languages for 1974-75. *Comm. ACM*, **19**, 12, 655-669.

Zahn, C.T. (1974). A control statement for natural top-down structured programming. In Proc. *Symposium on Programming Languages*. Paris.

Chapter 12

NEW DIRECTIONS IN COMPUTING

Andrew Arblaster

Contents

1.0 Introduction

In this chapter we will consider the impact of some possible changes in computing on the ordinary programmer. In the field of computing it is difficult, as a consideration of the history of computing shows, to predict what will be important for future developments. We can distinguish many important influences on computing. Those which we will consider here are:

• Theoretical Computer Science (including those activities in theoretical computer science which are called 'Artificial Intelligence').
• Hardware developments.
• Software developments.
• Changes in methods of working.
• Changes in applications of computers.

Advances in any of these areas can change the work of programmers. Some of these advances are relatively easy to predict in themselves. However, problems arise when trying to predict the effects of the interactions between new advances in one area and factors in the other areas, even assuming that the other areas remain static. If there is one lesson that is plain from history it is that the other areas are not going to remain static. The effects of interacting changes in different areas make prediction much more difficult.

Other influences which are at least as important as those which have just been mentioned are sociotechnical factors, external management factors, political and even legal factors. These will not be considered explicitly here, but they lie in the background to any assessment of possibilities and should not be forgotten.

We will now consider some examples of the importance of advances in each of the areas with which we will be explicitly concerned, and the ways in which advances in these areas can interact.

Theoretical Computer Science. This may be expected to continue to be a very important, and probably underestimated, influence on future developments. In the past, the ideas of Post, Turing, Von Neumann and others were in a field regarded as the purest of pure Mathematics. These men worked on the decision problem for predicate calculus, the problem of finding a general algorithm to decide for each given expression in the predicate calculus whether it is valid. They wanted to solve this problem because the various branches of mathematics can all be derived in this formulation of symbolic logic. On the face of it this work had no immediate application. However, this theoretical work came to be of immense practical importance when developments in electronics led to the possibility of these ideas being realised physically and developments in applications led to a perceived need for machines which could be easily changed for changing problems. The developments in applications in this case were the need for methods of solving problems in ballistics in the United States, which led to the development of ENIAC in 1945, and the need for solving cryptologic problems in Britain, which led to the development of the COLOSSUS in 1943. Both of these projects were undertaken under the impetus of urgent military need during the second world war.

Hardware. There is no likelihood that the pace of hardware development will slacken. Advances in hardware have obviously been an important influence on programming problems and methods of working. Their obvious nature has tended to obscure the effects of advances in other areas. One example of the way in which changes in hardware affect the computer user is the development of mass storage devices in the 1950's. When these devices (e.g., drums, discs, and slow store) were developed computers were normally used by the programmer booking time on the computer, usually subject to some constraints, setting up his own job and operating the computer himself. At first the development of mass storage devices made the programmer's job more complex. Programmers had to learn to manipulate the levels of store themselves. Later the development of operating systems and the concept of one level store, a software development, made it less necessary for programmers to worry about the details of manipulating mass store. But the developments also led to a change in methods of working under the pressure of scarce computing resources. Now the programmer handed his programs to an operator for running and collected the results later. The interaction of factors from different areas led to a profound change in the programmer's task. This sort of complex interaction is typical of the computing field.

Software. Again this is very important. In the past new software such as the development of compilers for high level languages led to new methods of working, new types of programmers, and new types of hardware specially designed to run programs in high level languages. The development of operating systems is another example which has been mentioned above. Both of these examples required considerable theoretical foundation. New advances in software will lead to equally great changes in computing.

Methods of working. These are influenced by other factors mentioned here and by external management aims. Changes in methods of working have also caused changes in the other areas. Examples of developments in computing which have been caused by a desire to alter the way in which programming work is done are the introduction of interactive computing, which is designed to optimise the work of the man rather than the computer, structured programming which is a discipline aimed at making programming a process of design rather than of coding, and distributed computing which aims to take advantage of the possibilities of communication between computers.

Applications. An example of the role of an application in forcing change has been given above in the case of the development of the first electronic computers. Computers are now applied to a vast range of problems in science, industry, commerce and government. But the potential for new applications is also vast. This potential has been underestimated on many occasions. One notable example is the doubt by Ferranti Ltd. in 1957 that many Mercury computers could be sold at $240,000—less than the rental price for one year of any comparable American machine. A member of the development team later admitted "We greatly underestimated the potential demand for computers.". Again, in 1947 (admittedly the year before the unveiling of the first stored-program computer at Manchester University), Professor Hartree of Cambridge University said that a computer for the solution of problems in Mathematical Physics might need as many as 5,000 store locations. At the present time the computers used for Physics problems at such laboratories as those at CERN and Lawrence Berkeley Laboratories have a capacity of many millions of bytes. Even IBM considered at one time that only ten machines could satisfy the entire US computing requirement.

Naturally it would be incorrect to become too uncritical in our assessment of the possibilities. The tendencies to underestimate the scope for change and to underestimate the effects of change are counterbalanced by a tendency to predict changes which are seen to be unlikely with careful analysis. In particular there is a seductive ease in predicting that trends of apparently linear or even exponential increase will continue throughout the forseeable future. This sort of basis for prediction seems to be behind an estimate in a recent IBM report that soon 25% of the population of the US would be engaged in Data Processing. We should remember that in 1200 A.D. a prediction based on the increase in the number of people becoming Cistercian monks over the preceding 50 years would have meant that by the end of the century nearly the whole population of Europe would have been living the life of Cistercians! We will see later that there is likely to be a substantial increase in the number of people who use computer facilities in their work but for most of these people the computer will be just a tool not the central focus of the work.

2.0 What's Going To Happen?

Our interest in this chapter is mainly in the impact of developments on the 'ordinary programmer'. For this reason, his/her methods of working will mainly be considered as a dependent area, though as we have seen changes in methods of working have their own impact in other areas. We will examine probable developments under whichever one of our headings will contribute the greatest impetus to the development, considering contributory effects from other areas at the same time.

2.1 Theoretical Computer Science

Developments in this field are the hardest to predict because of the difficulty of the field. The burning issue in theoretical computing, and an issue which is likely to remain prominent for a long time, is the problem of concurrency, how to organise computations in which more than one operation can be performed at one time.

For our purposes theoretical work can be divided into that which is at present very theoretical and which will come to fruition in the longer term, and work which is less theoretical and which is likely to be of importance in the near future.

The most immediate impact is likely to come from work on new computer architectures, on networks and on the theory of concurrent processes. Theoretical work on new architectures is helped by experimental work which is itself made easier by cheaper microelectronics. The most notable ideas in architecture are those which move away from the idea of a comput-

TYPE	EXAMPLE
Serial	Most general purpose computers, e.g. DEC PDP11.
Pipelined or Confluent	CDC 6600 (Thornton, 1970), MU5 (Ibbett and Capon,1978).
Vector	CDC STAR (Hinz & Tate, 1972), CRAY 1 (Russell,1978).
Array	ILLIAC IV (Barnes, 1968)
Multiprocessor	CM* (Swan et al., 1977), DAP (Gostick,1978)
Dataflow	LAU (Syre et al., 1977)

Fig. 1. A Classification of Computer Architectures (after Treleaven, 1978).

er as a processor operating on a linear array of store—the Von Neumann or Turing model. In this model a computer has a central processing unit (CPU), a store, and a channel between them. The CPU can only do two things to the store—it can fetch a word from a specified place in the store or it can send a word to a specified place, using the channel in either case. The two principal reasons for moving away from the Von Neumann model are first that this model is clumsy semantically—the sorts of programming languages which one might want to use for convenience are difficult to define in terms of a Von Neumann architecture; and second that it is difficult to exploit the possibilities of greater concurrency to gain greater efficiency.

Six types of computers may be distinguished, see Figure 1. The first five of these architectures share the problem that though their data may be operated on concurrently, using more powerful instructions than are possible with linear store, they are still limited by having essentially a single stream of instructions. Array processors allow concurrent operations on a nonlinear matrix store. They are intended mainly for use in solving numerical problems where large volumes of data are being manipulated. Analysis of common computations has shown that even with current algorithms there is an enormous amount of parallelism which can be exploited and inherently sequential steps can be surprisingly few (Gentleman, 1978). Newer algorithms can be designed, using newer programming languages to take advantage of parallelism. An array processor developed by ICL, the distributed array processor, uses a multiprocessor architecture but the processors still use a single instruction stream. The firm have recognised that traditional programming languages are deficient for this type of processing,

```
     REAL VECTOR FUNCTION SOLVE(A1,B1)
C    DECLARE A1 AS MATRIX, B1 AS VECTOR
     DIMENSION A1(,),B1()
     REAL A(,),B(),MULTS()
C    STORE A AND B TO AVOID OVERWRITING
     A = A1
     B = B1
     DO 1 K = 1,64
     S = A(K,K)
     MULTS = A(,K)/S
     A(.NOT.ROW(K)) = A - MATR(A(K,))*MATC(MULTS)
     B(.NOT.EL(K)) = B - B(K)*MULTS
     A(K,) = A(K,)/S
1    B(K) = B(K)/S
     SOLVE = B
     RETURN
END
```

A subroutine to find the solution of a set of simultaneous linear
equations. This function implements the algorithm:
  1. Calculate the elements in the pivot column divided by the
      pivot element, a(ik)/a(kk), where a(kk) is the pivot element.
  2. For each row except the pivot row, multiply the pivot row
      by the appropriate multiplier and subtract from that row i.e.,
      a(ij) = a(ij) − a(kj)*(a(ik)/a(kk)) for all i,j.
  3. Do step 2 on the right hand side: b(i) = b(i) − b(k)*(a(ik)
      /a(kk)) for all i.
  4. For the first row divide each element by the pivot, i.e.,
      a(kj) = a(kj)/a(kk) for all j and b(k) = b(k)/a(kk)

Fig. 2. A DAP Fortran subroutine (after Gostick, 1978). (For simplicity the program does
not use maximum element pivoting).

but since they feel constrained to offer Fortran programming, their solution
is to define a special enhanced Fortran, illustrated in Figure 2. This shows
the dilemma which confronts both language and computer designers at
present: language designers were constrained by the traditional computer
architectures to produce languages which were suboptimal in terms of their
semantic structure and human factors features—now computer designers
have to be constrained by these traditional languages.

    Dataflow computing is a different approach to the inherent problem of
the Von Neumann model of computing, the problem of overspecification of
sequencing on a computation. Dataflow computing is designed to enable

operations to be executed concurrently as the data for those operations becomes available. The usual view of a computation is that more or less static data structures are being operated on by a program, which is conceived of as being dynamic, in a machine. Dataflow computing views the process as one where a static program of an assertional nature is operated on by the data, conceived of as the dynamic element, in a different type of machine. Dataflow computing languages may look quite similar to programming languages in common use at present, but this could be misleading. A superficial syntactic resemblance might prove to be a pitfall for the unwary programmer, used to a sequential programming language, who is lulled into forgetting the fundamentally different semantic nature of these languages. A language which has been suggested as a possible candidate for programming a dataflow computer is LUCID, see Figure 3. Others are Id (Arvind, et al., 1978) and DFL (Ackerman, 1978). The fundamental difference in semantics between these languages and traditional programming languages provides a link between work on new architectures and work on the semantics of computation which will be discussed later.

Recursion Equations
    root(n) = s(0,1,n)
    s(i,j,n) = *if* j>n *then* i *else* s(i+1, j+2i+3, n)

FORTRAN
    INTEGER I,J
    READ,N
    I = 0
    J = 1
10   IF(J.GT.N) GOTO 20
    J = J+2*I+3
    I = I+1
    GOTO 10
20   WRITE,I
    END

LUCID
(1)   N = first input
(2)   first I = 0
(3)   first J = 1
(4)   next J = J+(2*I)+3
(5)   next I = I+1
(6)   output = I as soon as J>N

Fig. 3. Recursion equations, FORTRAN and LUCID programs to find the integer square root of n (after Wadge, 1977).

Both the development of array processing and that of dataflow computing need considerable theoretical advances. They will also mean quite different sorts of programming languages and techniques, and, of course, a quite different set of problems for the programmer.

Networks and distributed computing depend as much on developments in hardware and software as in theory, but there are many theoretical problems which underlie these developments still to be solved. One of these is the replicability of results obtained from a program run on a network, given that the precise environment in which the program is run is not replicable. Another is the problem of determining the relative times at which events take place in a network—a pressing problem for those air travellers who are assured that their booking has gone through and that seats are available but who later find that their booking has been preempted by other bookings made later.

The third development, and one which is vital for progress in many areas, is an increase in the understanding of concurrent processes. This is necessary both for the new architectures mentioned and for the successful design of networks. Up to the present, work on concurrent processes has concentrated on problems of multiprogramming organisation, where the processes in question are not truly concurrent in the sense that their instructions can be executed simultaneously—the weaker idea of commutativity of atomic instructions is used. Control and synchronisation primitives using this idea have been grafted on to serial languages (Brinch Hansen, 1975; Conway, 1973; Dijkstra, 1968), but this forces a limit to the level of concurrency which can be encoded in programs. Their use can also in practice introduce undesirable side-effects and timing difficulties. In addition, Miller & Yap (1977) show that work based on this idea is not really suitable when complex systems of processes are being considered, but only for the toy problems in which the literature abounds. The solution of the more difficult problems will have enormous practical impact. The theoretical problems inherent in the control of simultaneous processes will be reflected in the complexity of software. As distributed processing and other uses of concurrent machines become more prevalent the ordinary programmer will need more understanding of these problems.

In the longer term the interesting possibilities are concerned with new models for the semantics of computation. Turing machines have been generalised to include machines having any type of abstract object associated with each cell. We can speculate that a realisation of an equivalent program machine might allow much more complex abstract objects than are now used as the basic primitive objects. Another possibility is the development of new types of machines and a new style of programming in terms of mathematical structures based perhaps on the ideas of Goguen & Thatcher, et al. (1976a; b; 1977a; b; c) (the *ADJ* group). This group have drawn together many apparently divergent approaches to the definition of the syntax and semantics of programming languages and data structures in a remarkable synthesis based on ideas drawn from universal algebra. The implications for language design of this exciting work have not yet been fully evaluated—indeed the impact of the work is such that its full ramifications may not be explored for very many years. ADJ show how programming language at present in use are related to their formulations, but the possibility of working in the opposite direction—to use these algebraic formulations as a basis for the design of computing languages—is obvious. It may seem that a language based explicitly on these ideas would need to be used by a skilled mathematician, but it was believed in the past that skilled mathematicians were needed to program conventional computers: in fact an advertising leaflet for one of the first commercially available computers emphasised that "our staff of trained mathematicians are available to program the computer.". Perhaps, therefore, ADJ languages would become commonplace within a very short time of their introduction.

John Backus, who played a leading role in the design of FORTRAN and the implementation of the first compiler for that language and who was also prominent in the design of ALGOL, has recently suggested that the Von Neumann computer and the corresponding programming languages are seriously inadequate. Backus claims that Von Neumann languages create enormous and unnecessary intellectual roadblocks in thinking about programs and in the creation of the higher level combining forms necessary for a really powerful programming methodology. He presents an alternative where the programmer specifies his algorithm in a functional, non sequential way, and programs are combined using relatively natural combining forms (Backus, 1978).

Lastly, we should mention the artificial intelligence field, if only because this has been one of the most obtrusive and highly funded areas of theoretical computer science. Here we must distinguish between the contributions of this area to psychology and other neurosciences and its contributions to computing. Most of the latter have come from work close to the traditional theoretical interests. Most notable, and hopeful, has been the work of Luckham and others at Stanford (Automatic Program Verification I to V, *Stanford AI project*, 1972-76) on automatic program verification and the work of Burstall & Darlington (1977) on methods of program improvement. The work of Luckham and his collaborators involves making assertions in some predicate calculus about the operation of a program at various points in its text. The program, together with these assertions, are then submitted to the verifier, which checks it. This work has had some success with programs in Pascal, see Figure 4.

To sum up, the overwhelming trend in theoretical computer science is away from the Von Neumann computer and the languages based on that model of computation. When the ideas outlined here come to fruition as implemented languages and working hardware they will lead to a profound change in the ways in which computers are programmed and in the programming languages and methodologies which will be used. The implementation and widespread introduction of new kinds of computers is, however, unlikely to be rapid or suddenly disruptive—gradual, evolutionary change is more likely for reasons which will become clear in the discussion of hardware and software changes.

PASCAL

```
TYPE SARRAY = ARRAY[1:L] OF INTEGER;

        PROCEDURE EXCHANGESORT(VAR A:SAR-
            RAY;L:INTEGER);
        INITIAL A = A0;  A0 is defined as the initial state of array A
        ENTRY 1≤L;  The array is to have at least one element
        EXIT Issortedarrayof(A,A0);  A is A0 sorted

        VAR X:REAL;VAR K,I,J:INTEGER;
        BEGIN
        I: = L;
        INVARIANT Permutation(A,A0)∧Ordered(A,I+1,L)∧Parti-
            tioned(A,I)∧(I≥1)
        The invariant asserts things which are true in the loop
        WHILE I>1 DO
            BEGIN
            J: = 2; X: = A[1]; K: = 1;
            INVARIANT Biggest(A,J−1,K)∧(1≤K)∧(K≤J−1)∧
                (J−1≤I)∧(X = A[K])
            WHILE J≤I DO
                BEGIN
                IF X≥A[J] THEN GOTO 3;
                X: = A[J];
                K: = J;
            3:J: = J+1;
                END;
            A[K]: = A[I]
            A[I]: = X;
            I: = I−1
            END;
        END;.
```

The user inserts the assertions as shown in the program, and definitions of the expressions used in a separate file. In this program A is an array, L is the upper bound of A. Ordered(A,J,L) means that the subarray A[J:L] is in ascending order. Partitioned(A,J−1) means that A is partitioned into an upper part and a lower part, such that elements above A[J−1] are larger than or equal to those below A[J]. Biggest(A,I,J) means that A[J] is the biggest element among the elements of the subarray A[1:I]. Permutation(A,B) means that the array A is a permutation of the array B.

Fig. 4. A PASCAL sort routine together with verification conditions (after Suzuki, 1975).

2.2 Hardware

In speculating on the development of hardware we must make a careful distinction between three different aspects of the computing scene. The first aspect is new hardware based on advances in theory. These have already been discussed. They will be carried out in the first instance as experiments on a relatively small scale by teams at Universities and at the research laboratories of the larger computer firms. Those which are successful will eventually be marketed and will produce long term changes.

The second aspect is the mainstream of computing, involving the computer manufacturers who are making large, medium and mini computers— the traditional computer makers. The third aspect of hardware advance is the microelectronic industry with the spectacular advances which have been made there in recent years.

In the mainstream we will see cautious advance on the foundations provided by the machines being made now. There will be no quick changes in design but a steady, gradual change towards computers which will be faster, more reliable and more convenient for the running of the required software. The large computer firms depend on a measure of stability in their environment in order to plan their own corporate development. They are in a position to enforce a degree of stability by their control of the hardware and software markets.

Large computers will not be superceded. Indeed, their use will grow, though possibly more slowly than in the past. They will probably become the centres of computing complexes, with an array of intelligent peripheral devices including smaller computers. Each computer in the complex may be dedicated to a certain subset of the functions which the organisation using the complex needs, either running software dedicated to a particular function or, increasingly, having hardware designed for a particular function. Such ancillary computers may, for example, be hardware array processors or database controllers. Others may run software dedicated, for example, to warehouse control or production management. The use of minicomputers will also grow, both as stand-alone machines and in large numbers in networks. The market here will continue to be dominated by firms such as DEC, though they will be joined by newer firms from the microcomputer industry.

The third area of hardware development is the world of microelectronics. This is controlled by electronic device manufacturers rather than by computer firms. Some of the greatest changes caused by advances in microelectronics will be outside the mainstream of computing, in devices for appliances such as washing machines, games, cars, houses and above all in the manufacturing industries. In computing the principal change will be a continuation of the trend to cheaper computers and peripherals. The interactions between these three areas are, as we have come to expect, complex.

On the one hand these microelectronic techniques have been used and will be used to aid experiments based on theory, and by mainstream manufacturers to help in the design and construction of their products. On the other hand microprocessors, originally developed for electronic appliance applications, have been used to produce microcomputers which compete with the products of mainstream manufacturers. A microcomputer typically has a single chip processor, limited semiconductor store, ability to drive a limited number of peripherals, and is usually packaged as a machine needing no special power supply. A minicomputer may or may not be based on a single chip processor, can usually drive both a larger number and a larger range of peripherals, and can usually have a larger amount of store attached. The development of the computer industry in this complex way has come about in part because firms in the microelectronic applications industry have often been small, entrepreneurial establishments, depending on high technology but not on extensive corporate planning. This has led to some confusion in the industry, but this period seems to be coming to an end. Some of the smaller firms will fall by the wayside, others will grow and mature to the extent they will need to plan in the longer term themselves and, hence, will need stability, and yet others will be taken over by mainstream firms.

In practice the effect will be that the newer microcomputers will compete at the lower end of the industry with minis, without either displacing the other. Cheaper microcomputers will share a part of a new market for personal computers with cheaper minis. These small personal computers will be used by programmers, office staff and professional people to do their more clerical tasks. They will frequently be tied into networks.

We must thus envisage a situation where we have large computers at the centres of networks, communicating with each other and providing large scale computer power for large scale problems. Then around these will be a number of smaller computers, some of them specialised to carry out particular functions necessary to the user organisation, then a number of personal computers used for clerical tasks such as routine filing, word processing, and copying. Only the largest organisations will have all of these elements, but smaller organisations will have smaller replicas of this sort of network. The setting up of public networks is likely in the more distant future. Even where computers are not connected in networks these three types will be present.

As a result of these developments the clerical work of a programmer will certainly become easier. The work of the programmer who is concerned with a particular function in an organisation may well become easier, because certain hardware will be dedicated to his/her function and because of corresponding software development to be examined in the next section. The work of programmers with responsibility for larger parts of the computing complex will become harder because these programmers will need a greater range of skills and greater flexibility to carry out their increasingly complex tasks. For this reason, such programmers will be less likely to be directly employed by user organisations, except the very largest. They will be representatives of the computer manufacturers or of the software industry, and it is to software that we will now turn.

2.3 Software

In conjunction with the tendency for hardware to be dedicated to particular functions there will be an increase in the use of programming systems where the functions to be carried out can be specified at a very high level, rather than by explicit coding in a programming language. There will be widespread use of programming packages and systems where programming is carried out by altering parameters of the systems instead of by detailed coding and in this way very high level programming languages and systems will come into being. This trend is an echo of the speculation in the section on theory that programming may be done by functional specification rather than by manipulation of machine words, even when, as in present programming languages, these are disguised as 'variables'. These changes, growing from the current state of the art, will be reinforced by the theoretical ideas previously discussed and will lead to the sophisticated methods advocated by such people as Backus. High level systems and packages will be prepared and marketed by the software industry, including the software interests of the computer manufacturers, but also increasingly by independent software houses. The use of such systems will apply particularly to business systems in the immediate future. A notable example of this tendency is the large number of database systems now in use for data storage, retrieval, and manipulation (See Chapter 6).

We are moving into a world of programming systems products (Brooks, 1975). The software industry will increasingly provide well tried programming systems written in a generalised fashion with well defined interfaces between the system components. These products will be thoroughly documented. To accomplish this the software industry will itself need to reduce the uncertainty inherent in the use of current programming languages. Given the present enormous investment in programs written in current languages and in the training of programmers to use these languages, they will continue to be used for a very long time. However, the way in which they are used may change considerably. At the coding level, where conventional languages are being used, more programming aids will be available. Some of these aids will be program verifiers and testers, similar for example to those developed by the Stanford AI group for Pascal, already mentioned in the theory section. Others will be program improvers (e.g. Burstall &

Darlington, 1977), and preprocessors to move from a structured problem specification to a working program. These aids will normally be interactive and the emphasis will be on human-computer cooperation rather than on any attempt at complete automation. Structured programming is a methodology which has had considerable success in reducing the uncertainty that used to cling around the process of program development. Given its present success it will continue to be the dominant methodology for using current types of programming languages, and will continue to be refined with such techniques as that of Jackson (1975).

Comparatively, less programming in current languages will be done in user organisations on the larger machines, but what is done will also use these new methods.

A comment on some very unlikely developments is in order here. Some writers have predicted that the use of microcomputers will lead to the use of Artificial Intelligence techniques for the automatic production of a program from examples of its input and the corresponding desired output, or from a specification of the program in terms of assertions in a predicate calculus. The first of these predications is very unlikely to happen, because its realisation depends on breakthroughs in Artificial Intelligence theory which are themselves unlikely. In contrast to the prospect for automatic program verification, the synthesis of programs from assertions is again unlikely. There is no reason to expect, as some writers seem to, that the widespread use of microcomputers will somehow lead to the solution of problems which depend on theory, not hardware.

In contrast to the case with large computers and substantial program systems products, the use of some conventional programming languages on personal computers will grow. Such simpler interactive languages as BASIC and APL and possibly RPG will be used by people who are less skilled in programming. They will frequently be user organisation's functional line staff rather than professional programmers. The increased use of simpler languages, together with a trend to distributed processing, will make computing power much more readily available to both professional and semiprofessional programmers.

In the less than immediate future the development of public data networks is likely, putting together developments in networks and in database handling. The new profession of information broker, an expert in the retrieval of desired data, will be increasingly prominent (See Chapter 6). There may also be a role for the yet newer profession of Computer Sabotage Consultant (Brunner, 1975).

2.4 Methods of Working

Nearly all of the things we have discussed so far will have their effects on methods of working. We will summarise the likely changes here.

The interactive use of personal computers will grow. This will lead to an increase in the number of less skilled programmers using simple high level languages and very high level programming systems, and in the use of computers by semiprofessional programmers—those who are professionals in other fields than computing but who need to use computers in their work, such as engineers, doctors, managers and others. Most highly skilled programmers will also use personal computers for their more clerical tasks. The coding part of their work will become less obtrusive, helped by aids to the design and production of software and by design methodologies. This is necessary because of the need of the software industry to reduce uncertainty. The distinction between programmer and systems analyst will become less because the skilled programmer will be able to concentrate more of his effort on systems design and problem solving. Programming groups will become problem solving groups led by people who will not necessarily be programmers.

2.5 New Applications

Computer techniques will replace older clerical methods in more and more fields. This expansion will, of course, be aided by the developments discussed above. One obvious effect of cheaper hardware and more easily developed software will be the computerisation of businesses which have been regarded as being too small for the viable introduction of data processing methods. Another growth area will be medical computing, partly due to the same effects as those which will lead to greater computerisation in small businesses, and partly due to the development of systems for providing medical information, advice, help with diagnosis, and other aids such as are discussed by Taylor (Chapter 9). Office automation has been given an enormous impetus by the introduction of word processors, systems where text is typed up on a screen and can be filed on a disc, recalled, modified and printed on a high quality printer. Most of the systems at present in use are capable only of a small finite number of operations, but it is likely that these will prove to be too restrictive in many cases. Word processing systems in the future will also allow computing and will include text-handling programming languages which can be used either directly as interactive languages or to write programs which can be stored to provide additional features for any office's system. In this way some typists will come to be programmers. Kraft (1977) cites examples of typists and other office staff who do programming as part of their jobs. (And of people called 'programmers' who never see a computer—typically salesmen.)

3.0 Conclusion

Programming per se has been subject to a continuous process of de-skilling over the last thirty years. At each stage higher and higher level programming languages and operating environments and more advanced methodologies for program production have come into use. As this has happened programmers at these levels have needed less skill for the programming part of their tasks. This has not made the skills of programmers of basic software obsolete. In absolute terms more skilled programmers working at the lower levels have been needed, but relatively their number has fallen. This paradoxical process will continue. Nearly all of the developments discussed will lead to a relative increase in the number of people using simple high level languages such as BASIC and RPG. These people will be recognised more and more as programmers. As a result the level of skill devoted to writing programs used by the programming profession will fall, but the absolute number of highly skilled systems, software and applications programmers will rise. In fact, as machines grow more complex the skill required at the systems and software levels will rise. But more of this skill will be skill in problem solving and less will be skill in coding. More of these skilled programmers will work for software firms and fewer for users.

Programmers oriented towards solving problems in their speciality, rather than towards some particular computer or some particular language will find the transition fairly easy. Some of those who think of themselves as, for example, IBM COBOL programmers will find niches for themselves in a declining trade. Others may find that their work becomes more routine and uninteresting. But those who are ready to meet the challenge of new ideas will find their lives and their work enriched.

References

ADJ GROUP (Goguen, J.A., Thatcher, J.W., Wagner, E.G., and Wright, J.B.)
(1976a). (EGW, JBW, JAG, JWT). Some fundamentals of order-algebraic semantics. *Lecture notes in Computer Science 45, 1976*, 153-168, Springer-Verlag, New York.
(1976b). (JBW, JWT, EGW, JAG). Rational algebraic theories and fixed point solutions. *Proc. 17th IEEE Symposium on Foundations of Computing*, 147-158.
(1977a). (JAG, JWT, EGB, JBW). Initial algebra semantics and continuous algebras. *JACM*, **24**, 68-95.
(1977b). (JAG, JWT, EGW). *An initial algebra approach to the specification, correctness and implementation of abstract data types*. IBM Research Report RC 6487.
(1977c). (EGW, JWT, JBW). *Free continuous theories*. IBM Research Report RC 6906.
Ackerman W.B. (1977). *Preliminary dataflow language*. MIT Computational Structures Group, Note 36. Cambridge, Mass.

Arvind K, Gostelow P. and Plouffe W. (1978). *The (preliminary) Id report: an asynchronous programming language and computing machine.* Tech. Report 114, Dept. of Info. and Computer Science, Univ. of California at Irvine.

Ashcroft E.A. and Wadge W.W. (1977). Lucid, a nonprocedural language with iteration. *CACM*, **20**, 519-526.

Backus, J. (1978). Can programming be liberated from the von Neumann style?. *CACM*, **21**, 613-641.

Barnes, G.H. et al. (1978). The ILLIAC IV computer. *IEEE Trans. on Computing* **C-17**, 746-757.

Brinch Hansen, P. (1975). The programming language concurrent Pascal *IEEE Trans. on Software Engineering*, **SE-1**, 199-207.

Brooks, F.P. Jr. (1975). *The mythical man-month.* Addison Wesley, Reading, Mass.

Brunner, J. (1975). *The shockwave rider.* J.M. Dent, London.

Burstall, R.M. and Darlington, J. (1977). A transformation system for developing recursive programs. *JACM*, **24**, 44-67.

Conway, M.E. (1973). A multiprocessor system design. *AFIPS FJCC*, **34**, 139-146.

Dijkstra, E.W. (1968). Cooperating sequential processes. In *Programming Languages* (Ed.) Genuys. Academic Press, London

Genteleman, W.M. (1978). Some complexity results for matrix computations on parallel processors. *JACM*, **25**, 112-115.

Gostick, R.W. (1978). *Introduction to DAP FORTRAN.* ICL Research Region Doc. AP 20.

Hintz, R.G. & Tate, D.P. (1972). Control Data Star 100 processor design. *COMPCON-72 Digest of Papers*, IEEE Comp. Soc. 1-4.

Ibbett, R.N. & Capon, P.C. (1978). The development of the MU5 computer system. *CACM*, **21**, 13-24.

Jackson, M.A. (1975). *Principles of program design.* Academic Press, London.

Kraft, P. (1977). *Programmers and Managers.* Springer-Verlag, New York.

Miller, R.E. & Yap C.K. (1977). *Formal specification and analysis of loosely connected processes.* IBM Research Report RC 6716.

Russell, R.M. (1978). The CRAY-1 Computer system. *CACM*, **21**, 63-72.

Stanford AI Lab. APV GROUP (D.C. Luckham, N. Suzuki, F.W. Von Henke, S. Igarashi, R.L.) London.

(1975). (SI,RLL,DCL). Automatic Program Verification I: Logical basis and its implementation. *Acta Informatica*, **4**, 145-182.

(1975). (NS). Automatic Program Verification II: Verifying programs by algebraic and logical reduction. *Proc. Intl. Conf. on Reliable Software*, SIGPLAN notices, June, 473-481.

(1975). (FWVH, DCL). Automatic Program Verification III: A methodology for verifying programs. *Proc. Intl. Conf. on Reliable Software*, IEEE, 156-164.

(1975). (DCL, NS). *Automatic Program Verification IV: Proof of termination within a weak logic of programs.* Stanford AI Memo. AIM-269.

(1975). (DCL, NS). *Automatic Program Verification V: Verification oriented proof rules for arrays, records and pointers.* Stanford AI Memo. AIM-278.

Swan, R.J., Fuller, S.H. & Siewiorek, D.P. (1977). CM*: a modular multi-microprocessor. *National Computer Conference*, **46**, 637-663.

Syre, J.C., Comte, D. & Hifdi, N. (1977). Pipelining, parallelism and asynchronism in the LAU system. *Proc. Intl. Conf. on Parallel Processing 1977.*

Thornton, J.E. (1970). *Design of a computer—the CDC 6600.* Scott Foresman.

Treleaven, P.C. (1978). *Exploiting program concurrency in computing systems.* Tech. Report, Univ. of Newcastle upon Tyne.

SUBJECT INDEX

Problem-oriented programming, 328–331
Problem-solving, 144, 302–314
Process control, 60–62
Production scheduling, 16
Production system programs, 53–54, 63, 150, 310
Program complexity, 326–327
Program maintenance, 325
Program structures, 328–331
 conditionals, 290–291
 GOTO statements, 276, 311, 312
 processes, 336, 345, 356
 subroutine, 311, 312, 325–326

Question-answering, 32, 136

Radiology, 250–254
Relational structures, 132
Representation, 25, 74, 206, 208–210, 213, 302
Responsibility, 13, 42, 250, 259, 262

Self-embedding (*see* Syntax)
Semantics, 297–299, 358
Simulation (*see* Models)
Social factors, 10–13
Software engineering, 19, 304
Software physics, 312
SOPHIE, 150
Speech, 34
Stepwise refinement (*see* Structured programming)
Strategies, 74, 78–84, 193, 232–233, 250, 292
Structure diagrams, 283–285
Structured programming, 19, 44, 276, 303–307, 315, 328, 329–330, 345, 362
Subconscious processing, 70–72
Syntax (*see also* Notation)
 discriminability, 288, 313–314
 features, 284, 312
 nesting, 290–291, 295–296
 signals, 281–284, 291, 296
Systems analysis, 121

Task types, 15, 74–78, 161
"T.J. Hooper" rationale, 45
Teacher, and Computer Assisted Learning CAL, 130–131
Teaching Classification, 132
Telegrams problem, 338–342
Theoretical computer science, 352, 354–360
TICCIT, 138
Top-down programming (*see* Structured programming)

Understanding a program, 52, 307–311, 314–315
Users
 end-users, 22, 166
 mid-users, 19
 system-support, 18